W9-CFT-670

"BEGINNING WITH THE FIRST CHAPTER, FRANCO DRAWS THE READER INTO HIS BRUTAL WORLD. . . . THERE IS NO LETUP IN THE ACTION, AND BY THE TIME YOU REACH THE FINAL PAGE, YOU FEEL LIKE YOU KNOW FRANCO AND HOFFA." —UPI

A SHOCKING, EYE-OPENING ACCOUNT OF THE AWESOMELY POWERFUL TEAMSTERS, THE COMPLEX AND RUTHLESS JIMMY HOFFA, AND THE MOST TURBULENT ERA IN AMERICAN LABOR HISTORY.

HOFFA'S MAN

"COLORFUL, PUNCHY, AND OTHERWISE BRUTALLY CANDID." —*Toledo Blade*

"FRANCO'S A GREAT STORYTELLER!" —*The Sun* (Baltimore)

"A GOOD HAIR-RAISING READ."—*Fortune* magazine

"INTRIGUING . . . FASCINATING SNAPSHOTS OF THE FRICTION-RIDDEN RELATIONS BETWEEN HOFFA AND THE KENNEDYS." —*Kirkus Reviews*

"THE ENTIRE BOOK IS SHEER DYNAMITE." —*Waldenbooks Crime Time*

"A CHILLING STORY . . . THE BOOK PICTURES IN DETAIL THE ROUGH-AND-TUMBLE ATMOSPHERE OF A UNION THAT FOUGHT AND ARGUED WITH THE GLOVES OFF." —*John Barkham Reviews*

OTHER BOOKS BY RICHARD HAMMER

The CBS Murders
The Vatican Connection
Mr. Jacobson's War (*novel*)
An End to Summer (*novel*)
Hoodlum Empire
Gangland, U.S.A.
The Illustrated History of Organized Crime
The Last Testament of Lucky Luciano (*with Martin A. Gosch*)
The Court-Martial of Lt. Calley
One Morning in the War
Between Life and Death

Hoffa's Man

The Rise and Fall of Jimmy Hoffa as Witnessed by His Strongest Arm

JOSEPH FRANCO
with
RICHARD HAMMER

A DELL BOOK

Published by
Dell Publishing
a division of
Bantam Doubleday Dell
Publishing Group, Inc.
666 Fifth Avenue
New York, New York 10103

ISBN: 0-440-20223-X

Reprinted by arrangement with Prentice Hall Press

Printed in the United States of America
Published simultaneously in Canada

June 1989

10 9 8 7 6 5 4 3 2 1

KRI

DEDICATION

When I told my editor I wanted to thank the people who've touched my life he said to make a list. I taped an hour's worth of names and it still wasn't finished. My editor told me we'd need another book.

So many people have been a part of my life: my family, my Teamster colleagues, those friends who've been there when the times were the toughest, those who've let me share happiness when times were good.

I owe many, many people and I'm sorry space prevents me from thanking them by name. I think they know how I feel, at least I hope they do.

But I have to say thank you and forgive me to Cindy who has always had a special place in my heart. Come back to that place, Cindy.

To Barbara: I still love you; I wouldn't trade you in for ten thousand elephants.

—J.F.

INTRODUCTION

We are a people who live in the present. We are obsessed by it and our dreams of a glorious future. We ignore or choose not to remember the past. In the midst of progress and plenty, we act as though there is no stagnation or want. Retrogression is impossible. And so we forget or ignore the reality that not long ago, in the lifetime of many of us, perhaps a majority of the nation lived on a thin edge between hope and despair, the present filled with anguish, the future bleak and without prospect.

This is a story of our world as it was and of how, in some measure, we got where we are. It is a story that touched and still touches the lives of all of us. There are few altruists or idealists in this story. This is a story of men who believed they did what they had to do, men who inhabited a realm most of us would prefer to believe was only the figment of distorted and perverted imaginations. But this is a true story of men who built the Teamsters union into the largest and most powerful labor organization in the United States, with the potential of bringing the economy to a sudden and complete halt. It is not a pretty story. It is, perhaps, a cautionary tale.

Unions are now accepted as a basic part of society. At some time or another most Americans—laborers in factories and offices, people who earn their daily bread in industries and enterprises controlled by others who pay them—have been members of a union. I have been a member of two—the Newspaper Guild and the Writers Guild of America—and my wife is a member of three —the Actors' Equity Association, the Screen Actors Guild, and the American Federation of Radio and Television Artists. We join sometimes because we have to, as a condition of employment, or because we owe something to the union that has obtained for us higher wages, better benefits and working conditions, and speaks for us to management. We pay our dues; they are deducted from our salaries. Occasionally we may attend a general membership meeting and we may even take part in bargaining sessions. But mostly we have only a peripheral concern for what the unions are doing.

And so we have watched the unions grow fat, satisfied, and lazy. Their officers are isolated from members, often acting like their supposed antagonists, the businessmen. As these leaders have grown rich at our expense and distant from our desires and needs, Americans have increasingly turned away, and union membership has declined. Who needs a union when management will take care of us?

There was a time, though, when to talk union, to join a union, was to risk great danger. Until the Depression of the 1930s, a business-dominated society preached that a man could be whatever he dreamed if he worked hard enough. Unions were the work of the devil—un-American conglomerations of radicals, subversives, anarchists, low-lifes, and unwashed foreigners. It was public policy, backed often by the weight of government arms and laws, to strangle unions at their birth, to jail the leaders, to fire the members and blacklist them from further employment. If violence was called for, violence was used. Armed police, troops, and strike-breakers put down the railroad strikes of the 1870s, and, in the process, washed the streets with blood. The McCormick Harvester strike in the 1880s led to bombs in Chicago's Haymarket Square, to the death and crippling of police and bystanders, and to the hanging of four supposed anarchists who probably played no part in the violence. There was violence and death in the coal mines, textile mills, garment factories, steel mills—everywhere men were striking for higher wages, better working conditions, and the right to organize unions.

Until the Depression and the arrival of the Roosevelt New Deal, with its National Recovery Act, Wagner Labor Relations Act, and other legislation that gave labor a bill of rights, unionism remained nearly stillborn in the United States.

The leaders of industry might stand discredited, but they had no intention of capitulating without struggle to the demands of increasingly militant labor and its emerging leaders. Workers realized that alone they were weak and defenseless, at the mercy of the bosses who gave only what they wanted to give and who held the power to hire and fire at whim. In unions there was strength.

Workers united were a force to be reckoned with by employers. The 1930s were a time to fight, to link arms and raise voices, and to take as an anthem the song of Joe Hill and the "wobblies," the Industrial Workers of the World:

> It is we who plowed the prairies, built the cities where they trade,
> Dug the mines and built the workshops, endless miles of railroad laid;
> Now we stand outcast and starving mid the wonders we have made.
> But the union makes us strong!
>
> Solidarity forever!
> Solidarity forever!
> Solidarity forever!
> For the union makes us strong!

The militancy of labor was, of course, met with equal militancy from industry. Wave after wave of strikes shut down industry after industry, the workers hitting the picket lines for higher wages, humane working conditions, and the right to organize. Out came the strikebreakers and the scabs. Violence once more erupted, in the Little Steel strike, the Big Steel strike, at Ford and General Motors, and in the coal fields, which led John Llewellyn Lewis, the head of the United Mine Workers, to say, "Labor, like Israel, has many sorrows. Its women keep their fallen and lament for the future of the race."

It was from this cauldron of violence that a generation committed to unions emerged. And it was from these fires that men emerged who led labor into a new world where it could force its demands on industry. If union leaders were all dedicated to the labor movement and the rights of the working man, they could not have been more dissimilar in other respects, including their approaches to the problems they faced. Leaders ranged from the leftist Harry Bridges and his west coast longshoremen to the racket bosses who ran the east coast docks; from the visionary liberals like David Dubinsky of the International Ladies Garment Workers to the conservatives like Dan Tobin of the Teamsters; from the liberal pragmatists like Walter Reuther of the United Auto Workers to the cautious and practical George Meany of the plumbers union; and there was Phillip Randolph who led the Pullman Porters not only toward better wages and working conditions, but to being treated as human beings—a status not normally granted to black men.

And there was James Riddle Hoffa of the Teamsters.

This is the story of Hoffa and a man who served him loyally and without question for nearly thirty years. It is the story of Hoffa and the Teamsters, not from the view of government investigators who saw Hoffa as evil incarnate, or of reporters who plowed through the files of the investigating committees, or even of dissident Teamsters seeking Hoffa's overthrow. This is the view of a man who never deviated from his admiration and idolatry of Jimmy Hoffa, who saw Hoffa in good moments and bad, who could present the Hoffa that he knew in detail as a man he worked for, whose bidding he did, whom he did not judge. It is a portrait of Hoffa that will confirm, and even go beyond, what many outsiders believed, and it will dispel some of the myths that have grown about the Teamster leader.

It is based on over a hundred hours of interviews, conversations, and tape recordings with Joe Franco, a Teamster to his soul in the Hoffa mold. Indeed, there is about Joe Franco a sense of the Teamster, of myth and legend of the Hoffa Teamster that is unmistakable. Franco is a big man, towering six feet four or five, and weighing well over two hundred fifty pounds, with the kind of powerful arms a man would need to drive an eighteen-wheel tractor trailer or fell an enemy with one blow. There is nothing benign about him, dressed as he often is in black pants and a black shirt open halfway down his chest. There is nothing gentle about that strong face with its Roman nose, fringe of white hair, and drooping white bandit's mustache, or in those eyes behind thick glasses that can turn to frozen balls in anger. To see those eyes freeze, to hear that midwestern voice turn menacing when told that a deal has turned sour, or even when questioning what he considers overcharges on a hotel bill, is to believe that Joe Franco is capable of much. The stories he tells of his life before he met Jimmy Hoffa and while he served Hoffa have the ring of truth.

—R.H.

JOE FRANCO REMEMBERS . . .

I never heard of James R. Hoffa until the morning I met him in the spring of 1946. In fact, I never even heard of the Teamsters until that day.

It happened like this. Back at the end of 1945, I was working as an organizer for the United Mine Workers. What we were trying to do was organize the cab drivers in Detroit and they sent in a kid to help me do the job. Well, it turned out to be a very bad experience because I found out that he was not the kind of stand-up Italian that I thought he was. He ended up getting chased out of town by the guys the owners hired to stop us from organizing, and so I got a very bad taste about labor unions from that, and I went to work for Radio Cab Company. We formed a committee from the drivers and I told them that if anybody from the unions comes around or if anybody's got any problems, I'll go to Pete Theodore who owned the place and tell him we'll handle our own grievances and we'll handle our own problems and fuck the unions, because I didn't want no more part of unions.

We didn't have any trouble for a while. Then, in the spring of 1946, I was working nights and we had radios in our cabs, and the dispatcher puts out a call to my cab number, which was RC-130. He says, "Joe, get over to Peterborough and Woodward. There's a union guy here talking to some of the guys at the cab stand."

Immediately, I went there and there was this gray 1930s Buick parked at the cab stand. The dispatcher pointed it out and he says, "There's the union guy." The guy was on the inside, sitting with a couple of cab drivers, talking about trying to organize them. I took my cab and I poked the Buick. Then I hit him again and again, until finally he got out of the car and started to come over to me.

Now, every cab driver carries a piece of pipe or a lug wrench or something to defend himself if he runs across somebody who gives him a hard time. I had a lug wrench. So, I hefted the wrench and got out of the car and this guy comes toward me. He was a big guy, big as me, but he was in his fifties and I was in my twenties. I look at him and he looks at me and he says, "You must be Joe Franco."

"Right. Who are you?"

"I'm Tom Burke."

Well, I don't know Tom Burke from a pile of crap. But then he says a couple of words in Italian.

"Where'd you learn that at?"

"From Chicago. I was born and raised in an Italian neighbor-hood."

So, I put the lug wrench down and I says, "Okay." And I'm saying to myself, he's expressing himself in Italian so he can't be all that bad, so I'm going to listen to his bullshit. So, we pick up a conversation and I listened to him and it was like two o'clock in the morning. He says, "How about if we get a cup of coffee or something?"

We ended up in a restaurant that was owned by a guy named Pete Parker, who was an old-time bookmaker. And Tom Burke keeps telling me about the Teamster movement and what a great movement it is, and what a great union, and how it's headed by this guy named James R. Hoffa and what a hell of a guy he is. He says, "I know where you come out of and I know you'd appreciate this guy. He's one of us. He's a real street guy. He's a real tough son of a bitch. He's out in front. You don't have to worry about him standing behind or sitting in his office calling the shots. He's out on the streets with you and he'll fight toe-to-toe with any son of a bitch." He tells me a story about Jim taking on six cops at one time, jumping into picket lines with baseball bats, beating the shit out of guys. Well, this was the kind of deal I was used to, because that was the kind of neighborhood I came out of. I says, "He sounds like one of our guys. I'd love to meet this guy."

"I want you to. I think you're gonna be happy."

It got to be about eight-thirty, nine o'clock in the morning and he says, "Come on. We're going over on Trumbull Avenue. That's our headquarters." Jim's office was up on the second floor. We went up there about nine o'clock and we went into the business agents' office and I got introduced around to the guys. Everybody in that room was big. If you were six feet four like me, you were a midget. I mean, they were big, big guys, like Marshall Dubeck, who was an ex-wrestler, and Jim Langley, who was Hoffa's brother-in-law; Langley was about six feet eight and weighed about two hundred ninety pounds.

Well, I liked what I met in the business agents' office because this was my neighborhood; these were the kind of guys I grew up with. If I had to talk to somebody, I didn't have to turn around and wait for somebody; they were right alongside me, or out in front of me. So, right there, I kind of took a liking to the idea of meeting this guy, Hoffa.

Burke knocks at the door and a voice hollers out, "Come on in." Burke ducks his head in and then we walked into the office, and Tom and I, we stood by this guy's desk. The big wingbacked chair was turned so that the back was facing us and we couldn't see the guy who was sitting in it. He was on the phone, talking against the wall. Bert Brennan was there in his chair at his desk, sitting there with his leg over the arm like he always used to sit. Jimmy and Bert Brennan shared the office. They didn't do anything without one another knowing about it. They were strictly up-and-up partners. Bert had a habit of taking a cigarette and holding it between his teeth. He would bite it and carry it between his teeth and he always wore a hat with the brim down. He showed a very, very cold personality and I think he took a dislike to me right away at that first meeting because, basically, I don't think he liked Italians. But, big as I was and cocky as I was, I didn't give a shit about him or anybody else. I was kind of waiting to see what this guy Hoffa looked like, where the hell he was coming from. Hell, I'd already gotten burned by two or three different unions, so I wasn't really looking to get back into the movement.

All the time, Hoffa is in the chair with his back to us, talking on the phone. I mean, he was screaming into this phone. He's saying, "You cocksucker, you. I don't give a fuck, just do the fucking job, get it done and get the goddamn thing done with. I don't want to hear your bullshit on the fucking phone. You want to talk to me, get your goddamn ass over here. Get that goddamn contract straightened away. I don't want to hear nothing." That's the way he used to talk in those days. I mean, he couldn't say five words without three of them being curses and swear words. This thing went on for about ten minutes. Finally, he hung up and he swung his chair around.

I looked at Burke and I says, "Is this Hoffa?"

He says, "Yeah." Then he says, "Jimmy, I want you to meet Joe Franco."

I reached over and I shook hands with him. Then he stood up. He was about five feet six and he probably weighed about a hundred and seventy pounds, but he was a really solid-built guy.

"I understand you're working for Radio Cab."

"That's right."

"Tommy wants to organize Radio Cab. What do you think?"

"Well, I organized them once before, with a UMW guy."

"That asshole couldn't organize a pimple on a whore's ass."

"They chased him out of town. Those fucking goons they got down the street, they chased the son of a bitch right out of town."

"Well, they ain't gonna chase us. I've assigned Burke to it and I'd like to see them do that to Burke."

I look at Burke and I'm saying, "Does this fucking kid know what he's doing?" Because he was only about ten years older than me, in his thirties, and he used to carry his hair in a real short brush cut, and he had a baby face and a big, beautiful, butter-eating smile and beautiful front teeth. I just couldn't put him with the stories I'd been hearing for eight hours from Burke, about him being such a tough guy. And I'm saying to myself, I could reach across the desk and slap him in the face. He couldn't last two minutes in my neighborhood. They'd spit him out. Hell, I'm going to work for somebody that's not as tough as me, for chrissake? I kind of leaned over to Burke and I whispered in his ear, "Hey, this guy's too little, too young. I'm going to have to fight his battles from here on out. No wonder you got fucking giants in the other room. This guy can't do shit."

Burke says, "Shut up. Don't let him hear you. He'll throw you right out that fucking door."

"He's got two chances. One dies and the other went back to fucking Chicago. I told you this morning, I ain't looking for this fucking union business. I wanted to meet him because of the stories you told."

Now, Jim was bending over the desk, doing some kind of

paperwork. He jumps up and he says, "You want to be a fucking organizer?"

"Yeah."

"Think you got the fucking balls for it?"

"I got more fucking balls than you got hair on your head. That ain't the problem. It's you. You're my problem. You got the balls?"

"I got more fucking balls than the height you got. Don't ever question my balls. I'll take you any fucking time you want to go."

"That goes both fucking ways, pal." And we got into one hell of an argument. That's how we ended up being friends, due to the fact that I opposed him the first day I met him. So he took a liking to me.

He turns to Burke and he says, "I like him. Teach him. Put him under your wing. Teach him everything I want him to learn. Everything. Every trick. Everything you know about the trade. Teach him how to shoot. Teach him how to throw dynamite. Teach him every fucking thing. I want him to be your partner." He turns to me and he says, "You've been assigned to Burke. You listen to Burke and you'll learn. If you learn, you'll be a good organizer. If you don't, you'll be out of this fucking building in two seconds."

"Okay. I like Burke. As far as you're concerned, we'll see how things come out. Now how about a paycheck? What do we do about that?"

"For the time being, you're a commission organizer."

"What the hell is a commission organizer?"

"If you organize somebody, I'll give you the initiation fee and 50 percent of the first month's dues." In those days, the initiation fee was like ten dollars, fifteen dollars, and the dues were like four, five, six, seven dollars a month.

"That don't sound all too bad." I figured if I organized a hundred people a week, that's a thousand a week, and at the end of the month, I get half the dues. So I says, "Sounds good. But what do I do in the meantime?"

"Burke'll bring you out to the house every Saturday and I'll pay you in cash. How's $150?"

"That'll keep me going."

We left there and I says to Burke, "He's going to have to

really prove himself. His size just don't speak his character. But I like him. He's cocky, a little bantam rooster."

Burke turns to me and he says, "Remember our jurisdiction."

"What's our jurisdiction?"

"The Teamsters' jurisdiction is anything that's got wheels. You got a wristwatch on? That's got wheels. That's our jurisdiction. As long as it's got wheels on it, it belongs to us. Don't let any other fucking union bother with it. Trucks, cabs, whatever. As long as it's got wheels." Then he gave me five hundred to a thousand application cards.

So, that's how I met Jim Hoffa and that's how, within the week, I was a street guy, an organizer for the Teamsters.

Part I

That day in the spring of 1946, what was it that Jimmy Hoffa, still a relatively unknown yet highly ambitious local labor leader, saw in Joe Franco that made Franco seem a man for Hoffa's purposes? In the years that followed, what was it that led Hoffa to place increasing trust in and responsibility on Franco? There was, certainly, Franco's size and there was his obvious strength; there was his self-confidence, arrogance, and fearlessness—the marks of the Teamster organizer. But there was more, and the answer must be found in who Joe Franco was and in the forces that shaped him.

He was born Joseph Valenti in 1924 (it would be two decades before he adopted the name Joe Franco), in Detroit's teeming lower-east-side ghetto—a neighborhood of immigrant Italians and Jews and a growing number of blacks lured from the south by tales of the economic opportunities in the motor city. It was, like ghettos of immigrants everywhere, a neighborhood of grinding poverty where survival was a daily battle. He was the youngest of eight children—five boys and three girls. His parents, Frank and Maria Valenti, natives of Palermo in Sicily, were part of that massive wave of pre-World War I immigrants from southern Europe. The family lived upstairs from the restaurant and beer garden that Frank and Maria Valenti owned and operated, serving homemade wine and beer during Prohibition. With repeal and the arrival of a liquor license, the Valentis sold harder stuff. Their restaurant was a gathering place for men who were or would become famous, or infamous—whose names stirred fear in others.

Franco's father was what he called a fixer and peacemaker, something of an arbitrator and mediator. His work took him to Chicago two or three times a month and occasionally east to Cleveland, Pittsburgh, Philadelphia, and into New Jersey, "but he never went into New York." That work was on several levels. On one, he arranged marriages and contracts between families.

★ ★ ★

The two sets of parents would call him in and make an agreement and they would pay him a fifty dollar bill or a hundred bill and it was for a lifetime contract and he had to enforce it. He would talk to the children and make them understand that they were getting married and that their parents had agreed to it and what was expected of them. Now, say, two or three years down the line, if the boy went bad—if he became a drinker or a gambler, beat his wife and his kids, whatever it was, or if the girl turned around and became a whore or something, didn't treat the children right, whatever it was—then the parents would have the right to call my father in and say, look, this is what's happening to our daughter or to our son and we'd like you to straighten them out. Then, if it was the boy that was doing the wrong thing, my father would call the two kids in and sit down with them and find out exactly what was wrong. Then he'd explain to the boy that he'd better mend his ways and straighten out his way of life or my father would have to come back in again. It would be the same thing if it was the girl that was doing the wrong things. That first time would be just a warning. But if he didn't straighten out, then my father would have to come back in and do some damage, maybe break his legs or something, put him in the hospital, depending on what the parents wanted done. Sometimes the boy might have gone too far and they might ask my father to dispose of him and end the marriage. My father would do it because that was part of the contract.

But I would say he had a lot less trouble with the girls. Usually a woman has more sense. When she's talked to and warned, she straightens out her life. And I would say that 95 percent of the time when my father talked to the boy, the boy would straighten out his life and those marriages would last thirty, forty, fifty years. It seems like a prearranged marriage in those days lasted a lifetime. Of course, there was no such thing as divorce then.

Frank Valenti did more than just settle marital problems.

If there was a dispute between two rival outfits, they'd call my dad in and he'd resolve it. There was no such thing as organized crime in those days. There were neighborhood gangs and they would need somebody to go from one gang to the other gang and say, we want to make peace because there's too much killing and it's come down to where everybody's shooting everybody. So they would use my father as a mediator. He would go to one person, the head of one gang and talk to him, and then go to the head of the other gang and make peace arrangements, where they could live in the same neighborhood or the same city and live amongst themselves in whatever business they were in. There were many meetings at my home where gangs would come in and sit down and my father would settle things between them. There was never any trouble, never a fight or an argument, because my dad and mother wouldn't stand for it.

Through these years, whenever Frank Valenti went to Chicago, two or three times a month, he invariably took his youngest son with him.

We would go to the Michigan Central Station and take a train and when we got to Chicago, there would be a big car waiting for us to drive us to Melrose Park. That was a very, very heavy Italian area; it was the hub of the Italian people. Melrose Park was like 99.9 percent Italian in those days. We used to go there and we'd stay with my *padrino* and *padrina*, Phil and Anne Benedetto; they were my godparents from my confirmation. My dad used to take me over to a place called the Lumber Gardens. Maybe Al Capone had his headquarters in Cicero, but Melrose Park was the real headquarters that ran the Chicago area and whenever there was a problem that had to be resolved, it came out of Melrose Park, and whenever there was a sitdown to resolve those problems, a lot of the times it was held at the Lumber Gardens. They had pool tables and bocci games in the back and they used to sit around and drink coffee and drink wine and play cards, and they would have their meetings and take care of their business. I would always go over to the pool tables and throw the balls around the tables, and my dad would sit with the guys. My dad and my *padrino,* Phil Benedetto— I called him Uncle Phil—they were very close friends of Al Capone and Big Jim Colissimo and a lot of the other people in Chicago. And my father was one of those that would bring them together with people they were having trouble with and set up meetings and make peace.

Frank Valenti was a fixer and a peacemaker, and he was a gambler.

He loved to play cards. He loved to play bocci. And they gambled for money, for big money. In those days, fifty or a hundred dollars was big money. My mother would send me to look for him because sometimes he would be gone for several days playing cards. I remember one time he had been gone for a couple of days and I was walking down the street and all of a sudden a cab pulled up and my mother was in the cab and she hollered at me and I got in the cab. She says, "Have you seen your father?" I knew where he was at and I knew where he was gambling. But I saw she had a pistol in her pocketbook and I think, "Uh-oh, if she catches him, she's gonna give him a shot or two." So, I says, "No." In those days driving around in a taxicab wasn't the greatest thing in the world because money was very hard to come by, and I saw that the meter was running like seven dollars and that was like you were very lucky to make in a week. But she was bound and determined to find him wherever he was at, whatever he was doing, because she figured he was like shacked up with some broad. But he was at somebody's home playing cards and they had been playing two or three days. We didn't have a telephone in those days so there was no way he could have called to let her know, and I wasn't going to let her know because I figured if she found out he was gambling, she'd raise all kinds of hell about it. I probably got him into more trouble than he would have deserved, but I couldn't say anything to her in the taxi, so I just let her run around the city trying to find him. He finally got home and there was all kinds of hell, but they eventually got that patched up.

There was another time that they had a very bad argument. My mother was as hot tempered as he was and he had a real short fuse. Anyway, he took me to a burlesque show. In the old days, they used to give you two movies and then the revue, a burlesque and slapstick, and during the intermission the vendors used to walk up and down the aisles and sell you a box of candy kisses, which were twenty-five cents, and inside the box was a gift. I asked my dad if he would buy me a box of candy. So, I got my candy and opened it and found a pair of black silk stockings inside. I put them in my pocket and I figured, well, I'll bring this home to Ma, and I'll give them to her and say that my dad sent them and that would make peace between them, maybe that would resolve the argument. So, we left the burlesque and we went home and my dad was standing on the corner outside the house and I went upstairs and gave the stockings to my mother, and I says, "This is a peace offering from Pa." She went into a rage and she pulled out a gun and opened the window and cussed at him in Italian. What it was was that sending a pair of black stockings was an indication of death, and my father didn't know I was giving them to her—he didn't even know I had the stockings. She thought that he sent them and that was like sending something saying that she was going to die. She opened the window and took the gun and started shooting at him, and I saw him running down the street, ducking.

One day in 1936, I was sitting in the kitchen and six federal marshals walked into the house, and they took him and turned him around and handcuffed him and didn't say nothing to me at all, and took him and rushed him out of the house. All I did was sit there and wait for my mother to get home. I told my mother about the six guys who looked like policemen and who put handcuffs on Pa and took him away. She immediately started to make some telephone calls to find out where they had taken him. She found out within a day or two that they had him on Ellis Island. She went to New York right away and when she came back she told me that he was all right and that they had sent him back to Sicily. He was what they called an undesirable alien. I guess he had a reputation, enough so that the United States government didn't want him here in this country.

To his family, he was the baby. To his friends and those who knew him, he was Jo-Jo, and years later he would be simply "the kid." To many others, in and out of Detroit's lower-east-side ghetto, he was trouble.

Of all my family, all my brothers became hard workers and lived normal lives. My sisters, too. My oldest sister was a college graduate and she became a social service worker, a truant officer, a policeman, and she worked in the courts. Anytime I got into trouble, they would call her up and say, "Hey, your kid brother's in trouble." She'd say, "Which one?" They'd say, "The baby, what else?" That was the saddest thing. What else? The baby's in trouble, what else?

So, I was the black sheep. I don't know why. I guess there was something in me. I didn't want to grow up poor. I wanted to be something and I didn't find it in school. So I had to find it the only way I knew how. That was by using my head, by being a hustler.

Almost from the moment of memory, at five or six, in the darkest days of the Depression, he hustled his way into trouble, into deeds small and not so small, into acts he saw as helping others and acts he saw as helping himself reach that only dimly perceived goal of not being poor. Always there was the philosophy and the rationale that would last through the years: "You did what you had to do to survive or you didn't survive."

It began, if memory can be trusted, like this:

I don't remember ever being a young kid. All I can remember is that I had to steal in order to survive. Back in those days, they had what they called penny pantries and soup lines. For a penny apiece, you could stand in line and buy a cup of soup, two slices of bread, meat loaf, and mashed potatoes with gravy. You could stand in line once a week and the government gave you a pound of flour and a pound of grease that had a little package in it that was yellow, and when you mixed it with the grease they called it oleo, and you got a two-pound can of corned beef hash, and that was your food allotment for the week. I remember standing in those lines with my mother and that was the most embarrassing, degrading thing I can ever remember having to do other than having to go to prison. I swore right then that I would never stand in line again.

We had our own gang in those days, when I was six or seven, and the oldest kid in the gang was ten. We swore that we would do what we had to do in order to have our families and our neighborhood survive. We knew where the government stored the food they used to pass out, so we used to break into that place and steal whatever we could get and take it around the neighborhood and pass it around. We'd tell the people to go ahead and continue to stand in line just so that it wouldn't be obvious that they weren't receiving their weekly allotment. That way, they'd have three, four, five bags of flour to make bread and spaghetti and have oleo to cook with instead of spit.

So, Franco and his gang—J.T., Eugene, and Charlie, known as the Four Musketeers, sometimes joined by a kid a few years older named Rudy—helped provide the food that enabled their families and friends to subsist. They tried to help ensure shelter as well.

Back in those days, the majority of the homes were owned by outside people and if you didn't pay your rent in thirty days, the next day the landlord would come with two or three guys and take all your furniture and put it out on the street and you were out of your home with no place to live. They didn't have eviction laws like they do today. We'd go to the homes that were vacated by eviction and we'd strip them. We'd take the bathtub, the doors and doorknobs, all the electrical fixtures, the wiring, everything—we'd even strip the siding so there was nothing left but the shell, some two-by-fours. We'd take all the stuff to junkyards and sell it and make enough money to go to the families that were evicted and put them back into another home in the same neighborhood. When the landlord came by in a couple of days, he'd find his home was just two-by-fours standing and what it amounted to was he had a vacant lot. Then we'd go and talk to the landlords. If you can imagine, a bunch of little kids going to talk to the landlords, but that was the way it was. We'd tell him that he ought to let the people stay there free, even if they couldn't pay the rent. At least that would protect the property, because the people that was living in them wouldn't bother the homes, and the people that was wrecking the empty homes, which was us, would stay away because there was people living in them. The landlords finally got to understand what we were trying to do, which was to make sure that everybody had a place to live and eventually, when times got better, these people would pay the rent because they didn't want to live there free. Well, they got to understand it and we had no more evictions in our neighborhood.

I had a little wagon in those days. It was homemade. My dad probably made it, or my older brother, I can't remember who. I used to follow the milk wagon with my wagon and it used to deliver in the richer neighborhoods, on the upper east side up toward Woodward Avenue where the wealthy people lived. In those days, the milk and the cream was in bottles and on the bottles they used to have a big three in a circle, which meant there was a three-cent deposit returnable to any grocery store. I would follow the milkman and watch when he put the bottles on the porches, and as soon as he went up the block, I'd run up to the porch and grab whatever there was and put it into my wagon and go on to the next house, until I had a wagon full. Then I'd go back to my neighborhood and go to the families who needed milk and give it to them. I told 'em they would have to give me the empty bottles back, like I was a regular milkman, when I gave them a new bottle. Then I'd take the empties to the grocery stores and collect the three-cent deposits off it. That way, I was helping them and making a little money for myself, and it was a matter of doing what I had to do in order to survive.

On the edges of the ghetto stood the Eastern Market, a major farmers' market in the Detroit area. Every morning, in the darkness of three or four o'clock, the small farmers from the outlying countryside—some in Model T trucks, some unable to afford trucks, in double-hitch wagons—would haul their produce to the market for sale. The slow-moving vehicles, crawling at under ten miles per hour, were easy prey for Jo-Jo and his gang.

We'd spot those wagons coming in and we'd line up two blocks ahead. If this guy had a load of potatoes, there'd be a kid waiting at each corner and we'd jump on the wagons and dump off the sacks of potatoes and they'd pick them up. Whatever it was, potatoes, onions, watermelons, anything, we'd do the same thing. But we never took more than we needed. We wanted to take care of our families and our neighborhood and so we took enough for that. The farmers, they never said a word about it. They put up with it because it was tough times and we never took more than we needed. I mean, we could have taken everything. We could have pulled him over and taken his horse, his whole load if we wanted. We did it to one guy. This guy got real nasty so we knocked him off his wagon and we took his horse and wagon and drove it into the schoolyard. We let the horse go. We got a can of kerosene and we set fire to the wagon and we all stood there and had a bonfire at five o'clock in the morning. Well, that taught the farmers. Hey, all we wanted was enough to live on. Don't get out of line, don't get tough, don't get smart, just do what you have to do. You help us and we help you, so, when you come to our neighborhood, nobody will touch you. It was kind of a protection deal.

Protection became something they soon brought to a certain perfection.

There was this little Jewish man who used to sell bushel baskets and gunnysacks to the farmers at the market, and they used them to bring their crops in. When you finished with that basket you'd bring it to this Jewish man and sell it back to him. Well, we used to break into his yard every Friday night and steal enough baskets and sacks to sell back so we could go to a movie on Saturday afternoon. This Jewish guy caught on, because he saw that every Saturday we'd bring him back twelve bushel baskets and twelve gunnysacks, no more and no less. He says to us one day, "You kids, would you kids like to have a job? I'll tell you what I'll do with you. I'll give each of you fifty cents apiece and you make sure that nobody breaks into my joint anymore. If you catch the guys, I leave it to you what you want to do with them." Well, what he was offering us was just what we'd get for selling him back the twelve baskets and twelve sacks, and it was enough for the movies. So, we were on his payroll.

But then we started to figure, why should we pay to get into the movies? We ought to be able to get in free. In those days, you got vaudeville and two movies and it cost ten cents, and ten cents was a big thing. We started to figure how could we save the dime. What we did was, we all chipped in and we went over to a novelty shop. They used to sell stink bombs for twenty-five cents a box and there was six stink bombs in a box. We bought two boxes, and we all chipped in for the cost. Then we went to the first theater in the neighborhood and we told the manager that we wanted in free every Saturday, otherwise the show would be empty. He told us to get the hell out of there and never come back. We says, okay, and then one guy pays for a ticket and he goes to the side door and opens it, and three of us run in and we run up and down the aisles throwing these little stink bombs. In about ten minutes, the show was empty, because it stunk to high heaven.

After we done that a couple of times, we figure how the hell can we save the fifty cents we were spending on the stink bombs. The way was, we would make our own. Rudy was pretty hep on chemistry and his mother, who was with the Follies in New York, had bought him a chemistry set. He said if we took film, negatives, and roll it real tight and wrap it in paper and set fire to it and let it burn for about a minute and then put it down and step on it, they'd smolder and they'd fill the theater with smoke. Boy, did they stink. And it was cheaper because everybody had film. That's what we ended up doing to every show in our neighborhood. Then, every Saturday when the manager saw us coming, he'd say, "Boys, come on in, take the best seats in the house you want, only I don't want anybody else coming in through the side doors, and I don't want anybody throwing stink bombs." After that, we never paid to get into a theater, and we were like on his payroll. Maybe it wasn't right, but by God, we had to survive and that's what we did to do it.

He was still a kid, not even ten, and the neighborhood was becoming too small to contain him, despite warnings that to venture out was to venture into a strange world with new dangers.

I lived on Mack and Russell, and Hastings was the next block. Whenever we went across Hastings we took our lives into our own hands because that was an altogether different neighborhood and there were different gangs. But I ventured out to Woodward Avenue and I saw the bright lights and I said, oh my God, this is a whole different world here, this is for me. I liked the bright lights. I liked the action that was going on. My neighborhood was for nothing.

So, I walked up and down Woodward Avenue, taking everything in. There was a restaurant called Greenfield's, right off the corner of Woodward and Charlotte. They used to put the desserts in the window and I used to put my nose up against that window and wish that someday I could go in there and buy one of them. There was a guy there who was probably in his thirties or forties and he was built like a bull, and that's what they called him, Bull. He was the newspaper man. He had that corner and about six other corners in the area and he was making a lot of money for those days. I figured this is the greatest place in the world to have a newspaper stand, right in front of Greenfield's where guys were going in and out all the time. So, I went over to this man, Bull, and I asked him if he wanted to sell his old newspaper stand.

"Sure."

"How much do you want?"

"Twenty cents."

"Okay. I'll buy it off you."

"Give me the twenty cents and it's yours."

"Okay. I got to get my wagon and I'll be back and I'll give you your money and I'll pick up the stand."

I ran home and got the wagon and I got a spike, a railroad spike, and I went back and gave him the twenty cents and picked up the old stand and went right in front of Greenfield's, and there I was, a seven-year-old kid with a handsledge pounding this railroad spike into the sidewalk through the length of the newspaper stand. My God, you know, that spike's still there. I got that done and then here comes Bull. He says, "What the hell do you think you're doing? Get that goddamn stand out of there. You can't put it there. This belongs to me."

I knew I had to do something. So, I grabbed the sledge in my hands and I looked at him, like looking at the top of a mountain was what it seemed like, and I says, "You son of a bitch, I'll hit you with this sledge hammer right between the eyes if you don't get the hell away from me." I would have killed him if he got close enough.

He's screaming and hollering and out of Greenfield's walks a guy named Charlie Resnick, and he's with a guy named Moe, a guy named Bananas, and a guy named Bubbles, and they're all gamblers. [Charles Resnick later went on to become a major figure in Las Vegas, one of the owners of the El Rancho casino and hotel.] They didn't look like the Depression. They were dressed in beautiful suits, white-on-white shirts, ties, and they used to eat at Greenfield's twice a day. Charlie walks up to Bull and he says, "Hey, what's the matter? What're you picking on this kid for?"

I says to Charlie, "Mister, he wanted twenty cents for that stand. I gave him twenty cents cash. I want to sell newspapers."

He turned around to Bull and he says, "The kid pay you?"

Bull says, "Yeah."

Charlie says, "Then leave the kid alone. Don't say anything to this kid. Don't you bother this kid. If you didn't want him to have it, you shouldn't have sold it to him. Now leave the kid alone or you'll answer to me." Then he turns to me and he says, "Kid, if he bothers you, you come into the restaurant and get me." And he tells me that everybody's gonna buy their newspapers from me.

They used to have newspaper trucks and jumpers who'd come by and throw out a bundle of newspapers. The papers cost a nickel and I'd have to pay two-and-a-half cents for them. So, the truck comes and the jumper throws out the bundles in front of Bull. But when he comes by me and I wave him down, and tell him I got enough to buy six newspapers, he says, "Sorry, kid, I can't sell you." Bull told them not to sell me any. When Charlie and the guys come out of the restaurant, they see me standing there with no newspapers. Charlie says, "Where's your newspapers? You can't sell anything if you ain't got nothing to sell." So, I told him that the newspaper trucks won't stop for me. He says, "Okay, we'll take care of that tomorrow."

The next day, I come back over to Woodward to get my newspaper stand and Charlie's standing there waiting for the driver to drop the newspapers off with Bull. When he comes by, Charlie flags him. He tells the driver, "Whatever this kid wants, whether it's two papers or ten papers or thirty papers, if he's got the money, sell it to him. If you don't sell it to him, you'll answer to me."

From that time on, I had no problems. I never bought more than ten because there was ten guys used to come in there and they had a way of reading the newspaper that I'll never forget. They would fold it and quarter it and read it, quarter it and fold it and read it, and when they got finished it was like brand new. And they'd come out and give it back to me so I could sell it again. And they would give me not a nickel but a dime. I was earning like two dollars a day. My dad was working at the time and he was making eight to ten dollars a week, and my brothers, if they were lucky, they were working maybe two or three days a week and making about a dollar a day. I'm making two dollars a day seven days a week. I started to flash it around the neighborhood, buying candy for the kids and other stuff. My family starts asking, "What're you doing? Where are you getting all that money?" I says, "I'm newspapering. Come and see me." So my older brother comes up and sees that I was telling the truth and that I did have a newspaper stand.

The stand, though, lasted only a couple of months. There were other things and easier money that began to lure him. His reputation and that of his friends had begun to spread. A funeral parlor opened in the neighborhood. It was opened by a black man and he was not greeted with much equanimity.

He was having some problems. One day, he called in the gruesome foursome, which was me and J.T. and Eugene and Charlie, and he asks if we would work for him and make sure that nobody would break his windows or anything else, and he would pay us fifty cents a week. Every week we would go by and collect our fifty cents and he never had any problems. He was a very nice man, very intelligent and educated, and his name was Mr. Diggs. A long time later his son became a congressman from the city of Detroit.

One night we were sitting on the curb, trying to figure how we could score for some money. Being that I had been on Woodward Avenue and I had been on Second and Third Streets, I knew a lot about what was happening. I didn't know what prostitution was in those days, but I was sitting there telling my three partners about all these beautiful girls that I would see standing in front of these homes on Second and Third Streets, and I says, "We can go up there and I know how we can make some money." Now the girls in those days, I don't know what it was, but they were beautiful, all of them. Maybe it was because I was like eight years old. But they used to wear the fox stoles and fox furs and jackets, jewelry, and they were blondes. We went up there and we'd start at the corner of Third going south toward Grand River and we would stop at every location where there was one or two or three girls in front of an apartment or a home. We'd sit on the curb in front of these girls and if a car pulled up, we would scream out, "Get the hell out of here. That's my sister." And the cars would just continue to roll. So the girls would come up and say, "Hey, kids, get the hell out of here. You're ruining our business." Then they'd turn around and give us a quarter apiece, and we'd go down to the next house where the girls would be standing and we'd do the same thing until we got all the way down to John R. and then come back up the street on the other side.

Now, the word got out that these four kids were putting the muscle on all the pro girls for a quarter, and this went on for two or three weekends. And they got to look on us like we were their kid brothers and we were protecting them for a quarter apiece. The thing was, I fell in love with this one blonde girl. Even being young and little as I was, I wanted to tackle her, I wanted to get on her bones and get into her body even if it cost me five dollars. I saved every quarter, every buck I could save until I got my five dollars. Every time I came by her place, I'd say to the guys, "Ah, leave her alone," and we never collected from her. Well, she took a liking to me and I told her, "Would you let me if I had five dollars?" She says, "Sure, why not?" So, this one Saturday, I got all spruced up, took a bath, and went down there and worked the street until we got to her. Then I told the guys, "I'll see you later. I'm going in there and jump on this girl's body."

She was waiting there for me and she looked beautiful. She invited me into the house and through this dark hallway with a red light and excited as I was, anticipating what was going to happen, I walked in, not thinking anything other than she was just giving me the sign to come forward, up the stairs to her room. Well, I had just hit the staircase when all of a sudden I felt a hand on the back of my neck grab me. It spun me around and slapped me right across the face like I'd never been slapped. And the guy looked at me and he says, "You little son of a bitch. I've been waiting to catch you. I hear you've been shaking all my girls down." I looked up at him. Surer 'n hell, he was my cousin. I always wondered what the hell my cousin did for a living, how he could dress the way he dressed, how he could hang around with the beautiful women he hung around with, with a big, brand new sixteen-cylinder LaSalle convertible. I always wanted to be like him. Well, I found out how he did it. He was a pimp. And the girl I wanted in the worst way was his wife who used to work for him as a hooker.

"You got the five dollars?"

"Yeah, I got the five dollars."

"Give me the son of a bitch."

He took it off me and then he kicked me in the ass, knocked me down the flight of stairs onto the porch, and he says, "Now get on your own side of town and stay there. Don't ever let me catch you on Third Street again." That was the end of my career of shaking down hookers.

There were other things to take its place. There was, for instance, burglary.

The grocery and candy stores used to have machines to sell candy and cigarettes and stuff, and we used to break into the stores and bust open those machines and take the candy and the cigarettes and the money and all those boxes of junk jewelry and those phony rings with those phony little stones they used to carry, figuring I could use them with some of the girls in the neighborhood. Those machines used to be loaded with dimes and nickels and pennies, because cigarettes used to cost twenty cents a pack and the candy was a nickel or a penny.

This one night, we broke into a store. I would always go first because little as I was I could squirt through the vent in the upper part of the door like a snake and then open the door for the other guys. We cleaned out the place and then we heard the cops outside. We beat it like hell and got away and headed for the barn where we used to go up into the hayloft to cut the swag. Well, this one guy that was with us that night, his name was Tarzan, and as we were running away, he was limping like he had a bad foot or something and he just barely escaped. When he got to the barn, we said, "What's the trouble?"

"I hurt my foot on that goddamn machine."

"What'd you get?"

"I didn't get nothin'."

"What do you mean you didn't get nothin'? You didn't get no cigarettes? No tobacco? Nothin'?"

"Nah. I screwed around with that goddamn machine and I didn't get nothin'."

We looked at one another and we figured there was nothing wrong with his foot to begin with and so how the hell did he end up with a sore foot coming out of there. So, we jumped him and we held him down and we took his shoe off. We found out why he was limping. His foot was full of dimes. He had broken into the machine and took all the dimes out and stuck them into his shoe and he didn't want to cut it up with us. Well, that was the end of him as far as we were concerned. He never stole with us after that. He couldn't cut it up fairly so he couldn't have no part of our operation. We beat the shit out of him and we never did forget or forgive.

But sometimes he got caught.

There was this one time when we were tearing down a house to protect the people from the landlord. My friend Albert was up on the roof and I was on the bottom with a crowbar, ripping the sides of the house out. The cops came up the front of the house and I went down the side of the house toward the alley. Albert jumped from roof to roof. That was our means of escape. If you stayed on the roof, you didn't have no problems. You always had your problems when you stayed on the ground. So Albert got away but I ran through the alley and the gate opened up and there were these two huge cops. They just grabbed me and picked me up in the air and took me down to the Hunt Street station, which was the toughest station in the city.

There was this young lieutenant there when they brought me in that night, and it was my first time. He knew my family and he was on the desk. I'm screaming and hollering and crying, about how little I am and don't put me in jail. Well, he called my mother and he told her to take me home and give me a bath and make sure I don't do it again.

The thing was, of course, it happened again, two or three times. But my sister was working in the courts then and they used to call her and she always got me out. So, I never went through what some of the guys did. You could always tell who got caught in the neighborhood doing something wrong. They had this detention home on the corner of Forest and Rockville and you were sent there if you got caught. If you were seven or eight, they only kept you overnight; later on, they kept you longer, a week or two weeks or three weeks or even a couple of months, depending on your age. The thing was, once they got you in there, they gave you a baldie. So you could always tell how long a guy was in there by his head. I mean, if he came out bald, he was only in overnight; if he had a little stubble, he was in a week or two; if he had a brush cut, you knew he was in for a couple of months.

He was lucky, and his luck held as he moved deeper into more serious crime.

I couldn't have been much more than twelve or thirteen when this guy I knew, Tony, who was about twice as old as me and an old pro, came to me one day and he asks me if I want to make like ten dollars a day, maybe more. Well, times was still rough and ten dollars a day was a lot of money, so I said, "Sure."

"All you got to do is take this bag into this Chinaman's shop, into this barber shop, and he'll give you another bag and you bring it out to me."

"Hey, sure. No problem." I didn't know what I was doing, but this went on for about two months, and I'm dropping these bags off and picking these bags up and giving them to him, and at the end of a couple of hours in the course of a day, I got ten dollars. All of a sudden, I'm making fifty, sixty dollars a week.

Now, one day my oldest brother comes to me and he grabs me by the back of the neck and he says, "Where the hell are you getting all this money? You can't be getting it off a newsstand because you ain't sellin' newspapers no more. We know you got rid of that. Where's this money comin' from?"

I had to get off the hook, so I says, "I'm working for Tony."

"Tony who?"

I tell him Tony who, and I got a whack right across the side of my head. He says, "Don't you know what the hell you're doing?"

"No. All I'm doing is taking paper bags in and bringing paper bags out."

"You goddamn fool. You're delivering dope. That's marijuana you're delivering. The Chinaman's dealing it. Tony's got a reputation. He's one of the biggest dealers in town. He's giving you ten dollars, and in case you get caught, he takes off and you sit there, you jerk. You're the guy that's goin' to jail for fifteen years, not him."

"I didn't know. Now you told me, I'll go away from him."

The next day when I was supposed to see Tony, I see him and I says, "I'll blow your goddamn head off for what you got me into. My family's into my face. You got me into more trouble than you know what to do with."

That was the end of that deal. I never did it no more after that.

But when he told Tony that he would blow his head off, he meant it, and Tony knew he meant it. For violence was always on the edges and often at the center of his life from his earliest memories. He was witness to it. He was accessory to the acts of others. And he committed violent acts of his own.

He had gone to Chicago, to Melrose Park, on one of the regular trips with his father and as usual they were staying with his padrino, *Phil Benedetto.*

About a block away from my Uncle Phil's home there was a barbershop and the barbershop was on a sharp corner, and there was a cement staircase with six steps going up to it and the door had a bell which tinkled when you opened it. I was sitting on the first steps, me and two little girls from the neighborhood, and we were just sitting there and talking. Here came two guys, just as normal as two people would be going into a barbershop to get a haircut and a shave. There was several people in there already and I think there was four chairs in there and four barbers.

These two guys walked in, and they must have had machine guns with them because all we heard was bow-bow-bow-bow-bow, and out these two guys came. When we heard these shots, we just got up and ran like hell to get out of the way. These two guys come running out and jump into a car that was driving up and off they went. We didn't bother to go inside because I knew that they had already killed one or two or three people in that place. All I could see was one of the barbers coming out and screaming for somebody to call the police for help. I just took off and ran about a block and a half away to where my uncle lived and told my uncle, "They just had a big shootout over at the barbershop." Him and my dad took off and told me to stay inside the house. They came back a few hours later and I could hear them talking in Italian that they had killed three guys in there that were supposed to be in town to hit somebody from Melrose Park. So, instead of them hitting somebody, the outfit from Melrose Park found out about it and hit them before they had a chance to do what they came for.

There was another time in Melrose Park, I was walking home from my uncle's place over to my aunt's sister who lived about a block away. I saw a car parked on the side of the street, on 28th Street, which was the main drive, and I saw a man on the opposite side of the street come walking across the street. This was about ten o'clock in the morning and there was nobody on the street at that time. He walked over and started to talk to the man in the car. I was just passing the car and all of a sudden I could hear in Italian, cussing out, disgraceful words and hollering out in Italian —*Morte di veni*—death to you, death will come to you. And all of a sudden I hear, pow-pow-pow-pow, four shots. I turned around and I see the guy running with a pistol in his hand and he's running like hell right down the street. I took off down the goddamn street and made a quick turn around the corner and headed for my aunt's sister's house. I told her and she took me home and told my dad what took place. He said, "Keep your mouth shut, you see nothing, you stay in the house until we're ready to go back to Detroit."

So, I was introduced to this type of life at a very young age. God, there was a lot of it going on in those days. Revenges between families. I mean, legitimate families. Vendettas between legitimate families, just regular ordinary families would have vendettas against other families over disputes or neighborhood arguments or maybe somebody said something. It was a thing that was basically brought over from Italy. You show disgrace to another family, well, the only way to save face was to do damage, either you put him in the hospital or you kill him. I've seen them shoot one another over playing bocci. I've seen outrageous fights over card games. Anything.

He was witness. And he was accessory.

I was raised by the guys that belonged to the gang in our neighborhood. I was like a mascot. They adopted me because of the fact that my father was in the business, whatever you want to call it. They were never scared to talk in front of me, and they spoke Italian, which I spoke fluently since the people associated with my family spoke Italian and nothing else. They used to hang around my mother's beer garden and they never hid anything from me. I knew when they were going to rob or do a job or hold up something.

They used to tell me to be on the corner at a given time and I'd be sitting there on the curb when this touring Model T with four or five guys sitting in it drove up, stopped, somebody called my name out, "Jo-Jo, come here." They gave me a gunnysack and told me to take it and hide it in the usual place, which was in a hayloft in an old barn that was still standing in our neighborhood. I went down the alley, went up into the hayloft, looked into it. There were shotguns, machine guns, pistols, there was enough equipment to start a war. This one time, I must have been six or seven, they had held up a bank on the corner of Canfield and Russell.

Those were the days of John Dillinger and he got the blame anytime a bank was held up. But a lot of times it was the gang that used to hang around my mother's place. Later on, these guys merged with a group that was called the River Gang and the key people, the ones I grew up with, who made me the mascot, were a guy named Mr. Joe and guys named Mr. Pete and Mr. Sam. Our people, the way we have of showing respect to an elder, we'd always say, "mister," and if you were on close terms, you were allowed to say "Mr. Joe" or "Mr. Sam" or "Mr. Pete," and if you weren't, you had to say, in due respect, their last name. You always said mister, not Sam or their first name. If you did, you'd get a slap across the side of the head.

So, I was their mascot and every time these guys would pull something off, instead of taking a chance of getting stopped by the cops, they'd always ask me to station myself someplace where they'd drop off their armament and I would go and hide it in that same hayloft. And they'd always take care of me, give me change out of their pockets. I was the pet of the whole group and they taught me a lot, they taught me how to behave with people.

And there was the violence he was directly responsible for.

Now, some people are going to say it's hard to believe, here's a kid at the age of six or seven who's already killed somebody. But it's true. I was either in first or second grade and there was a kid that was sixteen or seventeen years old and he used to wait for me every day on the way to school. In those days, the mothers would give you a penny and for that penny in school they'd give you a carton of milk and two graham crackers. This kid would grab me and shake me down for whatever money I had on me, and since I was making money off the milk bottles in those days and other things, I always used to have like fifty cents to a dollar, which in those days was like having a thousand dollars in your pocket. He'd grab me and beat me and take my money away from me. Well, that went on for quite a while until finally I got tired of it. I talked to my older brother, Jim, and he says, "Hey, kid, do what you have to do."

So, I got up early one morning and I took a baseball bat and got in between houses, and I waited for this kid to come looking for me. When he did, I came down on his head with that baseball bat and I split his head wide open. There's no question that I killed him, because the baseball bat had a lot of fragments on it and I took it home and washed it off and went to school.

That tells you what I was made of. There was something in me, I don't know what it was, but I wasn't going to let anything or anybody stand in my way or let anybody come down the pike and muscle me.

The second occurrence of my actually killing somebody came just after the end of Prohibition. I was probably about nine. There was a man that was trying to break into the side entrance to our restaurant and beer garden with a rock. It was summertime and it was like three-thirty or four o'clock in the morning and this guy was banging away with a big rock, trying to knock the lock off. I woke up when I heard my dad shouting in his broken English, "You get away from the door." I looked out the window and saw this guy banging away and telling my dad to go to hell. I turned to my dad and I says, "Go get the gun."

My dad says, "No. Don't touch the gun."

"Bullcrap." I ran into his bedroom and reached under the pillow where he kept it and I pulled the thirty-eight out and went over there and cocked it and aimed it and shot and hit him right in the head with it. Killed him deader than a doornail. This sent my father into a frenzy. He says, "Oh my God, you killed him." We went downstairs and we opened the place up and called the police department. The cops wanted to know who did it. I says, "I did it." The cops looked at me and they said, "You're one hell of a shot, kid. Now, let's take him and drag him inside so we don't have to arrest you because now we can say he broke into your place and you shot him while he was in your place."

That's how they squashed it, because I don't think they wanted to take a nine-year-old to court for a murder trial. And, anyway, the guy was trying to break into our building.

There was another kid whose last name was Diverto, who was about a year or two older than me. Rudy, this kid I used to hang around with, was like two or three years older and a hell of a lot bigger. Back in those days, our weapons were ice picks. We would steal those ice picks off ice wagons and then we'd drill the back end and fill them with lead and balance them so we could throw them. And we used to practice by the hour in the backyard with an inner tube. If you hit the inner tube, naturally you had to patch it up. So, you made damn sure never to hit the inner tube. We got to be pretty good with it.

Now this Diverto kid got out of line. He came into our neighborhood, our area, and he started going the milk bit with me, stealing my milk bottles, stealing things that would belong to us. So, Rudy and I grabbed him one day and we tied him up against the barn in what you call spread-eagle. Rudy says, "Okay, I'll go first."

I says, "You do what you got to do." He came real close. I don't think Rudy wanted to do anything. Me? I aimed right for his Adam's apple and that's exactly what I hit, smack in the Adam's apple, pinned him right up against the barn door and left him there.

Well, there was a lot of hell going on in the neighborhood at that time because Diverto's brother, who was about ten or twelve years older, was looking for the guy that killed his kid brother. But nobody knew other than Rudy and I. Not even my own brothers knew. But we never had no more trouble after that because they kind of felt we were it and nobody wanted to mess with us.

Even if anybody was sure, nobody would have said anything. The cops investigated, but they couldn't come up with anything. Back in those days, nobody ever said anything about anybody. If you squealed on somebody or if you fingered somebody, well, you could look right down the pike because you'd be the next one to get hit. You were marked. They used to mark you. They'd either cut your face or cut your throat and that was the sign of the stool pigeon. They'd give you a scar on your face or they'd cut you on the neck, not to kill you, but to identify you that you're a stool pigeon and not to trust you. So, somebody could have been standing right there looking at it, but they would never say anything about it. If the families wanted revenge, then it would be amongst the families to get revenge. But the families knew that if it came down, it would be one after another after another. So, it would get resolved somehow. And nobody would open their mouths up, absolutely nobody.

There was something in me. Damned if I know what it was. I showed no remorse about anything. I showed very little sympathy about anything. About the only thing I had a guilt feeling about was what I did to my mother. She was a beautiful lady and I respected her because she was a woman, but I only became close to her when I got older. Maybe it was because I had an uncontrollable temper. I couldn't have been more than five or six and my mother was trying to discipline me on something. I picked up a fork and flung it at her. I meant to throw it but I didn't mean to hit her. But I did. It hit her right in the eye and it blinded her eye. But even at that point, knowing what I did to her, I felt no remorse or anything other than the fact that I was going to get my butt whipped.

That was my temper. I didn't get it from my mother. I didn't get it from my dad. I don't know where the hell I got it. You got me mad, that was the end of it. Maybe what made me what I was was my temper and the times and the people I grew up with, the adults that I dealt with. I always hung out with guys that were ten,

fifteen, twenty years older than me and that did the things they had
to do. I was the black sheep of the family. My brothers were all
hard-working stiffs. I was the one that had to go out and do what
he had to do.

Maybe it was some of the things I had to do for a living that
made me able to do the things I was able to do. Like when I
worked at the Eastern Market. There were two or three slaughter-
houses there and I used to go and beg for the innards of any animal
they were intending to slaughter, and they would give me a liver or
a heart or they would even give me the head of a sheep, which I
was able to take home and skin and saw in half and then bake and
we would eat the brains, which today is a top delicacy in a restaurant.

In order to get more, I asked one of the black men that was
running the job what I can do to help. He says, "Have you got the
stomach for it?"

"I guess so. I been watching you for a couple or three weeks
and I guess if I'm watching you and I see what you're doing, I can
do it."

"There's a big difference between watching and doing it."

"You just show me and we'll go on from there."

The first day I worked there, they were working on sheep. The
sheep would get their hindquarters into this trap and up they
would go, and you'd hear them hollering *baaa, baaa, baaa,* and the
guy says, "What you do is, you grab them by the ears, pull their
heads back, twist it back, and that leaves the throat wide open, and
then you take the knife and start from one end of the throat and go
all the way through. Don't worry about whether you're going to
hit bone. Just make sure you cut all the way through, make sure
you cut the lung and the blood vessels so they'd bleed and be dead
by the time they got down to the far end."

After that, they slit the animal open, pull out the innards, skin
it, make the rough cuts and all the rest. Well, I got used to doing it
and I got used to blood and blood didn't bother me and neither did
cutting, and it didn't bother me to take the sledge hammer and hit
one of the animals on the head first, and after I'd been doing that
for a while, they let me reach in and pull out the innards. I became
very immune to it. They didn't pay me any money but I would be
able to take home the heart—they wouldn't give me the calves liver

because that was very salable—but they'd give me beef liver and sheep heads and other things.

I could do it and I did it. Maybe the next guy couldn't do it, but I did it. People say, "Hey, Joe, these are fantasy stories." I say, "Yeah, you're right, these are fantasy stories." I wish to God sometimes they were. Sometimes I say I can't believe what I did when I was that young. I look back at myself and I can't believe it anymore than I could believe that I would accomplish all I did in the labor movement and the people I associated with, and that I would even have dinner with the President of the United States. Here was a kid that came from the wrong side of the tracks, that committed crimes that nobody knew about but me, but even then I knew that there was something that someday would be and that had to be better than what I was doing in those young days. And when I found the labor movement, I said, "This is it."

2

But that would not be for a time, not until he was grown. Meanwhile, he continued to hustle, to try his hand at a hundred different things, to grab a buck wherever he could, to build a reputation as someone to watch, someone to be wary of. At thirteen, like hundreds of ghetto kids looking for an exit, he found boxing.

★ ★ ★

I was big. I was tall and lanky. I was five feet eleven and I weighed 128 pounds. I fought featherweight as an amateur and I looked like a good prospect for becoming a pro fighter. In those days, even though you were an amateur they paid you. I fought in school and in the Golden Gloves and then I went into what they called the Frank Barbera White Hope Tournament, which was sponsored by Frank Barbera, who was a nightclub owner back in those days. I was listed as a top candidate in the state of Michigan, as an up-and-coming prospect, probably because of my size and the length of my arms. Most of the kids my age were four or five inches shorter. They used to give you six dollars as an unknown, and once you became known, they paid you twelve dollars for two-rounders.

There was this beautiful Jewish synagogue on the corner of Brush and Alexander and downstairs in the basement there was a gym, and they used to have these fights down there twice a week. In my class, I had no problems. I could fight anybody within 128 to 138, but very seldom could they find anybody to fight me because of my reach and my height and the fact that I was very fast with my hands and my feet. In fact, my nickname was Twinkletoes. I could do the double shuffle that Ali introduced in the ring, the rope-a-dope, and all that. All us kids could do it back in the thirties.

Then, one day I was down in the gym and they had a fight going on and somebody didn't show up. My trainer, who was Al Dinopoli, and he was one of the best cornermen in the business—Jake LaMotta used him later—he came up to me this one night and he says, "Joe, we're short a fighter. You want to fight? There's four bucks in it."

I generally kept my stuff down there in a locker, and my brother Jimmy was with me and so was my brother Blackie, and they says, "Yeah, go ahead. Come on, we want to see you fight." They hadn't seen me fight in a long time. I went down and I got dressed and Jimmy taped my hands for me and put the gloves on and we go up to the ring and I go in and looked at the far corner and I see the guy I was gonna fight. The son of a bitch was six feet tall and he weighed 178 pounds. I says to Jimmy, "Holy God almighty, if he ever hits me, he'll kill me."

Jimmy says, "Box him."

"Box him? What d'ya mean, box him?"

"Foot work. You know, go get him, Twinkletoes."

"Ah, shit, I'm gonna get the shit kicked out of me tonight."

Well, I went out there and just jabbed and ran like hell, jabbed and ran like hell. Finally, he nailed me, and when he nailed me, I thought the ring came up and hit me right in the face. I saw stars like I didn't believe the heavens had. I just grabbed him and hugged him. I wanted to bite his ears off. Now he had me mad. I wanted to bite his throat, I wanted to suck his blood like a vampire. And I says to myself, "If I got to kick him, I'm gonna street fight him. There ain't no way I'm gonna fight this gorilla straight." But I couldn't do nothing. I boxed him and twinkletoed him and I stepped on his foot and I held him and punched him, I did everything I could think of. It didn't faze him. He could stand there and take my punch all day long. For three rounds, this guy beat the hell out of me. At one stage, I turned my back and ran to get the hell away from him. It didn't help. He got me in a corner and beat the hell out of me. When the fight was over, they had to pack my face in ice and I still got a scar on my nose from that fight. I turn to Al Dinopoli and I says, "I'll never fight in the ring again. After what you guys did to me, I'll never fight again." I never did, at least I never fought in the ring again. I had a lot of street fights but never in the ring. I couldn't trust those guys again.

I was getting the reputation as being a tough guy, real good with my hands and other things. And people started to come to me and the other three guys in my gang and ask us to do things for them. If somebody wanted somebody's house set on fire, they would come to us and offer us so much money to set fire to the house or the garage or a store or break windows or whatever it was. It was always me and J.T. and Eugene and Charlie, depending on if I needed three guys or two guys or one guy besides myself. If I could do it myself, I did it, and the majority of times I did it myself. I would burn houses or garages or whatever under contract or destroy storefronts with rocks and slingshots, whatever I had to use. My specialty was setting fires. In those days, we didn't use dynamite. We didn't know what it meant to have dynamite. Later, when I was sixteen or seventeen, I learned where to buy it. The farmers were able to buy it in order to blow up tree stumps and I found that out and I made a connection for it with the people who used to hang out around my mother's beer garden. But I never liked dynamite. It was too tricky and too dangerous and a long time later I had a very bad experience with it. Probably I got a lot of my training and my knowledge from my dad when I traveled with him to Chicago and other places when he would accept contracts. Without him realizing it, I was picking his brains. I don't think my dad ever wanted me to do what I did. My mother? I think she realized it, to the point of saying to me one time, "Don't get caught. If you get caught, you're going to pay the consequences." That's the extent of it.

It was not long before he added another specialty to arson.

People started to come around and ask me to do other things and I started to accept contracts about doing bodily harm. Those I did by myself, always. I wouldn't have any partners who would turn around and say at a later date, "Jo-Jo did this" and "Jo-Jo did that." Maybe somebody's daughter got raped or somebody's son got beat up by a gang or somebody beat somebody out of money or whatever it was. One day, someone came to me and said, "We've heard of your reputation. We've heard that you're trustworthy. We know it will never come back. If something should come down, we're told that you're a standup kind of a guy and will accept this kind of a contract." And that was to hurt somebody and put him in the hospital.

I started accepting contracts to break somebody's legs, break his arms, break his hands, break his collarbones, put him in the hospital. Like some people would say, take care of my son-in-law and break his arms, break his knees, break his legs, because he beats up his wife and his children, so leave a lesson to him that he should stop or the next time it would be worse. I believe this is a tradition they probably brought from the old country, where you did something wrong with your hands, they would punish your hands, like cut them off, or if you did something with your mouth, they would cut your tongue out, like if you were a squealer to the cops and talked about them, or even if they thought you were a squealer, and they wanted to make sure that you never talked again. What I used to do was, I didn't want to break the limbs where he would be crippled for life or anything else. So, I would use a baseball bat or a pipe, if I accepted a contract to put somebody in the hospital, and then I would break the collarbones, either one or both collarbones, which would put the arms into a cast and put the guy out of commission for a couple of months. I never wanted to hit anybody in the head because you might take a chance of killing him and then you'd end up violating your contract, which said they only wanted him put in the hospital. So, I stayed away from the head. I'd break the collarbones or the elbows or whatever they wanted and that way the family would be satisfied and I would have fulfilled my obligation and they would pay.

Then one day somebody came to me and wanted me to go ahead and kill somebody. The money was like $3,000 and in those days I could have bought four homes with $3,000. I was fourteen when I took the first of what I would say would be professional contracts. There was this guy that was married to this girl and he used to beat her up constantly and he abused the children and didn't take care of his family. The girl's mother and father objected to this and they didn't want to put up with it anymore. In those days, the old Sicilian families didn't put up with that kind of thing. So, they had had just about enough of this guy, but they didn't know who to go to. But they knew me from the neighborhood and they asked me to take it on. I accepted.

Guns were a dime a dozen and I had a stash of everything I wanted, from pistols to machine guns to shotguns, in that hayloft where the older guys used to hide them. I got a double-barreled shotgun and I went to this guy's house and I hid behind a tree and waited for him. When he was coming home, and he was just going up the staircase of his house, I let go with both barrels and hit him plumb in the chest and blew him right up the staircase, knocked him right onto the porch, and he was dead on the first step. That's the impact that kind of shot with a Double-O would have when it hit a guy. With that, I just took off and took the shotgun and put it back in the hayloft where it had been and then ran home and just minded my own business. That was my first $3,000 job.

It got to be a known thing not only in my neighborhood but around the city. Families would say, "Why don't you go and see Jo-Jo and tell him what's up. If your daughter got raped by those kids, go see Jo-Jo and maybe he'll do something. If you're looking for revenge, you tell him what kind of revenge you want and he'll tell you how much it's going to cost you."

Sometimes, it was like the first one where I just killed the guy and left him there. Sometimes, I'd have to dispose of the body. It wasn't like today where you read that they found somebody in a trunk or in a plastic bag. In those days, it was in the water. Not just me, but other guys that were doing it. What you'd do was throw the body in the river between the Detroit Bridge and the Ambassador Bridge or right next to the Detroit Stove Works, and it would be washed out with the sewage and if it was weighted down, there'd be nothing left. Eventually a skeleton would come up or it would just be washed all the way down and by the time it came up, there'd be nothing left for anybody to identify it.

I think there were eight or nine of those agreements that I took on. Maybe because of working in the slaughterhouse or whatever it was, but it didn't bother me, I became immune to it. I could walk up to somebody and just take a knife and stick it into them and it wouldn't bother me.

At fifteen, in the eighth grade, he quit school.

I had reached the stage of maturity, and that meant that I was able to go to work in a legitimate way. I went to work for New York Bedspring. All the guys in the neighborhood worked there, it was like a neighborhood shop, doing piecework, and I was earning like seventy-two cents an hour. I told the guy I was sixteen, which meant I didn't need a work permit, and he put me to work. And while I was working there, I had my first introduction to the labor movement.

I had to belong to the union and that union was called the Upholsterers Union, and the international president at the time was a guy named Sol Hoffman, whose mother was Italian and whose father was Jewish. And while I was working there, people recognized my ability, they knew what my reputation was, and they didn't look at me as fifteen, and so they asked me to become a union assistant shop steward, which meant that in case the shop steward wasn't there, I would be the temporary steward. Because of that, I was invited to attend the general meetings that were held once a month at the Labor Temple. It was my responsibility to go to these meetings and listen to what they had to say about union contracts, working conditions, and everything else. I liked what I saw and I started sniffing around to see where there's an advantage there, when I could make a living, and how I could make something out of myself. This looked like something I could really get into. I just had a good feeling then about this union business.

So I made it my business to make myself known to Francis X. Martell, who was the head of the AFL at that time. I called him one day and asked if I could see him. He was gracious enough to allow me to come up and sit down and talk with him, and he asked me some questions about who I was, my nationality and how old I was and other things.

"What makes you want to talk to me?"

"I like what I see. I like the labor movement. I would like to learn."

"One thing about the labor movement, young man, you either give it your whole life, be willing to put your life on the line, or don't get into it. It's not a thing you get into if you think you're just going to get in and get out and you're not going to stand up.

You either believe in it with all your life and all your heart, or you don't get into it at all. You're going to be labor conscious, you're going to be labor union, you're going to be a labor leader, and you'd better believe it. If you don't believe it, don't get into it."

He spoke like thunder. He was a short stocky guy with bushy eyebrows and a very rough way of talking. I was pretty much taken by him. It surprised me that busy a man as he was, he gave me close to an hour with him. Then he asked me to go and check with a man called John Paris, who was head of the Laundry Workers Union in Detroit and who was one of his protégés. I did and John and I became very good friends even though he was about ten years older than me.

As a matter of fact, a lot of years later, I introduced Johnny Paris and Faschi O'Brien, who was Chuckie O'Brien's mother, after she came to Detroit. She was very close to Josephine Hoffa, and Jimmy pretty much took care of Chuckie like he was his own son.

I says to Faschi one day, "Fash, I got a guy for you. You'll like him. He's a handsome guy, good Italian people, a nice Italian boy."

"Who is he?"

"Johnny Paris."

"Oh, I know about him. Go ahead and set up the introduction."

I did and they took to each other and it was only a matter of months before they got married.

For a year, he stayed on at New York Bedspring, working there and cementing his contacts at the Labor Temple and with the Upholstery Workers Union. Then he left, going to work for Ford Motor, and became involved with the United Automobile Workers Local 400.

I was not involved politically with Local 400 until somebody came to me and asked me if I wanted to become involved. This was around 1940 or 1941 and I was working on the main floor, and I had some girls working under me as riveters and I built up a reputation of being trustworthy, and a lot of the girls took a liking to me because I was a tall, nice looking kid with a lot of hair and I looked older than seventeen. They came to me and they asked me if I would run on their ticket to become a committee member, which was like a union steward only a little higher. The UAW had a different structure than the other unions. I says yeah because I still had that good feeling about the labor movement. It didn't matter to me whether it was the Upholstery Workers or the UAW or the AFL or what, as long as it was the labor movement. I liked what it stood for.

Three guys on our ticket got elected and the rest of us, me included, got beat. Then the guy who was the incumbent and who got reelected figured the best way to protect himself was by getting rid of me and he betrayed me and got me fired. I filed a grievance but it didn't do any good. Some of the guys who were on the ticket with me and who won asked me if I wanted to become the athletic director for the local. I figured I might as well do something as long as I was there.

In the meantime, a young redhead who was on his way up in the UAW, named Walter Reuther, sent out word that he wanted to establish what they called flying squadrons. There could be twelve to twenty-four guys in a squadron, and in case there was a problem in any other plant that was on strike, the flying squadron would go out. And if there were any scabs or anything else, or if there were any problems, this squad was the head busters—we would make sure that everything was peaceful and everything was taken care of. I signed on for certain duties within the flying squadron, like going to different meetings that we would have to protect, and bodyguarding areas where there would be negotiations or other things going on, and doing other things that had to be attended to. I stayed with it for three or four months while they were supposed to be handling my grievance and protecting me, and then I saw I wasn't going to get any help, so I started to get a little bad taste in my mouth in regards to unions, especially the UAW, and I walked away. But let me tell you, that Local 400 flying squadron was one of the best in the business. We were well recognized as the toughest bunch in the UAW. I suppose it says something that we were known as the flying squadrons and we were kind of heroes in the labor movement. Later on, when the Teamsters were doing the same kind of thing, they were called goons.

Still, he managed to keep busy. He was not one to let an opportunity pass by, and opportunities kept arising.

There was this guy, Danny, that used to hang around with my older brothers, but they had all got married and he was looking for somebody to hang around with and I was the next best thing. So, we started hanging around together. One day I says to him, "Danny, you know all this shit that I've got to go through. I've got to bomb this joint, I got to do this and that. Sooner or later, the reputation's gonna catch up with me. I'm getting tired of this and if I ever get caught, bingo, I'm gone."

Most of the guys in the neighborhood who were doing things in those days were carrying guns, some guys used to carry two guns. I never carried a gun unless I was gonna do something with it. A gun I thought I could get in trouble with. It was too easy to reach in and shoot. What I used to do was carry one or two sticks of fused dynamite. All I had to do was pull it out and everybody in the joint would run. It was the quickest way to empty out a bar or anyplace. I figured with two sticks of dynamite, I don't need a gun. But I was getting worried.

So I says to Danny, "How else can I make money?"

"Joe, I don't know what to tell you. But when I was in the joint, doing some federal time, I met this engraver."

"What the hell is that?"

"A guy that makes plates. For money."

"How the hell can he make money with that? He's still in jail."

"Well, before I left he taught me how to make molds and castings to make silver. The only problem is that we got to find a type of metal that will ring like silver does."

"That's no problem." I had a friend who was a foreman over at a plant called the Gray Iron Foundry. I asked him for a job as an apprentice mold maker and he took me on. While I was there, I made damn sure I got friendly with a metallurgist and I asked him if he could give me a book about metals. I read it and I found there was different metals that had different alloys in them that would be right, something that was used in the automotive industry to coat the motor pistons so they would last a hundred, two hundred thousand miles. It was very, very hard and silvery and it was what I was looking for. I went over to this big supply house and asked if they carried the stuff. It just so happened they had about six bars and I bought them all.

I went home and Danny and I, in my mother's basement, started to make molds out of dental plaster of paris to make half dollars. It was very slow work and we would make a hundred to two hundred molds at a time. We stood down in the basement, three, four, five days at a time, twenty-four hours a day, and we made half dollars and quarters and we made them look aged. The quarters we used in cigarette vending machines and then we'd end up selling the cigarettes. The quarters cost about a penny and a half each to make, and the half dollars cost a little more because we had to use more metal. The thing was, they not only looked real but if you tapped them with your finger or dropped them on the floor or anything, they sounded just like the real thing. The way we aged them was to put mascara on them and put them in the oven and bake them, and then take a cloth and rub them, and you'd have a coin that looked like it was a hundred years old. Then we put them in grape boxes and each of those boxes would have like five hundred dollars worth of half dollars and we sold them two-for-one, two hundred fifty dollars for five hundred dollars worth. When we had about a hundred cases, we would go to some of the old-timers who were with the gang that used to hang around my parents' beer garden.

I went to Mr. Pete and I says, "I got this silver. You want a piece of it."

"I'll take it all, all you can give me."

For about six months, Danny and I made this stuff and we scored on it pretty good. Then we had some trouble, and we figured it was time to get out. We had to take a load of the stuff into Chicago, and what we used to do when we were away was to leave everything in the basement and cover the table in the work area with a tarp, and I instructed my mother never to touch anything on that table. Well, sometimes some of the coins that we would make would be faulty because the mold hadn't filled completely or the temperature hadn't been completely right or something, and we'd leave them there until we could work on them again. Well, this time when we were away, my mother went down there and she didn't know any better, she saw the tarp and lifted it and saw half dollars sitting there. She took them and went down to the Eastern Market and bought everything she could buy. Well, Danny and I figured it would be very easy for someone to say she was the one that passed those counterfeit coins and we'd be in a lot of trouble. So, we just packed everything up and stashed it away and that was the end of us making counterfeit coins.

Then I got a telephone call from someone asking me if I would come over for a spaghetti dinner. I says, sure, and I went over to the house and sat down. This was a Sunday. And this guy tells me he has some friends that are in from New York, and he introduces them and, after dinner, the women all went into the kitchen and the men went into the other room and had a drink and a smoke, and we all sat down.

My host turns to me and he says, "We understand you're getting out of the counterfeiting coin business. My friends would like to know if you'd like to sell the whole operation. They will take everything and just operate out of New York."

"We'd be happy to sell out."

"So, how much do you want?"

"I'll take fifteen thousand for the whole works. Give me fifteen thousand and I'll give you five days of my time. I'll show you how to make the molds, I'll give you the equipment, everything we've got, sell you the metal, because that's the most important part, and I'll show you how to do everything."

What they were really buying was the type of metal I was using; without it, they wouldn't have been worth shit. They agreed and I went and picked up the box, got hold of Danny and went over there, and they gave us fifteen thousand cash. It didn't take me more than three hours to show them what was going on. They left and I never heard from those people again.

About six months to a year later, there was a big story in our papers that New York was being flooded with counterfeit coins. Instead of doing like we did, they got an engraver and made a metal plate, which I didn't know how to do. I tried but it never worked out. And they punched those coins out by the millions. Nobody could detect them because they had the ring. The only way you could detect them was if you melted them down and found out they didn't have silver in them. It took the government almost a year to find out they were counterfeit. After that, I didn't hear no more about it and I didn't want to hear no more.

By then, the United States was in World War II and he was drafted.

They called me and I went down to the induction center. Maybe some guys volunteered, but I don't think the majority of guys wanted to go into the army and they'd do anything they could to stay out. A lot of guys that got called would go out the night before and get stinking drunk and eat excessively so their heart rhythm would be out of whack and they would get a 4-F rating, do anything to get that. I know that one of my brothers went out and ate God knows how many pizzas and drank wine and stayed up until he had to go to the induction center, and they found his heartbeat was out of whack, so they said, go home, you're 4-F. And then one of the guys behind him in line says, "Like hell he is. That son of a bitch is healthier than I am." So they took my brother and put him in another room and let him sleep there for two hours, and then they woke him up and the wine had worn off and the pizzas wore off, and his heart went back into the regular rhythm and into the service he went.

Now, my turn comes and I was down there and standing in front of one guy and he sticks his finger up your rectum and turns you around and makes you cough and then pats you on the ass and tells you to move on. You go to another guy and he tells you to go down a tunnel and he says something to you and you'd have to repeat it, which was to check your hearing. Now the guy in front of me really broke me up there. He went down and the sergeant that was giving the test yells out, "Face me." The guy's still looking around, walking around, looking at the sky. Nothing. The sergeant says, "Can you hear me?" The kid's still walking around, pretending like he couldn't hear nothing. So the sergeant finally says, very quietly, like under his breath, "Okay, come on out." And the kid just comes walking out. The sergeant says, "Well, if you heard that, pal, you can hear and you're in the army." That just broke me up.

Now it comes down to the psychiatrist. They're all colonels, top officers, and they're all dingbats. This guy starts asking me questions, like do I like girls, do I like guys, do I do this, do I do that?

I says, "Hey, cut the shit. You want me in the army, you take me. You want to ask questions like, do I like to get laid, I'll tell you, yeah, I like to get laid. You want me to hit you one in the ass, I'll hit you one in the ass, too."

He says, "Oh, you're a tough guy."

I says, "You keep talking the way you are, I'm going to whack you one across your face. I don't go for nobody asking me personal questions."

"Oh, you like to fight."

"Yeah, I like to fight. So what? What the hell do you think I'm doing in line here? I want to fight for my country and I'm going to beat your ass, too."

"You want to fight too much."

"Hey, get out of my goddamn business." And I got up to hit him.

He reaches back and he says, "Here's your papers," and he stamps it and he says, "Keep moving."

Well, I never looked at the goddamn papers, so I went onto the next doctor and he looked at them and he stamped them, and just kept moving. After that, it seemed like just zip, zip, zip, going through. Finally, I end up going to the room where you get dressed and this army colonel called me in. He says, "Joe, come on in."

I says, "Ah, shit." I wanted to get into the navy and I figures, sure as shit, now the army's got me. He sat me down and he says, "You know, Joe, some guys are going into the army and fight for their country. But it's just as important for some people to stay home and work in defense work in a factory and make sure that the equipment that's sent over to the guys that are fighting is good equipment." I'm looking at him and trying to figure what the hell this guy is talking about. I figure he blew his stack or something.

"What I'm trying to tell you, Joe, is that we classified you 4-F."

"What does that mean?"

"It means that you can't get into the service."

I don't know whether to laugh or smile or cry. I'm saying, shit, I can stay home. I can do anything now. He came over and put his arm around me and he says, "Don't feel bad."

Well, I walked out of there and there's the whole crew, everybody from my neighborhood. They're hollering at me, "Hey, Jo-Jo, come on. We're gonna take our oath and then we're going off to Camp Custer." I waved like, I'll see you later. They're all screaming, "Don't let him go, colonel." And the colonel says, "Don't worry. I'm sending him on a special detail." So the guys never knew that I got rejected. Being that I got rejected, I figure at first that I would go back into a defense plant, and I did that for a little while.

As always, though, he was on the lookout for better and easier ways to make money, and, as always, something came along.

I bought a 50 percent interest in the Igloo Restaurant on the corner of Peterborough and Woodward, right next to Greenfield's. I had some money put away and I figured it was a good investment. Well, my partner, Dominick, got into trouble, so I ended up owning the Igloo, which was an ice cream parlor, by myself. After a little while, there were these three pretty young girls, about eighteen or nineteen, that came up to me and asked me if I would sponsor them because they wanted to be hookers. A lot of soldiers and sailors were hanging around there at that time and they figured they'd make a killing. I says, "I don't care. If that's what you want to do, that's your business. But I'll give you jobs as waitresses or soda jerks, if you want it." They says, "No, we want to make big money."

So, I took them over to this residential hotel, the Palmetto. I used to stay there once in a while, in a suite, and the manager knew me. I told him what I wanted. I wanted a three-bedroom suite fully furnished and I would give him a piece of the action. He agreed and we took the girls up there and stocked them all up with booze and everything, and they went out and got negligees and started working, and I went back to my ice cream parlor and ran my business and never paid any attention to them. But I used to send service guys I knew wanted to get laid up there, telling them that there were these three beautiful girls up at the Palmetto. I knew they were getting ten, fifteen dollars a pop. They were supposed to put all the money in a sugar bowl and at the end of the week, they were supposed to cut it up, give me the rent money, give me my expenses out of it. The understanding was that every Saturday I would go up to the apartment and the girls would divide the money up, minus all the expenses of the apartment that came up during the week, and I would take care of the manager.

The first week I went up there and everything was fine. I didn't take anything except my expenses because I was making a quick buck over at the Igloo and I just let the kids make the money. Now, this went on for three or four weeks, and then for a couple of weeks I didn't bother to go over. Finally, about the third Saturday down the line, I figured I'd better go and take care of the rent and take care of the guy because I know he's looking for the bread. I get there and there's no sugar bowl, no girls, no nothing. I don't know what the hell to do. The rent's like three hundred eighty and the guy's got two hundred coming. I see the booze is like half gone, but there's still booze around. Where the hell have these three bitches gone?

In those years, they used to have a neighborhood called the Black Bottom with a lot of night clubs. I went down there and I walked into one joint, and I walked into another, and I walked into a joint that was owned by a guy named Cash.

"Cash, my girls here?"

"Yeah, your girls are at that table. Do me a favor. No trouble."

"What's the matter?"

"The three bitches are with three of my guys."

"Cash, are they with your guys?"

"No, I mean my people."

"I don't give a shit. Let the three bitches be with the devil. I just want the goddamn money to pay the rent, to pay the man that's got the money coming because he gave us the okay to use the joint. I'm five hundred eighty dollars stuck as of right now. Tell the bitches to give me my five hundred eighty and I'll walk out of the joint."

He walked up to the three girls and they saw me and they shit. Now, the three guys that were with them don't want to do nothing because they saw me talking to Cash and they knew I was friendly with Cash. So, the bitches reached in, they all chipped in, and give me the dough. I walked out and that was the end of my career as a pimp. I figured that was enough. There had to be a better way of making a living.

There was. The war was on. Everything was in short supply. There were people who had ways of filling the demands. There was the black market.

I was in the black market from 1942 all the way to the end of the war in 1945. I sold gas stamps, sugar stamps, nylons, rubber tires, whatever I could get that was needed. I would make a deal and sell it on the black market. But the biggest score I ever made was in gas stamps.

When I was working at Ford, I met this southern boy from Tennessee. I didn't work there anymore, but I used to hang out at a restaurant right across the street, called the Manchester Inn. One day, this kid comes to me and he says, "Joe, I got something that's worth millions. I know where you come from and I know your reputation and I think I can trust you."

"Hey, you couldn't find anybody better to trust. What've you got?"

"I got two sets of plates. They're counterfeit plates to make gas stamps."

Now, the stamps were classified *A* and *B*. The *A* stamp would be entitled to so many gallons of gas and the *B* stamp would be entitled to so many gallons of gas, and it depended on where you're at, what kind of job you had. If you were classified *A,* you would get more gas because your job required you to have more gas. What he had were plates for *A*'s and *B*'s, and they were beautiful plates. They weren't counterfeit. They were legitimate and they were still sealed in a kind of very hard wax, which you could see was like government material. So, I went to a friend of mine who was very, very big in the racket.

"Angie, I think this guy's got something. I've been hustling all my life, and I've been hustling stamps since they came out, and I think this guy's got a set of plates that are genuine plates. The only problem we have is finding paper. If we can find genuine paper, we're multimillionaires overnight."

"Find out what he wants, bring him to me, let me see the plates."

I went back, met the guy and I says, "I talked with my guy. He wants to see the plates and he wants to know how much you want for them."

"I want $50,000 a plate, that's $100,000 a set, that's $200,000 for both sets."

I went back to Angie. "He wants $200,000 for the two sets. That's like one runoff, we make that."

Angie says, "Don't worry about the money. Tell him to bring the sets." I made a meeting and Angie looked at the plates and recognized right away that they were government plates. He says, "Okay, we got a deal."

"What do we do about paper?"

"We get the plates first, then we worry about the paper." Then he told the guy, "Okay, take the plates with you. Joe will meet you tomorrow night. I'll give Joe the $200,000 and you turn the plates over to Joe."

The guy left and Angie and I took a walk. Angie turns to me and he says, "You feel like spending $200,000?"

"Shit, no."

"Then I'll give you a briefcase with a lot of paper in it. I'll put some money in it, fake a stack, so when he opens it, he'll see the hundred-dollar bills. You turn the briefcase over to him, you get the plates, then it's up to you what you want to do. Because once he opens the briefcase up, he's gonna find out you stiffed him, that you gave him like $1,000 instead of $200,000. You handle it whichever way you want."

"Wait a minute, Angie. He won't come looking for you because I'm the guy who's gonna do the payoff."

"You do what you want to do."

"Thank you. Now, what are we gonna do after, with the $200,000, with the plates?"

"We're fifty-fifty."

"We got a deal, partner." Then we shook hands.

The next night, I called the guy. "Okay, I got the money in a briefcase. Where do you want to meet?" There was a bowling alley called the Casino over on Woodward and Charlotte. We agreed to meet out in the alley back of the Casino. As soon as he gave me the plates, I stuck them in my shirt. He took the briefcase. I pulled out a thirty-eight and I went a-boom, a-boom, a-boom, and I blew him away and I left him there.

I took the plates and gave them to Angie. About two weeks later, Angie calls me up and says, "Come on over. I want to show you the finished product." Now, there was a way you could test gas stamps in those days. You took Roman cleanser and it would take all the color out of a phony stamp, turn it white. If you put it on a government stamp with legitimate government paper, it wouldn't do too much. Now, these stamps were absolutely beautiful and we started to do a little work selling them, for twenty-five, thirty cents apiece, and they went like hot cakes. We were making a ton of money out of it.

Among those to whom he tried to unload these stamps was his padrino, Phil Benedetto, of Melrose Park. He had stamps he and Angie had made, and he had more stamps that he had taken on consignment from other sources in Detroit. He had stamps with a street value to consumers of about $1 million. He got in touch with Benedetto and told him he had something that might be of interest and of mutual benefit. Benedetto suggested it might be a good idea if he took a trip to Melrose Park, so they could talk more about it. The stamps were put in two suitcases and loaded into the trunk of his car, and he went with an old partner, Danny, with whom he was working again.

We got to my Uncle Phil's home and we sat down with him and I told him we had stamps with a street value of a million, which a big operator could wholesale for about a half million. I says we'd like to see at least $250,000 for them. He asks how fast can I make delivery. I told him, in twenty-four hours. I didn't want him to know that I had them with me, even though I considered him part of my family. I didn't trust him; I didn't trust nobody knowing that I was walking around with that much in stamps because it would be just as easy for him to finger me and end up with what I had and nobody would know the difference, family or no family.

He says, "Come back tomorrow and I'll give you an answer. I have to contact some people. I can't handle it all myself. I have to bring in some other people." We had dinner and when we're leaving, he turns to me and he says, "Where are you staying at?"

"We're not staying anyplace yet. We're gonna find a place." We got out of there and when we're back in the car, I says to Danny, "When we find a place, whatever you do, don't you dare tell him. He may be my uncle, my *padrino*, but $1 million is $1 million. Keep your mouth shut and let me handle it."

We went down about fifteen miles from his place and we checked into this little dumpy hotel right off an alley, and I give the kid at the desk a fifty dollar bill and I says, "Anybody comes around here sniffing, flag us." The kid would have done anything in the world for fifty bucks. So we had a lookout. And we got a room on the second floor where we could get out the window in case we had to. Then we go back to the car and stash the stamps in the trunk and bring the empty suitcases into the hotel and up to the room, pretending like we've got the stuff with us in case anybody was following and checking.

The next day, we went back over to my uncle's, leaving the suitcases in the room. We sat down and we had lunch and he says, "I talked to my people and we'll give you $100,000."

"No deal. We told you what we want. One million dollars on the street, $250,000 for us. I got people I got to listen to. I ain't making the $250,000 myself. I got other people involved. Danny and I are cutting up the pieces. Other people got bigger pieces. So, don't tell me you've got people to check. Either they make a deal or they don't make a deal."

"Well, you stay around for a couple of days, maybe I can find some other interested parties that would go for what you want. Where you stayin' at?"

"Forget that. You tell your people to give you the money. That's the only way we'll come down on this."

So we left and I turned to Danny and I says, "I dunno, I smell a rat. I got a funny feeling. I think we're being tagged. I think we're gonna get followed as to where we're at and they're gonna knock us off and steal our stuff." We went back to the hotel and sure as hell, we walk in and the kid's kind of nervous. I says, "Any calls?"

"No calls."

"Okay. We're going upstairs to take a nap. Anybody comes around, starts snooping around, you let us know."

We went upstairs and for some unknown reason, Danny calls down to get something cold to drink. The kid answers and he's very, very nervous and you could hear some people talking in the background. Danny turns to me and he says, "I think we're getting set up."

"Let's get the hell out of here." I didn't go out the window. I went down the stairs. We left the suitcases there, thinking that if they were going to shake us down, if they saw us go out with the suitcases, then we would have got into trouble. As long as we walked out of there without the suitcases, we were all right. So, I walked downstairs and walked out by myself. Danny went out through the window and went down the fire escape and got into the car and he had the car going when I went out. I says to the kid as I'm going out, "Listen, I'm going up to the corner to get something cold to drink for my partner. I'll be right back." There were three guys sitting around the lobby pretending like they were reading newspapers. I knew goddamn well what they were going to do. They were going to run upstairs, break into the room, and take the suitcases. I don't think they intended to hit me or Danny. All they wanted was to grab the merchandise. They saw me walk out without the suitcase, they didn't say nothing. They waited until I left.

When I walked out, I turned right around the hotel and walked to the parking area, and Danny had the car and off we went and we headed right back to Detroit. When I got home, I got a call from my Uncle Phil. "That was pretty cute, your partner ducking out the window, you walking out the lobby, and you left the empty suitcases."

"Well, you see, Uncle Phil, you want to play games, I can play games. I want to know where you're coming from and I found out. I can never trust you again, no matter what I ever get into. You're still family, but I can never do business with you again." So, we gave the stamps back to Angie and the other guys and that was the end of that.

It was the end, too, of dealing in counterfeit stamps. The government began to crack down, began to do some serious checking, and the dangers began to outweigh the potential gains.

Genuine stamps were something else again, if it was possible to get hold of them. But they were jealously and closely guarded.

Then, in the latter part of 1943, a couple of guys came to me and wanted to know whether I wanted to go with them to pull off a job. I asked what the hell kind of a job. "We're going to go where they take all the stamps."

The government had a depot where the stamps would be turned in by the gas companies, which had to collect them from the gas stations when they made deliveries so that everything matched up. The government would burn those stamps at the depot. There were millions and millions of stamps there. I agreed with these two guys to break in and steal them. We got a panel truck and we broke into the joint and we loaded up like fifty, sixty huge high crates that cigarettes come in. The next day, the newspapers come out with big headlines: "Gas Stamps with a Street Value in Excess of $25 Million Taken."

We divided the stamps three ways and we agreed not to put them out on the street for at least three to five months, until the heat cooled down. And we built up territories to distribute them. Gas in those days was like sixteen, seventeen cents a gallon with the real stamps and fifty and sixty cents a gallon to guys that didn't have stamps. Now, the thing was, the gas stations had to have stamps to turn back to the companies to show that they were selling gas on the up and up, even if they wasn't. So, we were supplying the gas stations and we were supplying private customers who need lots of gas, and we were getting like a buck and a half a stamp because we didn't flood the market. Like, I had one account that was a bookmaker and he had twenty-three guys driving for him as pickups in his betting and numbers operation. He needed gas for all twenty-three cars. I used to go to him every two, three days, and I was selling him stamps for a buck apiece, and I was making a couple of grand every couple of days on that account alone.

This went on all the way until February or March of 1945. And the money I was making was taking me into another area. The money was getting me into money people and getting me into politics, and I was starting to hear from educated people that the war was going to come to an end pretty damn soon. The three of us had a meeting and we agreed that we should start holding off because we were sure that the government was going to ask for an accounting, and all these gas stations are going to have to account for all the gas they've been selling and all the gas stamps or else the government was going to come down on them, and there was a five-year prison term involved. At that point, we could ask for two bucks a stamp, maybe more, and we could make a real killing.

Then, all of a sudden, I get a telephone call. Get the hell out of town, fast. There was big heat coming down. There was an investigation relating to that holdup we made. Somebody in the neighborhood was starting to say, hey, these guys are showing up with a lot of money, and that's all it took, the next thing you know, there's feds in the neighborhood up to your ass.

I jumped a train, the first train out, and I asked the guy where it was going. He says, Newport News, Virginia, which was the naval base. "I don't give a damn where the hell it's going, just give me a ticket." I got off at Newport News and didn't know what the hell to do there because the joint was loaded with sailors. So, I asked a cab driver where the hell you could go to get away from all the service people. He says there's a city about twenty-five miles outside called Virginia Beach, which is a resort.

"How much is it going to cost me?"

"It's going to cost you twenty-three dollars."

"Take me."

I stood there a couple of months and then there's big headlines about a bomb on Hiroshima and the war is coming to an end. A couple of days later, I get a call telling me to get my ass back home because we're going to have to go to work getting those stamps out to the gas stations so they could account up to the government.

I come back home and I get a telephone call from one of my partners as soon as I get off the train, and he comes over and he says, "You might as well take all your stamps and burn them because the government's not asking for any accounting. The gas stations are all off the hook."

"How do you know this?"

"I got a call from somebody in Washington."

"The word out yet?"

"Not for a couple more days."

"Hey, why don't we get out and sell all we can until the son of a bitch hits the papers?"

"You do what you want to do."

So, I went out and I dumped the stamps at twenty-five, fifty cents apiece, whatever I could get, like I was giving everybody a real bargain. I must have dumped about $200,000. And three days later, bingo, it hit the papers. And guys are calling me and saying, "What am I going to do with all these stamps? I don't need them."

"I don't need them neither. You bought them, you keep them. What do you think I'm running, a rebate deal where you can get a refund? What if the thing came the other way and the government wanted an accounting? You go to the can."

And they was saying, "Yeah, but Jesus Christ, Joe, all these years we been buying. . . ."

I says, "Hey, it's over with. Forget about it."

That was the end of the stamp business. Whatever stamps I had left, I just took them out and burned them. And the money. If I'd have invested it, I'd be a multi-multimillionaire today. But I spent it. As it came in, I spent it.

Part II

3

So the war was over. As the celebrations died, the euphoria of those glorious moments of victory gave way to hard and grim realities. The world was changed beyond measure, and those who dreamed of a restoration of the old ways and the old times were doomed as dinosaurs. Peace was no simple thing and the future stretched out uncharted. Allies of an earlier time were now locked in deadly struggle, those alliances of convenience during wartime now being shattered beyond repair in the reach for shares of the spoils.

As Winston Churchill would say, an iron curtain was descending across the devastation that was central Europe. On one side was the paranoid and despotic "workers' paradise" of Joseph Stalin, nearly prostrate after four years of raging battle on its own soil. This side was determined to shield itself from all outside and liberalizing influences as it tried to recover and, at the same time, begin to spread its own hegemony and so claim the spoils that would mean world dominion. On the other side of that line that stretched from the Baltic to the Adriatic, the United States and its European allies, battered by years of struggle, were compelled to gird for new and unwanted battle, this time against a foe who moments before had been the ally of convenience.

At home Harry S Truman confronted problems that might have paralyzed a less self-assured man. He had to find ways to lead his country and his people into the new world of semipeace. It was a staggering burden. Often he seemed isolated, hemmed in on every side by antagonists.

On his right there were the Republicans, out of power since the Depression and smelling victory that would return them to power, in Congress in 1946 and to the White House in 1948. Basically conservative, they wanted to undo the New Deal. They wanted an end to the controls and the restrictions of those years of recovery and of the war, they wanted a return to a free and unfettered economy; if there were to be restrictions at all, they wanted them placed on labor unions. And they were aided in their cries and demands by their natural allies, big business, which had grown fat and sassy with the profits made during the war.

On the left there were the unions, the traditional allies of the Democrats. They should have been the source of Truman's strength, but they were suspicious of him, uncertain just how deep his support of them and their causes went, and that suspicion deepened initially.

For the most part, throughout the war the unions had played the role of loyal patriots. Their members had worked long and hard to turn the United States into the arsenal of democracy. They had chafed under the restrictions of wage and price controls, which seemed to affect their pocketbooks a lot more than they had the coffers of industry, but save for an occasional strike, they had gone about their work certain that when peace arrived they would get their rightful share. Now peace had come. The factories were humming as they had rarely hummed, turning out consumer goods hardly fast enough to meet the pent-up consumer demand for everything from cars to refrigerators, from clothes to houses, from food to fuel.

There was work for everyone who wanted it—for those who had manned the assembly lines during the war and for those who had fought in the war and had returned to the civilian world and rejoined the labor force. Profits were staggering. Business had rarely, if ever, been so good. The workers, backed by their unions, wanted a piece of the pie. But industry seemed to have no inclination to share with anyone, other than stockholders and executives, certainly not with the average working stiffs. Demands for major wage increases, benefits, shorter work weeks, for all that would make up for the years of deprivations were met with adamant resistance. To some, it looked as though the nation were in for another wave of labor troubles to match the bloody strikes of the 1930s.

Beginning with a walk-out at Ford Motor in the fall of 1945, strike followed strike. Picket lines were thrown up around automobile plants, textile mills, steel mills, coal mines, everywhere. Some of the strikes stretched out for months and there were echoes of earlier days of violence. If the unions thought they could depend on President Truman for help, or at least to maintain a hands-off policy, they were wrong. Their initial wariness was nearer the mark. Truman watched the first wave of strikes with a growing anger, especially as the predictions of some economists seemed to be coming true, that a spiraling inflation would be the inevitable consequence of high wage and benefit settlements. The president's rage reached its peak in the late spring. The mine workers were out again and now the railroad brotherhoods announced a strike of their own, thereby threatening to tie up the nation's vital rail transportation system. Truman called in the union leaders, saying, "If you think I'm going to sit here and let you tie up this whole country, you're crazy as hell."

The railroads ignored him and walked out. Truman announced that he was going to draft all railroad employees and then order them, as members of the military of which he was commander-in-chief, back to work. Told such a move was unconstitutional, he snapped, "We'll draft them first and think about the law later." He prepared to go to Congress for authority and to the public for support. His advisors persuaded him to tone down his speech before delivery, in which he was going to denounce labor leaders, especially John L. Lewis, head of the United Mine Workers and the major labor leader who had called strikes during the war, and Philip Murray, president of the Congress of Industrial Organizations, and his "communist friends." They were, he declared, "liars . . . traitors . . . men who place their private interests above the welfare of the nation." The president's threats, supported by Congress and much of the nation, and his actions, which included an executive order seizing the mines, ultimately broke both the railroad and the miners' strikes and resulted in heavy fines for both unions for contempt.

But his actions won him union antipathy. The CIO called him the nation's "number one strikebreaker," and more than one union declared that it would spend every last cent in its treasury to defeat him if he ran for the presidency in 1948. That proved an ideal threat, thanks to the Republican opposition. In a Congress controlled by their party after the 1946 elections, the Grand Old Party (GOP) struck down the Norris-LaGuardia and the Wagner Acts, which labor considered its bill of rights. They were replaced with a hated Taft-Hartley Act, branded as antilabor, and passed over Truman's veto. The GOP nominated Thomas E. Dewey as their candidate for president in 1948, a man who was something less than lukewarm in his support of labor. Declaring Truman the lesser of two evils, the unions threw their weight behind him and provided many of the votes that allowed him to score the most remarkable electoral upset in the nation's history.

The unions had become militant with the coming of peace, a militancy that was galvanized as industry stubbornly resisted the demands of workers. Realizing that their strength was in numbers, the unions began massive organizing campaigns, determined to turn every American worker into a union member, by persuasion or by force or by any means at their command. Industry was equally determined to prevent unionization, by persuasion or by force and intimidation, by any means at its command, save on rare occasions when it voluntarily matched or topped what the unions were claiming they could provide in wages and benefits. The battle lines were drawn. Both sides gathered armies, sometimes called goons or scabs or strikebreakers. Often, workers found themselves caught in the middle of a violent and bitter struggle, threatened and beaten if they joined a union or even listened to an organizer, and threatened and beaten if they refused to join a union.

In the unions, change was occurring. The old guard that led the way through the anti-union fervor of the 1920s into the gradual emancipation of the 1930s was being challenged and, in many cases, supplanted by newer and younger leaders, schooled on the bloody picket lines of the prewar decade and now anxious to take the power and plot the course for the future. Nowhere was this drama played out more explicitly or with greater implications for the labor movement and the nation than in Detroit, and in the steel center of Pittsburgh, the most heavily industrialized areas in the country, the bastions of militant unionism. And it was this arena in which Walter Reuther and James Riddle Hoffa, two young and ambitious labor leaders still in their thirties and bloodied in the labor wars of the 1930s, were making their moves toward prominence and power.

Walter Reuther's union, the United Automobile Workers, was young, born in the ferment of the 1930s, welded in the violent confrontations at Ford and General Motors. UAW members were laborers on an assembly line, interchangeable parts in a modern industrial machine. Disdained by the older and more conservative craft unions that formed the AFL, the UAW joined with other newly emerging factory-based unions to form the more liberal and militant Congress of Industrial Organizations (CIO). Reuther epitomized the UAW and the CIO. His father, a German immigrant, had been a Socialist and a fiery labor leader in the Brewery Workers Union. He had grown up admiring the radicals Eugene Debs and Big Bill Haywood, and had campaigned for Socialist candidate Norman Thomas for president. He was a man of both ideas and action, working in factories during the day and going to high school and then to Wayne State University at night.

Fired from Ford for union activities, Reuther went to the Soviet Union to see for himself the workers' paradise, worked in a Russian factory for two years, and returned home. He was disillusioned by the Soviet experiment, but deeply committed to liberalism, social justice, and the rights of labor, and preached endlessly of the need for worker solidarity. By the end of the war, he had emerged as the dominant personality in the UAW, president of Local 174 and head of the General Motors department. In 1946, he was elected president of the UAW. But he was not satisfied. The CIO beckoned, and by 1952 he would lead it. Still not satisfied, he dreamed of a consolidation of all labor in one house, and so worked for and finally achieved the merger of the AFL and the CIO. He was a realist whose realism was leavened by idealism. He was a brilliant organizer, a tough and masterful negotiator, a man other men followed.

James Riddle Hoffa belonged to the International Brotherhood of Teamsters, Chauffeurs, Warehousemen, and Helpers. Unlike the UAW and the other industrial unions, the Teamsters, pillar of the old AFL craft unions, displayed hardly any militancy until the arrival on the scene in the late 1930s of men like Hoffa in the Middle West and Dave Beck on the West Coast. Founded in 1903 as a loose confederation of city deliverymen—those who drove milk, ice, bread, coal, and other wagons and trucks—it numbered fewer than 100,000 members by the time of the New Deal. Its president, Dan Tobin, who had ruled from headquarters in Indianapolis since 1907, seemed to disdain major organizational drives. "We do not want to charter the riffraff," he declared. Hoffa, Beck, and a few others were to change that.

Born in rural Indiana, Hoffa with his family migrated to Detroit after the death of his father. At sixteen, he dropped out of school and the rest of his education, he often said, came in the school of hard knocks. He found unionism on the loading docks of a produce warehouse where his organizing abilities and natural pugnaciousness brought him to the attention of emerging militants in the Teamsters. From Farrell Dobbs, a radical Trotskyite, he learned the lessons of organizing and bargaining, of the strength that came from numbers, including the riffraff like the drivers of longhaul over-the-road trucks. If he rejected Dobbs's politics, Hoffa took the other lessons to heart, including that you took your allies where you could find them and if it cost, well, everyone was on the take and the end justified the means. He was tough, aggressive, brutal, profane; he could be a bully and a sadist; he was devious and often unscrupulous; he was unforgiving and hated with a passion; and he was smart, natively intelligent, with an ability to learn quickly, master what he needed, and retain what was necessary; he could be charming and winning; he was a brilliant organizer, a terrifying negotiator, and a leader who inspired unswerving loyalty in his followers.

As their unions differed, so Reuther and Hoffa differed. Reuther was the idealistic realist who would carry the day with the force of his intellect and the logic of his arguments and rightness of his cause, all backed by the power implicit in his union and its numbers and its solidarity. Hoffa was the cynical realist who believed, as he would tell Joe Franco often through the years:

> You will never receive loyalty or respect by being a nice guy. Nice guys run second. They always get shit on. What you got to remember is fear and money make power. If you've got

enough to make a man fear you, he'll show you respect and he'll show you loyalty. It may be phony, but you can depend on it if you've got the power and you got the money and you create the fear. Those are the things you should work for. Fear will keep everybody in line. You think all the people who work for me like me? You think the guys on the other side of the table like me? Maybe they do. But if I turn my back, they'd go in fourteen different directions if they weren't afraid. It's the fear. They know that I'll retaliate. One way or the other, they stay in line. They've got respect and they've got fear. Have people fear you and people will respect you and they'll show you loyalty.

This was, then, a basic difference between Hoffa and Reuther. Still, there were many similarities, and they went deeper than both shunning worldly pleasures—drink, tobacco, casual affairs, and the like. Both went in for long and hard labor for what they believed in. Both were dedicated to the need for unions. Both were willing to sacrifice themselves and their families to advance their causes. Both believed that what they did, they did for the ultimate good of their followers. Franco says: "They were never that far apart, the redhead and Jimmy, so they couldn't sit down and talk and resolve issues. They both understood that they were labor and that if there was antilabor legislation or pressure coming up, they were going to fight it. Even in politics, where they were always on different sides, it was a case of you take one guy and I'll take the other guy and if I win, you'll have to come to me and if you win, I'll have to come to you. They were labor and that was it and that was where they were at."

And, as Hoffa would one day tell writer John Bartlow Martin:

We knew each other in the rough and tumble days. For some reason, it's kind of inexplicable, we drifted apart. There's no reason we should have any arguments. He depends on us and we depend on him. . . . If Walter would have stayed in the labor movement rather than getting into politics, we'd never have had any trouble. We still see each other. He's all right. What the hell, he's got his problems, I got mine. At least he knows what the union business is all about.

By 1946, Reuther had reached at least one of his goals: He was president of the UAW. Hoffa still had a long way to go. He might be president of Local 299 in Detroit and he might run the city's Joint Council of Teamsters, but he was little known to the world, and even in the Teamster movement he was considered only a newcomer. But he was about to change that. One way would be to gain more power, and one way to gain more power, strength, and respect was to organize, to make his local grow and grow.

4

On that spring morning in 1946 when Franco first met Jimmy Hoffa, his name was no longer Joe Valenti. During the war years, as he dug his way deep into illegal enterprises, he learned that there was another Joe Valenti. That Joe Valenti was a man of some importance in the organized underworld. While pursuing his own criminal activities, he might be mistaken for his namesake. He decided to choose another name. All around he was seeing ads for Franco-American spaghetti. He became Joe Franco.

Now twenty-two, Joe Franco was trying to give some meaning to his existence. He had made and spent fortunes in the black markets of World War II and had little to show for them. But when he walked out of that meeting with Hoffa, he was into unions; he was a Teamster organizer and, he hoped, he had found what he was seeking. He told Tom Burke, "I like him. He's cocky, a little bantam rooster and I like that." Burke turned over a thousand application cards to Franco and the next morning he went to work.

I was a street guy. I drove a hack and I knew everybody, starting at the foot of Woodward out to the seven-mile line. I had been in business on the street, newspapers, the ice cream parlor, usher in one of the movie theaters, other things, so I knew everybody. I says, "Oh, shit, let me attack what I think I can grab the fastest." I went around to every theater and signed up all the ticket takers. They sold tickets off a wheel, so they had wheels, so they were in the Teamster jurisdiction, which was what Burke told me. Then I went to the dime-and-dance joints. There were four or five at the time on the street and they had maybe five hundred girls working there. I signed them all up, because they wore watches and watches had wheels in them, and so they were in our jurisdiction.

One of the joints, the Hollywood Ballroom, was owned by a guy named Sol Bloom who was a friend of mine before I got involved with organizing. He sees what I'm doing and he says, "Franco, what the fuck are you doing to my girls?"

"They want to be unionized. They want to stabilize the thing. They want to get two-bits a ticket. All I'm doing is signing them up. You're going to sit down with a guy named Burke or a guy named Hoffa and they'll eventually straighten this thing out. Don't worry about it. You won't get hurt."

Well, I guess he did something, because the girls picked him up and threw him down the stairs and damn near killed him, and then they went out on a wildcat strike. There they were with these handmade signs saying, "We're on strike. We're Teamster members." It hit the fucking fan. The newspapers grabbed it and the next morning it was all over the front pages about Teamsters organizing the dime-and-dance girls.

That morning, I went over to the Book-Cadillac Hotel where Burke was living and he had the papers all spread out and he's looking at the headlines. He says, "Holy shit. You do this?"

"Yeah. Here's the applications." I must have signed up almost two thousand people that week—ticket takers, ushers, dime-and-dance girls, the drivers at Radio Cab, everybody. I'd see people walking down the street and I'd say, "Want to belong to the union? Okay, sign here and you're in the union."

Burke says, "Holy shit. Sure as shit the phone's gonna ring and the old man's gonna want to see us." And there goes the phone and Burke picks it up and he looks at me and he says, "Come on. He's one hot son of a bitch."

We got to the office and the carpet was rolled out in front of his door. What I found out was that if the carpet was rolled up, it meant he wasn't in. If the carpet was rolled out, it meant he was in and that meant to some of the guys in the business agent's office to get the fuck out of the building or else they was gonna end up with some detail they may not want. Well, the carpet was out and the door opens and here comes Hoffa. He looks at us and he says, "Get in here, you dirty son of a bitch. Both you guys. You, too, you dago bastard you."

Well, I don't like this and I says to myself, oh, oh, that does it. I don't like this guy. This guy's bullshit. I don't like to be called a dago bastard. This guy gets too wise, I'll knock his fucking head off. I don't want to hear that shit.

We walk in and I'm steaming and he says, "Who the fuck is organizing them fucking whores? That's all I need is to see headlines Hoffa's organizing dime-and-dance whores. I ain't got enough trouble? Goddammit, who the fuck did it?"

Burke points over to me. Hoffa says, "Listen, kid, who the fuck told you to organize them? How can you organize dime-and-dance girls? They're not truck drivers."

"But they wear wristwatches. Burke says if they wore wristwatches, they got wheels in them and they belong to the jurisdiction of the Teamsters. Every one of these girls got a wristwatch. I made sure of it."

He could hardly keep a straight face. Jimmy never laughed. I knew him almost thirty years and I never heard him laugh. He had a tendency of putting his chin down and he'd give you a thick smile with a kind of hiss, never a hah-hah. So, he kind of put his chin down and he had a half-assed grin on his face and he says to Burke, "Burke, did you tell him the wristwatch bit?"

Burke says, "Yeah."

He says, "Well, you go back there and you tell these girls to go back to work. Tell them we can't organize them. They don't belong to our jurisdiction. Tell them if they want to join somebody's union, find another union than the Teamsters. Goddammit, I don't need this kind of publicity. We don't want to be known as organizing whores."

I says, "Yes, sir," and I go back and straighten that out, got the girls back to work, and then went over to the hospital and saw Solly and told him I was sorry about what happened and it was all straightened out now.

Well, the next day, Burke grabs me and he says, "Jesus Christ,

Franco, you son of a bitch, you've been here two fucking weeks and you've already got me enough trouble and now I think we're in for more."

"What the fuck did I do now?"

"I dunno, but he's screaming."

We get in there and it's the same fucking thing. The door opens and he's screaming, "Get your goddamn fucking dago ass in here, you son of a bitch. You, too, you fucking Irish bastard. Get in here." We walk in and he says, "Who the fuck organized all the movie guys?" There were six or seven hundred applications.

"I did."

"Jesus Christ almighty. How the fuck are you organizing ticket takers?"

"They got wheels. Fucking tickets come on wheels."

"Burke, you son of a bitch, tell this kid this union is made of truck drivers, warehousemen, and we'll pick up some factory people if they're there. But what we're basically interested in is truck drivers. That's what we're here for, not ticket takers and not dime-and-dance whores."

And there's a guy sitting right alongside of Jimmy and he's an Italian guy and he was the head of the movie operators union. He went and beefed to Jim because what was happening is that when he would negotiate a contract, he'd hold the ticket takers and the ushers over the employer's head, and that's how the movie operators got such high pay rates and you had two guys in the projection booth. Instead of a strike, he would threaten to organize the ticket takers and the ushers. Once I organized them, he didn't have that sledgehammer anymore. So he went to Jim and beefed and Jim said, don't worry about it, I'll call him in. So now he says to this guy, "I want you to meet Joe Franco." And he says to me, "We've got to give those cards back to him."

"Wait a minute. So far in two weeks, I've organized about two thousand fucking Teamsters. You told me the girls are fucking whores so we had to give those back. Now I got six, seven hundred ushers and ticket takers and I got to give them to him. How the fuck do I make a living around here?"

"Go out and organize truck drivers. That's how you make a living."

"Burke, you fucker you, from here on out, you and I are

working together and you tell me what to organize and what not to organize."

From that time on, Burke and I were together I'd say twenty out of twenty-four hours every day. A couple of days later, we were out looking for trucks, cars, or something that we could organize. We ended up finding a restaurant firm and we saw about twelve trucks at the warehouse there. We figures there could be fifty, sixty employees of this restaurant supply house. We followed this one truck out, and the first stop he made, we pulled up behind him. Now Tom and I made a deal. One day, he was the bad guy and I was the nice guy, and the next day he was the nice guy and I was the bad guy. So, he walks up to the cab of the truck and tells the guy to get out. He says, "I'm Tom Burke of the Teamsters and we'd like to organize you. We'd like to bring you into the union, get you better wages and increases, a pension program, we'll get you an insurance program, vacations."

The driver was a big black guy and he says, "I don't want to fuck with no union. Shit, my boss would fire me if I ever said anything about a union. I'd get fired in a minute."

Burke walks to the back of the truck and drops the tailgate. He says, "Look, I like you. I know you got a problem. But see that kid over there?" He points to me. "He's fucking nuts. He's crazy. I can't control him when he gets mad."

I jump up on the tailgate and I went over and picked up a box of plates and I stood on the edge of the tailgate. The black guy looks at me. "Hey, man what the fuck are you doing with that box? Don't drop that motherfucker. That's full of plates."

Burke says, "I can't control him when he gets mad. He can't hear nothing. So, you want to join the union?"

"I can't join the union. I'll get fired."

I dropped the box and the plates go flying all over hell.

"Goddammit, you done did it. I'm gonna get my ass fired for sure." I got another box. "Oh, shit, man, don't drop two boxes. They gonna take it out of my fucking pay now. I ain't gonna have nothing left."

Burke says, "You'd better sign the fucking application. See what happens with that kid. He won't let you down. He'll go to that fucking employer and he'll shake him by the throat. Don't worry about getting fired. He'll protect your ass."

"He ain't protecting my ass now. He's fucking ruined me." I let another box go. "Ah, fuck, give me that fucking application. I'm fired anyway. I'm going with you two guys. You two guys are fucking crazy." He signed up right on the spot. "I ain't gonna make the rest of the deliveries. I'm going back and do the fucking thing and get it over with."

We went right back to the warehouse and he introduced us to all the guys. "These two motherfuckers are crazy, they just broke a couple of boxes of my plates."

Well, we explained who we were and that we wanted to get them better pay and benefits and before you knew it, we signed everybody up.

That was pretty typical of organizing in those days. We'd pick up a truck and we'd tail it into the terminal. If we found it was an organized trucker, forget it. If he wasn't organized, we'd take on a truck at a time and we'd follow it for forty-eight hours, and never let him go into an organized terminal, and if he went into an unorganized terminal, we'd make a report on it and that was the place where we'd start out. Sometimes, we'd tag a truck four, five days. I think the longest time we had a truck was three weeks. Every time he stopped, we'd stop. One of us would sleep, the other would be awake and drive and watch. The trucker, if he ran in to get something to eat, I'd run into the joint and grab some sandwiches and bring them out. We'd dog him. If he took us to an organized warehouse, we'd tell the guys there, "He's an unorganized truck, don't take his merchandise." And the warehouse guys were solid Teamsters. They'd say, "Hey, get the fuck out of here or we'll smash your fucking truck up and down." And he'd take off. Eventually, he'd get so tired he'd end up signing up. That's how we signed up truck drivers. We were signing up like two hundred truck drivers every week. And sometimes we'd be lucky and grab an industrial plant, too.

Saturday was pay day. We'd go out to Jim's house, me and Burke and the other guys that was roving business agents and organizers, and Jim would be out back. Jim Jr. was about five or six in those early days and Barbara, who's so much like him it ain't funny, she was about eight or nine, and they'd be sitting out on the steps and Josephine would be in the house most of the time. Jim would reach into his pocket and pull out the cash and pay us in cash whatever we had coming. In those days it wasn't always that easy for him to come up with the dough. He didn't drink and he didn't smoke and he was not a sex person. I really don't think he ever gave a damn about sex. But there was times in those days when he used to gamble, go into a back alley crap game to pick up enough so he could pay the guys what they were owed.

The late 1940s were years of constant ferment, of organizing the unorganized, of strikes. Much was marked by violence, which was not foreign to Franco and Burke and the others brought into the Teamster organizing effort by Hoffa.

Steve Schultz was the head of Local 283 in those years and he was organizing parking attendants, and Burke and I were helping him. We threw a strike on and the majority of the guys walked out. But a few of them stayed on and scabbed. We went to Jim and he says, do what you have to do, but no more scabs. Now, in those days, we used to ride two, three, or four in a car, and one of the tools of the trade was a hunk of chain that you used if you were chasing somebody or you wanted to whack a windshield or whack somebody in the head. Instead of a pipe or anything else, a chain was stock in trade. You knew how to use a chain, you could do a lot of things with it, you could do a lot of damage or you could do just enough damage. If you're dealing with a baseball bat or a pipe, then you've got a problem. You may overdo it.

One of these guys kept scabbing. He kept going across the picket line and we kept telling him, "Don't go across the picket line because you're causing a problem for us." He told us to go to hell. Now, we have to take care of business with this guy. We watched him and the first time he left, he went down Washington Boulevard. We watched him go down Adams and over to Woodward and from Woodward over to the highway. So, we seen how he went home, once, twice, three times, and always at five-thirty, six o'clock. So, three of us laid for him. As soon as he showed up, Maury Coleman and I jumped out of the car with chains in our hands and we gave him a shot across the head. With that, he started to run across Woodward. Now Maury was a little older than me and probably more out of shape, so Maury just got in a couple of shots. But I kept chasing him and I'd hit him just enough across the side of the head so the kid would run even faster. I got about four or five licks in and this kid just kept running like you wouldn't believe. Every time I hit him, he just went faster. Now, I was getting out of breath so I pulled off and went back to Maury and we got back into the car and went back to the picket line.

Two days later, this guy shows up and he looks like a Hindu. His head is all wrapped up. He comes over to me and he says, "I want to apologize. I ain't never gonna cross another picket line as long as I live. I'm not holding any grudges. I deserve what I got. I should never have become a scab." We shook hands and the kid was a friend of mine for years after that.

Now there was another kid there that was a troublemaker, too, and he was a scab and when we told him not to scab, he told us to kiss his ass. So, Tom Burke and I walked up to the corner where the old Greyhound Bus Station used to be, and Burke walks into Cunningham's Drug Store and he buys a large can of lighter fluid. I'm not asking any questions but I'm trying to figure what the hell he's going to do with the lighter fluid. The time of the year was the fall and you wore heavier clothes because it got kind of chilly at night. This kid had a plaid wool lumber jacket and it was about six o'clock and just starting to get dark when he walks out of the parking lot. Tom says, "Come on, follow me."

While we're following, about five feet behind, Tom takes the cap off this lighter fluid and he starts spraying and hits the kid in the back with the lighter fluid. And he keeps squeezing and squeezing and the fluid's going all over the kid's back. I says to him, "What the hell are you doing? If you ever put a match on this, the kid's gonna blow up. You got him saturated." We get to the corner and the kid catches a red light. And Tom is still pumping the damn lighter fluid onto him. He says to me, "You got a match?"

"Yeah."

"Take the whole book and as soon as it turns green, light the whole book and throw it at him, hit him in the back with it."

"Okay."

The light turns green, I light the book, the whole book exploded and I threw it and hit the kid in the back and that kid went right up in flames, *voom*. He took off down Washington Boulevard and he looked like what you see in the night sky, a comet. A streak that must have been ten feet long went out behind him. The lighter fluid just went up in a flash. It didn't burn anything, it just flashed. He must have went fifty yards before it extinguished itself. I broke up laughing and I goddamn near peed in my pants. Burke says, "Come on." So we go down to the Greyhound terminal and we go into the toilet and he says, "Get into the booth and put your feet up on the toilet so nobody can see your feet and sit there until I tell you." He jumps into one booth and I jump into another and we stayed there about a half hour, and I'm laughing, I can't stop laughing, and he keeps saying to me from the next booth, "Shut up, you son of a bitch, somebody's gonna hear you."

"Tom, we've been in here a half hour, ain't nobody gonna hear shit. In the meantime, I'm gonna take a leak." I'm laughing so goddamn hard I had to go to the bathroom. Then I says, "Come on, let's get the hell out of here." We didn't have no more trouble with that kid after that, and we got the attendants organized.

In 1947, I was running a picket line for Local 299 against a Ford distributorship out in Southfield. There was some bad feelings between the owners of that Ford dealership and James R. Hoffa, and I'm sure there were bad feelings toward me because during that three-month strike there were only two of us picketing the place and we kept it closed. Then we found out that they were starting to bring in new cars because the salespeople had run out of cars to sell because we had stopped all deliveries. When the trucks would arrive with cars for delivery, we would just say, "299," and we would show them our ID and tell them to take the trucks and the cars and take off and go back to the dock area, and dump them in the lots and leave them until further notice. And the guys would go along because they were members of Local 299. I then found out that some of the drivers were being told to take the cars to a warehouse about three miles away and they didn't know the warehouse was part of this Ford distributorship, so they didn't know they were violating Local 299's rules as to the conduct of good members. I called Jim. "Jim, he's got about fifty to a hundred and fifty automobiles stashed in this big warehouse and the sales guys are driving in these new cars and shoveling them over to the dealership during the night. We were wondering where they were getting cars from and now we know."

Jim says, "You do what you have to do. Talk to me when you

get to the office in the morning and tell me what it takes," meaning what his costs would be for me to resolve this problem.

Without their knowing anything about it, I proceeded to go home and went down to my basement and used electric bulbs and with a glass cutter went around the brass rim and took the brass off and filled it with paint, and then put a cork in and soldered the brass back on so they would act as paint bombs. I made a couple of them and picked up some other chemicals that could be put into these electric bulbs that would eat the paint off, acid-type things. We had access to all the chemicals we needed; all I had to do was ask for them, tell them what I was intending to do and they knew exactly what they had to give me.

A couple of nights later, I went out and did a number on all these cars by just throwing these bulbs and hitting these cars with paint bulbs and acid bulbs, and without any dynamite or anything else, I probably destroyed better than 80 percent of the automobiles that were in that warehouse.

The following morning, I went on the picket line and the owner came out and he started to threaten me and the guy that was with me, a young man named Bill Bagley. "I know you guys did it. I'll get even." I didn't pay any attention to him. A couple of nights later, Bill had to go home and I stayed as late as I could to make sure they weren't bringing cars in from other areas. I just sat in my car and watched and I stayed until about eleven or eleven-thirty.

Then I started to head for home. I came down Telegraph and circled around because I had a feeling I was being followed, and I found out in a few minutes that I was. Around the Seven Mile Road area, all of a sudden a car pulled up alongside. I had a new black four-door Ford. I hadn't reached the pinnacle yet of Jimmy supplying me with a big black Cadillac, which most of the agents that were with 299 got to drive around in and organize, to show the power and strength. I got mine a little after this. Anyway, this car drove up alongside me very fast and I knew I was in trouble. All of a sudden I could hear pop-pop-pop, gunshots. I swung over to the right, went up the curb, and saw there was on open field there, and swung across the field. The other car just took right off and never stopped. I guess they figured they hit me because of the way I swung over to the right and went into the field and was going back and forth. What I was doing was running up the field and trying to control the car; eventually I got full control and I started to come back on Telegraph, and I was ready to chase them, and I was prepared to do whatever I had to do at that time because I had the necessary equipment to retaliate. But when I came off the field and hit the street, I was going full blast. I dodged this fire hydrant and I looked straight ahead and there was one big huge metal telephone pole. There was nothing I could do to dodge that. I hit that telephone pole and the pole came right up in the center of the motor, and the motor was jammed up in front, and I was pinned because the steering wheel was jammed right into my chest. I turned the ignition off because I was thinking the car might catch fire. But I couldn't open up the car doors.

Some people stopped and the next thing you know, the police department was there. They crowbarred the door out and asked me if I was hurt. I said, no. I didn't feel it at that time and I didn't want to get into a big thing about it. They took me out and drove me down to a hotel in the center of Detroit and I took a room there. I was having severe pains in my chest, like as if I was having a heart attack. It turned out that the steering wheel had hit me so hard in the chest that it had bruised me and caused swelling and I was in pretty bad shape for a couple of days.

I talked to Jim and told him where I was holed up and he told me to relax and take it easy until I felt better, and when I did, to go back out to the picket line. I did and when I went back out there, the owner came out with a smile on his face. I shook my fist at him and I says, "Well, that's round two. I won the first. You won the second. Now let's see who wins the third."

"What do you mean by that?"

"You know what I'm talking about. You know the best shot you've got going for you, pal, is you pick up the goddamn phone and you call Hoffa and you settle this strike, because I'll tell you something, three strikes and you're out, because there ain't nobody else I'm gonna be looking for. I'm holding you responsible for what happened. So that's one for you and one for me, and I'll tell you something, if you start shooting at me, pal, you got a problem. Because if it ain't today, it's gonna be tomorrow, and if it ain't tomorrow, it's gonna be a year from today, but I'll get your ass. You belong to me, pal. So, you better get your little ass on the phone and settle this goddamn strike."

Well, he picked up the phone and he called Hoffa and he told Hoffa he'd like to meet with him. Within a week, ten days, that strike was resolved. He didn't want any more problems.

We hit a big electrical company with a strike. They had about forty or fifty trucks, closed panel trucks, and we had them on strike for about four weeks and it started to drag. After the fourth week, I decided something had to be done to get this thing off dead center. I started getting into the trucks and started putting sugar and molasses in their gas tanks, and I did it to better than 50 percent of their trucks. The funny thing about the whole goddamn thing is that the first day I didn't expect anything to happen, but I felt that by the second day, these trucks would start spitting and sputtering and then would jam up because the sugar and the molasses crystallize and freeze up the piston and destroy the motors, and they would have to buy all new gas lines, carburetors, fuel pumps, motors, the whole works. It would have been a very costly thing to replace that many parts in the twenty, twenty-five trucks I fixed up. But the thing is that the next two, three days, those trucks would start up and start roaring like you'd think I put some power in there. They never backfired, they never smoked, they never did a goddamn thing, they never ran better. It was like whatever those trucks needed it wasn't gasoline, it was sugar and molasses. They just ran beautifully. I couldn't believe it. I have never seen a truck react to this shit and operate and still be running after ten, fifteen days. Those sons of bitches should have been jammed up tighter than shit.

I told Jim and he broke out with that grin of his, those beautiful teeth of his shining. He says, "Well, what are you going to do now?"

"Well, I got to bring that son of a bitch to a head." The guy that ran the company was a real hard-assed German. He wasn't going to give up for love or money. He was going right down the pike one way or the other. So I says to Jim, "Let's bring this thing to a complete halt."

"Go ahead and do what you have to do and let me know what the costs are."

So I went ahead and I start doing some numbers on the trucks. I blew up about half a dozen at different locations where they were parked, making sure the drivers were all out of them and then popped them and went about my business. All hell started to break loose because now this old German called the police department. The state troopers came in and there I am with just two pickets plus the guys that worked there on the picket line. Let me tell you, I never asked any employee that walked out on strike with me to ever do anything that was improper or any violence or any violation of any law. I would do it, and I would be held responsible for it. I would normally tell them, stay the hell out of it. All I want you to do is picket, carry the signs, be good pickets, mind your own business, don't get sassy with anybody. If there's anything that's got to come down, that's what I get paid for, that's my job.

With all the heat that's coming down because of what's taking place with the trucks, I found myself going home late. It was like ten o'clock and it was dark, and at that time I was going with a girl who had just bought herself a brand new Mercury, and it was beautiful. She used to let me use it at night. I was coming home on Forest Avenue, which was a one-way street, and there was parking only on the right side. I was in the right lane alongside the parked cars. From out of nowhere a car comes right alongside of me and with a shotgun blast hit my right fender and tire and blew the tire out. I swerved into the curb area to get away from him and I heard another shot that probably hit the back end of my car. That didn't mean anything because at that point I had already impacted with my car on the parking side and this beautiful new Mercury was right up the backside of the car that was parked. It went right on top of it and across that one and a second one and a third one and a fourth one and stopped on the fifth one. I was on top of the fifth car before my car came to a stop. I had destroyed five parked cars and the car I was using from the girl. They were all totaled out. The insurance company paid all the damages.

Eventually, we put some more heat on and we got the thing resolved. But it's a very costly thing when a strike goes on too long. The people that are out on strike lose income, their families suffer from it, so the best thing is to have a quick strike and get it resolved as quickly as possible the best way you know how, and get the people back to work. Bobby Holmes, who was the secretary-treasurer of Local 337 in those days, and who was a very level-headed guy with his feet on the ground, not the kind of guy to go out and, say, blow up a car, a guy I used to confide in a lot, asking his advice, he would say, "Joe, you'd be better off if you'd call the man up and tell him you'd like to have a cup of coffee. You'll settle more contracts, more labor disputes over a cup of coffee than you ever will with a stick of dynamite." I took his advice on many, many occasions and found it did work. But there were times when you found out that the employer was stubborn and you knew you were in for a long drawn-out fight and then you went to the next step and used whatever means were available to you to resolve the strike and get your people back to work.

These were the years when Hoffa was carving out his empire, spreading his jurisdiction into whatever areas he could. He did not take lightly any encroachments on what he considered his rightful preserve. Thus, when the longshoremen moved into something he felt belonged to him, he acted.

We were attending the Wayne County convention at the Detroiter Hotel when all of a sudden word got to Jimmy that something had broken loose on the waterfront. The longshoremen were trying to take over the jurisdiction of driving automobiles onto the boats. That was the time when boats were starting to deliver cars from one port to another instead of by truck, and the longshoremen felt it was their jurisdiction to drive the trucks out of the parking lots where they were brought by Teamsters and unloaded and then load them onto the boats. Jim felt it was our jurisdiction to drive the cars onto the boats, and after they were on the boats, then it became the jurisdiction of the longshoremen.

So we were called out of the convention. Whenever there was a convention or a conference in Detroit, we all attended. Jim wanted the whole staff there at all times, and the whole staff was about thirty-five or forty guys. We all jumped in our cars and went down to the waterfront. We went around the side of the street where the cars were behind the fence in the yard and the longshoremen were lined up on the opposite side of the street. We were pretty well matched off. There were maybe forty or fifty of us and forty or fifty of them, and in the middle of the street there must have been twenty or thirty cops. Words were being thrown back and forth, and threats were being thrown back and forth. Hoffa walks over to me and he says, "Franco [he never in his life called me Joe, it was always Franco or the kid], get out there in the middle of the street and call Muscles out in the middle of the street and start a fight with him."

Muscles was this big longshoreman who looked like a wrestler, a big, big guy who looked like he could break you in half with his little finger. So I look at Jim. "Are you kidding? You picked me? I'm the littlest guy here, for chrissake."

"Get your ass out there and do what I told you to do. Don't worry about it. We're all here. We're not going to let you go out there and fight that big bastard."

"All right."

I went out in the street and I started to aggravate the hell out of this Muscles. "Come on you big musclebrain, you big piece of shit." The cops came over and I says, "Hey, you guys stay the hell out of this." And everybody on the side of the Teamsters is yelling the same thing and Jim's hollering, "You guys stay the hell out of it. You guys stay where the hell you belong and we'll stay where we belong. Just leave the kid alone. If he wants to start a fight, let them fight between the two of them. I think I'm sending in a lightweight compared to the heavyweight, so if that Muscles got any guts at all, let him come out in the middle of the street and fight the kid."

I knew what Jimmy wanted to do, so I kept calling him everything under the sun to aggravate the hell out of him. "You chickenshit son of a bitch, you ain't got the balls to come out in the middle of the street and have it out with me, and I'm twice as little as you are. Look how big you are and how little I am." And I'm yelling that this guy don't want to come out and fight and it just goes to show the rest of those longshoremen what kind of a leader they got because Jimmy sends out the youngest guy and the lightest guy and this Muscles still won't come out and fight. Well, the thing was this guy knew that once he comes out there, all hell is gonna break loose.

Then Jim called me back over. "All right, you and Burke get the hell out of here." Tommy and I walked away and we had parked our car way up on the corner. Tom says, "Come on." We walked around the corner and we went two buildings over and went up to the roof of the building which was a three-story building. It had kind of a ledge, a three-foot-high ledge on it, so that we could look over and look down and we could see all that was going on. Then Tom pulled out his pistol. I says, "What are you going to do?"

He says, "Watch me." Now, Tom was a crack shot. Not only a crack shot, but he was a trick shooter. He could shoot with a mirror backward. The man was amazing with a pistol. He reached over the edge and he says, "Now you watch. Watch his left foot. I'm gonna blow his big toe off."

"What? From this high and this far away?"

"Watch me. What we do after is we get the hell out of here. They won't know where it came from, so we'll have enough time to get away."

"Tom, you got to be kidding."

He was holding a .32-long barrel that I gave him. We had a twin set and I had one and he had the other, and they were target pistols. I says, "That's great for target practice, from like twenty yards. But you're talking about fifty, seventy-five yards, and we're up on the roof so you're shooting downward."

"You just watch, Franco. The old pro is going to show you something." He got his hand up there and he took that .32 and laid it on his arm, in the knee of this arm, put it on top of the ledge and let go. You could hear the crack. Muscles from the longshoremen jumps up and grabs his foot and falls on his ass. And the cops and everybody else is looking up to find out where the hell the shot came from.

I says, "Jesus Christ, let's get the hell out of here."

So, we took off and got downstairs and got in the car and went back to the building. Burke says, "See. I told you I hit him in the toe."

"How the hell do you know you hit him in the toe? All he did was grab his whole goddamn foot."

"I guarantee you I blew his goddamn toe off."

We got back over to Trumbull Avenue and waited for Jim and our guys to get back, which they did once Jim got it resolved.

That night, the late news came out that the guy that was the head of the longshoremen was shot and had his big toe on his left foot blown off and they took him to the hospital. When the news came out, I was sitting with Burke and Hoffa. I says to Burke,

"You son of a bitch. You're one hell of a shot." I turn to Hoffa and I says, "Jim, you know where the hell we were at?" I told him.

Jim says, "Franco, this man can shoot."

"I hope to tell you. I just wish I could shoot just half as good."

That took care of that. After that, the Teamsters took over the jurisdiction of driving the cars onto the boats and we never did have any more problems with the longshoremen.

So, Hoffa protected and expanded the jurisdiction of his Teamsters. And he gathered allies in other unions and other locals by coming to their aid when they were in trouble. He supported them in their strikes and organizing efforts.

There was this lovely lady, Myra Wolfgang, who was married to a sweetheart of a guy named Moe Wolfgang. Myra was probably the warmest labor leader in this country, she was as good as any man, she was just great in her work. She represented the Hotel and Restaurant Employees Local 24. But her strength came from James R. Hoffa and she knew that she could never resolve any of her problems unless the Teamsters were 100 percent behind her. And the reason that Jimmy gave her the fullest cooperation was that he felt she was the most capable labor woman in the United States.

Now, there was a time when Myra was starting to organize drive-in hamburger joints. I was on another assignment, so I was late getting there the night all the Teamster agents were assigned on her strike, and Jim went along. It was summertime and it was about nine o'clock and getting dark when I got there. I pulled up and saw the old man sitting on the curb holding his head. I came over and wanted to give him a report on what I had been accomplishing, and he looked at me and he had the biggest goddamn black eye you ever saw and he had a hunk of beef laid up against the eye.

"What the hell happened to you?"

"One of those goddamn seventeen-year-olds that hang around the joint took a sucker punch at me. I wasn't even looking. The son of a bitch gave me a real shiner."

"That's one hell of a black eye, boss. That's gonna be a

beauty. You're gonna have one hell of a time explaining that one to Josie."

"Quit laughing, goddammit. It's nothing to laugh about."

"What happened to the kid?"

"They haven't come back yet."

Roland McMasters and Hy Bushkin and a couple of other guys went after the kid and Jim was waiting for them. So I sat there with him and smoked a cigarette, and then here comes Mack and Hy Bushkin and a couple of other guys, and they proceed to tell Jimmy that they chased the kid down the street and they came to this house and there was this old couple sitting out on the porch in rocking chairs, and the kid ran right up there thinking he might get some help. But once he ran up those stairs, he knew he wasn't going to get no help from them, and he went right through the screen door, didn't even stop to open it, went right through the house and went right out the back door, right through the screen door, and didn't stop to open it, either. And who's following him? Mack and Hy and the other guys. The old couple is sitting there with their heads going back and forth like they was watching a tennis match. They must have thought they were seeing one of those Keystone Cops deals. Anyway, they finally caught up with the kid and they gave him a pretty good beating, enough so he'd never sucker punch another union official. Now Jim was listening and he was giving that shit-ass grin of his and hissing, trying to picture what it must have looked like. Myra comes over and she was very sympathetic to the fact that Jim had a black eye. And, of course, Jim helped her win that thing and organize those places.

Anytime she needed help, she would always say to Jim, "Send me Tom Burke and send me the kid," which was me, and that would be enough. And Jim would always assign us to Local 24 for any problems they might have. They used to have sitdowns where we would bring fifty, sixty people into a restaurant and no other customers could come in because we were sitting and drinking water and taking all the tables. And we'd do that day in and day out until the guy that owned the restaurant would probably give up and say, "I can't stay in business this way," and he would agree to sign up with Myra. A few times, though, she would go in and have the people signed up and the owner wouldn't recognize it. So, Tommy and I would have to go inside and talk to the owner and say, "Look, one lump or two lumps?" And if he says, one, he got one, and if he says, two, he got two, and that's the way it would be until he would say he was willing to recognize Local 24. Then we'd call Myra and say, "Send this guy an agreement," and he would sign it and that would be the end of it.

There would be times that Myra would be having trouble organizing clubs, and orders would come from Jimmy to me and Tom where certain restaurants and certain clubs would have their front doors blown off. If Myra was trying to organize Club A, we would go to Club B and blow their door off so that Club A would know and would get the message, and he would know what happened to the other club that wasn't being organized, so he would sit down and bargain with Local 24. It was Jimmy's way of saying, "Hey, listen, you'll learn. We don't want to hurt your club. But that other guy, we don't even want him in the union, we'll blow his door off. Let that be a lesson to you." That was the way Local 24 got Jim's support and Myra, knowing that she had the full cooperation and support of Jimmy—she was very beautiful. She built one big local union, it had in excess of twenty thousand members at one time.

And Hoffa came to the aid of union leaders who were on his side and who were under attack from dissidents, facing the possible loss of their locals.

The majority of assignments Jimmy gave out were to Tom Burke and myself, and to Al McNally, Roland McMasters, Davey Johnson, Jimmy Cliff, and a couple of others. These were the key guys. And Jim did everybody favors. If you needed something, you went over and asked him and he would help. Earl Bush was the head of the bartenders union in those days and he went to Jimmy when his local was being taken into receivership by the international. He thought they had no right to do that so he asked Jimmy for help. So, Jimmy intervened and he assigned me and Tom Burke and Al McNally to sit shotgun, which meant that we would walk into a local union and take over the books, put them in a box, and sit there. Each of us would have a shotgun or a pistol and we would let nobody come in, whether it was from the international or members or anybody else. Nobody could touch those records or the charter. As long as we controlled those books, the records, and the charter, the local stayed intact until Jimmy and Earl Bush could sit down with representatives from the international bartenders union and resolve Earl's problems. It might last a day, might last two days, if it lasted a week, we were not allowed to leave there. They would send us food and they would send us whatever he needed, but we would have to stay in there and barricade the place and protect the books and the charter.

Now, Paul Allen of the riggers, he had a similar problem. He was being upset by a dissident group that wanted to take over by force prior to an election. So Jimmy assigned Al McNally, McMasters, Burke, and myself, and we were sent in there to shotgun it. We sat shotgun for almost five days. Nobody was allowed in, even though the dissident group wanted to come in and also had arms. We were up on the second floor, which gave us an advantage. They would have to try to come up the staircase and in through the door and we'd let out a blast, with a pistol or a shotgun, and they would get right the hell out of there. They tried it a couple of times and they never tried it again. So, until the election was held and the results were over with, we sat there. Paul Allen and his executive board members won the election, so we let them come in and they took over the books and the charter and proceeded to do business again as a bona fide union.

In his search for allies, Hoffa was looking outside his Teamster stronghold into other locals and other unions. He was also beginning to find friends in another world where there was immense power. The cost of that friendship was not cheap.

To begin with, Jimmy had no connections with the Italian element in that period of 1946 and 1947. He didn't know anybody who was Italian other than those who were in the labor movement. He had no connections with the Italian so-called organized crime groups.

Now, a man who was very well known in Detroit and had basically the same kind of reputation as Joey Gallo had a lot later, as an uncontrollable man, was Sam Perrone. He was so uncontrollable that everybody was scared of him. When he made up his mind to do something, that's what was going to be done and nobody was going to stop him or even try. The thing is, Sam Perrone was one of the people that I had known since I was a baby. There was a closeness between my mother and dad and him, plus his partners were actually my *padrinos* who had baptized me. Sam was, if you want to use the term, like a godfather to me in the real sense of a godfather and not the movie bullshit. Sam was a union buster. He represented the Detroit Stove Company, which employed about four or five thousand people, and maybe 75 or 80 percent of them were Italians and immigrants. Sam controlled them and he had their respect because they feared him.

I was just coming out of the business office one day and I was in the hall on the second floor between the office and Jim's office, talking to somebody, when I see Mr. Sam come walking up the stairs. I says to myself, what the hell is he doing here? I walked over to him and I says, in Italian, with all due respect, "Hello, Mr. Sam. How are you? What're you doing here?"

He looks at me. "Hey, Joey, how are you? What're you doin' here?" He spoke with a very thick Italian accent, so a lot of what we said to each other we said in Italian.

"I work here," which he didn't know; my segment of my people didn't know at that time that I was affiliated with the union; my family didn't even know it.

"I work for the Teamsters. I work for Mr. Hoffa."

"That's nice. You would do me a favor?"

"Sure. Anything you want."

"I'm looking for this goddamn Italian kid what's giving me goddamn trouble."

"What Italian kid?"

"This kid they call Hoffa. I want to meet this Mr. Hoffa."

He thought Hoffa was Italian because his last name ended in a vowel. For years, a lot of the guys thought Hoffa was Italian; they didn't know he was Irish and English and Dutch, or whatever. Mr. Sam says, "I want to meet this guy that's supposed to be a tough man." And I can see he's getting madder every time he mentions Hoffa's name.

I says to myself, oh, oh, there's gonna be trouble, and I says to him, "Is there something I can do? Maybe I can, you know, get him a message."

"That dirty son of a bitch, I'm gonna put one right in the

stomach," and he opens his jacket and sure as shit he's got a big fucking forty-five in his belt. I know this man. The man would have shot him in front of everybody and wouldn't have given a shit.

I'm saying to myself, Jimmy's in, because the carpet is out. Jimmy's in and I think if he comes walking out of that door and he starts screaming and hollering, somebody will say, okay, Jim—we always called him Jim or Jimmy or James R. to his face, but when we talked about him, we never said his names, we always called him the Little Guy, it was a thing taken from Little Caesar—and that will be it, Mr. Sam will shoot him right there and then. I'm praying he don't come out of the office.

"Joey, I want you should do me a favor. When this Hoffa comes out, you point him out to me and when you point him out, you get the hell out of here."

"Wait a minute, Mr. Sam. Look, hold it. Please, don't do nothing. If there's a problem, please, tell me what it is and let me try to get it resolved. He's a good man. Maybe there's a misunderstanding. Let me see if I can do something about it."

"He's giving me trouble. I got the goddamn thing over there and that fucking Italian don't know who the fuck I am and he's sticking his goddamn nose in my business. I want to kill him right now."

Then the goddamn door opens and here comes Jimmy. I see him and I'm giving him the off, like get the hell out of here. Well, he catches it and he pivots and he turns around and walks back into the office. I says to myself, thank God, because all we had to do was have somebody come out and say, Jimmy, and Sam would have known right away and it would have been bang-bang, goodbye Jimmy.

Sam turns to me and he says in Italian, "Who's that guy?"

"What guy?"

"Some guy, he walk out, he walk back into the office."

"That's where the clerks sit. You know, the guys who keep the books and stuff. Probably one of them."

"You find out if this young kid Hoffa, he's here."

"Yeah. Wait for me and I'll go into the business agents' office and I'll find out if he's here."

So I go in and I call on the intercom to Jim's office.

"Jim, don't come outside. Sam Perrone's here."

"What's he want?"

"I'll tell you later."

Then I go back out and I say, "Mr. Sam, he's out and he won't be back in today. I just talked to his secretary and she says maybe he'll be back around three or four o'clock if he comes in at all. Tell me what the problem is and I'll take care of it."

"You tell this dago, this Italian son of a bitch that he better see me before the day is over. Otherwise, I go to his house, I shoot him, I shoot everybody. You tell him Mr. Sam Perrone gives him that message."

"I'll tell him. I'll take care of it, Mr. Sam. Don't worry about it. Just let me handle it, Mr. Sam."

"You know what you're supposed to do. I know where you're coming from. I know you say you'll take care of it, you'll take care of it."

"Good. Very good. Mr. Sam, you've got my word. I'll get word to him. Five minutes after you leave, I'll make sure I get on the phone to wherever he's at and I'll get him back here and I'll try to get it resolved."

"You got a guy here name of Al McNally. He's a Siciliano. We like him. You and him can handle the meet."

"Good, very good. Mr. Sam, I'll take care of it right now. You going to be at the restaurant?"

He had a gas station directly across the street from the stove works and a restaurant where they used to sit around and have coffee, on East Jefferson, and that's where they used to make their office.

"I'll be over there all day."

I walked him down the stairs, walked him to his car and two guys were sitting in the car, and off they went. I wiped my brow and went back upstairs and got Al McNally out of the business agents' office.

"Al, come on, we got to talk to the old man. We got a problem. We're going to have to go on East Jefferson." He knew right away exactly what I was talking about.

We went into Jimmy's office and I says, "Hey, boss. You know who that was?"

"Yeah, I recognized him. That was Sam."

"Yeah, that was Mr. Sam."

"What the hell was he here for?"

"To hit you."

"What the hell for?"

"I can't find out. I was talking to him for fifteen minutes before you came out and he wanted me to finger you. I told him you were out but I'd make damn sure I would talk to you on the phone wherever you was at and get back to him within the next three, four hours. Soon as I reached you. He says that between me and Al McNally, he wants us over on East Jefferson and he wants an answer. He wants a peace talk."

"Jesus Christ, how am I going to get a peace talk without knowing what he's pissed about?"

"There's one way to find out. Al and I are going to have to go there."

"All right, Al, you and Franco go and find out what it's all about and if it's anything you can handle, your word is my word. You give them your word, Al, then your word is my word. Whatever you say is okay with me."

We both got into the car and we went over to East Jefferson. We walked into the restaurant and I took Al over to the table. There were four guys sitting there with Mr. Sam and they was the Five Council. They were all very close to my mother and dad and one of them, Mr. Pete, baptized me and another, Mr. Joe, was my father's best friend. I introduced Al to everybody, and Mr. Sam and Mr. Pete already knew him, and they shook hands and they said in Italian, "This guy is a good guy. He's one of us. He's a Siciliano. We can trust him." Coffee and amaretto was brought out and Al sat down and I just turned around to everybody and I says, "Gentlemen, my training and my school, you that are sitting here taught me everything that I know and one thing that you taught me was to excuse myself when I had no business here. You taught me that what you don't hear you don't know and you can't repeat if you're questioned. Now, you've got him and you don't need me. Please excuse me and I will go over there and sit down and have a cup of coffee. Mr. McNally has full authority to resolve the problems and make the peace. Whatever settlement you make with Al, Jimmy will stand by it. Right now, better I go over there and don't hear and don't know. Later on, if you want to tell me what took place, that's a different story. But now I shouldn't sit down at this meeting."

Mr. Sam looks at me. "You got good teaching. You're smart. Now, you give me your word?"

"You got my word. Whatever Al says, I stand for it and I'll make damn sure Jimmy stands for it, because Jimmy already said it, that whatever Al does is okay with him."

"All right, as long as you tell us, that's fine with us. We raised you. We trust you. Now, go over there and have a cup of coffee."

That was just fine with me, because even though these were my people, I never got into the personal shit, I always stayed away from it. They talked, I walked away.

It went on for about an hour and they were talking, talking. Finally, Al got up and they shook hands and I went over and shook hands and we say goodbye to everybody and we left. As we were leaving, I says, "I hope everything turned out the way you wanted, Mr. Sam."

"Joey, don't worry. Everything's fine. Goddammit, I thought that son of a bitch was Italian. I didn't know he was American. But it's just fine. We take care of it."

We turned around and we walked out of there and get in the car and Al says, "Holy shit, the old man came within inches of getting hit over nothing."

"What the hell's it all about?"

"They thought he was Italian. They thought he was fucking around with the stove works. I assured them it wasn't him. It was the goddamn UAW that was fucking with the stove works, and it was a couple of Italian guys in the UAW that was doing it. The thing was, they put two and two together and the guys that was doing it was Italian and they think Hoffa's Italian, so it had to be Hoffa that was doing it."

We got back to the office and Al told Jimmy it was all resolved and what it was all about. And Jim thanked us and a little later he met with the five guys and they all shook hands, and from that point on, they had the highest regard, the highest respect in the world for James R. Hoffa. They took a liking to him, they loved him because his word was his bond. Whatever was required of him, he kept his word. Whatever it was that was misunderstood, he straightened it out.

A couple of days later, I went over to see Mr. Sam and he says, "I like him and he's like me, he's a little guy but he's got a lot of guts." Sam was maybe five feet one or a little bigger, the fucking gun that he carried was heavier than he was. "It's too bad he ain't Italian." From that time on, every time I saw Mr. Sam or Mr. Pete or Mr. Joe or any of the others, they'd always say, "Give my best to Jimmy."

And Jimmy told me later that was really the first time he ever sat down with the so-called Italian element and got to know them. From that point on, he used it. Through them, the people in Detroit, he met and made contact with the people in Cleveland and they took a liking to him, and to the people in Chicago and other places.

Of course, what Franco refers to as the "Italian element" and the "outside element" might have been strangers to Hoffa at that time, but they were no strangers to others in the Teamsters or to the union itself. Since the 1920s and the age of Prohibition, they had played an increasingly important role. Bootleggers had bought scores of trucks, established trucking fleets, and they used them to transport their merchandise to eager customers. With the end of the Noble Experiment, they had not abandoned trucking; they had merely moved to hauling other wares, legal and illegal. Since their drivers were often their own men, and since they wanted no trouble with union organizers, they simply obtained Teamster charters and captured control of locals in the nation's vital centers.

Now they were forging new alliances in the Teamsters with a rising star, using Hoffa as he was to use them. They were not all Italians. They included men like Moe Dalitz of Cleveland, who controlled the laundries among other things, who had been a major bootlegger during Prohibition, who would go on to bigger and better things in Las Vegas and then in southern California where, with Teamster pension funds, he built the world-famous resort at La Costa.

And then there were those who came up with the ideas that led to the establishment of the pension and health and welfare funds, which would provide them and Hoffa with billions of dollars to use as they would. At the core were Paul "Red" Dorfman and his stepson, Allen Dorfman, from Chicago.

★ ★ ★

My acquaintance with Paul Dorfman goes back to the late forties or early fifties when I was working with Tom Burke. Paul Dorfman came into Detroit with Allen, who was just a young man in those days, about my age. They came in with a little man with bushy hair, a doctor named Leo Pearlman who was out of some insurance company in Massachusetts. He was working with Red and Allen to set up the health and welfare and pension programs for the Central States Conference.

We used to call Paul "Red" because that was the color of his hair. He was very friendly with Tommy Burke. During the course of their stay that time, I got to meet both Red and Allen, and they took a real liking to me. Red told Jim that maybe within a couple of weeks he would like Jim to send me and Tom in to see him in Chicago because he was going to have some labor problems. Paul was head of a large local union in Chicago that was into wastepaper and a lot of other things. About a month went by and Jimmy called Tommy and I in and he says, "Go into Chicago and see Red and he'll give you your assignments."

So, Tommy and I got into the car and drove into Chicago and went over to Red Dorfman's office, which was off of Clark Street at that time. That was before Allen built this tremendous building they got now that's the headquarters of many of the locals and the Central States Conference and the pension and welfare programs. Anyway, we went in and sat down with Red and he said hello to me and Tom and then he started explaining what his problems were. He had these wastepaper companies on strike because he was trying to organize some of them and trying to negotiate contracts with those he already had. It looked like he was going to have some trouble. He wanted us to do a few things for him and we assured him that we would do whatever he wanted us to do. Knowing Burke's reputation, he knew damn well that we both were capable of doing what we have to do.

He assigned us to three different wastepaper companies that we either had to blow up or set fire to. I think two we set fire to and one we blew up. We did it in two days and we never went back to his office. We went right back to Detroit and we went into Jimmy's office and we told Jim that we finished what we went to Chicago for, but we didn't go back to see Red Dorfman because we felt it would be better if we wouldn't be seen going into his office again. We were seen going in there once and that was enough.

We were compensated for it and we never heard no more about it, only that Red resolved his labor problems and he settled with the other companies that didn't want to be organized and he didn't have any problems negotiating contracts with those that was already organized.

Now, the question I asked Burke was, "I know Red's connected. What the hell did he want us to come into Chicago for when he's got everything in Chicago he needs and he can go to anybody that he wants because he's well connected?"

Tom says, "Sometimes, you're better off not calling on your own people in Chicago and going to the outside instead, because then you're not committed to them and you don't owe them any favors."

"I can understand that."

Paul was very well connected with the outside elements, so for him to use us was a way of not owing them any favors and at the same time getting very close to Hoffa. Now, the outside element respected Paul and he was always like a peacemaker for them, and he had the means to set up meetings between Jimmy and different people in Chicago so that there would be no war between the Teamsters and the outside sources. And he brought Jimmy close to people like Moe Dalitz. So, in that way, he was doing Jimmy a favor, too. It was one for him and one for Jim, all the way.

As time went by, I saw more of Red and Allen. Both of them, especially Allen, was in Detroit a tremendous amount of time when they were setting up the health and welfare and pension programs, and I used to go into Chicago at least once a month to see them. I remember one time when the program was just getting started, they needed somebody to front them in Detroit, and Allen says to Jim, "Why don't you give Joe the position?"

Jim says, "No, leave him alone. I want him exactly where he's at. We'll find somebody else to take care of that." Allen wanted to push me into that area so that I could get away from being a gofer and traveling around the country like I was traveling around in those days.

Whenever I went into Chicago, Red would always have me come in and sit down with him and he'd ask, "How're you doing, Joe? What's going on? Is Hoffa treating you okay? You know, if you've ever got problems, if you need something, don't be ashamed, you call me. If you need money or anything, you just come to me." In those days, Red Dorfman kind of adopted me and took a real liking to me. Jimmy used to throw shots at me and Red would say, "Leave the kid alone. He's a good kid and you're damn lucky to have him around." And then he'd say to me, "Don't pay any attention to him, Joe, if he throws shots at you. He's always testing you out."

"I know. It don't bother me." We got to be real close and I learned a lot from him and he gave me some good advice and told me how to handle myself.

And Allen and I became very, very close, close as close could be. We used to go out together in the early days when we were young, and screw around and go clubbing every once in a while.

Allen controlled all this money that was floating into the pension fund and into the health and welfare and he was getting a service charge for handling it. The pension fund became so wealthy and at first Allen was the director and he was investing into the stock market in real good blue chips. But the pension fund was growing so fast they had to find some other ways to invest their money, and they did that, they were putting that money into mortgages on hotels and different projects in Las Vegas and Florida and wherever. Of course, if you wanted a loan of $10 million, you got a loan of $11 million and $1 million would be kicked back, and Allen got some and Jim got some and later on, when he took over, Fitz got his.

One time, we were standing in a hotel and Allen says to me, "You know, Joe, a lot of the guys look at me and they're fucking jealous that this fucking Jew, he's got all the fucking money."

I know that for a fact. I heard a lot of Italian guys with the locals putting Allen down because, they says, he's Jewish and he tries to act like fucking high and mighty because he's got all that fucking money. I never say nothing. A couple of times, I did stick up for Allen, but it seems like that would just get me in trouble. So, most of the time, I just says, "Yeah, um . . ." and walk away, because if I stood there, I'd get into a fucking beef with these guys.

There was a tremendous amount of jealousy due to the fact that Allen was Jewish and he was very close and loyal to Jimmy and he had access to all those multimillions of dollars.

Allen says to me one time, "Remember just one thing, Joe. When you got two loaves of bread, one under each arm, don't think that you go home with both. Sooner or later, you got to reach out and shake hands with somebody and one loaf of bread is going to fall out." Meaning that he was paying somebody and taking care of somebody on the outside and he was sharing whatever money there was that had to be shared. That was a pretty clear understanding and everybody on the higher echelons of the Teamsters, which was where I was, knew it and accepted it.

There was lots of times Allen would say to me, "Don't think I'm eating by myself, Joe. I know a lot of the guys criticize me and a lot of guys are jealous of me. Hey, I was there, we started it. Jimmy put me there. I work for Jimmy, so do you and my dad!"

I says, "Allen, you don't have to tell me this. I understand the facts of life. If you think I thought you were making all that money and just taking it home and putting it in the bank, forget about it. I know goddamn well you're feeding people. It's a common thing. If I was in your shoes, I'd do the same goddamn thing. They're not going to let you eat by yourself. Nobody does. Everybody eats whenever there's a buck to be made. That's common knowledge among us. I know that and so do you."

5

His mentors were Tommy Burke, his partner and new-found friend, and Jimmy Hoffa, his boss and soon his idol. They were the professors in the advanced seminars in practical organizing and labor relations, as utilized by the Teamsters, other unions, and recalcitrant employers during the postwar years. Franco was a quick and adept pupil for all they had to teach him.

★ ★ ★

Tommy was a very good and thorough teacher. He didn't miss anything. He made damn sure that you had your best shot to survive, such as, he taught you how to determine whether you were being followed and how to shake the guy. He taught you to watch your rear-view mirror as much as you watched the front, and to watch every car behind you, to identify four or five cars behind and when you turned to see how many of those cars would turn with you. The police department and the federal departments had what they called lay-off cars; they would have four or five cars and one would peel off and go four or five blocks, then a second would peel off, and the third would stay with you for maybe a mile and then he would peel off, and all of a sudden you found the original one that had peeled off was back in the third position, and it was like a parade, and when you saw him sitting there again, you definitely knew that you were being followed by three, four, five different cars. If you weren't taught and you didn't have the experience to know what to look for, you'd never pick it up.

Another thing Tommy taught me was that one of our main tools of the trade was a shotgun. Of course, we stayed within the federal regulations about how many inches the barrel had to be. What we'd do was cut the handle off so it would be a small sidearm, and we'd take the barrel and cut it down to exactly the federal length, then saw the shoulder part and make a handgrip out of it, then make a drop hand where the injection was if you were using a pump, which you didn't have to do if you were using a double-barreled shotgun. One of the tricks of the trade was how much damage you wanted to do. Did you want to spread the spread or did you want a single penetration with a big impact? If you wanted a single penetration, you could use a Double-O and then take a razor blade and cut along the brass rim of the casing, but not all the way through; you had to know how and just where to stop, so that when you did eject a shot from the barrel, the only thing that would stay in the gun would be the small brass casing, everything else would come out in one solid piece, not like a normal shot. In a normal shot, what would come out would be the Double-O plus the padding in front, and that would give you a spread maybe twice the size of a basketball. We were in a barn once and Tom showed me what it would do at ten or fifteen yards. He ejected two of those shots and he tore a hole, not tore but collapsed almost a third of the barn wall so that you could have drove a Mack truck through it. I couldn't believe the damage that a shell ejected that way could do, whether it would be to an automobile or a garage or the back of a truck or anything else. We used it quite often on trucks that we were having some problems with, where a truck company was scabbing or something and we would pull up behind and let go maybe five rounds at the back door, and you could bet those doors were coming down or caving in and whatever was inside was destroyed.

There was a time I had a one-man strike on five wineries in the upper part of Michigan. The company was violently opposed to me and I probably came as close to being tarred and feathered as you could come. A Mr. Turner owned this company and he got all the grape growers, the vineyard owners, and the farmers to come down and support him because he was the biggest buyer of their grapes; because of the fact that I had them on strike, he was not able to buy their grapes and they were ready for picking. It was causing a great problem for him and for the growers. Now, I never did have a chance to talk to them before two or three hundred of them came down these dirt highways with baseball bats and I saw sacks of feathers and I knew what was going to happen. Some of the guys were even hollering out, "Let's tar and feather him!"

I just jumped into my car and got the hell out of there, drove into Kalamazoo and met with the officers of Local 7, the president of which was a guy named Brand. I told him what had happened and we had a good laugh about it, but it was damn serious. The more I thought about it, the more I got angry. I called into Hoffa. "Hey, I damn near just got tarred and feathered by about two, three hundred farmers up here. That son of a bitch, old man Turner, turned 'em loose on me."

"Well, do what you want to do and let me know what my cost is."

I put in a call to Tom Burke. "Tommy, what are you doing? I need help. Come on up and bring up some equipment." One thing about us: Whenever I needed help, Tom was always there, and if Tom needed help, I was always there.

Tom says, "What are you looking for?"

"I'm looking to pop wine tankers."

They had these truck tankers that they used to ship bulk wine into Detroit and sell to two or three wine bottling companies there. And I told him I needed steel because of the fact that we had to penetrate the steel tankers, so he'd have to bring up steel bullets. He came up with a two-seventy Magnum; he didn't think a two-thirty-aught-six would be strong enough and he didn't want to take any chances. I looked and I says, "I don't care what you've got, let's go to work."

We waited until early morning and then one truck pulled out and we got behind him and we let him get about fifty miles down the road, and I just took the Magnum and sat in the back seat and opened the windows and leaned out and pumped one on the bottom level of the tank so that it would open like a faucet. And then I pumped five or six more and there was wine coming out of those holes that I put there. By the time he would reach Detroit, which was a good three- or four-hour drive for him, there would be nothing above the line of holes I had made, and they would lose thousands of gallons of wine.

We went back and we waited for the next tanker and we did the same thing and we did it to four tankers in all. When they reported to old man Turner that they had lost those four truckloads of wine, that brought things to a head. Mr. Turner was obliged to sit down and recognize the union. I turned those guys over to Local 7 because it was too far for me to go back and forth between there and Detroit to service them.

From Tom Burke, Franco learned a plethora of techniques to deal with strikes, organizing, recalcitrant employers, and to ply his trade as an organizer for the Teamsters union and, especially, for Hoffa's Local 299. He learned more about dynamite than he had ever known, though he had used it himself in the past; he learned about fuses and caps, enough to be very wary of them as he watched the cavalier way Burke handled the explosives. Tom Burke was a man with connections. He had originated in Chicago where he had perfected his calling, had done services for more than a few patrons in more than a few places before signing on with Jimmy Hoffa and the Teamsters. He was, Franco says, "well connected with the outside element; they liked him and they respected him." Through him, Franco broadened his own ties to that "outside element" as he invariably calls it.

Burke was his partner, the man who worked alongside him, who gave him on-the-job training. Jimmy Hoffa was his boss. He not only had the street smarts to pass on, learned at cost through the labor wars, but he had his own theories about labor and the role of unions. And, in his persona, he revealed to Franco the model of the Teamster leader Franco should follow.

I had some of the best teachers in the business, from the time I was a little kid, but Jimmy was the best there was. He was so streetwise. He knew how to spot a cop and how to figure out an agent, he just had a sense about things like that. He was tough and rough and nothing could put him down. He was very hep; there was nothing that Jimmy didn't know about the streets, that man was raised on the streets, he came up the hard way, he fought viciously to get where he was at, so you knew he was no cream puff. He was a goddamn raging bull.

To this day, I still have the habit he drilled into me about getting into a car. I put my right leg in and my left leg stays out, and then I start my car. If the car is rigged and you start your car that way, you have a fifty-fifty chance of surviving, because if it blows up, it will blow you out of the car. You could lose your leg, or you might lose something on the right side of your body and it might cause a lot of damage, but you have a chance to survive. And when you get out of a car, you always lock it. That makes it a little harder for anyone to try to get in and rig it. All that gives you a little edge, and the way we survived through the forties and fifties and sixties, we needed that little edge.

Jimmy loved to fish and he loved to hunt and many times we would go up to his hunting lodge in the upper peninsula of Michigan, all the business agents, the general organizers, pretty much the whole staff. There would be twenty, thirty guys and we'd hunt and we'd fish and Jim would hold like seminars. Most of his questions would always seem to come to me because I was brand new and young and I guess he was trying to see where my head was coming from. He wouldn't go to one of the older guys because they knew exactly where he was coming from and he knew where they were coming from.

He turned to me one day while we were having breakfast and he was talking about labor and management. "Franco, if laws were passed in this country that would eliminate unions, would the employers revert back to the thirties and the twenties and pay their employees starvation wages and take full advantage over their employees?"

I didn't know whether he wanted me to follow his psychology and follow his theory or if he wanted an honest answer in my own honest opinion.

"Do you want my honest opinion?"

"What I asked you. I want an honest opinion from you."

"Okay. I don't think management would ever revert back to the old days of the sweat shops. I can't believe that. They've been taught. We've organized them and we've established working conditions for their employees and they've seen the advantages of those working conditions and the system for applying grievances and whatever problems may exist. My honest opinion would be, no, management would not revert back to the low wages and the bad working conditions and all the rest."

He looks at me. "Franco, you're full of shit. You give any employer a chance to cut his wages in half tomorrow morning and that son of a bitch will do it. Because he's money hungry and he's got greed and he's got larceny and the only way he can make money is by taking it out of the working man's mouth. Don't ever think different. If labor was ever stopped by legislation, or if labor should start to slide and management had the opportunity to reverse itself, management would completely reverse itself and revert back to the days of the sweat shops and if there weren't laws to stop them, they'd get back to paying seventy-two cents an hour like you used to make and like I used to make, whenever we could make it. Don't bullshit yourself, Franco. You're young. You're coming up, but, by God, you're naive. And I'll get that naiveness out of you if I have to beat it out of you."

Everybody started to laugh because they figured Joe Franco's stuck his foot in it by giving Jim an honest opinion. But that's the way Jim was. He appreciated the fact that I did it. It gave him an opportunity to expound on it because he wasn't only directing all of that to me, he was directing it to every guy in that breakfast room, so they would all know.

In those early years, Franco, still feeling his way into the Hoffa-Teamster mainstream, often served as Hoffa's whipping boy.

There was this day that Jim called in a bunch of key people from the Midwest and the East. Harold Gibbons was there, from out of St. Louis, and Bill Presser from Cleveland and Babe Triscaro from Cleveland and Babe Salupo from Cincinnati, Roy Williams from Kansas City, Sandy O'Brien from out of Chicago, Johnny O'Rourke and Miltie Holt and Johnny Dio from New York, and some of the other top guys. They were all standing around the hall waiting for Jim. And Tommy Burke and I were out in the hall. Tommy knew all these guys from way back and I was very much an unknown at that point. Tom made some quick introductions, like, "Bill Presser, meet the kid . . ." kind of thing. In those days, and for a lot of years . . . , nobody knew my name, they just knew me as the kid. Well, big as I was and the fact of being Tom Burke's partner gained me a little respect from those guys.

Then, all of a sudden, the door opens and Jim comes out of the office and he comes walking up to me and he starts punching me in the chest with his finger, because that's where he reached, not even up to my shoulder. And he starts yelling, "Now get the fuck out of here, you son of a bitch, you cocksucker you, didn't I tell you to go see that fucking guy and tell that motherfucker what I told you to tell him . . ." and he raved on and on. I'm looking at these guys around me and I know he's got all these guys saying, "Oh, shit man, this son of a bitch is a raving maniac, and this is going to be a tough goddamn meeting." He gets through with me and he opens his door and he says, "All right, everybody in my office," like he owned them all. And these guys walked into the office and he slammed the door.

Me, I'm already halfway down the staircase when Tommy Burke says, "Where the fuck are you going?"

I looked at him. "Don't you know?"

"No. What's the matter with you? Don't you know what he did?"

"Don't tell me he did it to me again?" because he did the same thing before, more than once.

"He sure did. Didn't you get it, all that crap about what's-his-name and whatchamacallit? He just pumped himself up on you, you asshole. He did a fucking number on you."

And Tom broke up laughing and so did I, because I was walking out of there, ready to go find what's-his-name and goddamn if I know who the hell he was.

"Jesus Christ, Tom, can you imagine what them guys must have felt like when they walked into his office?"

"What the hell do you think he did it for?"

The thing was, Jimmy used to pump himself up like that, get himself so angry he was ready to walk into a meeting all primed and the guys he was meeting with would be scared as hell. You could always tell when it was an act. When his ears got red, you knew he was a hot ticket. If his ears didn't get red, then he was just blowing off steam and pumping himself on some guy, in those early days, me. He did such a good job on me that day, though, that I was ready to believe him.

The first time he did it was when I hadn't even been there six months and I was ready to cold-cock him and tell him I wasn't going to be abused like that for seventy-five or a hundred bucks a week. I could do that driving a cab or a truck. But that day, Burke just told me to cool it. And then Bobby Holmes sat me down and he says, "I want to give you some advice. Every time Hoffa comes in here and starts screaming and screaming at you, and swearing at you, he may look like he's ready to hit you or something. For God's sake, don't let it get to you. As long as he hollers and screams and swears at you, that means he likes you. He doesn't mean it to you. He probably wanted to get to other guys in the room and he used you to get the message to them."

"You got to be kidding."

"No, this guy's psychology is really rough for the guy that has to be in front of him when he's using it. But leave it alone, Joe. You're young and hot tempered and Jimmy's the same way. The more he does that kind of thing, the more he likes you. Believe me when I tell you that."

From that point on, except for times when he really pulled one on me like the day of the meeting, I would just stand there and fold my hands in front of me and look him straight in the face and wait and then give him one of those looks like, go ahead, boss, do what you've got to do and let me know when you're all done. It got to the point where a couple of times he knew I caught him at it and he damn near, not laughed, because Jimmy never laughed, but grinned or smiled or something. But then I figured that was spoiling things for him and what he was trying to accomplish was going right down the tube. So, I figured, what the hell, go ahead and use me as a whipping post if it's going to help do what you got to do.

Forty years from the day he first met Hoffa, and a decade since he last saw him, Franco was still trying to figure out this complex man who had been his boss and his idol, the man he had followed almost without question.

I loved Jimmy. He had a lot of good points, but he sure as hell had a lot of faults. He had a tremendous Napoleonic complex. He used to read everything there was on Napoleon. He was always trying to get me to read books on Napoleon, like he got me to read *The Rise and Fall of the Roman Empire,* where you could find a lot of what Jimmy believed. I never read any of those books but I looked up the complex and there was Jimmy to a tee. He was out to conquer the world. He liked to have big men around him and show he was the biggest of all. He loved power. He didn't give a shit about money, only that money could buy him power and fear, which was what he wanted. In his life, the union came first, the Teamsters was way out ahead, and Josie and his family came second, a long way back.

He was like what he thought his membership wanted and expected him to be. He was rough, tough, arrogant, and all the words you can use, but that's what the membership wanted, they wanted strong leadership. They were truck drivers and they were tough individuals and they were tough guys to organize, so you had to show them that you were as tough as they were or tougher to begin with. That's what they respected and that's why they always respected Jimmy. And Jimmy created fear, even into his membership. As well as he took care of them, they still respected him and there was that certain amount of fear that they had. I used to hear a lot of our members walk out of a meeting and say, "I'd hate to cross him up because he'd be one son of a bitch that would get even with me. I'd hate to have him get mad at me."

One thing about Jimmy, he could not praise anybody to his face. All the years I worked for him, I never received a direct compliment as to saying, well done, job well done, very satisfactory. No praise, nothing. He'd give you a very heavy grunt, like, big fucking deal, if you couldn't do it, you shouldn't be here and, besides, I could do it better.

In fact, the only time I ever heard praise was while we were in prison at Lewisburg. There was a guy there with us named Bobby Baker, who was Lyndon Johnson's guy who had been sent to prison for tax evasion and fraud or something. Well, one day Bobby comes up to me and he says, "Hoffa really thinks you're the greatest thing that ever walked."

"You got to be kidding. Why?"

"Anytime your name is brought up, the first thing he says is that Franco is the best fucking organizer he ever had, bar none. He says, Franco's the best but then he got you young and he trained you and he taught you everything you know, so you ought to be."

And then I found out he told that not only to Bobby Baker but to the other guys on celebrity row there, like Carmine DeSapio and Carmine Galante and Joe Shipani and some others. He told them I was the best organizer, but it was because he trained me and taught me everything I knew.

So, Hoffa was his boss and he idolized him. Burke was his partner and he worked with him. And there was another man, somewhat older, who he got to know at the very start of his career in the Teamsters, and who was for a decade or more sometimes his partner partly because Franco pitied him. That man was Frank E. Fitzsimmons.

To be honest about it, Fitz was a gofer and a flunky for Jimmy and Bert Brennan and he was basically abused and I always kind of felt bad for Fitz. He got the worst assignments anybody in the building would get. There was a time when Jimmy sent him into Jackson, Michigan. It was a terrible rebel situation up there and they were just waiting for somebody from Jimmy's office to come up so they could beat the shit out of him. It was a terrible mess and Jimmy told Fitz to go up there and straighten them out.

Fitz came to me and he says, "Joe, will you please go with me? I'm scared shitless. I got another of them fucking dirty jobs like he always gives to me." Now, I think Jimmy must have fired Fitz twelve different times and Fitz would always go back and get it resolved somehow and get rehired, and Bert Brennan really didn't like him that much, which may be one of the reasons that Jimmy kept giving him the shit details and kept firing him. Anyway, he tells me, "I got to take this local into receivership and I understand they're just waiting for me to come up there and they're just going to stone me when I get there."

Well, I was the kid with the iron and I says, "Okay, Fitz, whatever you want. I'll go up there with you." I never refused the man.

We got there and I've got two of them with me and I'm loaded for bear. I figure if they start going for him, I'm going to start shooting up in the air and that'll quiet everything down and then

I'll get him the hell out of there before he gets the shit beaten out of him. He gets up and I'm standing up against the wall and nobody's around me, and I says to myself, oh my God, because everybody's shouting and screaming, "Get him out of here. We don't want that goddamn Hoffa in here, we don't want that shit. You're a Hoffa guy, get out of here."

Then Fitz starts giving them that carny talk of his, like he always did. He talked for almost an hour and nobody understood what he was talking about and they kept saying, "Get him out." But he kept up that carny talk and they were shaking their heads because it was totally something nobody understood because it didn't make any sense anyway. But he was doing something else. He taught me something in the years I worked with him. He says, "If you find one guy, Joe, and he's looking at you and he ain't screaming and hollering, at least you got his attention. So you direct all your attention to that one or two or three guys and you look straight at them. If you get them, and you'll find them, then you got the rebel son of a bitch that's screaming and hollering and he won't get up and fight even if he wanted to. That's the one cow that stampedes the thousand cows. That's the way to handle a rebel situation in a membership meeting."

That's the way it went. These guys are screaming and he captured two or three guys in the first couple of rows, and one guy was a big son of a bitch. He got up and he turned around and he says, "All you dumb son of a bitches, sit down and shut up and give the man a chance to say something." Now Fitz has been talking for an hour and he ain't said nothing yet, but he's talking his ass off trying to save his ass and they figure he must be saying something. Well, that started it and Fitz felt a little more secure knowing I was there with the iron, and he started to really work the front rows and pretty soon they're all telling everybody else to shut up and listen. Then he tells them that what Hoffa wants and what he wants is to select a group to act as an interim committee to go down to Detroit and sit with Jimmy, and Jimmy will go along and you guys can have an election and elect all new officers. In the meantime, the local's got to be put into receivership so it can conduct its business. Otherwise, the contracts are all going to go by the wayside and everything they've got will be destroyed. He was starting to make sense to them because he wasn't giving them that carny bullshit no more. And the guys said, "Yeah, that sounds like a good idea, thanks Fitz, thanks for coming up." They all got up and gave him a standing ovation and selected their committee.

Then Fitz comes to me. "Come on, let's get out of here quick, before they change their minds." So, we got in the car and I drove and he says, "Son of a bitch, if you weren't there, I would've shit in my pants. I owe you one."

I says, "Ah, Fitz, don't worry. We both got jobs to do. It just so happens you get the dirty work, that's all. Sometimes, I get some of it and it ain't too pleasant, either. So, don't worry about it."

So, we created a coalition between the two of us and anytime he had a problem, he would come to me and if I had a problem, I would come to him.

Now, in 1949 and 1950 and all the years I was first working with Burke, I didn't know there was money to be made. All I knew was the things that Larry Steinberg from Toledo taught me about labor and that Johnny Paris taught me about how to behave and the things Bobby Holmes told me. And Burke, he used to tell me to walk a straight line. That son of a bitch would take a hot penny from a hot stove. But I didn't know that. All I knew then was what they preached at me, that if you're labor, you're labor 100 percent and you don't do nothing wrong. I was young enough and naive enough to believe all this, and that's the way I conducted myself.

Then there was this strike that Fitz had and we got it resolved, and I helped him in that, and he says to me, "Let's get one thing straight. We're partners. We have an understanding." And he gave me that typical look of his and he starts giving me that carny talk which broke down to we split, fifty-fifty. I really didn't understand what the hell he was talking about at first and then I got it. If I scored $1,000 or $2,000 or $5,000 or whatever, half of it would be his. And then Tommy Burke tells me, "Be careful what you're doing." And sometimes Jimmy would even come to me and say, "Look, you're organizing this company, give them a soft contract and here's an envelope," and it would have like $5,000 or $6,000 in it. Naturally, I would take it and I would count it and I would call Fitz and he would say, "I'll see you at the house." If it was $5,000, I'd give him $2,500, and we did that for many years.

6

For Hoffa and those like Franco who had hitched their wagons to his accelerating Teamster caravan, the 1950s dawned with the promise of a glorious decade. For one, there was the Teamster leadership itself. Dan Tobin had held the reins for nearly half a century, since only a few years after the union's founding; his rule had been loose and was becoming looser as he aged. It was apparent to everyone that he would soon pass from the scene. The obvious heir was a Teamster vice-president, the head of the large and aggressive Western Conference of Teamsters, the Seattle-based Dave Beck. Under him, the membership of the Western Conference had soared in the postwar years, and he had pioneered major wage and benefit improvements for his members. Furthermore, Beck was politically astute and had mended his fences well, gathering enough support from Teamster leaders around the country so that he felt his election as president was assured anytime he decided to make his move.

But there was much about Dave Beck that did not sit well with some of the Teamsters. They began to rally to the side of the young, tough, aggressive leader from Detroit, the head of the Central States Conference, Jimmy Hoffa, whose reputation was spreading rapidly throughout the union. The differences between the two were marked.

Hoffa behaved as many Teamsters thought a Teamster leader

should behave. He was never far from the picket line and was often
out front. He was a tough and agile bargainer who won from employers as much for his members, or even more, than Beck had for
his. He was always available to hear their grievances. If he took
payoffs, well, who didn't, and besides, he seemed to use the money
less for his own personal aggrandizement than as the means to
amass the necessary power for himself and for his union. Everything about Hoffa was Teamster.

Beck, on the other hand, had begun to distance himself from
the rank-and-file, to act more like a suddenly wealthy businessman
than a union leader. The money that came his way from payoffs
and extortion went not to benefit the union, but rather to reward
himself with a manner of living he thought befitted his position. He
spent lavishly on homes and all the accoutrements of the rich. To
many, then, he seemed to have lost touch.

As the Teamster convention approached in 1962, it was apparent to everyone that the time had come for Dan Tobin to step
down. The pressure on Hoffa to challenge Dave Beck mounted.
Hoffa was tempted. He had set a timetable for himself and he
intended to be at the top of the Teamster pyramid before he was
forty, and so have plenty of time to accomplish all he desired from
that pinnacle of power. It had been his hope that Tobin would hang
on while he demonstrated his own abilities, cultivated the local
princes, won the unswerving support of them and the Teamster
rank-and-file, and so emerge as the man who could not be stopped.
And he wanted Tobin to hang on because he was sure that, in the
long run, he would have Tobin's support.

"Dan Tobin loved Jimmy," Franco says, "loved him from the
start, looked at him as a kind of son he would have loved to have
had. And Jimmy loved him. He always referred to him as his
father, as the old man, as pop. As far as Jimmy was concerned, the
old man was deserving of respect and he was going to stay there as
general president as long as he wanted and nobody was going to
move that man out until he was ready to retire."

But by 1962, Tobin was ready and Hoffa was not. He counted
his votes and realized he could not win. It was a bitter realization,
because Beck was still young enough so that he might remain in
office for the next twenty years or more, which would mean that
time would pass by Jimmy Hoffa. Hoffa was determined that

would not happen. Since he could not beat Beck in 1962, he threw the man from the West his support, in exchange for a Teamster vice-presidency. That support, though, was anything but whole-hearted. "That fat cocksucker," he told Franco one day, "he's got no more business being general president of the Teamsters than a fucking pig. He ain't even a fucking Teamster himself no more."

Hoffa watched as Beck wallowed in his new-found position and power, as Beck preened on the national stage as a labor states-man, as Beck spent Teamster millions to move the union's head-quarters from Indianapolis to a lavish palace overlooking the Capi-tol in Washington. And while he watched and waited, he planned Beck's downfall. The opportunity came halfway through the de-cade when Congress began to look into labor racketeering and the payoffs to labor leaders. It was the moment Hoffa had desired; he fed the congressional investigators the information they were look-ing for that would lead them to Dave Beck, that would reveal the scope of Beck's extortions and payoffs, that would eventually send Dave Beck from the presidency of the Teamsters union to a federal prison and leave that chair vacant for Jimmy Hoffa to occupy.

Hoffa's ascendancy could not have come at a more opportune moment for him and his union. America's love affair with the auto-mobile had led the administration of President Dwight David Ei-senhower to make a fateful decision. While much of the rest of the world was throwing funds and effort into modernizing mass transit to move people, the Eisenhower administration went a different route. Mass transit, and especially the railroads, became foster children. The government went on a massive road building cam-paign, to link every section of the nation, from the Atlantic to the Pacific, from the Mexican border to the Canadian border, from large cities to small towns, with a web of fast interstate highways. One thing that meant was that henceforth the nation's goods would move to market by trucks instead of trains. If trucking companies grew rich and powerful, the Teamsters union, which controlled the drivers, grew richer and more powerful. There were thousands of trucking companies but there was only one Teamsters union, and only one James R. Hoffa. Unwittingly, by spending billions of dollars to build the super-highways, the federal government had in essence put in Hoffa's hands the power to strangle the country and its economy. He might promise never to wield that power, but he had it. By the end of the 1950s, Hoffa had become a terrifying specter, not only because of the evil that was reputed to him, but because of the potential power that lay in his hands.

As Hoffa rose through the decade, Franco rose with him, from strong-arm organizer and whipping boy to a power in his own right.

★ ★ ★

One day, Ray Carroll from the Building Service Employees Union, Local 79, called Jimmy and asked him to send me in to help him with an organizational drive he was having to organize the mutuel clerks and the parking attendants at the racetracks around Detroit. So, I went out and helped him and it was a very successful, good, clean organizational drive with no bodily harm to anybody.

When we finished that, Ray decided he wanted to organize the janitors, caretakers, and everybody else in apartment buildings throughout the Detroit area because they were in the jurisdiction of the Building Service Employees. We were very successful in signing people up but Ray wasn't getting any contracts signed with the owners, so he asked me to go ahead and pull a strike to set an example. We were out for about a month and then I turned to Ray and I says, "Hey, you didn't ask for me to be assigned to you to do picket duty because this thing could be resolved in five minutes if you'd let me go."

He says, "What do you want to do?"

"Well, I'd take one stick of dynamite and go down to the basement and blow the furnace out. Without the furnace, those people upstairs ain't gonna get no heat. They're gonna complain to the management and the next thing you know, you've got a contract for the caretakers. We do the same thing in each building until everybody gets the lesson taught to them. Then, when you throw a picket line on them, they know they're gonna get their furnaces blown out if they don't come around."

He says, "No, no, no."

So, I found out at that point that Mr. Ray Carroll didn't have the balls the good Lord gave him and I reported back to Jimmy and I says, "This guy's got a yellow streak. He don't want to resolve his goddamn problems. I think all he wants to do at this stage of the game is probably to shake somebody down and grab money and get the hell out of there. Because we're not doing no good where we're at. You assigned me to that local but not for goddamn picket duty. He can hire anybody for that."

Jim says, "All right, come off it. Anyway, Bill McFetridge wants you in Chicago." Now, Bill McFetridge is the international president of the Building Service Employees. I go to Chicago and Bill McFetridge and Jimmy assigned me to a guy named Miles Berry who was trying to organize the country club golf courses and the dental technicians and the grave diggers. He had an assistant named Sol Gault, and Sol and I became friends and we worked together on the first project, which was to organize the golf courses. What we would do was we would go out and play golf and we would talk to the groundskeepers and the assistants and the guys you normally see around the golf courses cutting the grass and doing the other maintenance. Now the private courses around Chicago were all nonunion and they wanted to be organized and the Building Service Employees had the proper jurisdiction. I says to Sol and to Miles that the quickest ways to organize in a situation like this was to follow Jimmy's theory, which was you pick on the biggest one and if you're successful with them, the others will say, "Jesus, he took on the biggest guy and he beat them and now they're in the union, so you know damn well he's going to get us because we're a hell of a lot smaller."

We went out to one of the biggest and nicest country clubs and we had somebody who took us in as guests. We went toward evening, like around four-thirty or five o'clock, and played eighteen holes and by the time we came in, it was damn near dark. I took some chemicals with me and what I was doing at every hole was, after I got through putting or while the other two guys were putting, I'd take some of those chemicals and I would sprinkle them on the greens. Now the greens are watered in the evening after everybody's off the course, and then they get wet from the dew in the morning, and the water would set off the chemicals I was putting down and they would just burn up the whole green, destroy the life of the ground and the grass and everything. They would have to replace the dirt, the mounds, the grass, the whole thing, and in those days that would cost like $50,000 or $100,000 for each hole.

I did the whole eighteen holes on this big fancy country club on Lake Shore Drive. It hit the papers that this club was having labor problems and all eighteen holes on the golf course had been destroyed by chemicals and the club would be closed down for the rest of the season and maybe for the next season too. Two days later, we had all the people at that club signed up. Then we went around to the other clubs and we found it very easy to sign people up. The country clubs didn't even question us. They didn't bother. We just went around talking to everybody and we organized all the country clubs and we stuck them into the Building Service Employees Union.

I then went on to the next stage of my job in Chicago, which was to organize the dental technicians. We didn't have any trouble organizing the legitimate houses, the dental labs, that made the false teeth and the plates and everything else which they sold to the dentists. But the legitimate houses were having problems with the bastard operations. People who had been trained in the legitimate houses were going out on their own and setting up as independent contractors in basements and they were selling the plates and teeth and all the rest for about half what the legitimate houses were charging, and so they were stealing business from these legitimate operations, and they were really destroying the lab business for these people.

Now, we had about a thousand or two thousand people organized but before we could negotiate a decent contract for them we had to eliminate the bastard operations. Miles Berry called me in and he says, "What can we do?"

"I know what I would do. If you want me to do it, you'll have to call up Hoffa and get an okay from him."

He says, "What's that?"

"Well, we know this one and this one and this one that's operating out of their basements. We know it for a fact because we've been tipped off. What we'll do is we'll take a stick of dynamite or two sticks of dynamite and we'll blow up their basements and put their operations out of business. After we do about five or six of them, the rest will close up because they will know they're next in line to get blown up."

He looks at me. "Do you think that will work?"

"Well, I can't think of a better way and a faster way to do it. So you call up Hoffa and tell him you want to meet with him when he comes into Chicago. He'll be at the Palmer House."

They made an appointment and they met with Jimmy a couple of days later at the Palmer House and they came back and Miles says, "I talked to Hoffa and Hoffa says to go ahead."

"Okay. Did he tell you about money?"

He says, "No, he'll talk to you and he'll take care of that with you."

Later that evening, I went over to the Palmer House and sat down with Jim and we worked out the numbers. I says to him, "I need this and that and I need equipment, so get hold of Tommy Burke and tell Tommy that if he wants to come in and help out, I'd appreciate it and he should bring some dynamite with him."

I didn't mind timing fuses or setting it and lighting it, I didn't care what the hell I did with it. What I didn't like was the capping, the putting the fuse and the cap and the crimping it. That I didn't like because that could explode with no problem, if you just crimped it too much. And Burke used to do it with his goddamn teeth. I didn't like that. I heard too much about caps exploding, so I always left that up to Burke.

We came to an agreement on what we had to do and about a week later, Tommy came in and the first one we let go was a home. We laid it down in the backyard where you went through the door into a basement entrance. We laid it right at the back door and we made sure there was nobody around because we didn't want that problem. We only used a stick or two, just enough to blow in the door and cause a little damage, but not enough to cause any damage upstairs or to do anybody any physical harm, just enough to scare the shit out of them.

We let one go that night and Tommy and I did three the following night and we did two more the night after, and bingo, there were headlines about bombing and dental technicians being organized.

All of a sudden, Miles Berry calls a mass meeting of all the legitimate dental technicians and legitimate houses, and there must have been two thousand people there. He got up and he told them that we were being very successful in organizing the dental technicians. Miles was a very dramatic type of a speaker and very loud, he sounded like an announcer at a prize fight. He went through the whole thing, what he was intending to do and how successful he was being in organizing and the negotiations he was going through to get a good wage for these people. Then he went through introductions of all the people that was there, and he introduces the local business agent and an organizer and some other people. And then he points to me and he says, "Ladies and gentlemen, this young man, he's from the city of Detroit and he's one of our best organizers and by God, he's doing the job that you're reading about. This guy is one hell of a guy and he's doing one hell of a job for you people and he's getting rid of those bastards that we don't want in our industry, and I want you to meet Joe Franco. Joe Franco, stand up and take a bow."

I says to myself, holy shit, this guy just put me right out in the open. If a cop is sitting out there in the room, I'm going to prison. If these people go out and say what Miles Berry said, I'm gonna be up shit's creek without a paddle.

Well, the meeting got over and a whole crew of people came over to me and they says, "Joe, we know you're doing a hell of a job and we know what a risk you're taking." These people couldn't do enough for me. As a matter of fact, they were real nice people and I got all my teeth fixed for free by them.

Well, it didn't take more than a couple of more bombings after that to bring everybody down to the point of making the bastard operations disappear and getting all the legitimate houses organized and a damn good contract negotiated.

I got finished with that and then they sent me in to organize the grave diggers. They were not too difficult to organize because you're talking about guys with shovels. They didn't have steam shovels to come in there and scoop out a hole and get done in ten minutes like they have today. They used to have four or five guys digging a hole six feet deep by eight feet long by four feet wide and doing it by hand, and these guys were getting like fifty cents an hour. So, we came in and it was no big problem getting them organized. But the cemeteries didn't want to be organized because it was going to increase their costs and they were making a big buck up front for their plots and they didn't want to pay it to the people that was taking care of their property. So we pulled a strike, and I ran into a very difficult situation where we ended up throwing a picket line on one of the graveyards. We were out there mass picketing and all of a sudden one of the funerals comes driving up, the hearse and the limousines with the family in it following. All of a sudden out comes a woman who's got to be in her sixties and she wants to bury her son and she's crying and carrying on.

I look over to Sol Gault and I says, "I'm gonna tell you something. This is now three or four times I've gone through this. I can't take this no more. I don't mind doing what I do, but, by God, I'm not going to stop somebody from burying their loved ones. Let's find another way of organizing and getting these cemeteries to recognize us other than picketing, because we're going to get a bad press on it and we're gonna have public sympathy against us and I don't like this, I can't take this. I'm gonna call Jimmy up and ask him to pull me the hell out of there."

It just so happened that a couple of days later, Jimmy was at the Palmer House and he called me and told me he wanted to see me. I went over and Jim had three people up in his room. There was Joseph O'Neil, who was general president of the Distillery Workers Union, and Jimmy Devers, who was executive vice-president of the union, and Fitz. Fitz was still a low-life in those days even though he was a business agent. He was really only a gofer for Jimmy. But he was friends with Joe O'Neil and Jimmy Devers and he brought them together with Jimmy, and immediately they became very dependent on Jimmy as a means of supporting them and guiding them.

They were having a problem in Detroit at that time. They gave a charter of a local to some guy that was using it to shake down the distillers, for like $15,000, $20,000, $30,000 at a pop. This guy wasn't looking to organize the distillers. All he was doing was using the charter Joseph O'Neil gave him as a shakedown operation. Now Jim says to me, "Franco, how would you like to come back home?"

I says, "Thank God. I was just about to tell you that I want out of here. I'm running into a lot of problems organizing the grave diggers. Not problems that I can't do it, but I can't put up with the families. Jim, just get me the hell out of here."

He says, "Well, you want to represent this local union in Detroit?"

"Yeah, just get me back home."

"This way, Franco, you'll get back to Detroit and take care of this local for me and run this local for me and whatever has to be done, we'll do it."

"Great."

"But in the meantime, I want you to get back to Detroit, find the guy that's got the charter, and get the charter and come back here by ten o'clock tomorrow morning."

Well, it's like ten in the morning then, so I didn't waste any time. Because one thing you couldn't say to him was, "How the hell am I going to find this guy when he doesn't have a phone number and they don't have an address, they don't have nothing but the guy's name." And he's giving me like twenty-four hours to go find this needle in a haystack and then get back to Chicago and bring him the charter. If you said anything to Jim, if you questioned him, he'd just say, "Well, you're not the guy I need for this job. I'll see you back in Detroit and we'll work something out." If he gave you an assignment, you said, yes, sir, and you went out and did it. You didn't come back a failure, because if you're a failure, don't bother to come back because he's not going to put up with it.

Fitz grabbed me on the way out and he says, "Do you think you can pull this off?"

"Well, I'm gonna give it one hell of a try."

"Joe, you know with the old man, if you don't do it, if you come back tomorrow morning and say you can't do it, well, you know him. It was my recommendation to give you a shot at this deal, so for God's sake, Joe . . ."

"Thanks a lot, Fitz. But if I can't do it, you know goddamn well, there ain't nobody else going to do it."

"Well, that's true. Go do the best you can, and if you need any help, call me."

"I'll be back tomorrow morning, one way or the other."

So, I got into Detroit like two or three in the afternoon, going like eighty-five, ninety-five miles an hour down the old US-12, the old truck route because they didn't have any turnpikes or freeways in those days. Immediately, I went downtown and start spreading the word, does anybody know this Charlie, whatever his last name was, and I went and I went and nobody has ever heard of this guy.

I called a couple of liquor companies and asked them if they had any knowledge and nobody had any knowledge of him.

About one o'clock in the morning, I walked into this cocktail lounge in a hotel downtown and I was pretty disgusted. In those days, I used to have a drink every once in a while, which I don't do anymore; I haven't had a drink, except maybe a little wine, in more years than I can count. But in those days, I used to have a drink. I walk into the bar and there's a group of people down at the end, and there's a guy I've known since we were kids. His name was Chinky Sherman and he was one of the biggest bookmakers in Detroit. Chinky sees me and he says, "Hey, Joey, come on over and have a drink and congratulate me. I just got married."

"Great, Chink. God bless you. But I didn't come here to go to your wedding party. I got to find somebody and I've been looking all over for him."

"Who the hell are you looking for?"

I tell him and he says, "What do you want with that stupid son of a bitch?"

"Don't tell me you know him?"

"Sure I know him."

"Do me a favor, Chinky. Get on the phone and tell the son of a bitch to get down here right away because I got to get back to Chicago by ten o'clock in the morning."

He gets on the phone and then he tells me that the guy will be right down. I says, "What kind of a guy is he?"

"Well, he's got two guys working for him, Joe, and the two guys are a couple of heavy kids."

"What do you mean? With iron?"

"Yeah, and they also always carry knives."

"No problem. Because I got a piece on me so I ain't worried about them."

About a half hour went by and here comes this guy and he's got two young Italian kids with him. Chinky brings him over to the table and he sits down across from me. I says to Chinky, "Go tell the other two guys to go sit someplace else."

This guy Charlie says, "No. I want them to sit here."

I lean forward across the table toward him and I took a pistol out of my belt and held it under the table in my right hand where he couldn't see it. "I'm here alone but I got a midget under the table that's holding a .38 on your ass. If that midget lets go, you're gonna have a gut full of lead."

Chinky says, "Charlie, this kid ain't bullshitting you. If he tells you he's got a piece of iron aiming at you, he's got a piece aiming at you. Now, you want me to tell your guys to stay out of it or do you want this kid to open up?"

He says, "Oh my God, go tell the guys to sit in the corner." Chinky goes over and the guys sit down.

I says to this Charlie, "Listen, I work for Jimmy Hoffa and I'm Hoffa's man. I just left him at the Palmer House. You got a charter for Local 42 that belongs to the distillery workers for Joe O'Neil. I have to have it right now because I've got to be back in Chicago with it no later than ten o'clock in the morning. I hope we don't have no problems. I hope you'll be more than a nice guy and just turn it over to me."

He says, "I ain't gonna turn it over to you. Look, kid, I don't know who the hell you are."

"You want me to talk to the midget under the table?" Then I called Chinky over. "Chinky, I want you to bear witness to this. Jimmy sent me down here to pick up a charter this guy's holding. If I have to leave here without it, and Jimmy tells me to come back and hit him, I'm gonna come back and hit him."

Right away, this guy knows I ain't bullshitting. He says, "I'll give you the charter for ten thousand."

"Fuck you. Your life ain't worth ten thousand. You give me the charter and I'll tell you what I'm gonna do. I'm gonna hold your two guys here while you go and get the fucking charter. If you don't get back in one hour, I'm gonna hit those two guys. Because I ain't going back to Chicago and face Jimmy Hoffa with a no-no. I ain't gonna do it and you ain't gonna do it to me. Don't fuck with me because then you'll fuck me up with Hoffa, and if you fuck me up with Hoffa, I'm gonna fuck you up but good."

He says, "Well, okay. But can't I make no money out of this?"

"Just give me the fucking charter and I'll take it back to Hoffa and I'll tell Jimmy you want a few dollars. If Jimmy's willing to give it to you, hey, God bless you. But I don't have authority to say to you that I can give you a thousand or five thousand or anything. I was told to come here, find you, grab the charter, and bring it back to Chicago."

"All right. Only don't do nothing to the two kids."

I says, "They don't make a problem, they got nothing to worry about."

Chinky went over and grabbed the two kids and brought them over to the table and I told them in Italian, "You guys stay right here. Your boss has an errand to do."

They caught me real quick. They didn't move. Charlie left and he couldn't have lived too far away because he was back in about twenty minutes with the charter all rolled up. I took it and I says, "I'll do the best I can." I looked at Chinky and I kissed him and I says, "Chink, I'm sorry to have interrupted your wedding party."

Then I headed back to Chicago, driving through the night. I hit the shoreline about nine o'clock and I was really moving, and then I got stopped by a cop. He gets out of his car and he comes walking over and he's a big burly Irishman with the thickest brogue you ever heard. He says, "Jesus, you must be going to a goddamn fire."

"Believe me, officer, I'm trying to get to the Palmer House and I've got less than an hour and I've a meeting there with Mr. James R. Hoffa of the Teamsters and if I don't get there my job is on the line."

"Why didn't you tell me you were with the Teamsters? I know Jimmy well. A great man. But you're going to have to take care of me and my partner." I slipped him a twenty and he says, "Good boy. Now you follow us." He got in the car and turned on the siren and I followed him right up to the Palmer House, and I was fifteen minutes early. By the time I got up to the room, it was ten o'clock sharp. I knocked and Fitz opened up the door. He looks at me and he says, "You have any luck?"

"Yeah. I got it rolled up."

"Jesus Christ, how the fuck did you do that?"

"Shut up, Fitz, I'll tell you the story later."

I walked into the room and they're all sitting around having coffee and there's Joe O'Neil and Jimmy Devers and Hoffa's having tea like always. I says to him, "Here you are, boss. You wanted the charter, you got the charter."

Joe O'Neil was very happy. "Jim, you want to give the charter to this kid?" Then he looks at me. "Son, it's your charter. You can have it if you want it."

Jimmy says, "Franco, you take it. I will stand behind you. You take that charter, organize that industry. Go home and get set up. Do what you have to do and you bring it into my building."

After O'Neil and Devers left, I says to Jim, "Jim, the guy wanted ten grand, but I have no authority to okay it. But I'm sure the guy could use a couple of bucks."

"Okay, when we get back home, I'll give you three grand and you go take it over and you give it to him. He doesn't fucking deserve it because he's been using it as a fucking shakedown, but at least it'll make you look good."

I got home and the only place in the building that was left was a janitor's broom closet. I'm thinking, how am I going to organize people and have them come down to a meeting in a broom closet? I couldn't even put a desk in there. I didn't know what the hell to do. Then I start looking into the thing. Local 42 when I took it over had two plants organized, Arrow and Mohawk distilleries, and there was about a hundred and fifty people and no money except for a government bond for eight hundred dollars. I had a meeting of the executive board and I told them who I was and that I was taking the local into receivership until such time as I built it up, and then we'd have an election for officers. In the meantime, I told them that I was going to cash that eight hundred dollar bond and put the money in the treasury and start operating.

Now I got to have a place to operate from, and Jimmy said to put it into his building on Trumbull Avenue but there's no place there. So I called Fitz and Fitz at that time represented the film industry in Detroit and there was this Film Exchange Building. I asked Fitz if he had any connections. He said to go pick out a suite at the Film Exchange Building and tell the guy in charge that he sent me. I went over there and they showed me an office with red carpeting and an outer office for a secretary. It was perfect. Then I called Ray Carroll up and I asked him what he wanted for the desk and the furniture he had in his office, because I knew he was refurnishing his office. He tells me two hundred for the works. I says, "You got a deal. Ship it." Now, I got to pay for it and I got to pay the rent and pay expenses and I got to hire a girl and I got to put money down for first and last months' rent, and the goddamn local's got eight hundred dollars and that's it. I called President O'Neil to find out exactly what I could expect as far as support was concerned. He says they can give me moral support and legal support, but the only financial support that he can give me is he can put me on the payroll for $42.50 a week. I says, thank you very much, and I hang up.

So, now I got to figure what I'm going to do for money. I had all this stuff and I hired a secretary, Sherry Bushkin, who was Jimmy's old secretary who had left to have a baby and was ready to come back to work and she was willing for what little I offered. Fine. But where was I going to get even that little? I start thinking and I remember the old saying that when you need money, go to an old friend and he'll never say no to you. Well, there was this old friend of mine who was a bookmaker operating out of a gas station and I figured he'd be good for $3,000 tops. So I went over to the gas station, walked in, pulled a gun out and put it to his head and pointed for him to open the drawer because I knew that's where he kept the cash box. He opened the drawer and opened the cash box and I saw hundred-dollar bills stacked up full. I knew there was more than $3,000 there; there had to be anywhere from $10,000 to $20,000. It was just loaded with hundred-dollar bills. I damned near exposed myself by starting to laugh. I just picked the cash box up and ran out and down the street and got in the car and took off. He couldn't call the cops because he was running a bookmaking deal. I figured that someday somewhere down the line I'd go back and pay this man off; I knew I couldn't just go in there and borrow it from him, so I had to do what I had to do. When I got back to the house, I opened up the cash box and I counted out $17,500. I never got a chance to pay that man back because a year later he died of a heart attack.

That's how I started with Local 42. I went ahead and put $2,000 into a checking account, paid Ray Carroll for his furniture, got furniture for my secretary, told Sherry she would be making $250 a week, paid the first and last months' rent, put a telephone in, and then I called Mr. O'Neil up because I've got to cover myself because where the hell would I get all this money from? I asked him to give me a $2,500 loan and that I would pay it back to him in sixty days or I would give the local back to him, which was no problem because I had plenty of cash from the $17,500.

Now I started building up the local and organizing the whole state of Michigan. Using Jimmy's theory of going after the biggest guy first, we went after Seagrams, which was a combine of about five companies with a hundred and eighty not salespeople but what they call goodwill ambassadors who didn't sell anything but just went out and promoted the situation for Seagrams. Between Seagrams and myself, and not the Teamsters, but Jimmy Hoffa, who I was representing, the relationship came to a fight. Now, in those days the Truman administration had come out with a law forbidding the railroad brotherhoods from supporting any strikes or strike-bound goods, so even though I had Seagrams on strike, they were switching box cars full of cases of liquor. I did the only thing I could do. I went over to the railroad and I put signs up three or four hundred yards down the track before they came to the switching area, and those signs said there were sticks of dynamite every twenty-five yards ahead, but don't bother looking for them. If the cars were switched and came in, the dynamite sticks would go off as the cars went over them because there were timing devices attached. The thing was, I didn't have nothing down there, I just wrote out the signs.

Well, the railroad engineers saw those signs and the next thing you know they switched all the cars with liquor off on a side track before they got to the state liquor warehouses. That just shut them right down at a time when the warehouses were expecting a tremendous load of Seagrams products.

Two days later, I was in Jimmy's office and Jimmy got a call from an attorney in New York named Fred Lynn who represented Sam Bronfman, who was chairman of the board of Seagrams, and he set up a meeting with Jim at the Book-Cadillac Hotel. The next day, Jim grabs me and we went down there and we met with Lynn and a guy named Dave Blank who was a vice-president of Seagrams. Now the reason they called Jim and not me was because they knew where the power was. We went over to the hotel and Jim says to me, "Don't say a word, let me do all the talking." He walks in and he introduces himself and Fred Lynn and Dave Blank introduce themselves because they had never met before and Jim just sat down and he says, the way he used to talk in those days before he got the polish on him, "I don't know what the fuck you guys want, but if you don't want to sign the fucking contract, I'm busy, so let's get the fuck out of here." That was it.

Fred Lynn says, "Jesus, can't we sit here and have a drink?"

Jim says, "I don't drink and neither does the kid. Where do we go from here? You guys want to drink, you can drink after I leave. I'm busy. I got no time to bullshit with you. You guys want to recognize us, fine. If you don't recognize us, we'll keep your merchandise out of the state of Michigan until hell freezes over."

Well, they knew that Jim wasn't playing around. They didn't want to piss Jim off because Jim can control the distillery workers through Joe O'Neil and really shut them down because of the trucking system at other distilleries all over the country. So it came down that afternoon that they got up and they agreed to a gentlemen's agreement that they would recognize Local 42, which was part of the AFL, but was really under the direction of Jimmy Hoffa and the Teamsters Joint Council 43 with Joe Franco servicing them. We all shook hands and when we left, Jim told me, "You let me know if these guys don't come in and start signing up and getting everything straightened out."

I says, "Don't worry, I'll handle it from here. I can take care of it."

At that point, we organized Seagrams, all of it, which was the biggest company, and after that we straightened Schenley's out, and then we straightened Glenmore Distillery, American Distillery, all of them. I organized all the distilling companies in Michigan, and then I went after the distributorships, such as beer distributors, wine distributors, pop companies, whatever had white-collar workers, sales, advance sales, truck drivers, whatever. If they belonged to the Teamsters jurisdiction, I would turn them over, and if they didn't, I put them into Local 42.

After that, whenever there was a problem with distillers anywhere, Jim would send me in to resolve it. There was a distillers strike about that time in Kansas City and Jim called me in. "I want you to go on to Kansas City and meet with Roy Williams and the local there and get that thing fixed up."

I grabbed the first plane and as I was getting off—in those days, you didn't pull into a ramp, you walked off the plane on steps and then walked into the terminal—there were four guys waiting for me. I look at them and I say to myself, these guys are either Teamsters or I'm in a shithouse full of trouble.

As I was walking by, two of them came up on either side of me and they stopped me and one guy says, "Are you Joe Franco?"

"Yeah. What's the matter?"

"Look, kid, do yourself a favor. We understand you're Italian and you're our people. Get back on that fucking airplane. There ain't nothing you can do to help this strike out."

"Are you guys with the Teamsters?"

"Don't worry about who we are. We don't want you in this town. We'll take care of our own problems."

"You know I'm Jimmy's guy."

"We know it. That's why we're showing you the courtesy of stopping you right here, because we could easily let you come in and somewhere along the line, the next day or two, if you stuck your nose in, we'd probably beat your fucking brains out. We don't want to do that because we feel you're Italian and you're Sicilian and we'll show you respect, and we know you're Jimmy's guy and we want to show Jimmy respect because Jimmy's well liked here. So, you go back to Detroit."

"Thank you very much." I shook hands and I didn't even ask them their names. "It's a great pleasure being in Kansas City and one of these days I'd like to come in here and just see what the town looks like."

"Under any other circumstances, kid, you come on in here and you're our guest. But at this point, you go on back and tell Jim that we'll handle everything here."

I got back on the plane and went home and went back to Hoffa's office and I says, "Shit, I had a vigilante committee waiting for me. You know what I'm talking about? Four big fucking heavies were waiting for me and they were all Italian, brother, and in all due respect to you and in all due respect to me due to the fact that I'm Italian, they stopped me before I got into the situation and the message I was given was to tell you to stay out of it and they would handle it. They said you would know exactly what they meant."

He says, "Okay, no problem. I know what's coming down. Don't worry about it. It's been taken care of."

7

In the beginning Joe Franco was working with Local 42.
Franco was organizer, business manager, and overall coordinator.
He and his secretary, Sherry Bushkin, were, in fact, the entire
operation.

★ ★ ★

I was working my ass off and making a lot of progress. And I
wasn't making hardly enough to live. I was getting that $42.50 a
week from Joe O'Neil's payroll and Jimmy was still giving me
another $50 or $100 a week, whatever he could spare, and I never
pressed him. Thank God for the $17,500, or what remained of it,
because with that I was able to live and even get married. But it
wasn't going to last forever. But the local was growing. I had
organized all the distillers and I had over twelve hundred members
within the first six months and there was $28,000 in the local's
treasury, which I wasn't going to touch.

The first thing I decided was that I didn't need the damn office
that Fitz got for me anymore, which was costing me an arm and a
leg even though I was paying a bargain rate. I didn't think it was
necessary to put on the flash anymore, so I went back to Jim and I
says, "Jim, does your offer still stand? Because I would like to have
the janitor's broom closet."

Jim says, "Franco, I wish there was something bigger, but that's all I can do."

"Right now, I don't need anything bigger. I needed the flash for the sales people, but now that we got all these white-collar people in Local 42, I don't need it."

So, Jim allowed me to come back into the Teamster building and take over the janitor's closet, and we cleaned it out and we found there was enough room to put one little small desk in the front and another one back in the corner, about two feet away, which was my desk. But I didn't need any more than that because, eight, nine hours a day I was out on the street organizing. So all I needed was somebody to sit at that desk and take the phone calls and keep the books, and that was Local 42 at that point.

But things were very tight and I let Jim know that I would appreciate anything he could throw my way that might let me turn a little more. So, one day he calls me and he says, "Franco, come upstairs, I want to see you."

I got up to the office and there was this little short, stocky Jewish fellow smoking a cigar and talking out of the side of his mouth. Jimmy says, "I want you to meet Harry Karsh. Harry's organizing circus people, truck shows, train shows, carnivals. I want you to work with him. I want you to organize for him. He's going to bring the charter in and you supervise that charter for Harry and you do it through me. You need support, I'm always here for you. You need money, just tell me what you need. Harry will come and assist you when he can."

"Fine. I know a little bit about carnies."

"Okay. Go to work."

I found out where the carnivals were going to be through the year until they went back to Tampa for their winter quarters. Then I would spend five days a week, Monday through Friday, taking care of Local 42, and then Friday, Saturday, and Sunday I'd go after the carnivals. I would leave home about three in the morning, go to Jackson, catch a carnival there and sign them up, then go to Kalamazoo and catch a carnival there and sign them up, and so on. Through the summer, I was getting to the point where we were signing up a pretty fair number of employees and beginning to negotiate contracts. I would sign the people up and then Harry Karsh would come in and negotiate the contract.

Now it came time for the Michigan State Fair, and the state ran it and the concessionaires would put in bids to the state for the right to run the rides and the rest of the attractions. I walked in there and the contracts with the state had been assigned to the Wade Show, which was one of the largest carnivals in the state. They weren't organized, so I shut the whole state fair down until such time as Old Man Wade signed a contract with me. Old Man Wade was like seven feet tall; he was part of the sideshow himself at one time until he worked himself into a position where he bought his own carnival. He was a giant of a man with a big Texas hat always on his head. Sinelli Burns, who was the assistant to James Hare, who was head of the fairgrounds in those days—later on, he became secretary of state of Michigan—called me in and he called Wade into his office and he says, "Look, we can't afford to have labor problems here. You either recognize this local union or we're going to have to cancel your agreement and bring another carnival in."

Old Man Wade agreed to recognize me, but we struck a deal where I would allow him to finish out at the Michigan State Fair and then we would come to an agreement at his next location, which was at Marquette in the upper peninsula. We shook hands on it, me and Wade and Sinelli, and then I called Harry Karsh, who was in St. Louis, and told him what I had done so if he wanted to come in and sit down and negotiate a contract in Marquette, then come on.

He flew in and I picked him up and went to Marquette and I walked onto the carny lot and all of a sudden I start hearing, "Hey, Rube!" I'd been around carnies enough to know what that meant, Jesus, I knew what a John meant and a mark and all the games, the float games, the doll games, all the fix jobs, I knew the bag man and the kitchen men and all the terminology of the carnies. So, when I heard, "Hey, Rube!" I knew we were in trouble. There came one concessionaire that didn't want to belong to the union and he had a spike in his hands and his wife had a bottle of Coke in one hand and a bottle of Pepsi in the other and she was smashed out of her mind and so was he. And he's hollering, "Hey, Rube! Let's beat the shit out of him."

Picture this. Harry's about four feet ten and he weighs about two hundred and he's got this cigar that was about a foot and a half long and he's chewing on it, and he's telling all these people that are coming up that he wasn't going to stand for this shit. I kept looking at those people closing in and making a circle around us and this is one time I don't even have a knife in my pocket, even to pick my nails with. I came up there clean, not expecting no trouble. I went right up alongside Old Man Wade and I says, "You don't tell your people to back off, I'll . . ." And Harry's still screaming and hollering that we're not going to let you get away with this. I says, "Shut your goddamn mouth," and I gave him a kick in the ass. Then I look back at Old Man Wade and I says, "You don't call your people off, I'll cut you from one end of your stomach to the other. I'll open up your guts to your knees. Believe me, old man, I'll rip you open."

He says, "Hold it. I promised Joe Franco that we would recognize him when we got to Marquette and by God, my name is my bond."

They start screaming back, "We don't want to belong to the union."

He says, "If you don't want to belong to the union, get the hell off this lot."

I says, "Keep talking, old man." And I grabbed Harry by the collar and I says, "Keep your goddamn mouth shut until we get in the car." I dragged his ass out of there and we were lucky to get out. It looked like we were going to end up in the hospital. We got in the car and I started it up and took off and went ten yards and found I had two flat tires. They had taken two spikes and rammed them through my back tires. And while I was checking the tires out, cursing like a son of a bitch, I looked in my gas tank. In those days, you didn't have them in the back, you used to have them on the side. I had a big black Cadillac then. I saw that somebody had been tampering with it. I opened it up and they had loaded it with that sugar they make cotton candy out of right up to the brim. I says, goddamnit, there goes the motor. Somehow, I got the damn thing started and ran it on the wheel rims with the flat tires and made it the six, seven miles into the city. We got to the hotel and I got on the phone and called the Teamster local and got the big Swede that was running it and I says, "This is Joe Franco from Joint Council 43 in Detroit. I'm up here and I got a problem."

"Joe. Jesus Christ, how are you?"

"I'm up here about that carnival. They screwed up my car, they got my gas tank all screwed up, and now I want to go back and I want fucking revenge."

"How many pieces do you want?"

"Bring me one, and bring about a half a dozen guys with you, and be loaded for bear and I'll meet you outside the hotel. Pick me up."

Sure as hell, here comes three cars, and in one car which I got into there was a woman that had to be six two and she must have weighed two hundred pounds, and she had the two biggest western .45's you ever saw in your life strapped in her belt. Well, Marquette's an old mining town and these people are real tough, real miners. They don't take no shit from nobody because they had one hell of a time when they were organizing. I look at this woman and I look at the Swede and I says, "What are you bringing the girl for?"

"Don't worry about her. She'll outshoot you, she'll outpunch you, she'll outbeat the shit out of you. Don't worry about her."

She looked at me. "Sonny, I'll watch over you."

I says, "Sweetheart, you got the job." And then she hands me a .38 snubnose.

With that, we proceeded to go to the carnival lot. All the guys got out and I says, "Watch me. I'm gonna head for the cash wagon and when Harry and I go in, if you see any trouble, you guys cut loose. Don't shoot anybody. Shoot up in the air." So, they stationed themselves all around the park. The concessionaires see me and Harry walking through and they knew they were in a shithouse full of trouble.

I head right for the cash wagon where they keep all the money. Old Man Wade comes walking over. I says, "You get inside." He walked in. "Mr. Wade, I'll tell you what you're going to do. I want every concessionaire to come in here one at a time. Harry, you sit over there on the couch and you give them an application to fill out and sign, and you make triplicate copies authorizing the deduction of dues. And I want twenty-five dollars a month for the first month's dues."

"It's going to blow up, Joe."

"Don't worry about the goddamn thing. Mr. Wade, you just get the hell out of here and tell your concessionaires to come in here one at a time. I'll handle it from here."

Harry Karsh was shitting in his pants. He was so nervous, he didn't know whether to shit, piss, or holler, because he's never seen this kind of action.

In walks the first concessionaire. He sits on my left and Harry's on my right. I took the .38 snubnose and stuck it under some newspapers and just kept my hand there. I says, "Harry, give him whatever papers he's got to sign. Now, you, sign 'em." He didn't say a goddamn word. I says, "Harry, how much money does he owe?"

"Twenty-five dollars initiation fee and ten dollars for the first month's dues."

"Give the man thirty-five dollars cash, and Harry, give him a receipt."

That's the way it went, until it comes to the guy that was making all the trouble the first time out. I calls out to Mr. Wade, "I want him and his wife in here at the same time. I don't want 'em separated." They walk in there and I says, "Sit down, you, you mother-scratchin' son of a bitch that you are. And you, you're a whore, you're whatever I want to call you. Your old man ain't got the goddamn balls to say a goddamn word to me right now and I wish to Christ he would because . . ." and with that, I pulled out the .38 and I put it right in his mouth. "I'll blow his goddamn head off. Now, you bitch, scream and holler about how tough you are. And you, you asshole, see what you can do with a goddamn pistol stuck in your mouth." Harry Karsh damn near choked. He quit smoking a cigar, put the cigar down because he was choking on it. This guy pulled the pistol out of his mouth. I says, "Now, you got something to say?"

He says, "Mr. Franco, I saw you at the carnival in Michigan at the fairgrounds and I thought you were a nice guy. It's just that I was drinking too much."

"I don't want to hear your shit. Harry, give him the goddamn paperwork to sign." Harry gave him the papers. "Give his wife some, too. You both are going to join."

"Oh, yeah, we'll both join. Don't worry."

"Hey, I don't want to hear nothing. Sign those goddamn papers."

Then I turn to Harry and I says, "Harry, how much money does he owe? A hundred dollars initiation fee, isn't it, Harry? For both of 'em, that's two hundred. How much are the dues, Harry? Fifty dollars for the first month, each? You owe him three hundred dollars, mister. Give it to him in cash. Harry, give him a receipt."

The guy says, "Well, the other people only had to pay . . ."

"Don't tell me about the other people. You, you asshole, you wanted to hit me with a spike. You fucked up my car. Now, I'm gonna charge you for my car. I'm coming back tomorrow when I find out that they got to take my gas tank off and they got to give me two new tires. I'm gonna collect it off your ass. Now get the hell out of here."

By two o'clock in the morning we had cleaned up the whole goddamn carnival. Next day, I took my car into the service and the guy has to take off the wheels and put two new tires on and he has to clean out all the lines and grease the carburetor out, and it took the whole day. The next day, Harry says, "Let's go home."

I says, "Screw you, Harry. You know, you're made of shit, you got a stick up your ass. I don't. That son of a bitch is going to pay for it all."

He says, "I'm gonna call Hoffa."

"I don't give a damn who you call. You call Hoffa, I'll tell him what a chickenshit son of a bitch you are."

I went back out to the carnival and I grabbed that son of a bitch by the throat and made him pay three times what I spent as far as getting the car fixed. He paid it and he paid it very nicely. He was very happy to pay it. The funny thing was that after that, that man would have done anything in the world for me. He was so down the line that whenever I walked onto the carny lot and he saw me, he'd holler out, "Here comes the kid. All you assholes straighten out." He was 100 percent with me. Nobody would ever raise a finger to me as long as he was on the lot.

I went back to Detroit and reported to Jimmy what a chickenshit guy this Harry Karsh was. Jimmy says, "Don't worry about it. You just keep doing what you have to do." Now what we did was we put all the carnival people into the Jewelry Workers International Union and they appointed me an international vice-president because I had done such a great job organizing the carnies. Of course, I was Hoffa's man and whatever I was doing I was doing for Jimmy, and he was my boss and I reported to him and I took my orders only from him, which upset some guys, but that was the way it was.

After a while, I started going after the big circuses like Ringling Brothers, the tent shows and the train shows and the truck shows, and I was having very good success. I organized about twenty-eight hundred people into the union. But we didn't put them into the Jewelry Workers; we put them into Local 688 of the Teamsters out of St. Louis, which belonged to Harold Gibbons, and they were handled by an old friend of mine named Phil Rindone, who originally came out of AGVA and he did such a hell of a job there that the Teamsters picked him up and brought him to St. Louis and put him to work on the circuses. So, Harry Karsh had nothing to do with them.

A couple of years later, after the AFL and the CIO merged in 1955, a lot of bullshit came out about the Jewelry Workers having underworld connections and other crap and George Meany took the charter away. That meant that I didn't have a charter for the carnival workers no more. I took everything, the money out of the bank, which was about $28,000, and the books and the charter and I had a certified check made out and I sent the whole thing to Karsh. Then I went upstairs and I told Jimmy, "Hey, I sent everything to Karsh. I don't want it in the building because it may come back and hit us right in the ass and we may get bad publicity because it's here in the building. I figured, let me get rid of it. Nobody knows where the hell I'm from, so let it fly."

Jimmy says, "What did you do with the money?"

"I sent it to Karsh, with the books."

"Why you dumb son of a bitch. That means the charter's gone and it's out of business. All you did was give Harry Karsh $28,000. Why didn't you keep it for yourself?"

"How the hell am I supposed to know that? All I was told was to go out and organize and that's what I did, and I figured it belonged to him, for chrissake."

That brought the organizing of the carnival workers to a halt. Rindone kept on with the truck shows and the train shows and the tent shows and he did a hell of a job. But I didn't have no more to do with that.

Through the early 1950s, Franco was still running the Distillery Workers for Hoffa and Joe O'Neil, in addition to a thousand other assignments that Hoffa kept throwing his way. The Distillery Workers, though, continued to occupy much of his time and energy.

By far the most respected Teamster leader, in and out of the union, was Harold Gibbons. A political liberal and an intellectual who battled long and hard for the rights of minorities long before such battles became popular, he was president of Local 688 in St. Louis and of Joint Council 13 by the early 1950s; this gave him effective control of the organization in the area. He was a pioneer of many of the programs and reforms that were later adopted not only by the Teamsters but throughout the entire breadth of the union movement, including health and welfare programs for his members, retirement colonies for older Teamsters, social action throughout the social structure, and much more. He was an able bargainer and negotiator who was firmly committed to the good of his followers. In order to survive, he sometimes forged alliances with unsavory elements, but so did many labor leaders. He turned early for assistance to Detroit and to that rising Teamster star, Jimmy Hoffa. A friendship and a respect developed. Hoffa came to understand that he could look to Gibbons to support his ambitions, and Gibbons could look to Hoffa for whatever help he needed. Gibbons, the tough bargainer, often dug himself into pits where that help was essential.

★ ★ ★

One day, Jim called me in. "Drop whatever else you're doing. I want you to handle a situation in St. Louis. You met Harold Gibbons?"

"I met him casually a couple of times when he was up here. Tommy Burke introduced me."

"Well, he's going to be in Chicago tomorrow and I want you to set up a meeting between him and Joe O'Neil. Harold's got a problem and I think you can help him out."

It seemed like Harold had pulled a strike on Seagrams in St. Louis and Seagrams had got a permanent injunction against him to stop him from picketing, and they were going to sue the shit out of him for damages. Now, by then my relationship with Seagrams was on a very high level, and I could get things done. I had organized Michigan, Ohio, and Pennsylvania, which were monopoly states where the state controlled the sale of liquor on the retail level, and I had organized some of the open market states, too. So, Seagrams was pretty much under my control as far as jurisdiction was concerned. What Jimmy wanted was for me to use my influence to have them back off and not sue Harold. There wasn't much that could be done about the permanent injunction, but the lawsuits were something else.

Immediately, I went into Chicago and set up a meeting at the international office between Harold and Joe O'Neil. We sat down and Harold told me what it was all about.

I says, "Look, as far as Seagrams going after you, I can get hold of Fred Lynn and see what he can do. But you got the goddamn distributors on your ass and they're the ones that got the permanent injunction and I don't know if we can get them to go along."

Harold says, "Whatever you can do to get this thing off my back, I'd appreciate it."

I got on the phone to Fred Lynn. "Fred, Jimmy told me to give you a call and see what we can work out about this thing in St. Louis. He wants you to lay off Harold and drop the actions that you got against him."

Fred says, "What can we do to work this out, Joe?"

"Well, Joe O'Neil and Harold Gibbons are sitting here with me and I'm sure I can talk Harold into withdrawing from this whole goddamn thing as long as you withdraw and get your distributors to withdraw all these legal actions. Then we'll call the whole thing a draw and Harold can walk away and save face and your company can walk away and save face and that will be the end of all the problems."

"Hey, I'm willing to do that."

"Well, let me put Joe O'Neil and Harold on the phone and let's get this thing ironed out."

That's what I did and the whole thing was resolved right there and then. When it was over, Harold turns to me. "Joe, I'm very grateful for what you did. Now, what are your plans?"

"Well, I'll probably end up going back home tonight."

"Why don't you stay over and have dinner with me and then make the late flight?"

We had dinner that night at a place called the Chez Paree, which was a nightclub in Chicago in those days. There was Harold and me and a guy named Lefty O'Hearn, who owned a hotel off Rush Street, and what I didn't know at the time was that he was the guy behind the organizing of the carnival concessionaires which I was organizing with Harry Karsh. And there was a couple of friends of Lefty O'Hearn's that meant nothing to me or Harold and three or four girls. We had dinner and then the show was going to start and I found out that Johnny Ray was the star, which I didn't know before. The thing was, that when Johnny Ray was first starting out and nobody knew him, I heard him and I thought he had a lot of talent. So I took him to an after-hours joint in Detroit they used to call the Newspaper Club, and it was owned by a guy I knew they called Strawberry. I says to him, "Strawberry, do me a favor. Give this kid a break and let him play the piano and sing." That was about two-thirty in the morning and everybody from all the other nightclubs used to drop by the Newspaper Club after their shows to listen to the entertainment. Strawberry agreed and it was a break for Johnny and for a little while after that I was his manager.

Now, here we are at this place in Chicago and he's about to come out. I says to Harold, "Let's not sit up ringside because I know this kid and I know what he's going to do and he's going to embarrass me."

Harold says, "Come on, you don't know him."

"Harold, I do know him."

So, Harold promises, and surer than hell, he makes it so we would be sitting right next to the stage. I says, "Harold, if he embarrasses me, I'm going to get up and I'm just going to walk the hell out of here."

The show starts and they introduce Johnny Ray and he starts singing behind the curtains and then he comes out. He's a star by this time, and he used to have a habit of walking very pigeon-toed and he pigeon-toes out and he looks right at me and he recognizes me right away, and he comes over and sings directly at me, and after the song was over, he sat on the edge of the stage and sang another song within about two feet of me. I says to Harold, "Do you understand now? This kid feels he's obligated to me because I was his manager and I gave him to Al Green at the Flame Show Bar and that's when he started to make his big name." I mean, it was a mess, the way he was making over me, because everybody in the country knows he's gay. I got up and I walked back to the club they used to have in the back of the Chez that they called the Key Club. Harold came back and he apologized to me because he knew I was embarrassed.

After that, we left and we went out someplace else and then we had breakfast and I headed back for Detroit. From that point on, Harold and I became very close to one another and very intimate. We had a standing joke after a while that I was Harold's illegitimate son. Whenever I would call him and they would ask who was calling, I would say, "This is Harold's illegitimate son, Joe Franco." All his staff got to know it and got to know me and they thought it was pretty funny, and later on, when Harold married Toni, she always got a kick out of it.

A lot of years later, when I was in my forties, I was on an elevator out at Caesar's Palace in Vegas and Milton Berle got on. Milton and Harold were very close friends. I looked at him and I says, "Hey, Mr. Berle, I don't like to be forward, but I understand you're a very dear friend of my dad's."

He looked at me and he says, "Yeah? Who's your dad?"

"Harold Gibbons."

He says, like he thinks I'm crazy or something, "You're kind of old to be Harold's son."

"Well, I'm illegitimate."

The way he looked at me he was very happy to get off that elevator and away from this cuckoo clock that's saying he's Harold Gibbons's illegitimate son.

The next day, Harold calls. "I hear you bumped into Milton Berle on an elevator."

"Yeah. What did he do, call you?"

"As soon as he got into his room. I damn near broke up laughing. I told him, that's Joe Franco and Joe and I are very close."

I saw Milton Berle a few times after that and he always remembered and he always said, "Hey, you're Harold Gibbons's illegitimate son, aren't you?"

That's how close Harold and I became after that time when I straightened out the Seagrams thing for him. And I met a lot of beautiful people through Harold and he met quite a few through me, including Frank Sinatra. And through the years, I did a lot of things for him and he did a lot for me, and he would have done more if it hadn't been for some damn bad luck down the line.

Harold Gibbons became his closest friend within the Teamster movement. It was a different kind of relationship from the one he had with Hoffa, who was his boss and to whom he showed an almost blind and unquestioning loyalty. And during the 1950s, the tasks Hoffa was throwing his way carried increasing responsibility, and brought him into close contact with scores of other Teamster leaders and officials of other unions as well as many outside the union movement. These contacts often seemed to begin in friction but inevitably ended with friendship.

It was during these years that Franco became Hoffa's regent, running half a dozen international unions dependent on the Teamsters, including the Distillery Workers; the Building Service Employees; the Jewelry Workers; the Toy, Doll, and Novelty Workers; the United Steel Workers; and the Sheet Metal Workers. But always his basic loyalty was to Hoffa and to the Teamsters, which he considered his base, and he took directions only from Hoffa. On those few occasions when he acted as an independent, without checking with Hoffa first, trouble resulted.

★ ★ ★

I was assigned by Jimmy to organize the state of Ohio for the Distillery Workers and go in and straighten out the state. Jim told me that the key people I should make contact with would be a guy named Babe Salupo, who was head of the Teamsters in Cincinnati, and a guy named Babe Triscaro, who was out of Cleveland.

I got into Cincinnati and checked into the hotel and called Babe Salupo and we agreed to meet in the lobby. I went down there and sat around, which was what we usually did, and kept looking for a guy who would be like six three or six four, typical Teamster, who would come over and say hello. I sat around the lobby for four hours and I finally went over to the house phone to call my room to find out if anybody's been trying to reach me. The operator says, yes, a Mr. Salupo has been trying to reach you. And standing alongside me was this guy who was about five three or five four, a good-looking kid who was very sharp and a very sharp dresser. He turns around and he says, "Are you Joe Franco?"

"Yeah. Are you Babe Salupo?"

"Yeah. Jesus Christ, I been sitting here for three hours waiting for you."

"I been in the lobby for four hours waiting for you. I been looking for a six footer. Jimmy didn't tell me . . ."

"Don't call me small. I'm bigger than Hoffa. I don't want to hear that shit about being small."

"I'm sorry. I didn't mean to offend you."

These guys all have small man complexes. I don't know why. But Babe was a very powerful guy and a very tough kid. Anyway, we got to talking and I told him what I was looking for, that I wanted to organize the state of Ohio. He gives me the okay and he says to go up to Cleveland and meet with Babe Triscaro and his brother, Tony Salupo, who was representing the laundry workers in Cleveland in those days and he would meet me up there.

I went up to Cleveland and met him there and he introduced me to his kid brother, Tony, and to Babe Triscaro. They told me that a guy named Joe Fontana, who was head of the hotel and restaurant union and the culinary workers, had the charter for the distillery workers in the state of Ohio.

Nothing much happened then and I went back to Detroit. Then I got a call from three salesmen in Cleveland and they told me they wanted to be organized into the Distillery Workers and they weren't having much luck. This may be the only time it happened, but I didn't check with Hoffa. I called Joe O'Neil and he told me he would appreciate it if I would go into Cleveland and pick up the charter from this guy Joe Fontana. So, back I go to Cleveland and I get in touch with Tony Salupo and ask him if he knows where I can find this guy Fontana. He took me over to the office and it's a dingy little place and he says the office is upstairs, just go up the flight of stairs and it's the first office on the left. Some years later, Jackie Presser was employed by the culinary workers and he worked out of that local office.

I went up the flight of stairs and walked into this office and there was a guy sitting behind a desk, a big guy, and there were two big bruisers sitting on the other side of the desk who looked like they were big enough to be Teamsters. All three of them was just sitting around bullshitting.

I says, "Who's Joe Fontana?"

The guy behind the desk says, "I'm Joe Fontana."

I didn't even say who I was. "I understand you have the charter that belongs to the Distillery Workers."

"Yeah."

"You got any books and ledgers or anything that belongs to the charter?"

"Yeah."

"Can I see them?"

"Sure."

He opens the drawer in his desk and brings out the charter and three ledgers and the checkbooks. I picked up everything and turned around and walked out and went downstairs with them under my arm. It happened so fast the three guys didn't know what the hell was going on. They didn't even bother to ask me who the hell I was or where I came from. I was pretty pleased with myself because I didn't get into any beef and I didn't have to be nasty or anything.

I got into the car and Tony Salupo says, "What have you got there?"

"I was sent in by the international to pick up the charter and the books and I picked them up."

He says, "Are you crazy? Are you nuts for doing what you just did? Joe Fontana's nobody to play around with, and he's probably got two or three big guys up there with him."

"Yeah. So what? I got a job to do and I'm doing it. Now, take me back to the hotel so I can put this stuff away and then we'll go have dinner before I go back to Detroit."

We did that, and then we went over to the Theatrical Grill on Pinston Avenue and we had dinner, and some people came walking in and Tony introduced me to them, and then my cousin, Jimmy Valenti, came in and I introduced him to Tony and they kind of hit it off and they became friends for many years after that.

We sat around for a while and had dinner and it got to be about nine, ten o'clock at night, and we walked out of the place and walked over to the corner and we stood around talking. I was standing in the street and they were standing on the sidewalk because they were both little guys, about five two, and some other guys came up and they were introduced to me, and I was facing them, looking in toward the buildings. In those days, I used to wear a shirt and a tie, and after what happened then, I never wore a tie after that unless I had to go to a funeral or a wedding or the grand jury. Because, the next thing I know, I have some son of a bitch behind me and he put his hand in my collar and grabbed the back end of it and he started to choke me and me wearing a tie made it even worse. And then a big burly Irishman is standing on the curb, and I'm still in the street, and he's pointing his finger at me and he's screaming, "Who the fuck do you think you are coming into my fucking town? What gives you the right to come in here and stick your nose into our business? Who gave you the right to go up to Joe Fontana's office and take that charter and take those books and everything and walk out like you were King Kong? Who the fuck told you you could come into my town?"

He's screaming at me and I can't answer because this big gorilla who must have been at least six feet six is behind me and he's got me choked with his hand down my collar and I'm about to pass out. I figure, if I'm going to get choked to death, and get stomped on, I might as well take my best shot. The only thing I could do was to reach back and grab this son of a bitch by his balls, which I did, and I gave him a good rip and a tear, and he let me go and he just gave out a yell. I turned around quick and I gave him a swift kick into his balls and down he went. I was ready to step on his face and I could hear this big Irishman screaming, "Don't do it! Don't do it! If you do it, we'll have to shoot you! We're gonna kill you!" I backed off and he came up to me and he grabbed me under the arm and threw me up against the wall and he says, "Who the fuck are you?"

"I'm Joe Franco. I'm out of Detroit."

"Who do you work for?"

"James R. Hoffa."

"Why the hell didn't you say that? Goddammit, get in here."

He pulls me into a little restaurant and he gets on the phone and he starts to call Detroit. This is about ten o'clock at night, maybe later. I'm saying to myself, holy shit, this guy knows Jimmy because he's calling him at his house. Oh, oh, I'm in big trouble now because I didn't tell Jimmy I was going into Cleveland to grab the books and the charter. Well, he got Jimmy and he told Jimmy a guy named Joe Franco was there and he told Jimmy everything I did and the next thing I know, he hands the phone over to me.

I knew I was going to get my ass chewed out at that point. I picked up the phone and Jimmy's screaming, "You dumb fucking dago bastard you, what the fuck are you doing in an unknown area? I told you to deal with Salupo. I told you to deal with Triscaro. And you walk in there like King Kong and you pick up books and a charter. You goddamn asshole you, they could just as well shot you and got it over with. Get your goddamn ass back to Detroit and be in my office tomorrow morning. Now, put the guy back on the phone."

I turned the phone back to the guy and he got back on and he says, "Okay, Jim, don't worry about it." He hung up and we walked out and at that point he knew my name and now he introduced himself.

"I'm Bill Finnegan and I'm president of the AFL-CIO for the state of Ohio."

"Oh, Jesus. I came in here for the sole purpose of helping out Joe O'Neil out of Chicago who's the general president of the Distillery Workers."

"Jesus Christ, why didn't you . . . that's another mistake you made, goddammit. Joe O'Neil is a very dear and close friend of mine. If you had come in here and told me what you wanted and mentioned O'Neil's name and Jimmy's name, hell, I'd have got the goddamn books and none of this shit would have went down. Now you see what happened."

Well, that ended it and we went in and had some coffee and after that Bill Finnegan and I became very close friends. But during the course of the evening, all of a sudden, Joe Fontana comes looking for me with a couple of heavies, and they wanted to beat the shit out of me. Bill Finnegan stopped that and told him that everything was taken care of and he introduced me and Joe Fontana and we became very close friends until he died. And both Bill Finnegan and Joe Fontana told me that night when we were saying goodbye, "You know, kid, you're good enough to be one of us Clevelandites." Bill Finnegan's dead, too. One of my biggest problems is that everybody who was anybody and everybody that was a good and standup guy, they're all dead today. There's damn few of us left.

When I got into Jimmy's office the next morning, he really ripped me apart, and he taught me a lesson I never forgot. Never go into a strange town unless you cleared it with him and he told you who to go to, and always make sure you covered yourself by going to certain people that he would tell you to go to and say, "I'm here and this is what I'm here for and I'm not here to cause any problems, and if it's a problem for somebody, tell me and then I'll back off, but this is where it's at." Since then, I have followed that many, many times going into another city. I made damn sure all my steps were covered before I did anything.

But, out of that thing, I made a lot of good friends and my relationship with the people in Cleveland was always at the highest level. Bill Presser, who was Babe Triscaro's partner and Jackie Presser's father, and who was a beautiful guy and a standup labor guy, and a damn good Teamster and who was the head of the Teamsters for Jimmy in Cleveland, and I became very close and we had a standing joke. He used to say that before I ever came into Cleveland, I was to make sure I called him so he could prepare himself for the worst of it because every time I went to Cleveland I always got into trouble.

There was one time I was sitting in my office in the building when Mr. Sam Perrone called. He asks me if I know a guy named Petroff. I says, "Sure, he's downstairs here with me, right next to my office." Petroff was the head of the automobile salesmen and mechanics Local 376. At that time, he was busy organizing a Dodge dealership on the east side of Detroit. Now, it just so happened, which we didn't know, that they guy who owned the dealership was a friend of Sam Perrone.

He says, "I want to see this guy."

"What's the matter, Mr. Sam?"

"I'm going to shoot this guy Petroff and I'm going to kill him."

"Wait a minute, Mr. Sam. Don't go killing nobody. Let me come over and we'll talk about it."

He had his office in a gas station he owned directly across the street from the stove works on East Jefferson. I went over there fast and he told me the Dodge dealer had come to him for help. Now, Sam Perrone was the kind of guy if somebody came to him and told him that a guy was mistreating him, and he liked you and he had respect for you, he would put a slug into the guy in a second, in the blink of an eyelash.

I says to Mr. Sam, "Look, Mr. Sam, let me set a meeting and maybe we can get this resolved without going through this killing business." He agrees and he says he wants to meet Petroff on this deserted road that night. I can't do nothing but agree, but I'm thinking, holy shit, if he goes haywire on me and we're on a deserted road, it's nothing for him to just pull out that .38 and go pow-pow and that's the end of it. Not that he would do anything to me, but I know he'd blow the other guy away.

I wanted to be very careful with this, so I got there early and then Sam showed up and the last one to show was Petroff. I was parked and then Sam was parked in back of me and Petroff pulled up in front of me. I got in between Petroff when he got out of his car and Sam got out of his and came walking toward him. I grabbed Petroff right away and I says, "Stay right here. Don't move. You fuck around with this guy, this guy will put two holes in you real fast without even mentioning your name. So don't move from here."

Then I walked over to Mr. Sam and I says, "Mr. Sam, don't do nothing. You promised me there'd be nothing done tonight."

He says, "I keep my promise."

I says, "Let's see if we can resolve this thing."

We walk over and he tells Petroff, "You stay away from that car dealership. I don't want you around there and I don't want them to be organized. I no going to tell you a second time. I no want you to go there. I no want you to talk to nobody there. I want you to stay away. If I hear you come around there once more, I put two holes in your stomach. I make you die slow." That was typical of those guys at that time. If they had any feeling for you at all, they'd make you die fast, they'd give you a shot in the head. But if they hated you, they would give you a shot in the stomach and they'd make you suffer, they'd make you hurt for a long time before you died.

Well, we listened and I told Petroff, "You'd better back off from that fucking dealership because this guy ain't going to tell you twice." He believed me and he dropped the whole thing.

Jimmy called me one day and he told me he wanted me to organize Earl Scheib's paint-your-car business, which used to paint cars for $39.95 in those days. There were like a hundred and fifty to a hundred and sixty plants and they were all over the United States. Jimmy wanted me to put them all under the Teamster banner and then Harold Gibbons would handle the thing. Well, the first thing I had to do was go out to every city and every state and find them and make a survey to find out whether they were union or whether they were nonunion. I found out that some of them were organized and some weren't, and those that were organized were in all different unions, the United Mineworkers and the UAW and the Teamsters and whatever.

Then Jimmy said that I should make all the necessary deals with everybody that's got them so I could put them all in the Teamster house. I went into Michigan, Illinois, Pennsylvania, Indiana, Ohio, everywhere, and I got all the locals, and I made some deals with them, sometimes compensating them with money, and sometimes compensating them with members to replace the members they were losing, and sometimes just by saying that this is Teamster jurisdiction and they would automatically turn them over.

Then I got hold of Earl Scheib and brought him into Chicago and we had a meeting with Jimmy and Harold Gibbons. Jimmy told him what we were doing and he said he had no objection, in fact, he was grateful because he was having quite a problem because he had too many contracts to negotiate with too many unions, and so he would rather have everybody in one union and have one master contract covering the whole country.

Now, the place where he was having real trouble was out in California. There were two locals out there that had all the Earl Scheib plants in the state completely organized, and they were run by a guy named Tony who had three or four real bad kids working for him. Harold Gibbons had a young guy working for him, and Dick was assigned to work with me on things out there, and we went out and sat down with Earl Scheib in his office and told him what we were going to do. He says, "Anything I can do to help you accomplish it, you let me know."

I says, "Just stay the hell out of it. Don't stick your two cents in and don't have your managers spike me. I'll handle all the rest."

"What are you going to do with Tony here in L.A.? Tony's my biggest problem."

"Don't worry about it. I'll handle it."

I went back to Detroit and I told Jimmy about this guy Tony. He says, "Go back to L.A., tell Tony I sent you, and tell Tony I'll give him $50,000 if he turns over his independent unions to you and becomes affiliated with the Teamsters."

Dick and I went back out to L.A., and Dick was filled in on the whole arrangement so he knew what the hell was coming down. Dick and I had dinner and I told him, seeing that he was Jewish and Tony was Italian and I was Italian, I would meet with Tony and lay the thing out for him and if he agreed, Dick would handle the rest.

The next day, I met with Tony at Delmonico's restaurant, which was a place Earl Scheib owned, and Dick was there, too, but I did all the talking. I told Tony exactly where I was coming from and that Jimmy said for me to tell him that he would get $50,000 as soon as he turns over all the contracts and the books and everything to Dick and turns his members over to the Teamsters, and then Dick would give him $50,000 in cash. We came to an agreement right there. I turned to Dick and I says, "Go pick up the $50,000 and give it to Tony and he'll give you everything he agreed to. Now, you don't need me anymore, so I'm going back home to Detroit." With this, everybody shook hands and we had an agreement and I went back to Detroit. The next day, I got a telephone call from Tony. I wasn't home even twelve hours before he called.

"Joe, you and I agreed to $50,000. Right?"

"No problem, Tony. That's exactly what Jimmy told me to give you."

"Well, Dick's welshing on the deal. He says he's only willing to give me $25,000."

"Why would Dick try to beat you out of $25,000? Listen, I told you $50,000. That was my word. That was Jimmy's word. That's exactly what you're going to get."

"That son of a bitch is trying to beat me for $25,000. He's telling me he's only got $25,000."

"Listen to me, Tony, it's $50,000. He's got to give you $50,000."

"I'll tell you something, Joe. He's at Delmonico's right now. Dick's sitting in a booth with a couple of broads and we had words. I told him if he steps out that door, I already had two of my guys to blow his fucking ass off. They're ready to kill him."

"Don't, Tony, please don't do nothing. Give me a chance to get on a plane and I'll be there as quickly as I can. I'll be there. Stay there. I'll be there in three, four hours. I know it's gonna be hard for you to sit there and wait that long, but don't leave. I'm gonna call Earl Scheib and tell him if I'm late to keep the damn joint open. Close the bar off, but keep the joint open until I get there."

I got hold of Earl Scheib and told him that, and then I got to a plane and got out to California and took a car right to Delmonico's, and when I got there I saw three guys sitting in a car in the parking lot. I walked up to them and they knew who I was. I says, "Look, fellows, don't worry about nothing. You guys can go home now."

One of the guys says, "We can't unless Tony tells us."

"Look, if I tell you I'm responsible, don't worry about it. I'll take care of it. I'll resolve it."

Two guys got in another car and took off and the third guy waited for Tony. I went inside and I saw Dick sitting there with a couple of broads, and Tony was sitting way over on the other side of the room by himself and I could see he was steaming. I walked over to him and I sat down and I says, "Don't worry about it. I talked to the little guy and I told the little guy what happened and the other $25,000 will be made available and you'll get it all as of tomorrow before I leave Los Angeles. Now, Tony, go on home and relax. I'm sorry this happened. I should never have left here until this whole fucking deal was done. That's my fault, not his fault. He's an asshole, he's a chiseler, so what are you going to do? Go home. You got my word. It'll be taken care of. Tomorrow, meet me at the Beverly Hills Hotel around one, two o'clock and the money will be there. You bring everything with you and we'll make the transfer and we'll get it out of the way and this time I'll stay until it's done."

"Okay, Joe. But you tell Jimmy don't ever send a son of a

bitch like that to me again and don't ever send any son of a bitch like that out to California because unless he sends someone like you, I won't recognize anybody from his office. This guy's a piece of shit."

"Well, this guy's from Harold Gibbons's office."

"Then when I see Harold, I'll rip Harold a new ass for even having this kind of a guy around."

Tony got up and I walked him over to the door and said goodbye, and then I walked back and sat down in the booth. Dick was sitting there like he was scared shitless.

Dick says, "What's going to happen? Did you get everything straightened out?"

I says, "Yeah, you chickenshit son of a bitch. Didn't I tell you the old man okayed $50,000?"

"Well, I thought maybe you and I could score and cut up $12,500 apiece."

"Dick, you're so full of shit. If Tony would have taken $25,000, you would have put the other $25,000 in your pocket and that would have been the end of it. Who are you bullshitting? You know, I should smack you in the goddamn face. Because, I'll tell you something, you made me make two trips out here and I saved your life, you asshole, so you owe me. You really fucking owe me. I'm staying at the Beverly Hills. You'd better be in that goddamn hotel by one o'clock and bring the bag, bring the money with you, all of it. Not $25,000, you bring $50,000. And this time, I'll handle the transfer."

The next day, he brought me that $50,000. Tony showed up about a half hour later and I gave him the money and we shook hands and the locals were turned over to the Teamsters, and at that point, all the Earl Scheib locals all throughout the United States were in the Teamster jurisdiction and we put them all into one master agreement. And then I went home.

Part III

Part II

8

Through the 1950s and into the 1960s, Hoffa amassed ever
more power and wealth, and created ever more fear. He moved far
beyond his bastion in Detroit's Local 299 and the area's Joint
Council of Teamsters, took control of the Central and Southern
States Conference, helped engineer the downfall of Dave Beck, and
brought himself to the pinnacle of union power as president of the
international union. And he did so despite mounting troubles of his
own. The Senate committee investigating labor racketeering, led
by John L. McClellan of Arkansas and his chief counsel, Robert F.
Kennedy, was after Hoffa with righteous vengeance, calling him
and other Teamster leaders to testify about ties to the underworld,
payoffs, racketeering, and more. Government agencies, taking
their cue from the McClellan committee, began to gather like
storm clouds around his head. George Meany, president of the
AFL-CIO, under increasing pressure from the federal authorities
to clean labor's house, forced the expulsion of the Teamsters and
some other unions labeled corrupt and gangster-ridden from the
labor federation. Here and there, dissident elements within the
Teamsters rose to voice displeasure with the way the union was
being run by Hoffa and his cohorts.

None of this deterred Hoffa. He faced Kennedy and the senators with a belligerence equal to their own and, for a time, created
a stalemate. He challenged the government's right to interfere in

his affairs, and managed a standoff. He derided Meany, laughed at him, and went on to use the ouster to gather the other expelled unions under his suzerainty and begin raids on the ranks of unions that belonged to the AFL-CIO. He put down the incipient rebellions within his own ranks with little difficulty, if with some broken heads or worse. He stood unchallenged at the top of the Teamster pyramid, a man of immense power and wealth, a man who stirred inordinate fear not only in his enemies, but in his friends and allies.

Like the old story of Franklin D. Roosevelt as a tug carrying the harbor's flotsam and jetsam in his wake in his march to electoral triumphs and power, so Hoffa carried with him into ever higher realms the Teamster flotsam and jetsam, those who had followed his orders and done his bidding. Some, like Frank Fitzsimmons, Robert Holmes, and Dave Johnson, he made union vice-presidents and heads of Teamster locals, and more. Others, like Joe Franco, he made his regents in the control of unions affiliated with and dominated by the Teamsters. From all he demanded absolute loyalty and unquestioning obedience. From all he demanded recognition that there was only one leader, and that was James R. Hoffa, and the union was utterly dependent on that leader. The Teamsters, he declared and they believed, were synonymous with Hoffa as Hoffa was synonymous with the Teamsters. He stood alone at the top and beneath him, a long way down, was everyone else.

Those who showed their undeviating loyalty were well rewarded with positions and with money. By the early 1960s, Franco was one of the highest paid labor leaders in Michigan. At a time when the average hourly wage was about $2.25 an hour and the average weekly income of American workers was less than $90, Franco was earning $21,000 a year, plus another $6,600 in allowances and expenses. In the Teamsters, that was topped only by Frank Fitzsimmons's $37,000 from both Local 299 and the international, of which he had been made vice-president by Hoffa. The only other Teamster leader in the state close to Franco was Bobby Holmes, president of Local 337, who pulled down in salary and expenses just about an equal $27,600. Even Walter Reuther, head of the UAW, was making only a little more than Franco—$27,800 in salary and expenses. Salary, expenses, and allowance, though, hardly told the whole story of Franco's income. There was cash handed over by Hoffa whenever Franco needed more and asked— $5,000, $10,000, sometimes more. There were envelopes stuffed with bills handed across as a reward for negotiating a sweetheart contract, one an employer could live with without pain, or for walking away from an organizational drive at a non-union company—cash that he split fifty-fifty with his friend and partner Frank Fitzsimmons.

Whatever he was earning, he needed to support a growing family and increasingly affluent life-style. He had married soon after the war's end, a marriage primarily to legitimize the birth of a daughter named Cindy. His wife was young, Protestant, and the daughter of educated and affluent parents who looked on Franco— then driving a hack for Radio Cab and protecting that company from unionism—as a kind of strange and inferior species. Not only was he a low-paid laborer, but he was Catholic and Italian. A few months after his daughter's birth, Franco sent his wife back to her parents. A bitter custody battle ensued. Franco won, but was then persuaded to turn the child over to his wife's parents because they could provide for her a lot better than he could. They adopted Cindy, left Detroit for Florida, and raised her as their own child, as her mother's sister. It was a decade before Franco saw that child again, and then only from a distance while on a trip to Florida. He did not speak to her, did not approach her, and never saw her after that.

In 1950, he married Alice Thomas, a nightclub dancer. She was just the kind of wife he wanted and needed. As Hoffa threw more responsibilities Franco's way, she helped keep the books and records and do other union chores. She also followed the dictum required of the wife of a union organizer and the rules for a traditional Italian wife. She stayed out of the way, asked few questions, accepted whatever explanations Franco gave, and accepted when no explanation was given. Her role was to be the understanding wife and mother, and she gave birth to three daughters and a son.

Her rewards were cars, furs, jewels, possessions of all kinds, including increasingly lavish homes that, by 1960, meant one in the exclusive Detroit suburb of Bloomfield Hills. And her reward included whatever love Franco had to give her. With that was the

trouble that followed the life of a union organizer doing the things
Franco was doing for Hoffa.

★ ★ ★

It wasn't always easy in the labor movement. It was hard
being affiliated and a close associate with Jim. Every time Hoffa got
a blast in the papers, it would reflect on all the buffalo, meaning all
the business agents and organizers, in their neighborhoods, and
their children would be affected by it, and their families would be
affected by it.

Jimmy was being given some real bad heat and every day
there were headlines, and my daughter Victoria was only about
four years old. She came home one day with four teeth hanging out
of her mouth. Some kid hit her with a two-by-four. And it was all
over the fact that this kid heard his parents talking about Hoffa
and knowing that Hoffa had been in my home for dinner and I was
associated with Hoffa, he thought it was the same as if they were
talking about me, so this kid took it out on my daughter.

When I got home, my wife, Alice, showed me what had happened. I grabbed a gun and these people only lived just around the
corner from us. I wasn't going to hit the kid, because the kid was
only six or seven and he didn't know what the hell he was doing. I
blamed the parents for it. Alice was standing on the porch and I
come rolling past her and I go around the corner and his wife is
standing on her porch and she sees me and she hollers out to her
husband. They knew what had happened to Victoria. I went right
up on the porch and opened the door and he was going out the
back door and I let loose one shot and just missed him. He went
into the backyard and I'm chasing him through the yard and I'm
shooting at the son of a bitch, but I'm running so I can't aim and I
can't hit him. I took four or five shots and missed every time.

With that, some of the neighbors came running after me and
one of them says, "For chrissakes, Joe, they'll have the cops down
here and they'll have you in jail. Stop it."

I just put the gun away and walked home. Alice was very
upset about it. But those are the things we had to live with.

It even came down for Jimmy. He came running into the
office one day and he was very upset and he turns to Tom Burke

and me and says, "Get out to the house, go pick up Jim Jr. and take him to the hospital."

I says, "What's the matter, boss?"

"Some son of a bitch hit him in the head with a rock and the kid's unconscious. I'll be following you right out."

Burke and I went out. The thing had happened at school and Jimmy Jr. was still there, so we picked him up and took him over to the house and called the doctor. Then Tom and I went and found out who the kid was and went over to his house and grabbed the father by the collar and threw him in the car between us and I put a pistol right to his ear. "I'll blow your fucking head off you just move. You know what your son did?"

"Yeah, but I don't know why the kid did it."

"I'll tell you why. Because an asshole like you will read the newspaper and start making comments in front of a kid and the kid thinks that he's going to do something and he takes it out on the other man's kid. That's what the hell it's all about."

We took him over to Jimmy and Jimmy says, "What the hell are you bringing that son of a bitch in here for?"

I says, "Hey, your kid's hurt. His kid hurt your kid. Your kid's next to dying. What do you want to do with the son of a bitch? If your kid dies, this guy dies, whether you want it or not. I'm gonna kill this son of a bitch if Jimmy don't come out of it."

Jim says, "Aw, Jimmy's all right. The doctor's got him upstairs in the bedroom. He's got a busted head, a slight concussion, but he's gonna be all right."

"What do you want to do with this asshole?"

"Take him home. I think he's had a good lesson taught to him."

I says to the guy, "I hope you got a goddamn good lesson, mister. You leave that kid alone and you tell every other kid and you tell your son if he ever touches that kid again, you'll have a bullet stuck up your ass."

The sins of the fathers, according to Scripture, shall be visited upon the children. They seem also to be visited upon the wives. Alice Franco, certainly, did not escape. No matter how much Franco tried to protect her from what he was doing, he could not

*completely succeed. She suffered the harassment of her children.
And she suffered harassment directed at her.*

It was a hard life for any woman that was married to any man
that was in the labor movement, especially any man that was in the
Teamsters as an organizer or a business agent. We told our wives
very little about what we were doing. Alice knew that when I went
out on a detail, she had no right to ask any questions, because what
she didn't know she couldn't say to anybody. If anybody would
ever question her, she couldn't answer because she didn't know. I
was away a lot on assignments Jim gave me, sometimes for weeks
at a time, sometimes for months without coming home. I would
call her whenever I got a chance from wherever I was, but she
knew that as long as she didn't hear from me, everything was all
right. When she heard from me, it was either that I'm on my way
home or I was in jail or I was in trouble. So, most of the time, she
would rather not hear from me than hear from me.

But she used to constantly get threatening telephone calls.
People would call up and threaten her and threaten the children
and everything. She started getting telephone calls saying that I
was in bed with another broad in a motel in Toledo. The first ten or
twenty calls like that, a woman can pass them off as crank calls.
But when they keep coming, any woman would start to say, hey,
there could be some truth here. And the next thing you know, it's
"Where were you? What time are you coming home? Are you
screwing around? I got a call saying you were with a broad last
night. Is that where you were at?"

I'd tell her, no, I was on a detail. Besides, I'd say, "You're not
supposed to ask me what kind of a detail, but I wasn't with a girl,
be assured of that."

One night I was sitting right there and she gets a telephone
call from a girl telling her she's in bed with me in Toledo. Alice
says, "I hope you enjoy yourself." She says to me after she hangs
up, "Guess who that was? Some girl calling from Toledo saying
you were in bed with her."

I says, "Now does that prove a point? All this argument and
all this stuff that you've been going through all these years that
you've been thinking, now it's finally come out and you know the
truth."

I thought that helped and eased her mind, but one night I'm out of town on a detail and I come home and she comes running out of the house and she's got a goddamn pistol in her purse and she's taking off. She sees me drive up and she stops.

I says, "Where the hell are you going?"

"Two guys just called. They're with a girl. They wanted to prove to me beyond a doubt that this girl has been shacking up with you for years and they asked me to meet them where US-24 and US-25 cross, at the truck stop on the way to Toledo."

"Alice, what the hell's the matter with you? Don't you know they can't get to me, the next best thing that they can do is get to you? They won't touch the children, but they'll get to you. If they get you there, they would have held you until I showed up. They would have called me and then I would have had to come there and I would have been disposed of. How many times have I got to tell you, you get telephone calls, hang up? It was an out-and-out trap."

It could have been people that was hired by employers that I had organized because certain employers would be vicious son of a bitches, they'd go after organizers and some of them would even set fire to their own companies and make it look like a union thing because we had them out on strike. They would go and hire people to cause me a problem, to give me a beating or even shoot me. Hell, we did it for a cause. They did it from revenge. That was what was happening here and this was the first time she fell into the trap. I told her, "Don't ever do that again."

But the calls and all the crap kept coming and they were building up in her. Because of that, she ended up with a serious mental problem. She was treated by a psychiatrist and it was a few years before she seemed to come out of it. In the meantime, it was hell for her and hell for the children and hell for me.

9

No matter how high Franco rose in the Teamster inner circle, he never questioned that he owed it all to Hoffa. He never doubted that without Hoffa, he never would have reached what he considered an exalted station. And Hoffa never let him forget it, nor did he let anyone else in the union hierarchy forget that he was the leader and they were there to do his bidding. When Hoffa summoned, they came running. When Hoffa ordered, they did the assignment without argument, no matter how menial or degrading. For Franco, this often meant that one day he would be in negotiations with corporate executives and the next he would be setting off dynamite; one day he might be planning an industrywide organizational campaign and the next acting as a bodyguard; one day he might be acting with all the majesty of a union leader and the next with all the muscle of a goon. If Hoffa wanted something done, he had his reasons.

★ ★ ★

Jim called me into the office one day. "Get to Chicago and meet this guy at the Sherman Hotel in the lobby." He didn't give me a name. He just gave me a description and a message to give the guy.

Without question, I just got in the car and went to the airport, got the plane, went to Chicago, and sat in the hotel lobby for half an hour. In walks this guy and he looked like the description. He came up to me and he says, in a low voice like a whisper, "I'm being followed. Meet me at Brown's Hotel in Denver, tomorrow at eleven in the morning."

I just looked the other way and after he left, I walked out of the hotel and grabbed a cab, grabbed a plane and went to Denver, and checked into Brown's Hotel. The following day, at eleven in the morning, I went down to the lobby and waited. There he was, sitting down, reading a newspaper. I went over and sat down next to him. I didn't talk to him or anything. He turned and looked up from the paper and he says, "Don't talk to me. Meet me at the Beverly Hills Hotel in L.A. tomorrow, eleven in the morning." He got up and walked away.

I grabbed a cab, went back to the airport, got a plane, and went to L.A. I went to the Beverly Hills Hotel and checked in. The next day, I'm sitting in the lobby and here he comes. He turns to me and he says, "I can't talk to you. Meet me at the Sherman Hotel in Chicago. Tomorrow. Eleven in the morning."

With this, I'm starting to get a little upset by this whole goddamn trip and what I got to tell him is only three sentences. But Jimmy told me to do this, so I was doing it. I got back in the cab, went back to the airport, got a plane to Chicago, went to the Sherman Hotel, and waited until eleven the next morning. And here he comes, walking through. And it looked like I'm gonna take another goddamn trip. This time, I grabbed his arm and I says, "I don't give a shit who's following you. This is what Hoffa said. He said, 'Take the son of a bitch out. I don't care how you do it. Take him out. That's your message. Goodbye.' " And I walked out and went back to Detroit.

When I got home, I reported back to Jim and told Jim what the hell happened. He started to chuckle. "All right, Franco. As soon as I get a call, I'm gonna want you to go someplace for me."

I says, "Sure, boss. Anything you want." So, I left.

The next day, he calls me in. "I want you to do me a favor. Take this and go to New York and meet this guy that you met at the Sherman Hotel and give it to him." He gave me a nice-looking briefcase.

I took the briefcase and went to the airport and grabbed a

plane to New York and checked into the Warwick Hotel, which was where we always stayed in New York. At the specified time I was supposed to be in the lobby, I was there. Here comes the guy. He says, "What's your room number? I'll meet you there in fifteen minutes." Now, I didn't know what's in this briefcase. One thing I never did, if Jimmy gave me something, I never looked in it, never opened it. It was none of my business. It was just for me to follow orders and that was it.

I went up to my room and waited, and the guy came up in fifteen minutes, like he said. He introduced himself as Lou.

He says, "You got something for me?"

"Yep. Jim sent you a briefcase."

He took it and opened it up and then I saw . . . hundred-dollar bills, thousand-dollar bills. He started counting it out and it came to $380,000, and I'm shitting, because I figure it was maybe supposed to be $400,000 and this guy's gonna think I got the other $20,000. He counted out the $380,000 and I'm looking at him and he's looking at me as if he's got a question mark on his face, like where's the extra twenty? Then he turns to me and says, "Well, everything's here, everything's okay. Tell Jim that the thing is taken care of and the guy's out of the way."

I says, "Okay." He left and I waited about half an hour and then I went back to the airport and went back to Detroit and went back to Jimmy's office and told Jimmy. I says, "The guy's been taken care of, everything's all set. Whatever you had figured, it's okay. Now, boss, let me ask you a question. Why didn't you tell me I was traveling with $380,000? The other thing is, I shit when he started counting and he only got to $380,000, because he looked at me like he was going to say, where's the other $20,000? But the thing is, I'm walking around with $380,000 and I don't even know about it, and I don't even have anything to protect myself if some son of a bitch knows what I got."

"You see, you weren't nervous, you weren't uptight, you were relaxed. You got on a plane like you normally would do and everything you did was normal. If you had known you had $380,000 in cash, you'd have been nervous, fidgety, and people would have stared, and somebody could have spotted you. This way, it didn't bother you."

It was not unlikely for Hoffa to go outside his Teamster ranks to hire violence even though he had plenty of men around who could have done it.

The reason why Tom and I or anybody else in the Teamsters was never asked to go out and kill somebody was that Jim had different guys that he would use outside of his own Teamster help. He had his contacts wherever and whenever he needed them. He had two black guys that I remember he used as subcontractors and he would use others from the outside. I remember Tom told me that Jim would never ask us to hit anybody because he didn't want his own people involved where it might come back to him.

There was another time, it was years later, in the sixties, when the trouble was coming down by the shitload, Jim came in from Washington and he called me into his office. At that time, he had a young fellow who was his accountant and he was sitting there. Jim came in and he says, "Listen, I want you to go someplace for me tomorrow. Be here at nine o'clock in the morning."

The next morning, I showed up at nine o'clock and we both walked into the office at the same time. Jim reached under his desk and pulled out a big shopping bag like you get from the A&P. And the thing that got us was that when we first walked into the office it smelled like somebody had crapped. It was the most putrid smell you'd ever want to smell. I mean rotten, dirty, awful smell. Now, the bathroom was in the back of the office and I says to the guy, "Goddamn, something died in there."

He hit me, just a nudge, and he didn't say nothing. We both looked at each other. And when Jim pulled that bag out, we both knew where the hell the smell was coming from. The bag was full, jam-packed down full of hundred-dollar bills, five-hundred-dollar bills, thousand-dollar bills. Jim told us to stack and count it and put it in a briefcase. Then he left us there and we started stacking it up and we were ready to throw up because of the stink. The guy turns to me and says, "You know where the money was hidden?"

I says, "Nah. It had to be hidden in a toilet or something."

He says, "Jim has a habit. Everytime he scores, makes a buck, he stashes it away in a sewer drain, in a sewer trap in his basement. He's got sewer traps every five feet. If you ever go down to the basement, you take a look at it. It's the only home in the world that's got thirty or forty sewer traps. He's got them all over the basement. That's where he puts the extra money, so when you take it out it's got that stink all over."

I looked at the cash. "Hey, the son of a bitches are rotten." And then we stacked it all up and there was $1 million, cold cash. We packed it all up and put it in this nice-sized case. A couple of hours later, we're sitting there and Jim comes walking in.

"You got it done?"

"Yeah."

"How much?"

"One million."

"Nothing over?"

I think, oh, shit. I looked at him and I says, "Not a dollar short or a dollar over. You can bet money on it. Not even a dollar. You've got $1 million, so cut the bullshit. You know how much money was there. Now, what do you want me to do?"

"I want you to accompany him. Make sure nothing happens to him." Then he looks at the guy and he says, "You take that to Washington and you take that to the man and you tell him it's from me."

We got into a plane and went down to Washington and we went to a hotel and I sat down in the lobby and he got a cab and he came back in an hour or an hour and a half, and we picked up a cab and went back to the airport and went back to Detroit, and he reported to Jimmy and he says, "The money was given to the person and everything was fine."

Now, since I wasn't there when he delivered the $1 million, I can't say for sure who got it. But what I know, from the things he said and the things Jimmy said, there was an election going on at that time and Jim didn't have no use for the Kennedys who, he figured, was out to get him, and Jack was in the race. I think Jim figured he could kind of depend on the other side when the chips were down, and he was trying to make damn sure he could.

Carrying money and protecting money that was being carried were sporadic if not uncommon errands for Franco. Though his plate was filled to overflowing, he came when Hoffa called, and he did Hoffa's bidding without question. He knew what was expected of him.

Jimmy used me as a basis of representing at least five different international unions. I was the liaison between those international unions and Jimmy. If Jimmy wanted the president of that international union to do something, he would give me the message and I would go and say, "Hey, this is what the little guy wants."

Sure, there were a lot of paper locals in our union, the majority out of New York and Chicago, but it was a leftover from the old days. They came about as a sort of protection racket; they found the simplest way to tell an employer we'll protect you was to say, "We're union, join our union and we'll protect you, we're not going to represent our people, we'll handle the people, they're our members and we'll take care of them. This gives you labor peace and you'll never have to worry about another union." And if any other union tried to come in, these guys would say, get the fuck out of here, and give them a whack and throw them out.

Well, Jimmy said to me, and we had many talks about it, he says, "I need them. Basically, I need them." Because they were behind him and they were helping him get where he was going. He thought he could get them behind him and then make them change. He used to say to me, "These guys have to be taught that it's not the roaring twenties anymore, not even the thirties. There's grand juries and investigations looking into things and a lot of these guys are going to get dumped." So, he sat down with some of the major people and he said, "Look, reverse your ways of thinking. I'm gonna take all the heat because anytime you do something, you're a member of the Teamsters and they're going to come down on me."

But, the thing was, Jimmy had to deal with them because they had the power. It would be like the outside element would come to him when we were organizing a company and they would say, "Look, this company is our people and we understand you're trying to organize them and we wish you wouldn't. We'd like to see you walk away from it." Then we'd know the situation that existed between Jimmy and certain people. And sometimes they would say, "Bring Hoffa in, let Hoffa decide," because they respected Jimmy and they would sit down with him and he would act as a mediator. Jimmy would come into New York, for instance, and sit down with Albert Anastasia and Frank Costello and other people in that element and they would say, "Do me a favor, Jim." And if

Jim says, "Don't worry about it, it's taken care of," then it would be taken care of. There was a time when I was working on a thing and he would call and he'd say, "Franco, walk away."

"How can I walk away?"

"Because I'm telling you to walk away."

"But I'm deep into this."

"I've committed myself to somebody. Until I tell you you can go back, you walk away. I'll handle it and don't you worry about it."

Of course, it wasn't always a back off. Sometimes the outside element would come in and tell the guy that was organizing to take a walk, and the guy would get on the phone to Jimmy and tell him, and Jimmy would make a call and then there'd be a meet where Jimmy would sit down with the outside source that was maybe representing the employer and Jimmy would say, "Look, I want them in the union. Now, what does it take to get them in the union?" And the guy would tell Jimmy and he'd tell Jimmy the employer was afraid that he was going to get a wage structure he couldn't afford. So, Jimmy would say, "I'll give him a contract he can live with." If you want to call it a sweetheart deal, maybe it was, but it was a beginning. Because what Jimmy did was instead of asking for a boost of a buck an hour, he'd ask for a boost of twenty-five cents, twenty-five cents, and twenty-five cents over three years, which the employer could live with. And when that happened, everybody got a good deal; the employer didn't get a strike; there wasn't any bloodshed; the guys in the shop got the union behind them and wages and benefits they didn't have before; the outside element was still making the big buck representing the employer and making sure everything worked out.

Now, that doesn't mean that Jimmy was in love with every guy he met that was Italian, any more than he was in love with every guy who was Jewish or anything else, or that he was in love with every guy from the outside element. He used them, and I guess they thought they were using him. So, it worked both ways.

10

For years, he was known only as the kid, Tom Burke's partner, and Hoffa's man. Tall, muscular, good looking in that slightly dangerous way that made him attractive to many women, he exuded the aura of a man capable of doing efficiently whatever Hoffa assigned him to do. The closer he came to the center of Teamster power, the more his world expanded into what he called a "spiderweb," the strands intermingling in random patterns. One person brought him into contact with another from another world, and he began to move more easily through a myriad of spheres. As a rising labor leader, he became intimate with the captains of industry. He branched out into politics, not merely as a man on the fringes, but right in the center. He knew leading entertainers and counted many as his closest friends. And from his earliest days with the Teamsters, as Hoffa cemented deals and alliances with what Franco always calls "the outside element" and "the Italian element," Franco moved along with him. His contacts and friendships in these circles spread from the men he had known since childhood in Detroit to the realms of their compatriots throughout the nation.

★ ★ ★

I got to meet a lot of these people on trips into New York, which I made all the time because the Toy, Doll, and Novelty

Workers, which I was servicing for Jimmy, was based in New York, and the Distillery Workers was very big in New York, and some of the others also operated out of there. I would generally find myself in New York at the same time Jimmy would be there and I was always around him. If Jim was with certain individuals, he would automatically introduce me. "Meet the kid," he'd say. And in many instances, he would send Tommy Burke and me into New York to meet with certain people that was close to him and that was heads of Teamster locals in the area, like Johnny O'Rourke, who was head of the joint council, and Miltie Holt and Miltie Gordon and Johnny Dio and Tony Provenzano and a lot of others, and with other people who was with the outside element.

Tom knew everybody and he was always introducing me. That's how I got to meet Albert Anastasia. We had lunch with him three or four times at the old Sheraton Hotel, which was where he got killed in the barbershop. He was one of the few people I met in New York that I really didn't like. He was a very cold man and he was a little too rough for me. He had no polish. One thing about him, unless you made an impression or unless you meant something, he never made a comment as to recognizing you the next time he saw you unless you were back in Hoffa's company or in Tommy Burke's company, and then after you were introduced again, he'd go, "Eh, yeah, sure, I met you before."

[On October 25, 1957, Albert Anastasia, known as the "Lord High Executioner of Murder, Inc.," was shot dead while getting a haircut at the Sheraton. It was one of the executions ordered by mob boss Vito Genovese as he moved to consolidate his own power. The killers, according to underworld stories, were led by Joe Gallo, known as "Crazy Joe."]

I got to know Joey Gallo, too, through Tommy Burke, and we became friendly and I used to see him every once in a while when I was in New York. But I never got too friendly with him. He was a rebel, like Sam Perrone, and I sure as hell didn't want it to be known that I was friendly with Joey Gallo because I didn't know who the hell was his enemies and who was his friends and I wasn't taking any chances.

The thing was, seeing I knew a lot of these guys in New York and Chicago and Detroit and other places, there was people who thought I must be part of the families as they call them, part of what the federal people call O.C., meaning organized crime. Well, that's a load of horse shit. The only family I was a member of, the organization I belonged to, was the Teamsters. Sure, I showed respect to them, but it was a means of friendship with the Italian people and the Jewish guys that I met in New York and other places, and in all due respect to Jimmy, I showed them respect. But anytime if they required anything of me, I would always say, "You'll have to ask Jim because he's my boss." I respected nobody as being my boss but James R. Hoffa. That was it.

The one guy I really got close to, though, was Frank Costello, who was a beautiful man, one of the best dressed men in the country, a real classy guy you never had to be introduced to twice. My first introduction to Frank C. was through Jimmy, and then Tommy Burke brought us together on several occasions. In those days, Burke and Jimmy would always introduce me to people as "the kid" . . . "I want you to meet the kid." It was never my name. My name was very seldom used. People in other cities never recognized my name for years because of that. I was always the kid. But when I got introduced to Frank C., he wanted to know my name and he always called me Joe. I think one of the reasons he took to me was that he knew of my closeness to Jimmy, which automatically gave me a certain amount of respect, and there was the fact that Tommy Burke, being much older than me, had respect for me, for the young kid like I was in those early days, and he had me as his partner and he traveled with me, which meant I must know my trade. So, I got close to Frank C. I guess you'd have to call him my principal rabbi in New York, the guy I could always call on and depend on if I needed somebody. It got so whenever I came into New York, I used to call him and pass on greetings from Jimmy and we'd have dinner together.

Then there was this thing that happened one night. I came into New York to negotiate a contract for the Distillery Workers with Canada Dry, and we got through late and this Canada Dry vice-president named Skip Anderson decided to take me to this exclusive nightclub, which I had never been to but which I had heard a lot about. We got there about ten o'clock and the dinner hour was over, so we went into the bar, which was to the left as you came in. Looking down the bar, there was this young guy in a blue blazer with an open-collar shirt and a white pair of pants and

a medallion on the blazer like he was a yachtsman. He had three of
the most gorgeous girls you ever saw around him. As a matter of
fact, I can't ever remember seeing an ugly broad in New York in
those days. I turned to Skip.

"Who's the guy with the three girls?"

"He doesn't look it, Joe, but that's Frank Costello's right-
hand man. He works directly with Frank."

"You're kidding."

"No."

"He's a good-looking kid. You'd never think it. He does pretty
good with the broads. He's doing pretty good with the booze, too."

Skip says, "Yeah. He's a real clubber. He does very well representing Frank."

Now, I put him in a position as to where he was from and who
he's with. Going down the bar a couple of more seats, there's a
little Japanese guy, and he's got a couple of girls on either side of
him, and he's a little short, Dapper Dan kind of guy. I says, "He
looks like he's flash money."

Skip says, "Yeah. He's got a real bad reputation. I don't know
him, but I know he's got a real bad rep. He's supposed to be a real
tough guy. You don't mess around with him."

Now, I'm looking to score with a broad and this one guy's got
three and this other guy's got two. Skip warns me not to make any
passes because either one of the two guys could cause me a problem. So, I just kind of laid back and watched these two guys operating with their beautiful women. Then I notice there's a guy sitting alone at a table just away from the bar. I says to Skip, "Who's
the single-o sitting at the table?"

Skip says, "That's the Jap's bodyguard. He's a real tough Italian kid."

"No shit. The Jap's got a bodyguard. How do you like that?
He must be into something that he needs somebody to walk with
him."

Skip kind of agreed that whatever he was into wasn't legitimate and I let it go at that. All of a sudden, I notice that the Jap is
starting to make some beefs with this kid that belongs to Frank
Costello. The Jap gets up and the kid was standing up by his girls.
I see what's happening and I know that this Jap is going to do
something. I look over and I see that the Jap's bodyguard is getting

his hand into his pocket and starting to make a move. When Frank C.'s man and the Jap get nose to nose, the Italian kid at the table I could see was about to get up. I says to Skip, "Skip, stay the hell out of the way if something starts to bang-bang. Just get the hell out of the way."

He says, "What are you going to do?"

"You just get the hell out of the way and mind your business and stay out of it."

I just casually walked away from Skip while Frank C.'s man and the Jap are screaming and swearing back and forth and about ready to come to blows, and the Jap keeps looking over to his bodyguard. By this time, I got behind the bodyguard and I stuck my finger into his back and I says in Italian, "Do you work for him? Are you his bodyguard?" He nodded his head. I says, "Don't turn around and look behind because I don't want you to see who I am. Just sit down." He sat back down and I sat behind him and he still doesn't know what I look like, he doesn't know if I've got a gun, and he doesn't know anything, and he's got to respect that. I keep telling him in Italian, "Don't turn around. Let the both of them do what they got to do. Let them scream and holler. Let them fight if they have to. They started the argument, you stay the hell out of it. If the Jap is going to pull a knife, then the other guy's gonna have to handle it himself. If he's got a gun, then it's not a proper match, but let them solve their own problems. You're Italian and you know I'm Italian because I'm talking in Italian. I have no beef with your man and I don't know the other guy, but I don't like to see two guys on one. Let them beef it out."

The Jap took a look over and saw that I was sitting behind his bodyguard and his bodyguard was not getting up and he wasn't going to make any moves. Right away, the Jap backed off and the guy from Frank C. put him in his place and that was the end of the beef. With this, I told the bodyguard in Italian, "Thank you very much. Someday maybe I can do you a favor. See how they fight over broads. You could have got in the middle of it, over an argument over some girls, and they could have got into a real mess. Best that you listened to me. See, they're buying each other drinks now."

I went back over to Skip and the guy from Frank C. came over and he says, "I saw what you did and I appreciate it. I didn't have any problem with the Jap. The only thing I was concerned with was the bodyguard. I saw that you handled that very nicely. You showed me a lot of class, kid. I want to thank you."

"No thanks necessary. I just don't like to see two on one and knowing that you're Italian and I ain't that fucking crazy about the Japs. The kid that was sitting there, I know he's Italian, so I figured I'd talk to him in Italian and tell him to stay the hell out of it and you two guys can fight over your broads and see who's got the best looking broads. Which is stupid. You know, you're having a good time, you're drinking, so you get into a little trouble."

Now, I know he's Frank C.'s man, but he don't know who the hell I am. He starts to become a tough guy with me. He says, "I want you to know that Frank Costello's my boss and I'm his right-hand man."

"No shit. That's really something. I wonder what Mr. Costello would think about his right-hand man being in this club with three girls and drinking and getting into beefs over three broads. I wonder what the hell he would think about something like that."

"I probably would have got into a lot of trouble. I want to thank you again, but I want you to know that I'm Frank Costello's right-hand man and I'm his bodyguard."

"Well, I guess that makes you something, it must make you a big person around here. To tell you the truth, it really doesn't impress me."

"Hey, you're a cocky kid."

"Well, if I had a boss, I wouldn't pull off what you just pulled off if I had any respect for him."

"Where are you out of, New York?"

"No. I'm out of Detroit."

"What do you do?"

"I'm with the Teamsters."

"No kidding? My boss is very close to your boss."

"Who's my boss?"

"Well, Mr. C.'s very close to Jimmy Hoffa."

"Well, it just goes to show you. You brought the name up. Now, Jimmy's my boss. And Mr. Costello's your boss and they're both friends. So, it was my duty to go to your help because I saw you were going to get in trouble and Skip told me who you are. I figure I owe that much to a friend of my boss. I'm just wondering what Frank C. is gonna say if he hears about this."

"Oh, Jesus, nobody's gonna tell him."

"I'll tell you one thing. I think you should cool it. It's a bad scene for you."

He starts coming on with that real heavy New York bullshit, like I can take care of myself, I don't need you fucking guys, I don't have nothing to worry about it, I'm a real tough guy.

I says, "You can be the tough guy all you want. I just came in here to see the club since I've never been here before. Now, Skip, let's leave."

As we're leaving, he wants to shake hands with me. I says, "I'll tell you what. The next time I see you, I'll shake your hand, but it's gotta be in front of Mr. Costello. As a matter of fact, I'm having dinner with him tomorrow night and I would like you to be there when we're having dinner."

He says, "You're gonna have dinner with my boss tomorrow night?"

"Yeah. He called me up and he wants to have dinner with me tomorrow night and I would like to see you there because I want you to see if what you're telling me is legit. And maybe someday if you're in Detroit, I'll take you in and introduce you to Jimmy Hoffa so you'll know I'm not bullshitting you. Now, I'll see you tomorrow night at dinner."

"Holy shit." He put his arm around me and he says, "Wait a minute, kid. If I insulted you in any way, if I came on too strong with you, I owe you one as it is, but please don't say anything to Mr. C. because he gets a little mad at me when I go out drinking."

"I don't blame him. You got no business doing that because what if he needed you right now, what if he picked up the phone and says I need you? Are you in a position to go out and lead and do what you've got to do for the man?"

"You're right. Look, let me tell him. By tomorrow night, he'll know what took place."

The following night, I went over to this beautiful classy restaurant that Frank Costello had. It was about eight o'clock when I walked in and Mr. C. was sitting at a table in the back and so was his bodyguard. I walked over and shook hands, and in those days a handshake, you would shake with your right and your left would go around and it was a sort of semi-embrace.

Frank says, "How are you, kid? How do you feel, Joe?"

"Fine, Mr. C. Everything's okay."

"How's Jim?"

"He's fine and he sends his regards, like always. He said if I was having dinner with you, I should make sure to send his best regards."

"You do the same, you send my best regards to him and tell him to be sure to stay in touch. What are you in town for?"

"I'm here negotiating a contract with Canada Dry, which I have just about wrapped up."

We sat there and I had a little bit of white wine, which was all I drink, and he put his hand on top of my hand and he says, "I want to thank you for what you did last night."

"What did I do?"

"Come on," he started to chuckle. And then he says, "This fucking ape head over here . . ." I never heard the man swear before. But he was a little pissed off at his man. He says, "This fucking ape head over here, every once in a while, he gets a little loose and he gets a couple of drinks and he gets tough. Other than that, he's a good boy. I want to thank you for interceding. He told me the whole story and I told him he can thank his lucky stars that you were in the club that night and you backed up his play."

The dinner went very nicely and the food was very good and one time, when Frank got up to talk to somebody, the kid thanked me for not saying anything.

So, Frank C. and I got to be real close and as far as my loyalty in New York was concerned, it was to Mr. Costello. He was my guy.

They tried to kill him one time in the lobby of his apartment, and they screwed up the hit. I got wind of it right away and immediately I put a call out and asked if he wanted me to come into New York and if he needed help, I'd be more than happy to do what I could do. I got hold of Tommy Burke and then I got hold of Jimmy and I says to Jimmy, "I just called New York. I talked to Frank C.'s guy and in case they need some help, I'd be more than happy to go in."

Jimmy got real pissed at me. If they wanted help, the proper channels would have been that they would have called Jimmy and then Jimmy would have told me and Tommy Burke to go in there and assist Frank C. But Jimmy was taking a hands-off position, not knowing where the hit might have come from and it might come from another area that might have been as friendly to Jim as Frank Costello. He wouldn't put himself in jeopardy by saying that he would support Frank C. over whoever tried to put the hit on him. Jim stayed neutral on that. But I didn't know any better. I guess I'm a funny kind of a guy. If I'm friendly to you and I'm loyal to you, then I'm loyal to you. And I always felt a very close friendship with Frank C. And the many times I went to him for help, he never refused me.

[On the evening of May 2, 1957, after a quiet dinner with friends, Frank Costello returned to his apartment on Central Park West. As he headed for the elevators, an obese man, later identified as Vincente "The Chin" Gigante, stepped out from a hiding place, said, "This is for you, Frank," and fired off one shot before fleeing. The bullet grazed Costello's head. It was another step in Vito Genovese's plan to take control of the organized underworld, for Costello was a major rival, a long-time partner of Charles "Lucky" Luciano and Meyer Lansky. Money and casino tallies found in his pocket resulted in a jail term for contempt and an indictment for tax evasion for Costello and, essentially, the end of his power.]

Whenever I went into New York, I had a regular routine. I'd check into the Warwick and then I'd see Danny Stradella who owned Danny's Hideaway and I'd say I was coming in and have dinner there. There was a special booth that he always saved for me. This one time I was in the city and I went over to Danny's and we had dinner together and while we were having dinner, Alan Drake called for me. Alan was a very close friend and he found out I was in town. Alan says on the phone, "Joe, Tony Martin is opening at the Copa tonight and he wants you to come over and catch the show. I want you at ringside with me." Tony was a good friend, too.

"Okay, Alan, I'll come in. You go ahead and make the arrangements for a table, or I'll come over with Danny Stradella." Danny always had a standing reservation for a big ringside table at the Copacabana.

I came back to the table and Danny says, "Are you going over to the Copa to catch Tony?"

"Yeah. That was Alan on the phone and that's why he called me. You going?"

"Yeah. As soon as we get through with dinner, we'll go over and sit in the lounge upstairs until it's showtime."

I hadn't been in the Copa that many times prior to that. I had a way of life when I went into New York. I didn't go nightclubbing unless I was invited, unless somebody was with me or unless I told certain people that I was on the street and going someplace, and I never went by myself. I generally just took care of my business, went to my room, ordered dinner up there, and stayed there. I didn't like walking around or going clubbing by myself or looking for trouble. That's why I got in the habit of going over to Danny's, because it was second home, and Danny always looked out for me and everybody that worked there looked out for me. I felt secure there. And from there, I would end up back at the Warwick if we didn't go someplace together, or Frank Costello would call or have somebody reach out for me and tell me to have dinner with him at his club or someplace, and I'd make it my business to go over and have dinner with him. But there'd always be somebody to come over and pick me up, because I didn't know how to get around New York. As many times as I came into New York, I never learned my way around the city.

This night, we went over to see Tony and we were all sitting upstairs in the lounge, about fourteen or fifteen of us, including Jackie Leonard, who I was very close to, and other guys, and a lot of girls. Everybody was tied off except Danny and I. Danny never took a girl and I never took a girl because of my cautious way of living. Going into New York, I didn't want to put into a trick bag.

Now, the thing is that everybody in the club knew me except the guy that ran it, Julie Podell. I had never met him. The two guys at the door, Carmine and Angelo, they would always greet me and they were two tough kids, I would hate to tangle with both of them. But at that stage, I wouldn't have known Julie Podell if he sat in my lap.

We were all getting up to go downstairs and Alan Drake is coming up the stairs and he says, "Come on, the show's going to start."

I turn to Danny and I says, "Alan's giving us the high sign." This very attractive lady, she must have been in her middle or late thirties, and very well dressed and if they were phony stones she was wearing, they sure looked good on her fingers and around her neck, she was a very classy looking lady. She came over to me and she says, "Are you going down to see the show?" I tell her that's where we're going. She says, "Would you by any chance have one extra open chair? I would love to see the show but my date's not here. It seems that I've been stood up and I'd hate to miss the show."

I turned to Danny and I says, "Danny, this very lovely lady, I don't know her but she's a very pretty lady. Do we have another chair so we can invite her?"

Danny says, "Sure, we can always make room for one more person." And he kept walking down the stairs.

Well, the lady had a tab at the bar, so I says to the bartender, "How much is the lady's tab? Give it to me." It was like six dollars and I threw a ten-dollar bill down and I says to the lady, "Come on, follow me."

All of a sudden, I hear some guy hollering out, "Who the fuck do you think you are, picking some fucking whore up at the bar? And taking her downstairs to see the show?"

I don't know who he's hollering at. I heard all this commotion and it's going toward the staircase, by the hatcheck. I turned around and I see this very short chunky guy that's speaking like he had a frog in his throat, and he's screaming, "We don't allow goddamn hookers in this joint."

"Are you talking to me?"

"Yeah, I'm talking to you. You take that whore and you get the fuck out of here."

"Wait a minute. Who the fuck . . ."

It's starting to get a little boisterous and here comes Danny back up the stairs, and the little guy is backing off because I'm going to go for him. All of a sudden, I've got Carmine and Angelo grabbing me under the arms and looking the other way, and Carmine's whispering, "Please, Joe, don't start nothing with this guy, he's a fucking cuckoo clock. We work for him but we know how he is. Don't start nothing."

I says, "Carmine, do me a favor, the both of you, please, get your hands off me. I don't give a fuck who this guy is, he could be the fucking king of Persia, he ain't going to talk to me like that. I don't know this lady. She seems like a nice lady and here's this man calling this lady a whore. How the fuck does he know? She's liable to get a lawsuit slapped against him. And second, I don't stand for him verbally abusing me. Now, just wait a minute, Carmine, I'm not out of line. You may work for him, but I don't give a fuck." And this guy can hear me. He's leaning up against the counter at the hatcheck. I turn to him. "I'm going to tell you something, you dirty cocksucker that you are, come on outside. Don't have Carmine fight for you. You come out, you bastard, and I'll beat your fucking brains out. Now, I'm going to leave here, I guarantee that I'll be back. And when I get back, you be fucking ready for me."

I start to leave and Alan comes running up the staircase and he says, "Jesus Christ, Joe, Tony's upset."

I says, "Fuck you, fuck Tony, fuck everybody. This son of a bitch ain't gonna talk to me like that." And I turn to Carmine and I says, "Carmine, when I come back in, stay the fuck out of it. I mean it, stay out of the fucking way."

He says, "Please, Joe, please." But he knew I blew my fucking stack, and he got out of the way.

Well, I got outside and I grabbed a cab and I went over to Mr. C.'s place and he let me in. I says, "Mr. C., I've got problems." I tell him what happened and I don't know this guy they tell me is named Julie Podell but he had no call to act like that.

Mr. C. says, "Okay, Joe. I tell you what. Go on back there and let's see what the atmosphere will be like when you get back."

"Mr. C., if I go back, I'm going to tell you something. I'm coming here to tell you, I mean to go back in there loaded for bear."

"No, no, you don't have to. You just go back. Don't worry about it. This will never happen again. You just go back and play it real cool. You've got the upper hand now. Play it like you would play poker. You've got four aces wired, so play it cool."

"Okay. I don't know what you got in mind, but if you tell me, I'll do it."

"You just do what I tell you, and you come in tomorrow night and we'll have dinner."

So, I left and I got a cab and went back over to the Copa and got out of the cab and who's standing in the doorway is Carmine and Angelo and they've got the biggest fucking grins you ever saw on two guys. I walked up the staircase very slowly and Carmine winked at me and he opened the door and they walked me over. There's Julie Podell standing over there. By this time, the show was over and everybody's upstairs in the lounge. Julie Podell comes rushing over to me and he says, "Hey, I'm sorry, kid. I didn't know who you were. Why didn't you tell me who you are? I didn't know you were Hoffa's man. I found out you're Jimmy Hoffa's man from Detroit and I didn't know, and Harold Gibbons is in here all the time and I'm really close to Harold and I'm really close to Jimmy."

"You're full of shit. You'd have known I was Hoffa's man then, would it have made a difference, or is it because you got a fucking telephone call?"

He says, "Well, forget about that. Let's be friends. I want you to sit at my table."

He stuck his hand underneath my arm and took me over to his table, a little table right off the lounge where he always sat. We sit down and he raps that big pinky ring of his on the table and the waiters come running to get us whatever we wanted. He says to me, "You know, I'm really sorry. This club's yours anytime you want it."

And Carmine and Angelo are standing there and they got those big shit-eating grins on. They knew he got the fucking telephone call.

Now, Tony and Alan come upstairs, and they're both jumpy. Then they see I'm sitting with Julie Podell, and they start grinning, and Danny Stradella is laughing his head off because he sees I'm stuck now with Julie Podell, sitting there listening to his bullshit. The thing was, I could see he had damn little to do with that nightclub. He took orders from certain people, and he was fronting for them, and I know that Mr. C. had a hell of a lot to say about the Copa. From that night on, whenever I came in there, Julie always insisted that I sit at his table with him, which gave Danny Stradella and Jackie Leonard and the other guys a big laugh, and whenever Jackie played the Copa and I was there, he'd stand up there and he'd say, "Listen, Julie, do me a favor, let the kid come over and sit down so he can enjoy the damn show and he won't have to listen to your bullshit." To me, from then on, Julie Podell was a kitten. No more tough guy. He knew where I was coming from and he knew that I was very close to Mr. C.

Now one of the guys that Julie Podell was very closely associated with and who I understand had a piece of the Copa was Little Augie Pisano who later was killed out at the airport in a car with Alan Drake's wife, Janice. Well, my life crossed wires with Little Augie and crossed them very badly.

Augie was connected with one of the unions that I represented, the Distillery Workers. And there was a time I was having trouble with that union because I didn't show them any loyalty due to the fact that I had only one boss and my boss was James R. Hoffa and I made that known to everybody. The new president of that union was a kid named Mort Brandenberg and he disliked the idea that I did not show loyalty to him and anytime he ever asked me to do anything or asked me for anything or confided in me, I'd say, "Don't tell me anything about it. I don't want to hear about it. If you want anything, you call Hoffa, you tell Hoffa, and whatever Jimmy says, I'll do." What he wanted me to say was, "You know, Mort, you're the international president and if you want me to do certain things, well, being that you're the general president, my loyalty is to you and I'll do it." Well, that was the way I was with all the international presidents, and some of them accepted me as I was, as Hoffa's man, and a liaison between them and Hoffa. There was a couple that didn't and Mort Brandenberg was one of them. He opposed me and he hated me with a passion, and we had a very vicious argument one day.

Well, Augie Pisano was called into the picture. I was called on the carpet. Augie wasn't there. He never exposed himself. In fact, I never met the man and I only saw him one time. I knew what he looked like, that's all, and I knew his reputation.

Anyway, after this meeting, and during it, I was threatened and I heard there was a contract out on me and Augie Pisano was going to hit me. I called Mr. C. and he said he'd see what he could do. And I went to my people in Detroit, Mr. Sam and Mr. Pete. I explained the whole story to them, that I was a target because Augie was told that I was out of line and that I was going to try to take over the international, which wasn't true, and that I showed no respect and that I was strictly a Hoffa man and nobody could control me, and that was very upsetting to Augie.

They said that what they would do was follow the old ways, which was that they would investigate and make sure what was happening and then they would make a decision. But this time, by the time they did that it would have been too late and I would be killed. I explained that and they made a telephone call and the next day we were on an airplane going down to Florida.

Florida was neutral grounds, it belonged to everybody, and that lasted for many years. It's not that way anymore, of course. There was a meeting called, at this very good Italian restaurant where all the guys used to go. It was called the Plantation, but it doesn't exist anymore. But at that time, it was the meeting place of anybody from all over the country, from the east coast to California. If anybody wanted to see anybody, that's where you would go to see them. It wasn't a celebrity hangout. It was a hangout for all the guys. And that was the meeting place we had.

We got into Miami, Mr. Sam and Mr. Pete and myself, but they didn't go checking into any fancy hotels. They went up motel row, beyond the Diplomat, about a half mile, where there are like little apartments and the majority of people at that time were Canadians and it was very inexpensive. Since we were only going to be there a couple of days to resolve this problem, I was surprised because I figured these two guys who are very well off, they would be checking into the big fancy hotels. But they were very nonconspicuous, low key, they didn't flash. I stayed with them, and after we checked in, we had dinner at the Plantation.

We walked in and sat down and ordered and Mr. Sam turns to me and he says, "That's Augie Pisano sitting over there," and he was at a table with ten or twelve other people.

I says, "Mr. Sam, I don't know him. This is the first time I've ever laid eyes on the man." I turned around and looked and I saw this short, not thin, not heavy, on the stocky side, guy. We finished eating and Mr. Sam says to me in Italian, "You sit here. Don't move. You don't move. Mr. Pete and I will take care of what we have to take care of."

I says, "I don't want any trouble now," knowing Mr. Sam like I knew him, and knowing that he was uncontrollable, that he had a vicious temper, that he was about ten times worse than Joey Gallo when something got to him. So, I says, "If you're going to talk, talk. Anything else besides talk, let's get out of here and go home. I don't want you people to get into trouble. I can take care of myself when it gets down to rock bottom."

He says, "No, no, you just sit here and mind your business. I take care of that son of a bitch. I gotta find out what's going around. He's going to hurt you, he's gotta hurt me first."

I think both him and Mr. Pete was loaded for fucking bear. They both went over to the table and I could see Mr. Sam pat Augie on the shoulder. Augie got up and shook hands and they embraced. Mr. Sam looked like he was about to say, who needs this shit. I came here to find out what's wrong.

They excused themselves from the table and they went back in a corner where there was nobody, and the three of them sat down. I could see Mr. Sam pointing his finger and everything, and Mr. Pete stuck his two cents in there. And Augie's shaking his head, yes, yes, like he's agreeing. And then the three of them got up and they all shook hands. Augie went back to his table and when he went by me, he gave me a look like, now I know what you look like and now you know what I look like, and now I know where you come from. It was like a recognition look, like, now I know you're not just a Hoffa man, you come from good people that are related to you.

We left the Plantation then and jumped in a cab and Mr. Sam tells me that when he and Mr. Pete and Augie Pisano were off in the corner, he told Augie in Italian, "This man that you want to kill, he is our *figlioccio* that we baptized and confirmed and we don't want nobody to threaten him. He's from Detroit and he's our man." He made it very clear to Augie that I was related to him, and Mr. Pete made it very clear that I was related to him.

After that, there was a different relationship with Augie and Mort Brandenberg and the rest of the crew from out of New York that was with the international union and me.

[Augie Pisano, whose real name was Augie Carfano, was a leader in the Genovese crime family. During the Genovese campaign of violence against Frank Costello, Albert Anastasia, and others, Carfano-Pisano showed a certain wavering loyalty. Genovese took his time about meting out a reward. He waited until 1959, and then ordered Carfano-Pisano's execution. Little Augie was found shot in the head with former beauty queen Janice Drake, in his car parked at LaGuardia Airport in New York.]

So, things cooled off for a while and the international distillery workers just kind of laid back and laid off me. Then, for some unknown reason, there was a convention and somebody started a rumor that I was going to run for general president against Mort Brandenberg. I was down in Florida and Jimmy was general president of the Teamsters then and working out of Washington and he called me up and he told me to get into Washington right away because he wanted to talk to me. I left the convention and flew in and Jimmy says, "I got a telephone call from New York saying that you're going to run against Morty for general president."

I says, "Who the hell's starting that shit? I couldn't run for anything in that international union. I've got twelve delegates and that's what I'll get, twelve votes. I'm not looking for nothing. If I was looking for something, wouldn't I come to you and tell you first?"

"That's what I told them, I told them Franco would never go in unless he tells me. All right, go on back and I'll call them and get it straight."

I went back and old Morty comes over to me and shook hands because he'd been told I had no intention of running against him and everybody jumped the gun. I got up and made the announcement that I was not a candidate and somebody started that and I didn't want it, so please don't put my name up. I'm not a candidate for anything, I told them, and I don't want to be a vice-president and I don't want to be a trustee, I don't want to be nothing. Well, they ended up making me a trustee anyway, and I didn't like that and I resigned it. Let me tell you, I didn't want anything to do with that international union because everytime you did something, they would run like a thief to Jimmy or somebody else and cause you nothing but trouble.

A while later, I was sitting in my office in the building in Detroit and I get a telephone call from Jim and he's down in Florida. He says, "Franco, get down to Florida and be here at nine o'clock tomorrow morning."

Well, it was then like one in the afternoon. I says, "What's up?"

"Franco, don't argue and don't ask questions. Just get on the plane and get down here to the Fountainbleu. Now, do what I tell you."

"Okay, boss, I'm on my way." I hated to tell him that I didn't want to fly, but it would have taken me at least twenty-six hours to get there if I drove straight through without stopping. So, I was going to have to fly. A little time before that, in 1957, I had a bad experience being in an airplane crash where I hurt my back getting out, and I became a white-knuckler and I didn't fly unless it was absolutely necessary. Seeing that Jim told me and there's no way I can drive, I got to take the plane. I ended up drinking a half a bottle of Scotch, and since I don't drink, you can imagine what that did, and I took six Dramamines and then I got on the plane and passed out and the next thing I know, I'm sitting on a bench in the Miami airport. Somehow, they took me off the plane and they sat me down on the bench and they knew that I was drunk and I'd sleep it off. This girl was sent to pick me up and she got me and she sobered me up and got me over to the Fountainbleu at nine o'clock in the morning. Well, I walked in there and I was still a little drowsy and a little stoned from all that bullshit, but I woke up pretty damn quick.

Jimmy was standing over at the far end of the lobby, going to the pool entrance, and just before that there was a spiral staircase going to the mezzanine. I walked in and I saw Jimmy and he saw me and he raised his hand and flashed me over. I walked over and he grabbed me by my jacket collar and faced me toward him and he says, "I'm going to do something and I want to keep talking to you and I want you to look at me, and I'm going to look like I'm very angry with you. Whatever I do, and I'm going to look like I'm very angry, don't turn around and don't get upset and don't say nothing." With that, he gave me an open hand slap right across my face.

I looked at him and I says, "Boy, you must have a goddamn good reason for doing that." The slap was so goddamn hard it brought stars to me. He says, "Sit down. I've got to talk to you." He shoves me onto this little loveseat couch there.

"Franco, there's a contract out to kill you."

"Jesus Christ, now who's starting this shit? When the fuck are they gonna leave me alone? Still the same people from New York?"

"Yeah. One's up at the top of the staircase and the other's at the door. But don't turn around."

"Look, boss, I've gone through this with Little Augie. What is it this time?" I knew it wasn't Little Augie this time because Augie Pisano had been killed, so he's not around anymore.

He tells me that some of these people say I'm still causing them a problem. Only this time, they didn't go to anybody outside, to the outside element. Instead, they went to Johnny O'Rourke, who was the international vice-president of the Teamsters in New York, and they told him the only way they was gonna have peace was to get rid of me and they wanted his permission.

I says, "Jesus Christ, Jim, Johnny gave these two fucking guys an okay to hit me? Didn't they tell him who I was?"

He says, "Franco, they said Franco. He only knows you as the kid. He don't know your name. He knows you when he sees you. If they'd have said the kid, Jimmy's man, O'Rourke would have called me and it would never have gone this far. But he just heard their side of the story, which was a load of horse shit because I heard it."

Like Jimmy said, O'Rourke didn't know my name. When I used to go into New York with Tommy Burke, O'Rourke and Johnny Dio and Miltie Holt and the rest of the guys would know me as Tom Burke's partner, and I was a young kid and I was always introduced as the kid. The other guys got to know my name, but for some reason Johnny O'Rourke never did. To him, I was always the kid, even though I'd been to his home in Florida on a half a dozen different occasions with Jimmy and Josie, and my wife Alice and I would go there and have dinner with them. So, when they went to O'Rourke and asked for permission to hit Joe Franco, it was just a name of a guy he didn't know and he says, "If he's doing what you say he's doing, sure, go ahead."

All of a sudden, here comes Bill Bufalino walking by. Jimmy flags him over and he says, "Hey, Bill, take Franco down to the coffee shop. Johnny O'Rourke and some of the guys are down there."

"Wait a minute, Jimmy. Before I go down there, I'm gonna get up and turn around and see where these two cocksuckers are and what they look like."

I get up and I look. The guy at the door is named Max, loudmouthed dirty rotten son of a bitch that he is. The other guy, standing up at the top of the stairs to the mezzanine, is a fat kid out of Jersey. Both of them were pieces of shit. I turned to Jimmy and I started to laugh. I says, "Those are the two guys that are gonna hit me?"

"Yeah. They're waiting for you to leave the hotel. But I'm trying to get it settled with Johnny."

Now, when I saw these two guys, I knew it was all a bunch of crap. Up to then, I thought maybe I did something I didn't know about to hurt Johnny O'Rourke's team, but when I saw them, I knew. What it was was there'd been a situation out in Jersey that I was trying to get resolved for a Teamster kid named Andy, and these two bastards shot him in the leg over the deal. I went to them and I told them, no more, stop this shit unless you go to somebody and get an okay on it, otherwise I'll hit you two guys. I guess that's why they went to Johnny O'Rourke with their line of bullshit, not to get permission to hit Andy but to get the okay to hit me.

I says to Jim, "Do me a favor, boss. Take a walk. Walk away from me. Go someplace and get away from me. Because the guy at the top of the stairs, I'm going to fucking dump him off the fucking balcony. I'm gonna kill him first. And that fucking asshole at the door, he won't run fast enough. I'll catch him running down the fucking street and that'll be the end of him. I don't give a fuck who gave him the okay. That piece of shit belongs to me, he belonged to me four years ago. They went and asked for an okay to hit me? Bullshit. So, go take a walk, boss."

He grabbed me. "Don't start it, Franco. I got it about settled."

"Settled? It's only going to come up again, Jim. Those two assholes, everytime I sneeze, they run to somebody. I'm surprised they went to Johnny O'Rourke and asked him for the okay to hit me. I don't think they've got the fucking balls for it. I think they pulled a bluff and they got you to pacify them and to put me in a trick bag. This started a long time ago with Augie Pisano and we got it all straightened away and it was squashed. Now Augie's dead and they can't go to nobody else, they ain't got no other rabbi to go to, so they invent something else and they go to O'Rourke."

He says, "Don't do nothing now." He turns to Bill Bufalino and he says, "Take Franco down to the coffee shop and make sure you introduce him so Johnny'll know who Franco is."

We go downstairs and O'Rourke is sitting in the middle of the booth and next to him is his partner out of New York, Miltie Holt, and next to Miltie is Babe Triscaro, and sitting on the outside is Tommy Burke, who used to be my partner and who is still my friend and who I still work with sometimes. On the other side of O'Rourke is Bill Presser out of Cleveland and next to Bill is Johnny Dio. Everybody sitting there is very close to me, but O'Rourke is the only one that didn't know me by my name. He sees me as I walked over to the table and he says, "Hey, kid, how are you?"

Now Burke sees me and he says, "Hello, Joe, how are you?" I hadn't seen Tommy in four, five weeks. Now Babe Triscaro and I are very close and he started to get up, and Tommy got out and Babe got up and he gave me a hug and a kiss, and I could hear Miltie Holt saying, "Hey, Franco, when did you get into town?"

With that, Johnny O'Rourke looked at me. "Franco? Joe Franco?"

And Bill Bufalino says, "That's right, Johnny. Jimmy asked me to bring Joe down here and make sure you knew his full name, Joe Franco. Now, if you'll excuse me, I've got things to do." And Bill turned around and walked away.

I says, "Yeah, Johnny, that's me. I just talked to Hoffa and there's two assholes upstairs. I came down here for one fucking reason. Those two assholes are the ones that you gave the okay to hit me."

When I said that, Miltie started to choke. He was having a cup of hot coffee and the coffee came shooting out all over the table.

Babe Triscaro looks and he says, "What?"

Tommy Burke got up alongside me and he says, "Where's them two fucking assholes at?" Tommy always carried a piece and he always carried an extra piece for me. Tommy says, "Come on, let's go upstairs. We'll clean this fucking mess up quick."

Johnny O'Rourke says, "Hold the phone."

And Bill Presser turned to O'Rourke. Bill had a very dry sense of humor and when he was happy, he looked mad, and when he was mad, he looked like he was mad, he had that one kind of look. He had that look and he says to O'Rourke, "Since when do you give out okays to hit our own people?"

O'Rourke was embarrassed now. He says, "Jesus Christ, Joe, I'm so sorry. Goddammit, the name just didn't . . . I didn't tie the name in because I've been calling you the kid for so many years with Burke."

Johnny Dio is sitting there laughing his ass off and Burke keeps saying we got to go upstairs and do a number, and Babe Triscaro starts agreeing with him, and now everybody's getting a little upset.

Johnny O'Rourke says, "Don't nobody go no place. Sit down." He tells Babe to slide over and make room for me so I can sit down next to him and Miltie. Then he turns to one of the guys and he tells him to go upstairs and tell Jimmy that he wants the two guys downstairs right away.

So, here comes the two guys and they come in front of the table where we're at. O'Rourke looks at them and he says, "You two guys, you came to my office and you put a beef on this kid. You told me that a guy named Joe Franco is causing me nothing but problems and is causing nothing but aggravation to the international and he was looking to take over the international and he was causing problems with that, and you asked me for permission and I granted you permission. But you didn't tell me he was one of ours. Why didn't you tell me he was a Teamster? Why didn't you tell me he was Hoffa's guy? You came to me and you gave me bad fucking information."

Now, I'm getting steamed and O'Rourke is nudging Miltie and Miltie is nudging me, don't say nothing, shut up when Johnny's talking, he'll cut them new assholes.

Then Burke stands up and he pulls this fucking .38 like he'd stick it right up their assholes. He's ready to blow them out right there.

These guys didn't know what to do or what to say. One of them says, "John, we're sorry you didn't understand. . . ."

Johnny O'Rourke says, "I don't want to hear another fucking word out of you." Now Johnny was a cold, cold Irishman and he was nasty as nasty can be, and they knew it and they saw it and they was ready to shit.

And then Johnny Dio got up and went over to these two guys and he says, "Do you know how lucky you two guys are? If they would have let this kid go, if Hoffa would have let him go, if he would have walked away and let him handle you, he would have cut you up into fucking mincemeat and fed you to the sharks. You know how fucking lucky you two guys are? Because if he couldn't do it, if he couldn't finish it, you see the guy that's standing behind you right now? That's Tommy Burke and that's his partner and at the count of three, both of you would be on the fucking floor with your heads blown off. And you go to Johnny O'Rourke and you don't tell him that this is Joe Franco, Hoffa's man? Then you fucked with O'Rourke. Now, I think O'Rourke should do something with you two guys."

With that, I jumped up and I says, "Hold it. John, do me a favor. I've sat in on spaghetti dinners, and this is typical and we're going to resolve this thing. If you feel that they were in the wrong in asking you and they tricked you into giving them permission, then I'm asking you right now for your permission to hit them. You see them, so it isn't that I'm lying to you. And I give you my word of honor that this isn't the first time that this has happened. They went to Augie Pisano when he was alive and they asked Augie and I almost got into trouble with Augie until my people intervened for me out of Detroit. Now they come to you and they wanted to use you and I don't think either one of them has got the fucking balls. So, do me a favor. Give me an okay. I'll give them one minute. I'm in the booth and you've got me tied in and I can't get out. So, I'll give them one minute to get away from the booth and get up the staircases and if they ain't out of this fucking town by the time I get up those staircases, I'm gonna chase them and when I chase them, I'm gonna catch them, and then I'm gonna cut the fuck out of them. There ain't gonna be no fucking shooting. I'm gonna cut the fucking shit out of them. There ain't gonna be enough of them left to get on the fucking plane to go home with. Just give me the okay."

Now, Miltie's watching me and he knows that what I'm trying to do is scare the shit out of them. He says, "Hey, Johnny, you gave them the okay. The kid's got to have satisfaction. That's the way it's fucking done. He's entitled."

I says, "John, that's the way we operate."

Burke says, "Don't give 'em no fucking minute. They ain't got no fucking minute. O'Rourke, does the kid got an okay?"

Tommy's pistol is out and he shoves it into one guy's guts. He says, "When we walk out of here, we're gonna get in the car and that's gonna be the end of you two fuckers."

Now, Johnny Dio gets up and he says, "I'm going with you."

And Babe Triscaro gets up and he says, "I'm going with you. I want a piece of their asses, too, because these cocksuckers got no right to do what they done."

Now, Miltie nudges Johnny O'Rourke and O'Rourke gets it and he says to me, "Okay, kid. What do you want?"

"I want satisfaction." I says to Babe and Johnny Dio, "Will you excuse me, but they belong to me." Then I says to Burke, "Tommy, give me that thing in your hand." He hands me the pistol. "Now, I either hit them here in the hotel or I hit them out in the street. That's the way it is. That's my satisfaction. They belong to me. I can't go into your neighborhood, Johnny, because that would cause you a problem. But Miami is not your territory and it's not my territory, it's open territory. They're open game. You pulled 'em off and I want 'em."

Miltie says, "The kid's got his rights."

Babe Triscaro says, "Franco, I got one in my pocket. You take one and I'll take one and that'll be that."

"Thank you, but I don't need no help. I can blow both of 'em."

Burke reaches into his pocket and pulls his other pistol. He says, "Let me hit one of the sons of bitches right here."

"No thanks, Tommy. Leave 'em to me."

And these two guys are standing there and they don't know whether to shit or run, they're apologizing and they're pleading and they're sweating like two stuck pigs. One of 'em started to pee in his pants.

By now, O'Rourke's got it and he says, "Okay, kid, you got my okay. Hit them wherever you want. Just don't do it around the table because I'm having late breakfast and don't screw up my breakfast. Take 'em outside."

I start to get up and then I sit down again and I says, "Nah, John. With all due respects to you, they ain't worth the goddamn heat we'd have to go through. I make a gift of them. They belong to you. You do what you want with them. But if I ever see them in New York, if I ever see them in Detroit, if I ever see them any-place, don't say anything to me if they come up dead."

Johnny says, "You're a better man than these two assholes, kid." Then he turns to the two guys. "I want you to go back to New York. Now. I want you in my office when I get back to New York, because this ain't the end of it. I'll tell you something. You may need the Teamsters, but as of today, I don't give a fuck what you do, you will never get the support of the Teamsters in New York or any other fucking place in the country. Hoffa's pissed off at you and he's pissed at your organization, and believe me when I tell you, you are not going to get any cooperation from us. Now, get the fuck out of here."

Johnny gets finished with them and then Bill Presser tells them they better not ever come to Cleveland again, and the local they had in Cleveland they didn't have no more, and they didn't belong to the joint council in Cleveland no more, and wherever they had something, it didn't belong to them no more.

With that, those two guys turn around and they got out of there, they couldn't get to the stairs fast enough and they couldn't get out of the hotel fast enough and they couldn't get to the airport and onto a plane to New York fast enough. From then on, they were nothing. If they want to strike the distillers or anybody else, they had to clear it through Jimmy and they had to clear it through O'Rourke, and they never got an okay from anybody, and they were up shit's creek without a paddle.

11

Franco was a collector. He collected friends the way other people collect stamps, coins, memorabilia. Wherever he went, and during the years of his rise as a Hoffa prince he went everywhere, he came away with hundreds he considered close friends.

In the mid-1950s, for instance, Hoffa sent him to Montreal to organize the Playtex plants in Quebec Province, and then put him in charge of an office there with orders to mount major organizing efforts on behalf of the Teamsters and the distillery workers. For the next few years, until Hoffa decided to shut down the office, Franco commuted every few weeks between Detroit, or wherever he might be in the United States, and Canada. His organizing efforts were at least partially successful and less fraught with troubles than those south of the border. And his friends included the mayor of Montreal, government ministers and politicians, labor leaders and businessmen, entertainers like the Canadian comedian Jackie Kahane, and more. In Montreal, he found a young woman he took as his mistress for much of his stay, who bore him a son he has never seen. As he amassed friends, he also collected women, managing to find someone to comfort him in the lonely days away from his family and home in Detroit. It was something he never told Hoffa about, for it was something of which Hoffa, puritanical as he was, disapproving as he was of such moral lapses, would not have approved. There were some things you just didn't tell Hoffa.

What happened in Canada, with friends and girls, was duplicated on an even grander scale in New York, Los Angeles, Las Vegas, Miami, Chicago, Washington, and points in between. Everywhere there were the friends of Joe Franco and, to a large degree, they were entertainers—people who are often attracted to men of power, men who exude an aura of strength, mystery and a certain unsavoriness, as such men are attracted to them. There was a day not long ago when Franco sat down and tried to put together a list of these friends. It ran on and on and there were stories with every name, illustrating how these friendships began and flourished.

Franco remembers, "I used to have a dream when I was a young boy that I would drive up to my neighborhood on the corner where all the guys used to hang out, and drive up in this big beautiful convertible and I'd be with Clark Gable and Errol Flynn and Douglas Fairbanks, Jr., and Myrna Loy and Carole Lombard and all the sex images of that day. And I would blow the horn and the guys would all come out and look and say, hey, look at Jo-Jo, he's with all the movie stars. It was a fantasy and I never realized it would come true. But it did."

If not Clark Gable or Carole Lombard, still he came to know stars on a slightly less exalted level, and to relish the knowing. There was, for instance, Wendy Barrie, one of the lesser glamor girls of 1930s movies and one-time girlfriend of the notorious Benjamin "Bugsy" Siegel, the man who made Las Vegas. Franco saw her one day at LaGuardia Airport in New York, approached, and the approach led to other things. She was on her way to Grand Rapids; he was in New York on business. He went back to Detroit, showered her with flowers, and soon "we became very, very close and intimate friends."

There was Linda Darnell. He met her through Wendy Barrie and through Harold Gibbons, who seemed to know everybody and who gloried in his familiarity with entertainers. "Linda and I dated a lot and before she died in a fire, we became very good friends."

He dated Anne Baxter and got to know Jinx Falkenberg and did some good deeds for Mike Todd. Johnny Desmond was a close friend; they grew up in the same neighborhood. He was close to Jilly Rizzo, Frank Sinatra's man. Harry Guardino told him stories about how even the most successful actors stand in unemployment lines during long periods between jobs. He rescued a slightly drunk

Judy Garland from two guys who were abusing her one night at
Jilly Rizzo's joint and put her in a cab to take her home. He
introduced Buddy Greco to Bill Bufalino when Greco was going
through a bad divorce, and Bufalino straightened things out for
him. His friend Alan Drake introduced him to Robert Goulet and
he got two guys from Buffalo off Goulet's back when they thought
the singer/actor was coming on to their wives, after which he and
Goulet became close friends. He broke the camera of a guy who
was trying to take Tony Bennett's picture at an awkward moment
and that "created a great friendship." The names and the stories go
on and on.

There were some, though, that he didn't get along with. One
was Sammy Davis, Jr.

★ ★ ★

I was sent into Miami Beach to organize on behalf of the
laundry workers and the hotel and restaurant employees. Basically,
I was supposed to be organizing the doormen, the maids, the
cleanup people, the laundry people, but I was organizing anything
I could get my hands on, and I spent three or four months there
and I got to know a lot of people doing what I was doing, and I got
to know a few girls I used to bum with. I wouldn't stay at one place
too long because in those days, union organizers wasn't an accepted thing down in Florida.

In fact, the first time I was down there was with Tommy
Burke in the late 1940s or early 1950s, when Jimmy sent us down.
In those days, you took your life into your hands and you had to
know where you were coming from and what you had to do. If you
came into a town and you got threatened and they picked you up
and chased you out and you left, well, what you did was make it
very difficult for the next union organizer who showed up in that
town, because they got away with it once, they were gonna chase
his ass out, too.

When we went down there, the guy that was the head of the
local had his house blown up, his car blown up, there were shots
through his house with a rifle that damn near killed his wife and
two kids, and he just said, "To hell with this. It ain't worth it." He
packed up and went back home.

The employers down there at that time, they could get guys for $500 to come and beat your brains out and throw you in a field someplace or in the water. Two guys that was trying to organize down there just before us, they found them floating in the inter-coastal with their heads blown off.

And the legislature in Tallahassee passed a law stating that any organizer for any and every union had to go to Tallahassee first and register and get a license with your picture on it, and then the word went out that you were in Florida as a general organizer for the Teamsters, and they knew you were there even before you knew you were there.

I organized the America Jalousie Window Company, which had about fifteen hundred employees, but it was something, and when it was over, we came home and I told Jim, "Hey, I don't think the south's ready to be organized. They're a bunch of red-necks and crackers and they're nothing to fool with. They're walk-ing around with pistols in their pockets and if they see somebody trying to organize, they say, 'Hey, we don't want you around here, get your ass out of this goddamn city.'"

So, Jim called us off and it was a while before anybody went back down there to try again. It sure as hell wasn't like you see it in the movies where one Jewish kid from New York goes in and gets the textile workers all signed up and nobody runs him out of town on a rail or shoots his ass off. It's easier now, because of the laws, but it still ain't that easy.

So, that's why when Jim sent me down again I kept moving every couple of weeks and watching my step. Now, while I was down there, Harold Gibbons would be in and out and every time he showed up, we'd be in touch. I always knew when Harold was in town because he always stayed at the Fountainbleu and he used to go to a cocktail lounge called the Pink Poodle and to a couple of joints on the 79th Street Causeway, especially a joint called the Place for Steaks that was run by Petey Fox and that was like a second home to me. Anybody from show business would always go there to have breakfast or dinner, and Petey would tell me who was in town, and I used to make it a stop to see who was around or to leave word, like to tell Harold that I was at the Singapore or the Castaways or wherever.

One night I get a call from Harold and Skinny Amato, who

was a young man very close to Frank Sinatra. I was staying at the Castaways then and they came over to my room and Harold and Skinny say, "Hey, Frank is throwing a party tonight and he wants to invite you. And see what you can do to bring a couple, three girls with you."

I says, "Okay." I always heard the stories that when Sinatra threw a party, there were women up to your ankles. But he wants me to bring three, four broads with me.

Now, I was going with a very pretty Greek girl. After all, while I was there, I had to have company, so I picked up a really gorgeous one. And I had met three other girls that were working with me and helping me organize the hotel employees. One of them was a little blond girl about thirty, a cosmetologist who worked downstairs at the Americana. I got hold of Penny and I say, "Would you like to go to Sinatra's deal?"

She says, "Oh, God, yes."

And then I got hold of two other girls and I told them to meet me at the Castaways and we'd all go by car. We all went over to the Fountainbleu and walked into the Pink Poodle that was the cocktail lounge and it was the starting place. Then we went into a private room that was all set up with a buffet and everything else. Here comes Skinny and here comes Harold. I introduce Harold to my girl and Penny and the other two girls who were both models. Skinny grabs one and Harold grabs one and they take them over and introduce them to Frank Sinatra and Dean Martin and Joey Bishop and some other people that were standing around. Then Harold comes back and he asks my girl if she wants to meet Frank, which she sure as hell did, and I says, okay, go ahead, and Harold takes her over.

Then Harold comes back and he says, "Come on, I want you to meet somebody." He takes me over and meanwhile, I'm looking at this girl that I've met two or three times before through Harold, just casual types of introductions and always with a group and I didn't know who she was. It was always, hi, how are you, nice to see you again. But then I found out her name and it was Mai Britt and she was just starting out her movie career and starting to become a box office draw. Harold starts to introduce me and I says, "Harold, you've introduced me to her three or four times already."

We go over and Mai says, "Hi, Joe."

I says, "How are you, honey? How've you been?"

And then Harold introduces me to a very tall, I would say five nine or five ten, very striking woman in her early fifties. Absolutely magnificent looking woman. She was a princess and she was the sister of the Pope. Pope Pius. And she was with her daughter, who was about twenty or twenty-two, and exquisite, I mean, beautiful. Harold says, "Joe, you take care of the princess and her daughter and keep Mai company, and I'm just going to mill around."

I turned to everybody and I says, "Can I get you all a drink?" And I went and got them drinks and I stood there and I took care of them, and everytime they wanted a drink, I'd go and get it, and if they wanted hors d'oeuvres, I got them, so they didn't have to go to the table or anything. We just stood around and we talked, God knows what the hell about. I was more interested in having a conversation with Mai than anything else. We were laughing and joking.

Now, Sammy Davis was sitting in the corner playing the drums. I'd never met him. I was so involved talking to these people and other people walking up and saying hello, that I didn't notice that Frank and Dean and Harold and the whole crew were sliding out of the room and into another room that had two big security guards on the door. I see them, but I figure this is an open party and when this thing breaks up, there's a private party in the other room, but I've got no problem with that because I'm with Mai Britt and I got invited.

All of a sudden, with my back turned, I get a shove. It's Sammy. He grabs Mai by the arm and he says, "Come on. Come with me."

She's trying to give me the glass and making excuses. "Excuse me, Joe, I have to go." And he dragged her off like she was some kind of tramp or something and he was abusing her all the time.

Maybe he was stoned out of his mind, but it made me feel terrible because I felt like maybe he thought I was doing something that I wasn't and he made it like she was guilty or something.

He dragged her right into the private room and I'm still standing there with the princess and her daughter and some other people. Now, the princess is getting ready to leave and she says to me in Italian that she was very pleased to have met me and if I was ever in Italy, I should please call on her and let her know and they would take me to dinner and show me Rome the way Rome should be shown. And then they excused themselves.

Now, I walked over to the door where these two big security guards are standing, and I know my girl and the other three girls that I brought are in that room and I'm standing there and it looks like I'm the last of the Mohicans. I walk up and I says, "How do I get into this room?"

They had a place board in front of them with the list of names of people that was allowed to go into that room, and if your name wasn't on the list, you didn't go in. So, the one guard says, "Can we have your name, sir?"

I says, "Sure. Joe Franco."

He looked down the list and he says, "Sorry, Mr. Franco, your name's not on the list."

"Do me a favor. Will you go in there and get Harold Gibbons and tell him Joe Franco's outside?"

"Sorry, sir, we're not allowed to go in there, either."

I says, "Wait a minute. My wife's in there. I want to get her the fuck out. I want to go home. Now, if you can't go in there and I can't go in there, what do I do, leave my wife here?"

Well, we got into one big hell of an argument and I was ready to start kicking the fucking door down. I says, "I don't give a shit about the other three girls, but don't fuck around with the girl I'm going with." I was one hot son of a bitch. On top of what Sammy Davis done to me and the embarrassment with Mai Britt, now I lost four girls. All this big fucking talk about Frank Sinatra and all the beautiful broads and all the parties and everything else, to me I haven't seen a fucking party yet.

I went back to the hotel and it was about one o'clock in the morning. I turned on the TV and I just sat there and I dozed off and it got to be about five in the morning and the phone rings. Who's on the phone? Harold Gibbons. He says, "What are you doing, you dago bastard? Where did you disappear to?"

"You motherfucker, you. Harold, I'm gonna break your fucking head when I see you. You introduce me. You invite me to a party, the great Sinatra party, and I think I'm gonna have a good time. You take me over and you dump me on the princess, the Pope's sister. How'm I gonna get lucky with the Pope's sister? And Mai Britt, I was standing there talking and that little fucking midget comes over and grabs her by the arm and drags her off like she was a piece of shit. Embarrassed me, embarrassed her."

"Frank was looking, we were looking . . ."

"Don't give me that bullshit."

"Skinny and I are coming over right now."

"I don't give a fuck if you do or you don't." And I hung up.

About a half hour later, up comes Skinny and Harold. Harold says, "Come on, we're all going to meet over at the Fountainbleu down in the coffee shop and we're going to have breakfast."

I says, "Harold, I'll come there for one reason, to find out what happened to the girl I'm going with. I don't care what you did with the other three girls, but if I find out anybody fucked with my girl, first I'm gonna slap the shit out of her and second I'm gonna break somebody's fucking arm. So, expect that. You still want me to come for breakfast?"

He says, "Wait a minute. As far as your girl was concerned, nobody screwed around with her. That was your girl. How this thing got screwed up, Joe, honest to God . . ."

And Skinny says, "Honest to Christ, Joe, we didn't know your name was not on the list."

I says, "Hey, you know, Skinny, you're a nice guy. I love you. But don't bullshit a bullshitter. My name wasn't on the fucking list? You should have checked it before you went into that goddamn room. You should have come over and got me and said, Joe, excuse yourself, we're all going into the room. And if you didn't see me in there within an hour, then you should have come out and looked for me. You guys got no goddamn outs. You got bullshit here. Take your invitations, Harold, and tell Sinatra he can shove them up his ass. Don't invite me to no more of your fucking parties where I got to throw the party. All he did was supply the booze. I supplied the broads."

Well, I was one hot son of a bitch. They cooled me off and we ended up going down to the Fountainbleu about seven in the morning. Nobody's gone to bed as far as the whole crew is concerned. Peter Lawford's down there and Pat Henry and Jilly Rizzo and a shit house full of people. But Frank wasn't down there and he was upstairs in bed, and Dean wasn't there and Joey wasn't there and Sammy wasn't there. But there was my little Greek girl and she got up and came over and gave me a kiss and she says, "I sat there looking for you and nobody knew what happened to you."

I says, "We'll talk about that when we leave here."

As we were ducking out, Harold says, "I'm getting out of here this afternoon."

I says, "Okay. You know where I'm at. The old man's got me down here for the next couple of months. Leave word for me at Petey Fox's whenever you're in town so I'll know how to reach out for you because you know I don't like to stay in one place too long so I'm going to be jumping around like a grasshopper."

Now, about six months to a year later, and there's Sammy Davis again. There was a nightclub in Windsor, Ontario, one of the prestige clubs, and it was called the Elmwood Casino. That was like a second home to me. The girls in the line were all friends of mine and so was the house singer, a kid named Chris Columbo who was related to Russ Columbo, the original crooner before Bing Crosby. Al Segal, who owned it, and his wife were very dear friends of mine, and so was everybody who worked there. A young Japanese guy was working there at the time and he was teaching me to speak Japanese and I was teaching him to speak Italian, and I would introduce him as the only Japanese Sicilian in the world. All the biggest stars in the world appeared there.

Now, I walked in one night, not knowing, because I never looked to see who was appearing, it was like me going there to have dinner instead of going home, and I was dating one of the line girls on the side. As I drove up, I saw the marquee and it says, Sammy Davis. I says, well, will you look at this. It hadn't been too long before that he and Mai Britt got married.

When I walked in, everybody was sitting back in the Cantonese Room and everybody says hello to me. I could hear somebody saying, "Joe, Joe," not too loud, just loud enough so I could hear. I looked up and on this little balcony back there was this little blonde girl sitting by herself and I says, for God's sake, it's Mai Britt. I didn't go up on the balcony. I stayed on the lower end and went over there and shook hands with her and congratulated her and wished her all the happiness in the world. I says, "I really didn't know that you and Sammy were going together that night in Florida, the last time we saw each other. I know you were embarrassed."

She says, "Please, Joe, honest to God, I was so embarrassed. It's not like Sammy. He'd been drinking that night."

"Honey, look, don't make excuses for the man. You love the man, you married him, I hope you have all the happiness in the world. If you ever need me for anything, you know you can always get hold of me through Harold Gibbons."

Well, from out of nowhere, here comes the little son of a bitch again. He comes over, sees me, doesn't say shit to me, grabs her again by the arm and drags her and pulls her down the stairs and goes back to the dressing room, which was all the way through the aisle, through the corridor, back into the nightclub, and to the back entrance to the dressing room. And you could hear him swearing and hollering at her, like as if there was a big thing between me and Mai Britt or something. Let me tell you, I was goddamn mad.

The next day, I got a telephone call from Chris Columbo and he says, "Joe, Sammy has this guy working for him as a bodyguard. A big black guy, must be six five and two hundred eighty pounds. He's real tough. And if you should come in here he is going to beat the shit out of you."

"You got to be kidding."

Well, it was about eleven o'clock in the morning. I says to Chris, "Tell the girls I'm coming over and tell the chef that I want to set up a lunch buffet for all the girls." I used to do that every once in a while when they were practicing a whole new show, which they were doing at the time with a choreographer that was in from Vegas.

Now, I had three agents working for me at that time, at one of the locals that I was repping, and I told all three of them to come over and grab iron and we're going to Windsor. We got something to do. And I says to them, "Here's what I want you to do. I'm going to sit down ringside with the girls and Chris Columbo. I want you three guys to sit back maybe eight, nine tables. And if this big black dude comes over to the table, as soon as you see him come over to the table and I have him sit down, I want you to come over and put the barrels in each of his ears and one in the back of his neck."

So, we go over to Windsor and we walk in and they sat where

I told them and I sat down with Chris. Chris says, "Oh, Jesus, Joe, don't start nothing."

I says, "Chris, go back there and kind of hint that guess who's out front buying the girls lunch."

So, he went back and he made it known and then here comes Chris on the stage and he gives me the signal that the big black dude is coming around the back end. Here he comes, through the back door, coming through the club. I'm at the first table where you come around the corner from the turn. He walks over to the table and he says, "Are you Joe Franco?"

"Yeah." I never stood up. I just sat there, holding my left hand inside my pants like I always do, and I had my jacket open. "Yeah, I'm Joe Franco. What about it?"

"Well, things don't look right."

"Hold it, friend. Before we go any fucking further with your conversation, number one, I don't like your fucking looks, number two, sit your fucking ass down because I don't dig the idea of looking fucking up to you. If anybody's going to do it, I'm going to look down on you. I don't want you to look down on me and I don't want to look up at you. Now, get your ass down on that fucking chair so you and I can talk."

As soon as he sat down, the three guys came over and two of them stuck a pistol in each of his ears and the other one stuck it behind his head. When they did that, I looked at him and I says, "Now, you were about to say something to me. What the fuck do you want? What were you going to tell me?" I went up this black cat's ass one way and I went down the other, and he turned white. I says, "I'm gonna tell you something, partner, I tell my guys to cut loose, they all pull the trigger at the same time, there's gonna be three slugs going through your head and if we do it right, all three are going to meet in the middle and you know what that's going to do to the inside of your head? It's going to blow the top of the roof off your head and it's going to scramble your brains up so there ain't nothing left inside your head, you're going to look like an empty fucking watermelon.

"If I was you, pal, I'd find somebody else to fucking work for. And I'm giving you some good advice. And I'm going to give you some more good advice. When you go into a strange town and you're going to do something to somebody, you'd better find out who you're supposed to do it to, you'd better check out and see who the man is. You know better than that.

"I'll tell you what you do. You're a nice kid. You seem like a pretty nice guy. Okay, you guys back off, take the barrels out of his ears because I think it's starting to bother him a little bit. Go back and sit down and have something to eat."

He says, "Goddamn, I'll tell you something. I never felt such cold iron. My ears are frozen. That iron was so cold, Mr. Franco, it went down to my toes. I never felt the hairs in the back of my neck raise up the way they did."

So, he took off. In a couple of minutes, Chris Columbo comes back on the stage and he's laughing so hard he's almost falling off the stage. Sammy didn't know which way to get out. There's only two ways out, through the back and through the club. He didn't know which way to go, only that he had to get out of there. He didn't know where to hide. Chris is laughing his ass off. He comes over and he says, "That son of a bitch just got the fuck out of there. He didn't go through the back, he didn't go through the club, he went through the other dressing room and came out through the kitchen and out of the Cantonese Room and out the backside of the joint to the motel."

I never saw Mai Britt after that. They had a couple of kids and then I read they got a divorce.

And then there was Frank Sinatra. But that was complex and involved a critical situation for Jimmy Hoffa. It came at another time and in another context.

12

Since the New Deal's emancipation of labor, the unions have been the handmaidens of the politicians, and the politicians have been the handmaidens of the unions. Anyone familiar with Washington or with the state capitals knows that when the legislatures are in session, one of the more familiar sights is the minions of labor wandering the halls, deep in conversation with the representatives of the people. That an alliance was forged between labor and the politicians, especially Democratic politicians, was no more surprising than the alliance that had long existed between business and the politicians, especially Republicans. Both had much to gain from such an entente. The politicians got labor's support when election time came and, if venal, a little cash on the side. Labor got support for legislation it considered essential to foster its cause and, when the right politician came along, unquestioning ownership of a vote.

Very early in his career with the Teamsters, Franco became a registered lobbyist for the Teamsters and the distillery workers and other unions allied with the Teamsters, both at the Michigan state capital in Lansing and the nation's capital in Washington. As such, he came to know everyone who was anyone in government, on both the state and national levels. He was on friendly terms with the Speaker of the House of Representatives, Sam Rayburn of Texas. He was able to ask and be granted simple favors, such as the appointment of the son of a friend as a congressional page. He was able to ask and be granted more important favors, such as the Speaker's backing of legislation that Franco and Hoffa thought was essential to their cause. Through Rayburn, he met and formed a casual relationship with another powerful Texan, Senate Majority Leader, Lyndon Baines Johnson. Although a Democrat, Franco did not ignore the Republicans if he thought they might be useful, and so he came to number among his close political friends the Republican governor of California, Goodwin Knight, whom he and Hoffa thought might make a good president.

The more Franco learned about politics, the more he became entranced with it.

I loved the intrigue of it. I dug politics. I was on the outside of it and never knew what was happening on the inside of it, and that used to bug me. When they would go into caucus rooms and I wasn't part of it and I wasn't a district delegate or anything, I'd always say, I'd love to be on the inside of that room and know the real fucking dirt that's coming down. What makes our government tick? What makes these candidates spend $300,000 or $400,000 for a job that's going to pay less than $50,000 a year? I could never figure that one out. There was one guy that was the purchasing agent for the state of Michigan for the liquor industry who used to wear $65 shoes and wear $45 gloves and he was a civil service employee making $21,000 a year. I says, there's got to be something in this politics. That's what really got me involved in it.

When I first got into the Teamsters, I immediately got involved with the Young Democrats in Michigan. Pretty soon, I was moving up the ladder. It wasn't that long before I was on the executive committee and then I became executive chairman of the Young Democrats for the state of Michigan and I was chairman of the screening committee as far as endorsements went in Michigan for COPE, which was the political action of all the unions. And I was one of the guys that started the Dearborn Senators Club and the Wayne County Civic League Club, which was where we would bring any politician for lunch that was running for something, like judge or congressman or anything, to listen to him and see if he would get our endorsement.

Of course, I was Jimmy's man and I was representing him and doing what he wanted done. Jimmy was a Republican, but that didn't mean he didn't have a say when he wanted to. He'd put out the word, "I want Franco there," and I'd be there. He knew I loved it and he knew if he told me so-and-so is running for something, make sure he gets an endorsement, he'd get the endorsement.

It wasn't that Jimmy loved politics or politicians or even wanted that much to do with them. He and Bert Brennan believed the same thing, that politicians were all whores and all they wanted was money, but when you needed them, they ain't gonna be there because they walk away from you because they're gonna get heat. So, his theory was, fuck 'em, give 'em the money and throw 'em out of the office. That's the way the Teamsters operated politically in Michigan most of the time and that's why the UAW had the political power and we didn't. The UAW was very much involved in politics and they would go out and canvas and they captured congressional districts and everything. A kid named Jimmy Hannan, who was a state senator at the time, and myself, we kept trying to get Hoffa and the Teamsters to recognize that the Teamsters ought to be completely involved in politics in Michigan and to let us go out and set up committees in all the congressional districts and everything else and not simply hand out money and secretly endorse candidates. But Jimmy didn't want to do that because he didn't have any use for politicians.

At the time, we had a governor named G. Mennen Williams, who they called Soapy because his family was in the business. Now when Soapy first ran for governor, he had Walter Reuther and the UAW behind him and, funny as it was, Jimmy also endorsed him, and he won. But his loyalty leaned toward Walter and the UAW, and anytime there was anti-trucking legislation coming up, we would send our lobbyists up to Lansing, but Soapy took pretty much a hands-off policy as far as the Teamsters were concerned. He never did anything for Jimmy, so after a while Jimmy didn't have any use for him.

Now there was a new election coming up and naturally all the politicians were coming around looking for money and endorsements. Of course, they don't come around themselves, they send a flunky and he says, "I'm representing the governor and he's asking for your endorsement and your support. We'd like to set something up and we'd like to know what kind of financial support and other support we can expect." Well, Jimmy says no, and that started a hell of an argument between Soapy and Jimmy, which never healed, and as far as Soapy Williams was concerned after that, anything that was Teamster and Hoffa, he was 100 percent against.

I'd walked into his office in the capital with Jimmy Hannan and he'd see the big diamond Teamster pin in my lapel and he'd always say to one of his aides, "What the hell is Senator Hannan doing with that goddamn Teamster because I don't want them around here?" But I not only represented the Teamsters, I represented the AFL at that time and later the AFL-CIO and COPE and I knew it used to aggravate the hell out of him whenever he saw me in the office.

Now there comes along a young man who was married into the Briggs family, which owned the Detroit Tigers and a lot of other things. His name was Philip Hart. He was a lawyer and he'd been a government attorney and the family wanted Phil to become a judge. I liked Phil and I remember times going into the governor's office and down the hall was this little office, about ten by nine, just big enough for a desk and a chair and another chair and that was Phil Hart's office. He was the legal assistant to Soapy. He'd come out when he knew Jimmy Hannan and I were there and with his finger he'd wave us down and we'd sit down with him and talk. He was like a lost entity and Soapy only put up with him because the Briggs family endorsed him and made a great contribution to his campaign.

After a couple of terms, Soapy stopped being happy as governor and he wanted to be a senator and maybe go on to the White House from there. There was this political commentator from Michigan who was working in Washington named Blair Moody and he was very well liked. It was decided that he ought to run for senator on the ticket with Soapy for governor and Phil Hart for lieutenant governor.

At that moment, in 1954, Blair Moody was one of the leading political writers in the nation's capital and moderator of a major political talk show. Three years earlier, in 1951, Williams had

*appointed him to the Senate to fill out the unexpired term of
Republican Senator Arthur Vandenberg who had recently died. At
Williams's behest, Moody, though he had no real taste for active
participation in elective politics, ran for a full term. He was
narrowly defeated in the Eisenhower landslide of 1952. But his
personal conduct in the campaign won him a legion of supporters
and his trenchant political writing and commentary further
enhanced his reputation, both on the national scene and at home
in Michigan. Williams and others began to put pressure on him to
run for the Senate once more, in 1954, against Senator Homer
Ferguson, a Republican of conservative bent whose standing with
Michigan voters was sinking rapidly.*

It was a great ticket, an unbeatable ticket. Blair was so well liked
and Soapy was very popular. The only weak sister was Phil Hart,
because nobody knew Phil other than that he was legal aide to the
governor. But that didn't mean anything because Soapy and Blair
would sweep him in with them. Now the deal was that once everybody won, Blair would quit the Senate pretty quick and Soapy
would resign as governor and Phil, who would be the new governor, would appoint Soapy to the Senate.

Now, Hoffa got the word that Soapy wanted to meet with him
to talk about the campaign. Jimmy refused and that built an even
bigger bonfire between them. So, what happened was I became
kind of a liaison between Jimmy and the governor's office.

We got word that Blair was coming into town and he wanted
to meet with Jimmy, and Jimmy liked Blair. So he says to me, "Go
to the airport and pick up Senator Moody." We were already calling him senator. "And bring him back to the office."

So, I went to the airport and Blair and I got to be pretty good
friends. He says to me, "I don't want to be a United States senator.
I'm a newspaper man and I love it. I would like to have my own
newspaper."

I says, "Is that what you're coming in to see the old man
about?"

"Yeah. And after I get through with him, I have to run up to
Lansing to talk to the governor."

"Well, if you want me to, I'd be more than happy to drive you
up there. But I'll tell you one thing, if he sees me with you, he

knows that you've seen Hoffa and that won't sit too well. So, we'll make some arrangement and we'll get you up to Lansing, don't worry."

We both damn near got killed that day. Driving back to the office from the airport, I had a front-end blowout and went off the road into a ditch and we were lucky we survived, because I was going about eighty-five miles an hour at the time. That really made us close because there was no way we could ever forget that thing.

Anyway, we went in and he sat with Jim and Jim gave him a commitment that he would assist him financially if he ran for the Senate, but he would have to sit there until Jim told him it was okay and then Jim would give him the money that was necessary for him to open up his own newspaper. They agreed to it and we got him up to Lansing.

Now, I had my leaks in the capital plus the fact that Phil Hart would always fill Jimmy Hannan in and so we found out that Blair made a deal with Soapy where he would run for senator and Soapy would replace him after a while and Soapy would give him whatever financial aid he needed to open up that newspaper. So, now he had two deals, and Jimmy knew about the one with Soapy but Soapy didn't know about the one with Jimmy. But Jimmy wasn't worried. Because he was willing for Blair to quit the Senate after a while and let Soapy move in, he just wanted Soapy to swing for a couple of months until he gave Blair the okay to get out and that would make Soapy pretty damn nervous.

Everything was moving along just right until one day we were having a labor convention up in Grand Rapids, and the Teamsters were still part of the AFL, and I'm walking in the door and this guy Johnny Williams is giving out a stack of cards. Johnny and I were very tight, friendshipwise and politically.

He says, "Help me out, Joe."

"What've you got?"

"I'm running MacNamara for the Senate."

I broke up laughing. "What? Are you nuts or something? Against Williams, Moody, and Hart?" Now, old Mac was a pipe fitter and he ran his own local union as well as he knew how to run it, but old Mac was a little sipper, he loved his booze.

Johnny Williams says, "Joe, you know we just can't let them run loose. They'll walk in with no opposition. This is just my way of getting a little at Soapy." He and Soapy didn't get along, but the only labor guy the governor got along with was Walter Reuther.

He gave me some cards and as people walked by, I'd give them a card which said, "Here's a donation of five dollars and I will support MacNamara for the United States Senate." I stood there and I'm shaking my head and I'm saying, "I don't believe what we're doing. We're gonna be the laughingstock of this goddamn convention." But sure as hell, guys are taking cards and filling them up and giving us a fin. Whether they would have ever voted for MacNamara would have been another question. But we got enough petitions filed to register him as a candidate to run in the primary.

Now, here comes MacNamara with a little bulletin that he's running, and here comes big posters, all kinds of posters from Moody and Williams and Phil Hart. Well, the old man upstairs has his ways of resolving problems. Without any notice, Blair Moody has a heart attack and dies just a few weeks before the primary. Who does that leave? Old Mac. I understand Soapy Williams opened up a window and wanted to jump out except his aides stopped him.

There's nobody left to run in the primary now with Williams and Phil Hart but MacNamara. And who's in back of MacNamara? Jimmy Hoffa, and Johnny Williams is his key guy. And MacNamara's headquarters is in the basement of my home, and he used my office at Local 42 of the Distillery Workers. And the phone is ringing all the time. Soapy calls and he has a big meeting with Mac. Walter Reuther calls and they have a big meeting and they agree to throw their support behind him because they got no place else to go. Johnny Williams comes to me and he says, "Jesus Christ, Joe, we got a winner." Everybody is trying to make a deal, through Johnny Williams, through me, and trying to get to MacNamara. And they're trying to work through Hoffa, because Hoffa's coming through with cash and advertising and all the bullshit. He calls me in and he calls Johnny Williams in and he says, "You got my full cooperation to get MacNamara elected, but I don't want to hear about Soapy Williams or anything else."

Now, Mac wasn't the smartest man in the world, but sometimes he knew how to handle himself. He had a meeting with G. Mennen Williams and he agreed to go on the ticket with him and Phil Hart, but in no way did he commit himself that he would retire so Williams could take over. Williams was stuck with it.

So, the ticket won and Mac became the senator and later Soapy quit as governor when Jack Kennedy was elected president, and became an ambassador, which he fucked up, and Phil Hart ended up being governor after all and then he got elected to the Senate himself. And Phil had an understanding with Jimmy and he was very pro-Teamster and very pro-UAW, whichever way he could help labor, he was always there. And he never forgot the days when Jim helped him and supported him financially and the fact that Jimmy Hannan and myself was always there in his support and he knew the work we did for him, like going out day and night and pulling down Republican posters and putting up Hart posters, and getting my locals and my people in the Young Democrats to work their asses off for him.

As for Mac, he tippled the bottle pretty good while he was in Washington. He was on one of the committees that was investigating Jimmy and the Teamsters and I remember Mac being up in the office and I was standing by the door, ready to come in, and Jimmy was just finishing up, and he was saying, "Listen, you dumb fucking Irishman, I put you in there, now just do me a fucking favor. Don't say anything good about me and don't say anything bad about me. Just sit there and shut up." That's exactly what the good senator from the state of Michigan did. He just sat there and never said a goddamn word.

Franco might have been a Democrat, not out of any deep philosophical commitment, but simply because the Democrats welcomed labor; despite Hoffa, the Republicans did not. Franco was probably closer philosophically to the Republicans than he was to his own party, for he was essentially a conservative who believed, for instance, that Senator Joe McCarthy of Wisconsin was right: There were communists lurking everywhere and they ought to be exposed and thrown out of government and everywhere else. As much as he knew politics and politicians, Franco maintained for a time a deep veneration of those who held the highest offices, especially Dwight David Eisenhower. He might reach into the governor's office in the state capital; he might

wander through the corridors of Congress; but he believed the
White House and its occupants were far beyond his reach.

Through Tony Martin down in Miami, I got to know Al
Brode, who was a big stockbroker and a lot of other things, and his
wife had a TV show down in Miami and people used to call her the
lady in red.

I remember one time we were sitting around the pool, Tony
Martin and Tony Bennett and I, and Al Brode came over and he
tells Tony Martin and Tony Bennett and me, "I want you guys to
go to the telephone, call your stockbroker, and I want each of you
to buy Chock Full o' Nuts." It had just come on the market and it
was selling real low. Tony Martin and the others went out and
made the calls. I didn't, because I wasn't really into the market
area. But the next day, we were sitting around the pool and the
thing jumped like five points and before you knew it was up like
twenty points. That's what kind of a guy Al Brode was, a real
classy man. If he saw a good stock, he would tip you off on it. I
don't think I ever had a loser with Al in all the years after I got
into buying stocks. He kind of taught me what to do and before
that I didn't know anything about the stock market.

Al and his wife kind of took to me. Now she had this TV show
and she was pushing Eisenhower for president because she was a
staunch Republican and she was one of the people that helped
convince him in 1952 to run. After he was elected, she remained
very close and tight with Eisenhower and she was in and out of the
White House a lot.

One day, Al Brode called me up in Detroit and asked me if I
was doing anything. I said no. He says, "Why don't you come into
Washington and meet with me and the wife and have dinner with
us." They didn't say where. He says, "Come on in, Joe, spend the
day and we'll do some talking and we'll have dinner and then you
can fly out in the morning."

I says, "Okay, that sounds pretty good to me." In those days,
I always wore and a black mohair suit. They were very fashionable.
So, I wore the black mohair with a black tie, white on white rolled
collar shirt. I wore a tie that time. I got into Washington and they
picked me up in a big limo.

I says, "Where are we going for dinner?"

Al says, "We're going to the White House."

"Whoa, hold the phone. I'm not dressed for that. You people are."

She was dressed up in a beautiful gown with jewelry up to your tush, and Al was all decked out in a tuxedo.

"Hold it, I'm sitting here with a suit. I just came out of an office, for chrissake. I just left my office. This is the way I left the house this morning. I'm not going to go and have dinner with . . . where you guys are going. You're going to the White House? Are you crazy?"

He says, "Don't worry about it. Just mind your p's and q's. You're with me and the wife, Joe, don't worry about it. Ike's a plain nice man and Mamie's a nice lady."

We went there and we had dinner, the five of us, in a room if I remember right was on the second floor. It wasn't the main dining room where they hold forty, fifty people for presidential dinners. It was very intimate and very small. It was a very nice room and that's where Ike and Mamie would have their own dinners. All five of us just sat there and, hell, I couldn't even hold a fork in my hands I was so goddamn nervous. A few times, Ike directed some questions to me and I'm saying to myself, oh, God, please don't ask me what my affiliations are, and I'm saying, oh, I forgot, I got a big Teamster button on my lapel with a diamond in it that I always wore. It got me into a lot of trouble at times and it got me out of trouble other times. And I'm saying to myself, oh, God, if he spots that, there's no way I can take it off because if I take it off, it's going to be very noticeable. I'm sure he saw it, but he was a very nice man, a very gracious man, and he never asked me my affiliation and I'm sure he saw it was a Teamster pin, you couldn't miss the Teamster emblem.

Ike and Al and Al's wife, they spoke about their own businesses. It was just a nice, quiet, sociable dinner. I was taught many years ago, if you don't know what to say, just keep your mouth shut and nobody will know how dumb you are. If a discussion comes up and you do know and definitely know what the subject is about and you can interject something that has meaning, fine, go ahead and say something. But if it doesn't have anything that would affect the discussion or be something that would be of some importance, keep your goddamn mouth shut. Just nod your head and nobody will know you're dumb or you have no idea what's going on. That's the way I handled myself.

But I was nervous as a cat on a hot tin roof. And Mamie, she was a lovely lady but she had her problems and I'm sure Ike put up with it for some years. Because during the course of the evening that poor soul, she just had a little too much, she became a little tipsy and she was very jolly and she was very friendly, which made me feel a little easier. I'm saying to myself, by God, they're just human beings. She drinks and he doesn't, or maybe he had a little this and a little that, but he wasn't that much of a drinker. So, Al and his wife and I were very comfortable with them and it was a very enjoyable evening.

I never became involved with the White House on that type of basis after that. And after I started to hit the front pages in the middle and late sixties, I kind of stayed away from Al and his wife and everybody who was part of my legitimate life that held high positions in politics or business, and I kind of lost contact with everybody. I'm sure if I would have continued my association with them, I would have caused them some embarrassment and I didn't want to do that to these friends.

By the early 1960s, Franco was considered a major power in Michigan Democratic politics. There were even some who thought, were it not for his close ties with Hoffa and rumors of friendships with the "outside element," that Franco might have been considered seriously as a candidate for governor of Michigan. With his good looks, winning personality, and power in labor and the Democratic party, he might have won. The governor's mansion was not Franco's mind, though; a seat in Congress was what interested him.

I kept working away in politics and then the congressman from the Fourteenth Congressional District in Wayne County, Louis Raubeau, died, so there's a vacancy. I says, "Hey, here's my shot. I'm gonna be a congressman."

I got hold of some of the Young Democrats and Jimmy Hannan and quite a few other guys that was very active in politics, and I told them, "I'm gonna take a shot at it. This is a predominantly Italian district and the name Franco, well, I'm getting a million dollars worth of free advertising with Franco-American Spaghetti." I went out and got petitions and I filed to run for congressman.

Al Barber came to me then. Al was a brilliant young guy and a good labor man, but he was UAW. Not that he was anti-Teamster, he was pro-UAW and his loyalty was to Walter Reuther. Al says, "Harold Rhine is going to be coming in front of the COPE screening committee and then coming in front of the executive committee and as far as COPE is concerned, we're endorsing him for Congress."

I says, "Hold the phone. Why?"

He says, "Well, he's a state senator."

"He's a piece of shit. He doesn't know what he's doing, for chrissake. If a bill comes up and the UAW tells him what to do, he does it. He'll vote whichever way somebody tells him to vote. Harold's a nice guy, but he should never be in politics."

Now, I had eight state representatives and six state senators that were dues-paying members of Local 42, and Harold was a member of my local. So, I had political clout. I knew that with all that, I'd have no problems. I knew I could win the primary because they would all come out behind me and so would the Young Democrats.

I called the guy who was the head of the Young Democrats at that moment. "Mickey, do me a favor. Get the committee together. I'm running for Congress."

He says, "Great. It's about time we got back into business."

"Okay. Now, find me four guys whose names is Harold E. Rhine and I want them all black."

Now Harold was Polish and this was a predominantly Italian and Irish neighborhood, but there was a strong Polish segment moving in. But there were damn few blacks. I was going to print up those little tickets they pass out and they would say, "Vote for Harold E. Rhine," and the picture on it would be of a black guy. Not that we were discriminating or anything, it was just a way of killing Harold Rhine's chances in the primary. We did just that. We went ahead and paid a hundred dollars and got the petitions in and went out for the printing and got five hundred of those cards for each of the four black guys named Harold Rhine and started handing them out.

It floated back to Al Barber and I got a call. He says, "I want to talk to you."

I says, "Okay." Now, Hoffa knew what I was doing, because I was telling him, "Hey, Jim, I'm gonna run for Congress."

He says, "Go ahead. You'll get all our support. You need money, holler." Jim knew exactly what I was doing all the time.

Al and I meet and he shows me one of the cards and he says, "Joe, don't bullshit me. This is a typical Franco political move."

I looked at him. "What makes you think I would do that to one of my own members of my local?"

"Because I know that you want to be congressman from the Fourteenth Congressional. But I'm the boss of the Fourteenth. If I endorse you, you're elected. If I don't endorse you, you ain't elected."

"I'll tell you something, Albert, we got a stalemate. He's got to come in front of the screening committee, and I don't approve him, he don't get approved. He's got to come in front of COPE and I don't approve him for COPE, he ain't gonna have any fucking money. Now what have we got? You gonna endorse him or are you gonna endorse me? I'm the guy you got to endorse. I'm on your executive committee, for chrissake. He's a state senator. I want to be a United States congressman. I think I'm entitled to it. I think I can win it."

He says, "Joe, we've already given our word to him. Solidarity House and the red head have already given their word they're gonna endorse him. How the hell do we back off?"

I says, "Just stay neutral. I'll fucking bury him in the primary."

In the meantime, another guy sees what's happening and he comes into the picture. His name is Lucien Nedzi and he's Polish and there's those Poles coming into the district. He files. So, now there's Harold Rhine and then four black Harold Rhines and Joe Franco and this Nedzi. I'm not worrying about Harold Rhine anymore. Now, I'm starting to direct all my efforts toward Nedzi, to find out where the hell did this guy come from.

Al Barber calls me up. He says, "Joe, we got a goddamn mess on our hands. Nedzi's gonna be strong with all the Poles and they're gonna put a lot of money behind him and they're gonna really push him. We've got a goddamn problem. Do me a favor, will you? Will you back off and pull all your goddamn bullshit off the street and tell your Young Dems to pull off? You do and I'll appoint you drain commissioner of Wayne County."

I says, "How much does it pay?"

"Twenty-eight thousand a year."

"How much time do I got to give?"

"You're lucky if you give two hours a month."

"Okay, but you got to promise me, the next shot that's open, I get it."

And I'm saying to myself, drain commissioner? It could be a hell of a thing. I says, "What about the guy that's in there now?"

He says, "Joe, I can use you because the guy that's in it, he doesn't know what's going on. I can appoint you right away and I can use you right away and you'd be perfect there."

"All right, we make a deal on that. The money's all right plus you're gonna commit yourself that the next congressional seat that opens up, I get it." I was still a young man then and I figured I could wait four or six years down the line. We shook hands and we made a deal and in a couple of months he would appoint me drain commissioner.

Then I start getting subpoenas and indictments and that was the end of my political career. Hoffa called me in and he says, "You know, Franco, if it wasn't for bad luck you wouldn't have no fucking luck at all."

I says, "What am I going to do? I would have been a United States congressman, would you believe it. I blew it because you get into a fucking argument with Bobby Kennedy. You got to start that shit, it reflects back on me and I get indicted, I get all this bullshit. What am I gonna do?"

It all ended up that Harold Rhine lost it anyway and Nedzi won it and he's a nice man and a good congressman.

13

The strands of Franco's life, the spider web as he called it, crossed and intermingled and meshed in intricate and complex patterns, ever changing and shifting. There was the union, the core of all things, and through the union he walked freely into the worlds of industry and politics and show business; and through the union he walked with equanimity, sometimes on a high road and sometimes on a low one, depending on what he saw as necessary and what Hoffa ordered.

If there were constants, they were his family, with all their problems, and he tried to keep Alice and the children separated from the pressures on him. He was not always successful. There were the girls who inevitably filled the lonely hours on the road, but they were only passing fancies. There was Hoffa, his boss and idol. By the end of the 1950s, Hoffa was in Washington much of the time, operating the Teamsters out of international headquarters. Franco still saw him whenever he came into Detroit, which was nearly every week, or when Franco was in Washington, or when they were both in some other city. Hoffa remained at the center of his life and Franco saw their relationship as basically unchanged and unchanging. Indeed, Hoffa was still not above throwing dirty work at Franco, jobs that required the kind of expertise Franco had developed in the early days and which Hoffa never let him forget or discard.

And there were his partners, Tom Burke and Frank Fitzsimmons. But in 1958, those relationships changed.

★ ★ ★

Jimmy called me and Tommy Burke in during the summer of 1958 and gave us an assignment. He was sitting behind his desk and he says, "I want you two guys to go into Cleveland and I want you to blow up this cleaning plant. Tommy, you take care of whatever has to be done and you, Franco, take care of it. I'm assigning two other teams to two other different areas to do the same thing."

He didn't tell us the names of the guys on the other teams, but one was to go into Pontiac, Michigan, and the other team was to go into St. Louis. To this day, I don't know who he sent into St. Louis. But I do know what happened up in Pontiac, because that hit all the papers when Frank and Doc Kierdorf blew the place and Frank burned himself up.

Now, basically, the Teamsters were not involved with the cleaning industry and we were not organizing them. It was another union, the laundry workers. Tom and I discussed it and we decided that Jimmy was doing a favor for Moe Dalitz who was the big boss of the laundries, giving a message to the guys that owned the plants and to the whole industry that they were being organized and they'd better not make any trouble.

At midnight on the right night, I went over to the Book-Cadillac Hotel where Tommy was living and we took off for Cleveland. On the way, I asked Tommy if everything was taken care of, like how many sticks of dynamite and what percent, 30 or 35 percent dynamite, because all Jimmy wanted was to have the front blown out to give the guy the message. Tommy says for me not to worry.

When we got into Cleveland, we stop and Tommy takes the satchel, like what you would take to a gym, and he opens it and takes out three sticks of dynamite and starts to tape them up.

I says, "Tommy, you told me you had that all ready. What the hell are you doing?"

"Well, I didn't have time. But I'll do it right now. We've got a lot of time."

"Goddammit, Tom, I tell you a million times I don't like that shit in the car. I don't like you doing it in the car. I don't mind doing what has to be done, but I don't want to be around it while you're setting the goddamn fuses, setting caps. I don't know anything about that and I'm scared to death of it. I don't want anything to happen to you or to me. In the fucking car, you fuck around with that cap and it goes, you and I are the ones that's gonna go, not the fucking cleaning plant."

I just blew my stack I was so goddamn mad. But Tommy just went right ahead and taped up the thing and took out a plug and plugged the dynamite and took a cap out and took a fuse out and put the fuse in the cap and then put it between his teeth and crunched down. At that point, I just cringed. I was expecting an explosion that would have blown his goddamn chin right off. It just bugged me and I told him so. I says, "That's it. You'll never do that to me again. For chrissake, Tommy, don't put me on the spot here. Did you check the fuse? Did you time the fuse? Did you put a stop clock on it?" You have to do that. Normally, you have to put a stop clock on the fuse to see if it's a good fuse or an old fuse that could be spotty, to see if it's running so many inches per minute or second so we'd know if we had a five-inch or a seven-inch fuse and it wouldn't have a bad spot on it and race like hell and then you'd find yourself short of time.

He says, "Yeah, don't worry, I got seven to ten minutes there."

"All right. Did you clock it?"

"Yeah, I took care of that. Don't worry about it."

"Okay. I'll set the dynamite and you drive."

We got off the road and we stopped after a couple of miles and we switched so he got in the driver's seat and I got on the passenger side. I was very upset with him. I took the five-pound bags of sand we had in the trunk, which we always carry and which we place up against the dynamite and it causes the dynamite to go inward instead of outward. Dynamite has a habit of reflecting off a wall or something, but with the sandbag, it would bounce back inward and would cause more damage. I put the sandbag in the back seat and got everything ready.

We drove up to the place and made sure everything was clear, and I finally got out and went over to the door and placed the three sticks of dynamite up against the door and put the sandbag up against it and grabbed the loose end of the fuse. I took out a cigarette and lit it and lit the fuse from it, and as soon as I lit it, I knew goddamn well it was not a normal seven-minute fuse. It just went like zippo, and I got up and ran like hell to get to the car. While I'm running, I'm telling Tommy to get the son of a bitch moving. He's slowly creeping away. As soon as I got halfway into the car, the door hadn't even closed yet, the dynamite went off and we felt the impact on the side of the car and I felt like someone slugged me in the back, and off we went.

We headed for Youngstown. We were going to stop over and see Joe Blumetti who was head of the local there. Well, the union office didn't open until eight-thirty, so we dillydallied around and stopped and got a cup of coffee and then we pulled into the parking lot about eight-thirty and walked into the office. I used to have a reputation of always kibitzing with the girls and partying around with the girls, so as soon as I walked in and we asked for Mr. Blumetti, some of the girls recognized us and says hello, and then all of a sudden one of the girls lets out a scream. With this, Joe Blumetti comes out and he says, "Jesus Christ, Franco, can't you stop screwing around with my goddamn help? Leave them girls alone."

"I didn't say nothing."

And the girls are all saying, "He didn't say nothing, Mr. Blumetti. But look at him."

He turned me around and he says, "Come on into the office," and he dragged me and pulled me into the office and he says, "Take your jacket off." I still didn't know and Tommy was standing there like he didn't know either. Then I realized that I was bleeding and I had been bleeding and by then it penetrated right through my jacket and down my leg and I was covered with blood and that's what made the girls afraid. They thought I got shot or something. Joe B. took my jacket and called the girl in and told her to take it and get it cleaned, and he took my shirt and gave me something to wear while I waited for the stuff to get cleaned and fixed.

In the meantime, I was pitching a bitch at Tommy Burke. I was screaming at him, "You see, you fucking Irishman you, you dirty son of a bitch, you fucking around and not doing it right, that's it. I'll never fucking work with you again. I end up with a piece of fucking glass in my back and just because you're a fuck up." I loved the guy but I was really pissed at him.

About nine-thirty, I called Washington, because I told Jimmy I would check in and let him know, because these things are synchronized so that all three places would be going at the same time, the one in St. Louis, the one in Pontiac, and the one we did in Cleveland. I says to Jim, "Everything went okay. I had a little problem but the problem can be handled."

He says, "All right. I want you in Washington. Send Tommy back to Detroit and you grab a plane and come into Washington."

"It'll be three, four hours because they had to send my clothes out to be cleaned. I'll tell you about it when I get there."

We made arrangements for a plane and as soon as I got my clothes back, I got on and got into Washington and took a cab over to the international building and went into Jimmy's office and told the secretary I was there, and she took me in.

Jim got up and shook hands. "How did everything go?"

"I had a little problem. Tommy fucked up. I'll never work with him again, Jim."

"What did he do?"

"One, he told me he had everything set, and then on the way there, he's fucking with the dynamite and he's setting fuses in the car and capping and biting down on the fuses. I don't mind doing what I got to do, but I told you right from the beginning, I don't know anything about fuses, I don't like fuses or caps, they're too tricky for me and I never worked in the goddamn coal mines. Of all the things for Tommy to do in the car, and it was our understanding he was supposed to have everything done and ready and finished before we took off, and he did this all in the car, and I blew my stack at him. And number two, I asked him if he clocked it and he said, yeah, we got seven minutes, and Jim, as soon as I lit the goddamn fuse, it took off like a goddamn scared rabbit and I just barely made it back to the car when she just let go. And it ripped the shit out of my back."

Jim says, "Well, all right, we'll talk about that later. Come on, we're going to go upstairs and get a cup of coffee."

While we're walking out of the office, he's telling me what happened to Frank Kierdorf when him and Doc blew the laundry in Pontiac and Frank came through the skylight, which he wasn't supposed to do because Jimmy didn't want the inside of the plant to be blown, he just wanted the outside so it showed things were happening against the cleaning industry. But Frank was the kind of guy that liked to do things very thorough, and if he's gonna do it, he's gonna blow the whole fucking building up. So he went through the skylight and set the dynamite up against naphtha gas tanks and lit the fuse and started back up and by the time he got just about out the skylight, the fuse hit the naphtha tank, not the dynamite, and the whole thing went up and blew him right out the skylight and through the roof and over the side and onto the ground where Doc was standing and he was burning and Doc put out the fire and rushed him to the hospital where he was dying.

Jim was telling me this and there was no feeling on Jim's part. He always felt shame on you if you got caught. If you did the job right, you got paid for it. If you did the job wrong and got caught, shame on you, that's not being professional. Not that he would walk away from you; he would support you and give you whatever you needed to get out of trouble. He wouldn't abandon you, he would just look down his nose at you and say, "You asshole, you got caught. In our business, you're not supposed to get caught." He felt like Frank fucked up and he didn't think very highly of it even though it cost Frank's life.

We were walking down the corridor and we got to an elevator just about the time we finished our conversation, and we got on the elevator with three or four guys that I guess worked for different departments within the international and they was carrying newspapers that had headlines about Frank Kierdorf. Jim turned around to one guy and called him by name and he says, "You see what we do. We don't fuck around. We torch 'em, we burn 'em, we blow 'em up. People we don't like, we get rid of them one way or another. Ain't I right, Franco?"

"Yeah, you're right, boss."

Those guys couldn't get off the elevator fast enough. That was one of Jimmy's biggest problems. He'd capitalize on something like that and it wasn't really the way he was. He was just trying to impress these guys with his toughness.

But that whole thing was the end of my partnership with Tommy Burke. I still loved the guy. I always loved him. And we worked together now and again after that, and people still thought we were partners. But it was never the same.

Franco's partnership with Tommy Burke had been one born in violence and maintained in violence, and it ended in violence. His partnership with Frank Fitzsimmons was less violent and more subtle, based on exchange of favors, based on exchange of money and other things.

Fitz was my sponsor and Fitz was my partner back from the beginning. He was the one that recommended me to Hoffa to take over the charter for the Distillery Workers, he was the one that got me the office in the old film exchange so that I could put on a front, a hell of a show so the people would say this is not the schlocky deal like they'd been used to. And I was the guy Fitz turned to when he needed help with the shit assignments Jimmy threw at him.

My relationship with Fitz went into many areas. I was there in Florida when Jimmy made Fitz a vice-president. I was there when Jimmy made him executive vice-president. I was there when Jimmy appointed him president of Local 299. I was always at Fitz's side at any of those big steps in his life. I'd always say, "God bless you, sweetheart, you're moving up the ladder." I was never anti-Fitz from day one. I liked Fitz. I always felt loyal to Fitz, but my number-one loyalty was to Jimmy because Jimmy was my boss. But Fitz was my friend and I felt a little responsibility because he was like my sponsor that really got me started representing local unions that would come to his attention and he'd always recommend me to take over and service those locals for Jimmy.

There was one time, I was in my car and I was going over to the gas station which him and his sons bought to keep the kids busy and make a living for themselves, and a car came right through a red light and hit me right at the tail end of my car and spun me around and totaled my car out. I didn't get hurt, thank God, but I saw red. I went over and opened the guy's car door and the guy's drunker than a bastard. I grabbed him by the collar and I dragged him over to the gas station which was maybe twenty-five yards away. Fitz and Don and Dick came over and they says, "Are you okay?"

"Yeah. This fucking bum smashed into me. He went right through a red light."

"Yeah, we saw it all. Is the guy okay?"

"Yeah, he's just drunk."

Fitz says, "What're you gonna do with him?"

"I'm gonna fix this son of a bitch up."

Fitz says, "Where are you going?"

"In the toilet."

I dragged him into the toilet and I took his head and put it in the toilet bowl and if Fitz and Don and Dick don't grab me and jump on my back, I'd have drowned him. I kept sticking his head in and flushing the toilet and shoving his head down a little further each time. If it wasn't for Fitz, I probably would have been up for murder.

These are the little things and I loved Fitz. And if I grabbed a buck someplace, I would always call Fitz and say, "Fitz, I've got a dollar, here's fifty cents for you and fifty cents for me." It could have been a dollar, it could have been $5,000, $10,000, whatever. Fitz always got half of my action because he was my sponsor at the beginning and later and he was my partner.

Now, there came a time that I was organizing a company called Harold Johnson Beverage, which was a beer distributor. I had a very tough situation and I thought I was lucky to get away with some members. But Fitz knew somebody in the beer business who must have told him that Joe Franco scored with Harold Johnson, which wasn't the truth.

Fitz came to me and he says, "Where's mine?"

"Fitz, there was nothing. So help me God, I was thankful just to get the members. I was thankful to get the strike over with. I thought I was going to lose the son of a bitch. If I'd have went the soft way with the guy, I . . . we probably would have scored. But I didn't."

He says, "Ah, you're full of shit. I was told you scored. That's all right. You want to single-O, that's your business."

From that day on, I had a nickname I got from Fitz, Single-O Franco. From that time on, Fitz and I were friends but the partnership was done. He went his way and I went mine, all the way up until the dead end.

On my fiftieth birthday, Fitz sat down alongside me up at

Shanty Creek and he looked at me and he says, "Joe, I always loved you like a son. But on that fucking day that you told me you didn't score with Harold Johnson . . ."

"Oh my God, Fitz, that was like almost twenty years ago. You still holding it against me?"

"I remember it like it was yesterday. And I remember that you didn't give me any money, too. And you would have been right alongside me, Joe, all through this whole deal. You would have been my executive assistant. Because I loved you for the things you did with me and you were always straight with me until that time."

"Fitz, I'm gonna tell you something. I don't care if you tell me to take a walk right now. I'll tell you again. I did not score with Harold Johnson. There was no money there. Believe it or not, all these years later, I'm telling you the same story."

He looked at me and he says, "You're still fucking Single-O. But that's okay. I love you."

One time it was Joe Franco and Tom Burke. At other times, it was Joe Franco and Frank Fitzsimmons. But after Burke and I split over the bombing and Fitz and I broke up because Fitz thought I scored and didn't cut it up and show the guy good faith by paying him half, I was my own person, I didn't have to worry about the other guy ratting on me or knowing anything about my private business or anything else. I was all alone. I did it by myself and nobody could ever say Joe Franco did this or Joe Franco did that because they had no knowledge of it. They maybe assumed it or they may have heard it or somebody might say, hey, that's one of Joe Franco's deals, but nobody was there so nobody knew it for sure. Only Jimmy knew it. And sometimes he would ask me, "You want to take somebody with you?"

I'd always say, "Nope, I want nobody." Burke was the only guy I would trust for those things. When I lost my trust in Tommy Burke, then I did it by myself.

14

And there were these scattered memories of those times.

When Jimmy became general president of the international in 1958, he made certain commitments to some of the business agents and organizers that were responsible for his rise to fame, guys like Roland McMasters, Dave Johnson, Al McNally, Jimmy Cliff, the guys he really needed and used to carry out his instructions and orders. For all the things I did for him, Jim never did commit himself that he would give me a big top job, but that was all right with me. But he did commit himself and make promises to Bobby Holmes that when he became general president, he would appoint Bobby as vice-president. First of all, he would appoint Bert Brennan, who was his partner, and Bert was a sick man and he committed himself that he would appoint Bobby Holmes when there was a vacancy.

Now Fitz wanted that job and he immediately ran to one or two of the Italian element that he thought he was close to and he pleaded and he begged that they would intervene in his behalf with Jimmy and ask Jimmy to make Fitz vice-president instead of Bobby. And they thought they could utilize Fitz in a top job in case anything was needed or a favor had to be done. Jimmy granted that request to Fitz's friends that intervened in his behalf.

At that point, Bobby Holmes was very hurt and very disgusted. I was in the office and Bobby was on the verge of packing it in and quitting because Jimmy didn't keep his word to him that when Bert died he would be appointed vice-president. I'll tell you, from that point on, Bobby had a bad feeling toward the Italian people because they intervened on behalf of Fitz. Bobby turned to me and he says, "I'm going to pack it in, Joe. Screw it. The little man never kept his word to me and he gave it to Fitz." Fitz and Bobby never did get along too well.

I says, "Bobby, I want to tell you something. You know, years ago you told me something about that man Hoffa and I listened to you. I grew to know and love that man. Now, you understand him and I'm sure if you're willing to give me that kind of advice, I'm going to give you the same advice. If Jimmy gave you his word, you know his word is his bond. If there was some intervention on behalf of Fitz, fine, Jimmy was put in a position where he couldn't say no. But sit back, don't resign, don't ask for retirement. Once in a while, just crack to Jimmy, remember, I'm still here, you did give me your word. Just tell him that way and you'll put him in a spot where he'll appoint you when there's another opening. Sit back and give the man a chance."

"Okay, I'll stick around for a while, but if it doesn't happen, I'm going to get the hell out."

Sure as hell, within six months to a year, all of a sudden there's two vice-presidents from the same city, Detroit, which was not heard of before in this international union. Never before and never after was there two vice-presidents from the same city out of the same joint council. Jimmy finally kept his word to Bobby Holmes and appointed Bobby a vice-president.

And I turned to Bobby and I says, "You see, you taught me something about the guy and you forgot what you taught me is to have a little faith in him because his word is his bond. He did come back and keep his word to you and now you're an international vice-president and you're happy."

Right after Jimmy appointed Fitz as vice-president of Local 299, somebody put a bomb in front of Fitz's house where he lived a few blocks away from me in Dearborn and it blew up his lawn. I don't know if that was a message to tell Fitz something, because I had no knowledge of it. But it was a way for somebody to get a message to him, whether it was the Italian element or even Jimmy or somebody else, I don't know. It could have been anybody, because Fitz was into anything that would make him a buck.

Anyway, I was sitting in Carl's Chophouse where most of the Teamsters and a lot of lawyers and judges and other people have lunch, and Fitz walks by me and says, "You can tell your fucking Italian friends that I'm not afraid and they can stop the bullshit."

I says, "What the fuck are you talking about, Fitz?"

"You know what they did to me."

"I don't. What the hell happened?" And I didn't know because I hadn't read the papers in years.

"Goddammit, Franco, you know goddamn well what happened. Just tell them it doesn't fucking bother me."

Then somebody I was eating with told me about the bomb on Fitz's lawn. So I got up and walked over to his table and grabbed him and I says, "What the fuck are you trying to refer to? Are you trying to say I got something to do with it?"

"No, not you. But you know who did it."

"How the hell do I know? I didn't even know it happened until somebody at the table just told me he read it in the papers."

"Aw, it's okay. Don't worry about it."

I think he was really trying to tell me, like I knew what was going on and I would pass the message that he was very upset about it. The thing was, Fitz really never did have the connections with the Italian people that Jimmy had. They trusted Jimmy on the basis that he was a standup guy and if anything ever came down, they could depend on Jimmy never to involve anybody, so they respected him. Fitz, they didn't like. They only put up with him because he was weak and they could use him to their best advantage whenever they needed to use him. But they never trusted him and they never respected him.

Jimmy hated stool pigeons. If anything came out in the newspapers that said so-and-so went in front of the grand jury and copped on somebody, he just flipped his pizza and he'd say, "The stool pigeon son of a bitch."

But, in the meantime, Jim had his own stool pigeons around the country, around his own local unions, around the building on Trumbull Avenue, and there was three or four of these guys that used to report to Jimmy on everybody and tell him what everybody was doing. It was common knowledge that Jimmy had wired everybody's office so that he could listen in anytime he wanted as to the conversations that were going on. We would have to be careful even in our own building what we would say because we didn't know when he would throw the switch and listen to what we would have to say.

The stool pigeons that he had, he would pretend he liked what they were doing. But I remember one day I walked into his office and one of the guys was walking out and as soon as the door closed, he says, "That fucking asshole, that stool pigeon son of a bitch, I can't stand the guy, Franco, that rats on people. He's a rat fink."

I says, "I thought he was one of yours."

"Nah. That son of a bitch, I wouldn't give him a fucking detail if my life depended on it. That rat stool pigeon. Can you imagine if this guy stool pigeons on you and Tommy Burke and everybody else, what he would do if he ever got caught? He'd rat on everybody. I put up with these stool pigeon son of bitches only because I got to know what's going on."

"Yeah? Is that why you're always checking me out?"

"Don't start it with me, Franco. Don't start it."

"Now I got you. You copped out to me."

"I told you, now leave it alone." Just about then, he turned around and he says, "Come here." There used to be an old building across the street from his window and it was vacant. He says, "Don't open the blinds, just crack 'em and take a look. You see that window over there on the left side? The federals got a camera over there aiming right into my office and they're trying to shoot and see who's here and when I open the blinds, they can make moving pictures of everybody who comes in and out of my office. That's why you never see the blinds open in here when there's somebody with me. And they got bugs in here so they can listen to everything we're saying. But I got my own devices to knock that out so they can't hear shit. And now they've found out about it."

Three or four days later, he bought that building and he paid $40,000 for it, about ten times what it was worth, and then he had somebody come in and rip that building right down. It's a parking lot now.

Jimmy couldn't stand weaknesses in an individual, he couldn't stand guys who weren't stand up. I had to go into Cleveland with Jim one time while Bill Presser, who was head of the joint council in the area, was in jail. We met with his wife and she was in tears, telling Jimmy that Bill was getting very ill and having a real tough time and taking it very bad. Bill was doing very, very bad time, and it was showing physically and psychologically on him. Jimmy consoled her and told her to tell Bill to just hang in there and we were doing everything we could to get him out and whatever he needed and whatever he wanted, just tell Jim and he'd make sure Bill got it. And it happened it wasn't much after that that Jim made a move and Bill did get out earlier than expected, but he came out a very sick man and I don't think he was ever the same after that.

But after that, there was this undercurrent of bad feeling between Bill Presser and Babe Triscaro and their friendship was broken up. And Jimmy said to me, "See that, you never know, Franco. Here's a guy, Bill Presser, that was supposed to be a tough guy, came out of tough people, he went to fucking prison and look what happened to him. I would have trusted him with anything. Now, you see, Franco, now that I know this, I can never trust Bill again. He shows me he can't do time, he can't even do a year. He constantly cries to his wife and he constantly cries to people and it comes back to me. He's a fucking weak man."

It was never the same between Jimmy and Bill after Bill came out. Bill would kowtow to Jimmy but Jimmy would never confide in Bill again. Whenever Jimmy had the feeling there was something wrong with an individual or a guy was weak, he couldn't trust him because he felt the guy would crack. It didn't matter whether the guy cracked or not, as long as he got that gut feeling, he would never have anything to do with him again. Not that he would ever do it as far as business was concerned, but he would never give him another assignment and he would never say anything to him unless he wanted to know it and he didn't give a shit if it ever leaked out. And sometimes he'd push stuff out to this kind of a guy hoping the guy would go out and say something and the word would get around without Jimmy having to say it.

Jimmy used to be very antiblack as far as his union was concerned in the early days. In many local meetings, I heard Jimmy telling the members that he would never allow a black man on the highways as an over-the-road driver. Underneath it all, it was picking up points with the members. But, let me tell you, if a black man ever went out on the highways in those days pulling an eighteen-wheeler, he would probably have got killed somewhere between here and Florida. It was an unheard situation having a black man driving cross country in an eighteen-wheeler. So, Jimmy was very safe in promising his guys, and he knew that if any black guy ever did it, he would never be safe on the highways, anyway.

In later years, when the civil rights movement got going, Jimmy was against it until the Ku Klux Klan and that Lester Maddox from Georgia with his ax handle and all that stuff started coming out. Jimmy became very anti-redneck. It was not that he became pro-civil rights, he just didn't like what was happening down in the South. There was many times he would say, "Franco, let me tell you something. Those sons of bitches, they're crazy. Today, they're doing it to the niggers, tomorrow they'll be doing it to the Italians, and then with anybody. They're white Anglo Saxons and there's not one of them that belongs to an organization that's got ethnic people." That made him more pro-black and more pro-civil rights.

And then when Martin Luther King came along and became effective, Jimmy felt that he was seeing himself again, that he was seeing a man that was doing what he was doing twenty years before, building up a principle, something you believe in and you'll fight and die for. Jimmy said to me, "This guy has got to be one hell of a guy. He's building up something and he'll get the black people to rally around and he's selling a principle. He'd be one hell of an organizer, Franco, the way he's organizing black people all over the country, and he's got Jewish people helping him. It kind of reminds me of what we used to do."

Later on, Martin Luther King came up to meet with Jim and I got to meet him then and several times, and he was one hell of a guy and I felt good about him and I knew what he was fighting for, he was fighting for the black people like I fought for many years against the defamation of the Italian people and Jimmy fought for the unions.

There was a time, in the sixties, when we were all ready to go to the grand jury and we were in the coffee shop and Jim was being tough and hard as to what should be done in front of the grand jury. He was praising himself for the fact that he had never taken the Fifth Amendment because of the fact that he knew how to handle himself.

Then he turns to me. "Franco, I want to tell you something. And I want you to tell me something." He'd just finished drinking a cup of tea and he took the cup and he says, "You see where the cup is. Can you pour something in that cup?"

"Yeah. The cup's open."

"That's right." He takes the cup and he turns it upside down. "Can you pour anything in that cup now?"

"No, because now you got it upside down. How can you pour anything into it?"

"That's what I'm trying to tell you. When you go in front of that grand jury, you open your fucking mouth, everything flows in and flows out. You keep your goddamn mouth shut and you won't get into trouble. That's the simple fact of what you have to do. If the cup is open, you can pour into it. If the cup is turned over, that means you can't pour nothing into it. You either go in front of the grand jury and you open up or you keep your goddamn mouth shut. You open up, you're in trouble. You keep your mouth shut, you may have to take your lumps but you prove you're a man and you'll have less trouble."

That was his philosophy as far as the grand jury was concerned or if you went out and did anything for him. The only one that could rat on you is yourself. So, if you wanted to rat on yourself, then shame, shame on you and you should go to jail. But if you go ahead and open your mouth, you're going to involve other people and eventually you'll end up in more trouble than you know what to do with.

There was the time when Fidel Castro was still a rebel fighting in the mountains of Cuba against Batista. I kind of got a little bit involved in a half-assed kind of way.

One of the international unions I was servicing for Jimmy was the Toy, Doll, and Novelty Workers, which was out of New York. One of the business agents there was a strong supporter of the Castro movement and he left while Castro was still up in the mountains fighting guerrilla war, and he joined up. Later on, when Castro took over, who the hell do you think was doing all the killing? And they gave him the nickname of the Executioner. Anyway, his wife stayed on in the office and she worked as the secretary to Harry Dimeno, who was the general president of the union. Every time I came into New York, we'd sit down and she'd keep me posted about what was going on over there.

And there was a guy named Gene San Souci who was out of Indianapolis and he was the head of the Teamster council for the state of Indiana. Gene was a very handsome man, a real man's man, like Clark Gable, solid as a brick, dressed great, golden sandy hair and a mustache. He was an all-around type of athlete, flying planes, driving on the Indianapolis speedway, good hunter, good fisherman. And we got very friendly up at Jimmy's hunting camp and I used to go into Indianapolis and go partying with him. He was a real ballsy guy that had his own domain and he loved Jimmy and had a lot of respect for him, but he wasn't above telling Jimmy to go take a shit if he didn't like what Jimmy was doing.

Anyway, one of the things Gene was doing in those days was flying stuff over to Castro. I remember up at the camp one time, Jim was talking to him and I was sitting in, and Jim says, "Are you still running that shit over to Castro?"

Gene says, "Yeah, I'm still taking it over to him. You know, Jim, one of these days he could be a hell of an ally for us. The American government is blowing the deal over there and they're going to be left holding the bag because this guy's gonna win and take over. If we're supporting him, we'll be in very good shape."

I guess Gene convinced Jim because Jim started handing over money to buy the arms that Gene was taking over in his plane. Then, just before Castro took over, Gene's plane disappeared coming back from Cuba and they never found any wreckage and they never found him.

Anyway, that didn't stop Jim, and for a long time he continued to give money for arms for Castro and they got on a very solid basis and there was a few times when Jimmy asked that Castro send people over here to do little jobs for him.

Meanwhile, when Castro got the power, the guy that used to be with the Toy and Novelty Workers and who was now the Executioner for Castro kept sending over invitations for me to make a visit. But I says, "There's no fucking way you're going to get me over there. Not the way them fucking people is lining people up against the wall and shooting everybody. That son of a bitch is liable to think I was playing around with his wife or something and shoot me, and nobody would know what happened to me."

Jim says to me, "You stay the hell out of Cuba. You stay home. Let the thing cool down. Don't worry, Castro is good people."

It wasn't often that people ever saw Jimmy relax and have a good time. But that didn't mean he never did. When I was handling Local 42 and I was home a lot, we used to have dinner parties and social affairs at my home and Jim and Josephine would always come as long as he was in town. And everybody was always very nice to him and glad to meet the famous James R. Hoffa. Now this one time, we were playing this parlor game where two people would get underneath a blanket and everybody would create a circle around them, and it was staged that the other person underneath the blanket with you had a stick and would hit you with the stick and cover himself up and the one that got hit would sit up and look at everybody in the circle and point to who did it, who hit him.

We got Jim under the blanket one night with one of our neighbors. She didn't want to go because she was scared to death of him, but I says, "No, go ahead. He'll get a kick out of it. It'll drive him crazy."

She was afraid to hit him. When he got underneath the blanket with her, she looked at me and she held the stick like she was scared. I went, "Hit him, hard," not so he could hear it but mouthing it with my lips. She gave him a pretty good shot and right away she covered herself up. He sat up and looked and he said, "That had to be you, Franco. Nobody else would hit me that goddamn hard."

Everybody tore up and the poor lady, she just about shit underneath the blanket. We went through that about a half a dozen times and she gave him good shots and he couldn't figure it out and everybody was roaring. He finally got up and he looked at her and he says, "You thought I didn't know you were hitting me."

She says, "I didn't want to do it. Joe made me do it."

He smiled and chuckled and he says, "I had a good time. I'm only putting you on."

She says, "Oh, thank you. I was so scared to death underneath there with you, I didn't know what to do."

It was good to see Jim relaxing in that fashion, and later he told me he had more fun that night than he could remember.

After Jim got to be president of the international and moved to Washington, he used to come back to Detroit whenever he could, especially on weekends. And a lot of Saturdays, I'd go into the office to clean up things. This one Saturday, I didn't know he was in town and I was working at my office and all of a sudden he came downstairs and popped his head in.

I says, "Hey, boss, what are you doing here?"

"I came in for the weekend. What're you doing?"

"I got some work, dictating contracts. I thought I'd come in and just clean it up and I wouldn't have to worry about it on Monday."

"Well, when you're all done, come upstairs to my office. I want to talk to you."

It wasn't all that unusual for us. A lot of times, he'd be there and I'd be there and we'd kind of rap and he'd let his hair down, and he'd be the real Jimmy Hoffa I knew and not the head of the union.

I went upstairs after a while and sat down and he says, "Franco, what the hell are you running all over the country for? Why are you doing what you're doing? Aren't you satisfied? What are you trying to prove? Do you make a good living, Franco, get a good paycheck?"

"Yeah, boss, you know I do."

"You take care of your children and your family?"

"Yeah."

"Aren't you happy where you're at?"

"Yeah."

"Then why the hell do you do this and do that? Why are you operating the way you are? Every time I turn around and give you another local to service, you take the son of a bitch. You got enough of them and I give them to you to test you out and see if you'll take them, and every time I throw one at you, you take it and go out and organize it and build it up. What are you trying to prove?"

"Boss, I take them because you want me to do it. I didn't want that last local, but you told me to take it over."

"Forget that. You're doing this, you're doing that, you're

down there, you're going here, every time I turn around you're there, you're like fucking horse shit. You're always around."

"Well, I want to be where you're at."

"Franco, do you want them to be on your ass like they're on my ass? You're starting to get a taste of it. Why do you want it? You got kids. It's too late for me. But you still got time."

"Boss, since I met you I've always said to myself that someday I'd like to be like Jimmy Hoffa."

He looked at me with a kind of look that said, goddammit, I'm sorry for you. And he says, "There'll never be another James R. Hoffa. Don't ever try to be what I am. I am what I am and there'll never be another one like me."

"Jim, you're my idol. I still would like to be like you. I run my whole operation like you do. I try to copy you and I try to think like you do."

"Franco, do yourself a favor. It's too late for me. I can't back out if I wanted to. I have too many responsibilities. Too many people depend on me, they depend on me to run this organization the way I run it. I can't depend on anyone else. You, I can ask you to do anything and I never have to question you about it. How many people do you think I have like you? That's why I'd like you to stay home, raise your children, mind your business, do what you have to do to survive, don't get into trouble, don't commit yourself to anything that you're stuck with for the rest of your life. You're still a free man. I'm not. I'm a slave."

Then he starts asking me about how the kids are and how everything is at home and this and that, and then he jumps up and he changes, just like that, and he's the hard, tough Hoffa. He says, what the hell did I do during the week, did I accomplish anything, have I organized anyone lately? That was typical of Jim. He would go from one extreme to the other in a minute without your hardly even realizing it.

We were the backbone of the Teamsters, Burke and me and McMasters and the rest of the buffalo. Jimmy was a great leader but you can't be a great leader without having apostles and we were the apostles. We loved him, we trusted him, we worked for him, and he was our boss. We followed him blindly and we did his bidding and we were well compensated. As Jimmy went up the ladder, so did we. We were the unsung heroes of the Teamster movement.

Back in those days, you said Teamsters, immediately you said, using the expressions back in those days, tough guys. You walked in and you said Teamsters and people would take notice and they would say, "Teamsters, oh, wow, you guys are rough, you guys are real tough guys." That was the reputation we built. We walked into a company and we said we want to organize it and they said, "Who're you working for?" We'd say, "Teamsters," and they'd say, "Yeah, yeah, you guys will really support us."

You said Teamsters and there was people who said, "Teamsters? Oh, you're part of the Mafia." Okay, that was fine, too, because at the time it was a good tool, a necessary tool. Whatever it was, we used it and we built the union for Jimmy.

Part IV

15

The first years of the Hoffa regime were years of ferment, change, and excitement for the Teamsters. The union, which had stagnated under Dan Tobin, which had begun to edge slowly forward under Dave Beck, exploded after Hoffa took power in 1958.

Hoffa and the Teamsters had energy, ambition, and an unquenchable thirst for more and more power. The vast change in the nation's transportation system was on the Teamsters' side. The government was building a network of interstate highways at a staggering pace, and that was forcing a change in the traditional means of carrying goods to market. No longer were suppliers, manufacturers, and others dependent on trains. Now the trucks were carrying everything faster and cheaper and more directly. The demand for trucks and men to drive them increased rapidly, and every new driver was a Teamster whether he liked it or not.

And there was something else, though few recognized it at the time.

George Meany, righteously indignant at the charges of corruption and underworld influence on the Teamsters, expelled the union from the AFL-CIO. If he thought this would isolate the union and force reform, he could not have been more mistaken. As John English, the secretary-treasurer of the Teamsters through the reigns of Tobin, Beck, and Hoffa, told Meany and the other leaders of the merged federation, that action saved the Teamsters $10

million in per capita assessments. The Teamsters were no longer
bound by jurisdictional agreements, and so the Teamsters could
take that $10 million and go out and organize everything and ev-
eryone they wanted to, whether there were wheels or not. The
world of labor would now fall within the Teamster purview. In
short order, the laundry workers, brewery workers, and other
unions that had been booted out of the AFL-CIO, along with the
Teamsters, merged and became part of Hoffa's empire. It was Hoffa's intention to merge within the Teamsters every international
union that had fewer than one hundred fifty thousand members.
He and John L. Lewis held a series of meetings before Lewis was
forced out of his union, the object of which was the ultimate
merger of the United Mine Workers with the Teamsters. That
failed to happen when Lewis disappeared from the scene, but it
didn't mean that such a merger vanished from Hoffa's mind. It
would happen, he was sure, sooner or later. And he had his eyes on
mergers with the railroad brotherhoods, the building trades unions,
and more. He told Franco that if he could rid himself of his troubles with the government and rule until it came time to retire,
perhaps until the 1980s, he would be able to create a union that
would encompass all of organized labor except for the giant
unions, such as the UAW, the steel workers, and a few more.

Even without the realization of his dream, Hoffa was able to
turn the Teamsters into the nation's largest and most powerful
union, with a membership of more than 2.25 million. He had the
power to bring the country to a halt by calling a nationwide strike
and stopping the shipment of everything everywhere. He won for
his members huge wage increases, bringing truck drivers and other
Teamsters into the middle class. He secured benefits for them that
more than doubled or even tripled their base pay. He created
Teamster pension and welfare funds, into which employers contrib-
uted, running into the billions of dollars. The power that he had
dreamed of was his, and yet he wanted more. The fear that he had
sought to inspire was his, and he wanted to create still more.

But there were those who were determined to stop him. To
them, the thought of Jimmy Hoffa ruling a vast labor empire with
the kind of potential that would lie within it were the things of
which nightmares are made. Chief among those who would stop
him was Robert Francis Kennedy, who was named attorney gen-

eral, the chief law enforcement officer of the nation, when his brother became president of the United States. Bob Kennedy had clashed often and savagely with Jimmy Hoffa, at Senate hearings, in private, and in public. He was determined to strip Hoffa of all those regal trappings and to put him in simple prison garb.

Hoffa's Teamsters had been thrown out of the AFL-CIO, but that had only given them new and greater power. Hoffa had been indicted and tried for wiretapping his own offices, and he had been acquitted. He had been indicted and tried for attempting to bribe John Cye Cheasty to steal documents from the files of the Mac-Clellan Committee, and even had been arrested with those files in his possession, but despite the confident predictions of chief counsel of the committee, Robert Kennedy, he had been acquitted.

But now Bob Kennedy was attorney general. Now he had power to array major task forces to find the evidence that would give him his victory over Jimmy Hoffa. And those task forces found what they considered enough evidence of Hoffa's misuse of pension funds to secure two separate indictments against him.

Bob Kennedy's obsession with Jimmy Hoffa was a worrisome thing to Hoffa, despite his outward displays of bravado. And it was worrisome to the friends of Hoffa and to the mutual friends of Hoffa and the Kennedys, who feared that the drive against Hoffa could rebound to the Kennedys' discredit, and who worried about what possible retaliation Hoffa might devise. Some of those friends tried to bring about a reconciliation, to create a *modus vivendi* that would lead to peace.

★ ★ ★

I was at the Belmont Hotel in New York, across the street from the Waldorf. I had done for the day negotiating with Seagrams and Schenley distilling companies and I was up in my suite partying with two chicks I had stashed up there and having a good time. Then I ran out of cigarettes, so I went downstairs to get some and while I was out on the street I heard some guy hollering out my name. It was a guy from Detroit and I went across the street and I says, "What are you doing here?"

"I've been in New York for the last three or four days and we knew you was here and we've been looking for you high and low.

Julia Skouras is looking for you. We're honoring Frank Sinatra upstairs, a big testimonial dinner for him and she's been trying to get hold of you and didn't know where to find you."

Through Harold Gibbons, I became very close to a lot of important people and two of them were the Skourases, George and Julia. He was Greek and she was Sicilian. I met them at the "21" Club in New York and we became very close because she was the national chairman of Boys Town of Italy, which I was very interested in. Whenever she ran into a problem, like if she would have a problem in Pittsburgh, she would call me and say, "Joe, we're having a problem in Pittsburgh. We're not getting good response as far as our tickets moving along and we can't get the house filled."

So, I would go into Pittsburgh and get things moving along and sell the tickets and raise as much money as we could for Boys Town of Italy. I was always at her beck and call because I loved the woman.

Anyway, that night, when this guy told me Julia—and I always called her Aunt Julia because we were so close—was looking for me, I says, "I'm here."

He says, "Come on upstairs."

"I can't come up like this." I was wearing white slip-on gym shoes and I got on a pair of baggy pants and a T-shirt. "You're wearing a tuxedo and look at me. I can't do that."

He says, "Come on. Just to show your face, because she's really gonna be hurt if she doesn't see you and she knows that you were here."

"Okay, but don't make me get embarrassed and take me in someplace where people can see me the way I am."

We went upstairs and he took me over to a little room they had set up for the so-called society top and the celebrities. Nate Stein was hosting the door and he saw me. Nate and I go back a lot of years because of his close association with Jimmy. Nate looked at me and he says, "What the hell are you doing here dressed like that?"

I says, "Shut up, Nate. I don't want to be here, but I understand Julia Skouras is looking for me and I bumped into a friend of mine and he wanted me to come upstairs to see Aunt Julia."

"I can't let you in looking like that, Joe. Jesus Christ, very important people is in there."

"Nate, I don't give a shit if you let me in or not. All I'm trying to do is stay the hell out of everybody's way and I don't want anybody to know who the hell I am or anything else. All I want is to say hello to Aunt Julia and get the hell out of here."

Well, we were arguing at the door, and I was getting mad as hell and I was wanting to whack him right out. All of a sudden, I hear Aunt Julia scream, "Sweetheart, sweetheart, you made it. Thank you, God bless you." She comes running over and hugging and kissing me and everything else and Nate Stein sees this and he don't know what to say when she grabs me and drags me into that celebrity room.

As I go by, I says to Nate, "See you piece of shit, this lady knows class when she sees it. She's taking the caretaker in and I got to clean the walls."

She laughs and she says, "You'll never change, will you. But I'm glad you're here, sweetheart. I've been looking for you." And she took me over and she introduced me to some real nice people. Then she says, "You'll have to excuse me because I have to get back into the dining room because in a few minutes we're going to set this thing up and we're all going to be marching in. Joe, you just sit here and eat whatever you want and do whatever you want and be sure you come in and sit down in the dining room. We don't care how you look. We love you and we wouldn't care if you had shorts on."

She left and then Nate came over and he says, "Come on, I want you to meet somebody." He was taking me toward the back of the room and the guy that was sitting there was Mr. Frank Sinatra. People always used to think I knew Frank before that and that we were buddies, because I knew everybody around him and I'd been where he was lots of times. But this was the first time we ever met to say more than hello. Nate takes me back there and he says, "Joe Franco, I want you to meet Frank Sinatra."

We shook hands and then Nate says, "Frank, this is Jimmy Hoffa's guy, Jimmy's man."

Frank says, "Oh, yeah? Come here." He grabbed me underneath the arm and he says, "Come back here in the corner, let's sit down. What're you drinking?"

"I don't drink."

"Well, grab a glass of water or something."

I grabbed a glass of ginger ale and he grabbed a drink and we went over to the corner and sat down and just talked a little common bullshit kind of stuff. Then I says, "Mr. Sinatra . . ."

He says, "Don't call me that, I'm Frank."

"All right, Frank. You know, you're quite a celebrity and Nate tells me you're quite a guy and what I read and what I see and what I hear, you know, I am very impressed that I'm here with you."

He kind of shrugged that off and he says, "Nate tells me you're Jimmy's guy. This is what I want you to do for me, do me a favor. When are you going to see Jimmy?"

"I'm going back tomorrow and I understand he's in Detroit, so I'll probably be seeing him when I get in."

"When you see him, give him a message from me. Tell him the party we were talking about, I talked to him and everything looks good and he will be in touch with Jimmy. Tell Jimmy I took care of everything and things are being set up so that they can have a conversation, so Jimmy should just sit back and relax, just hold on and not loose his cool, and the guy will reach out for him in a very short time."

"Okay, I'll tell him tomorrow when I see him. Only, how come you don't call and tell him yourself?"

"I don't trust the goddamn phones. You never know who's listening. I was hoping I'd run into one of Jimmy's guys tonight so he could pass the word."

After that, we talked about this and that for maybe fifteen or twenty minutes and then he says to me, "What are you going to be doing now?"

"I'm about to get the hell out of here. Look at the way I'm dressed."

He says, "No, no."

"Aunt Julia don't want me to leave either. But I feel like a bum."

"Don't worry about it. I'll let you sit next to Bill Vieck and he'll make you look like Beau Brummel." He calls Bill over from across the room, and he introduces us and he says, "I want you to let Joe sit next to you at your table." Bill Vieck's got a sport jacket and sport shirt on, at least, and here I am in gym shoes and a baggy pair of dirty pants and a T-shirt.

I look at him and then I says to Frank, "He's got a bad reputation? Look at me."

He says, "Well, you got the reputation now, you just won it from Bill."

Bill started to laugh and he says, "I look good compared to you, kid."

Now, Harold Gibbons comes walking by and I flag him and we stood there talking and then Frank says, "I got to go. I got to go up and sit at the goddamn head table over there and eat that chicken and peas. But do me a favor, Franco, don't leave. We're all going over to Jilly's and have some fun after this thing is over. We'll grab some broads and we'll go bumming."

Now, I didn't want to tell him I already had two broads stashed across the street, so I says okay. He took off and then we went inside the dining room and I sat between Harold and Bill Vieck and after about a half an hour of sitting there looking at people all dressed up in diamonds and gowns and tuxedos, and even Bill Vieck's at least got a plaid jacket on, I look real bad. I look like the guy that washes the walls and that just sat down at the table for some unknown reason. I turned to Harold and I says, "Jesus Christ, Harold, let me get out of here." I looked up at Frank at the head table and I put my hand to my ear, to make a sign like to call me, and I pointed to Harold, like Harold will know where to call me so we can get together when you're done with this. And Frank is shaking his head and going, no, no, no, and it drew all the attention to us. I says to Harold, "Now he's making it worse. Now everybody knows here's the caretaker of a clip joint and he's sitting here making signs at Sinatra and Sinatra's making signs at him, and the people don't know whether we're arguing or what. Call me when you're done and then I'll get dressed up and cleaned up and then we can go out. I'm right across the street at the Belmont and I'm with two broads over there. While you guys are fucking around here for another couple of hours, I can go up and get laid and have some fun and then when you're ready to leave, call me and I'll meet you at Jilly's."

He says okay, and I looked at Frank and motioned that I was leaving and pointed to Harold, and then I left, and Frank was making motions not to leave and even Aunt Julia was making the same kind of motions.

But I got out of there and went across the street and had a good time banging both of these broads and I'm thinking, fine if they call me and if they don't, screw them. I met Frank Sinatra after all the years of being with his guys and almost meeting him, and it was a nice pleasure and I'll give Jimmy his message when I get back to Detroit. I stuck around the room and I sent the girls home and I sat there and nobody called so I went to sleep.

The next morning, as I was getting ready to go out to the airport, I get calls from everybody and his brother. And Harold calls me and he says, "Where the hell were you?"

"Right here. Why the hell didn't you call?"

"We were looking for you."

"Harold, don't give me that shit. You went out with Sinatra and you had a good time. Good. And maybe you got laid and maybe you didn't, and you forgot all about me. Well, I don't give a shit. I had two broads up here and I got laid, so screw you guys."

Harold told me that Frank was real pissed at me because I didn't show up at Jilly's and he'd probably hold it against me for a long time because he was the kind of guy that held grudges against people he thought didn't treat him right. I told him that was too bad, but I didn't go over to Jilly's to meet them because nobody called me to say they was going over there.

I got back to Detroit and Jimmy was there and I went in to see him and I says, "Jim, I met Frank Sinatra last night at this affair for Boys Town of Italy where they were honoring him. He gave me a message to bring to you. He said to tell you he talked to the guy and he was setting things up where you and him could have a meeting or a conversation or something and make peace. I think he was talking about Jack Kennedy." In those days, everybody talked in riddles and nobody used a guy's name, especially in public. But knowing what was coming down, I figured it would be all right to use the name so Jimmy would understand exactly what I was talking about.

And Jim nodded and he says, "Fine, thanks, Franco. I know what Frank means. So, good, okay."

It wasn't too much after that when the thing came down like Frank said. Jimmy was in his office with John English and Jimmy Hannan and a couple of other guys, I'm not too sure I remember just who, but I think it was Sandy O'Brien out of Chicago and

Herb Grosberg. I was hanging around right outside, waiting for it to be over with because I was anticipating that there would be an agreement and we were going to have peace. When it was all over, Jimmy Hannan told me what took place.

Jim had one of those phone decks in his office where everybody could hear and everybody could talk and they all stood around. The conversation was kind of friendly to start with, and Jimmy and Jack Kennedy talked about burying the hatchet and making peace between them, which would mean getting off Jimmy's back and getting Jimmy and the Teamsters to back Jack Kennedy and support him when he ran again. Jimmy was all for making peace with Jack. He knew that the way things were going, the fight between him and the Kennedys was not going to stop and he knew who was going to win and who was going to lose. John L. Lewis told him before, from his own experience with Harry Truman, that you get in a fight with the federal government and the president, there ain't no way you can win, you're going to come out the loser. Jimmy knew this and he wanted to make peace. Not that he would enjoy it. But he was smart enough to know he had to. He used to tell me, "You get in bed with a whore, okay, and you live with her until she gets relaxed, then you kick her in the ass and throw her out. But if you get in bed with her and satisfy her, somewhere along the line you're going to be in a position where you can say, go screw yourself and get the hell out because I don't need you no more. So, if I have to get in bed with the Kennedys, I'll get in bed with them until I accomplish what I want and what I set out to accomplish and at that point I won't need them anymore and I can walk away and tell them to kiss my ass."

Anyway, there was some mention in that conversation about Jimmy making reforms and getting rid of certain people and coming up with big contributions to the Democrats and to Jack Kennedy's campaigns. Well, that got John English's back up. He was one tough old bird and he was the toughest guy in the world when it came to money and especially political money. He hated politics and he hated politicians and he hated to give them money. He got up and he started yelling so it went right over the phone that the Teamsters didn't need Jack Kennedy and the Teamsters wasn't going to bury the hatchet and why the hell should the Teamsters apologize when it was the Kennedys that was in the wrong. He told Jack Kennedy that they'd been after Jimmy and after the Teamsters, and all of a sudden they were looking to make peace and looking for big donations. Well, the Kennedys could go screw themselves and there wasn't going to be no peace and we were going to go on just like we'd been doing.

That blew the whole thing. And I guess after that the Kennedys just came down on Jimmy and everybody else in the Teamsters ten times worse than they'd been doing already.

16

As Robert Kennedy's "Get Hoffa" squad in the Justice Department gathered momentum almost from the first days of the Kennedy administration, and accelerated following the aborted attempt to negotiate a truce between the Kennedys and Hoffa, Franco's own concern with potential danger on the legal front was suddenly diverted. Hard as he had tried to shield his family from the storms that swirled around the union, and him, he had been only partially successful. But at least, he felt by mid-1961, Alice was making progress. She seemed to be emerging from the deep depression that had gripped her during the past several years.

She was being treated by a psychiatrist and she seemed to be coming out of it pretty good and me and the four kids could see that there was a tremendous change for the better in her.

Now, it was 1961 and we were living in Bloomfield Hills, in a big, beautiful house. I was downtown at Cobo Hall where there was a big toy and novelty convention and everybody came out of New York. Miltie Holt was there and other guys that served on the executive board of the union with me, and in the evening, they asked me to have dinner with them, and call up Alice and tell her come in and there would be boxes of toys and stuff to take home for the kids and things for her. So I called her and she was in an outrage, screaming and hollering over the phone, and I just didn't listen. I says, "Look, Alice, I don't know what else to tell you. They're here. I can't say no to these people. They're only going to be here until tomorrow and they wanted to see you." There was no way of controlling her, she just kept screaming. I says, "Look, this is part of my work. I'll be home late tonight and, if not, I'll be home the first thing in the morning."

All bedlam broke loose. She's screaming, "Don't do that. Don't leave me. Don't do that to me. Please come home, please come home."

Well, I had a bad back in those days, a ruptured disc, and I was wearing a brace and taking medication and I was feeling like hell, anyway. That was all I needed. I says, "Goddammit, here we go again. For four months, you've been fine and now it's starting all over again."

She says, "I don't want to hear about goddamn unions. I don't want to hear about those goddamn dinners. Get home now. I need you now."

I says, "Al, I'm in no mood. My back is out. I'm hurting very bad. I'm not coming out to the house if that's taking place again."

She says, "Please don't do this to me." And all of a sudden, she hung up.

Well, between that and hurting as bad as I was hurting, I just couldn't make it out to the house. I checked into a motel about halfway home and went to bed. In the morning, I got up and put on my brace and took the last pain pill I had with me, got dressed and got into the car to start driving home. I had a phone in the car and no sooner did I get into it than the phone rings. It's my secretary, Betty Martin. She says, "Joe, you'd better get home in a hurry."

"That's where I'm heading. Is something wrong?"

She says, "Why don't you pull over. I got some bad news to tell you."

"Something wrong with the kids?"

"No. Something's wrong with Alice."

I says, "What's the matter?"

"Alice is dead."

"Oh, my God. I'm on my way home."

She says, "Everybody's there. The police department's there."

"All right."

I knew what she was trying to tell me last night. Somebody was at the house, somebody had her and she panicked. It had sounded like she was having her old troubles, but now I knew that wasn't it.

As soon as I hung up from Betty Martin, the phone rang again. It was Fritz. He says, "Joe, I just got word. I just called Jimmy to tell him. Are you all right driving? Would you want to pull over and I'll come and pick you up? Where're you at?"

"I'm quite a ways out. I'll be home in about seven or eight minutes."

He says, "Hey, you call me if you need anything. We'll be out tomorrow, as soon as you make all the arrangements."

"All right."

I don't know what's coming down. I don't even know what's happening. It still hadn't hit me. The shock didn't hit me until a few hours later.

Then the phone rings again. It's Jimmy and he's screaming, "What the hell happened?"

"I don't know, Jim. All I know is I got a call from my secretary saying that Alice is dead. I don't know. I should be home in three, four minutes."

He says, "Are you all right? Are you driving?"

"Yeah, I'm all right."

"Are you sure? Now, if you need anything, as soon as you get home, you call me and tell me what's up. I want to know. I'm flying in and I should be there tomorrow sometime and I'll call as soon as I get in."

"All right, Jim."

By that time, I was pulling into my driveway, a big circular driveway. I got out of the car and ran into the house. The kids were all over at a neighbor's place. The police department, the sheriff, everybody was there. My oldest girl, Vicky, was the one that found her. She was seven and a half at the time. She got up in the morning and she couldn't find her mother so she went looking for her and she found the garage door was cracked open and the firewall door, between the garage and the kitchen and the laundry room, was not completely closed, and her mother was lying in the car with her head back like she was sleeping, and the motor was stalled out. When Vicky couldn't wake her, she ran next door and the neighbors called the sheriff's department and then they grabbed the kids so they wouldn't see what was happening. When I heard all that, I ended up punching the wall and I broke my little finger.

Well, because of Alice's history, they marked it down as a suicide. They said she had been drinking and was depressed and that was it.

I let it ride. But I knew that wasn't it. I'm looking around and I see the garage door is about two feet off the ground and the fire door is open and the car was jammed in the garage up against the lawnmower and the other side was jammed against a big stack of pop bottle cases, so how could she have got in or out if she wanted to? If Al was going to do a suicide, she would have closed the garage door and all the rest.

But I let it ride. If I went out and started doing something, there would be a blood bath situation and I might end up hitting the wrong people. But I knew what they had done. They had given her a shot or something, spread a lot of bottles around, then shoved her in the car, turned on the motor, shoved the lawnmower against the door so she couldn't get out if she woke up, and that was it. I figured if I didn't do nothing, that would wash it out and no attempt would be made on the children. If they wanted to come after me, I was wide open.

After the funeral and all, and everybody came from the Teamsters and the industries that I represented and everything, I went to Jim and I told Jim about it. I says, "Jimmy, she didn't do it. But I'm leaving it alone on the basis that they're classifying it as a suicidal deal. This way, there's no heat, there'll be no investigation and I'll be able to maneuver around and do what I have to do. They wanted me at the house. They didn't want her. When I didn't show up, they figured the next best thing was her because I imagine she panicked and caused them some problems. Somewhere along the line, I'll find out, it'll come back to me."

Well, two years later, I found out that two guys out of Toledo were hired. A very good friend of mine told me about it. This guy was going with this chick and she told him that two guys paid her to call my wife periodically and tell my wife that I was in bed with her in Toledo or wherever, and these were the two guys that were responsible for Alice's death.

I went to Jimmy and I says, "Jim, I finally found out. I'm going to Toledo and I don't know how I'm going to come out, but you know what I got to do."

He says, "Go ahead, Franco. Do your thing. Do you want Burke with you?"

And Tommy Burke was there and he says, "Do you want me to go with you?"

"No, Tom. This is one that I've got to do by myself."

And Jim says, "All right. Just be careful."

I says, "Don't worry about it."

"All right. I'll see you. Call me as soon as you're through."

I got in the car and I took my tools, my shotgun, with me and I got into Toledo. I was there for a week. I picked up the broad so she could finger the two guys for me since I didn't know what they looked like. We went around to the restaurants and nightclubs and the places they were operating, but they didn't show. Then it just so happened that this one night they went into the joint my friend owned to have dinner, and the broad was a waitress there and she fingered them for me. I waited outside. When they came out, I walked right up to them at their car and they rolled the window down and with that, I let two blasts going out right alongside them and the first blast hit the first guy with buckshot and it also hit the second guy. But I wanted to make sure the second guy was gone, so I let the second shot go into him, and I blew both of them away.

With that, I drove into Cleveland and checked into a hotel and got hold of my nephew, Jimmy, and told him to do me a favor and go buy me a shirt and a jacket because my clothes was pretty messed up. A couple of days later, I went back to Detroit and checked in with Hoffa and told him everything was okay.

After what happened to Alice and everything, Jim and I were closer than ever. He knew I was a widower and he loved the children and he was always asking about them, and always calling me when he was in Detroit for talks and things. If he'd see me pretty gloomy, he'd say, "What's the matter, Franco? Something wrong?"

I says, "Nah."

He says, "Come on, something wrong with the kids? How're the kids?"

"They're all right. They're in school."

"You need some help? You know where to come."

17

With the death of his wife, Franco was torn by conflicts and emotions, by an inner turmoil he had rarely experienced and only barely comprehended, by responsibilities he felt himself ill-equipped to assume. Sometimes overwhelmed by grief, he felt he was largely to blame for Alice's death; he should have recognized that her cries to him over the phone had been the cries of someone in trouble and perhaps he could have rescued her. There were the demands of Hoffa and all the unions he was servicing and ruling for his leader. There were his four small children, suddenly deprived of their mother, dependent totally on him for everything—for guidance, for nurturing, for love, for all the things he had not been able to give them in long absences.

I just kind of eased off. I met with Hoffa and I explained to Jim that I couldn't run around as much as I did before until I got the children settled and got my head cleared and knew exactly where I was heading for. I says, "Jim, I've got a couple of thousand members here and I really don't want to be the head of three or four business agents and two or three girls in the office. I can't do it. I'm trying to raise a family, take care of my kids, and I can't operate this big an operation."

Jim says, "Go ahead, take parts of your locals and assign

them to different locals within the Teamsters. Go ahead and do what you have to do and once you get your head cleared and get the children settled, then you can start going and getting your tail feathers back to work."

I took some of my members and put them in Local 337 and some of them in Local 385 and some in Local 299 and it came down to where I ended up with about eleven hundred members, which was enough for me and Betty Martin to take care of as a two-man operation.

But I had to do something with the kids. Georgie, the baby, was too young to go to school yet. When he was old enough, I was going to send him to a military school in Chicago. In the meantime, I hired a woman to stay with me and take care of Georgie so I had an opportunity to go out and do my job. The three girls, Victoria and Janice and Diane, I decided to put in a good Catholic school where they would be taken good care of and get a good education and where I could go and visit them every weekend. Let me tell you, they had the guts to do what they had to do in order for their dad to survive and to continue to work in his line of work. All they knew about that was that I just made a living.

There was a convent up in Adrian where I wanted them to go, St. Joseph's, and it seemed like the right place. But it was too late then to get them in, so until they could go there, I sent them over to Sacred Heart in Windsor. That place was close enough so I could run over there every weekend and pick them up and bring them home for the weekend. But they weren't too happy there, so after several months I worked things out to get them transferred to St. Joseph's of Adrian. But the thing about that was they were only allowed to come home one weekend a month, and that tore me apart, seeing them so little and then having to send them back.

While they were at Sacred Heart in Windsor it happened that the Building Service Employees were trying to organize the school. The laws in Canada are different from the laws in the United States. Up there, if a union is organizing, they file a petition with the House of Parliament and the House of Parliament sends out a notification to the employer that it's happening, and if the employer doesn't respond within a specific time, then the union is certified as the bargaining agent for the employees. Well, the mother superior of Sacred Heart, being a kind of unworldly lady, didn't know what to make of it when she got the notification and she didn't do anything and then she had the union on her back. So, knowing that I was in labor and with the unions, she called me in and asked me what advice I could give her as to how she could resolve her problem of being organized.

I says, "Don't worry about it, sister. I'll contact that union and I'll get that union out of here and you won't have to worry about it."

She says, "Before you do anything, I don't have the authority to give that authority to you to do that. You'll have to go to the mother general in Montreal and then she will give that permission. All I can do is ask your advice."

So, I'm saying to myself that I just got myself into a situation where I'm going to have to make a special trip to Montreal to take care of this with the mother general, and I don't speak more than a couple of words of French. What I did was, I called Jackie Kahane, who was a big comic and a French Canadian Jew that I got to be very friendly with when I was heading the office in Montreal, and who I helped out in some very difficult situations he had with some tough Italian guys in Chicago, who got sore about some of his routines about the Mafia. I says, "Jackie, I got a situation where I got to come to Montreal, so make yourself available and I'll be there tomorrow. I've got a meeting at the mother house for the Sacred Heart and I got to have somebody who speaks French and can translate for me."

The next day we meet and we go up to the mother house, which is a big gorgeous building. We knocked at these huge doors with these big knockers and it felt like you went back in time. Eventually, the door opened and there was these two tiny little nuns, they couldn't have been over five feet tall. And they were wearing little white slip-ons instead of shoes and they walked in a shuffle like little penguins. I darned near broke up laughing when I saw them, walking in pairs. She says something to me in French and Jackie says, "She wants to know what business you have here."

I says, "I have a meeting with the mother general," and Jackie translates it. With that, the two little nuns asked us to come in and wait, and we waited in this huge vestibule that you'd have to see to appreciate. It was a magnificent place. The wood was beautiful and all polished like you don't see anymore, and there was this huge staircase, and there go the little nuns and they got to the top and they disappeared, and then they came back over to the top and they beckoned with their fingers for us to come up to the second level. In French, they told Jackie that we should follow them. We did, and with that little shuffle they had, and I think the little white slip-ons was a matter of polishing the floors as they walked, because the floors were absolutely shining, no dust, no nothing, they led the way. All of a sudden, here comes a bunch more nuns, all walking in pairs, all with their hands in their sleeves, all shuffling along and so help me, they looked like a flock of penguins, and none of them could have been more than five two or five three, little tiny girls, some of them young, some of them old.

We were taken into a huge room that had a long magnificent table with a huge leather wingback chair at one end and six smaller chairs on either side, and there were two chairs in front of this huge table, which looked like it could have been used for the last supper. In those days, I used to smoke and I was as nervous as a goddamn cat and I'm saying to Jackie, "Jesus God almighty, I don't know what I got myself into. I want to do these people a favor, but here I am, running all the way to Montreal, which I don't mind, because then I can see you and the wife and some other people, but I got a funny feeling I stuck my nose into something I shouldn't have stuck it into."

While we're talking, whispering, because you couldn't talk out loud because you could hear it all through that chamber, and we're sitting in it completely empty, like two condemned guys at an inquisition, all of a sudden a door opened on the right side of the table and out came six little penguins, all shuffling and they shuffled right up to six chairs and stood there, and here comes six more shuffling penguins and they stood alongside the other six chairs, and a few minutes went by and here comes a six foot tall nun. She was overpowering. You couldn't paint a more magnificent face, it was like something God created with His own hands. She got alongside the big chair and she made a motion with her head and in unison, nobody out of step or out of line, they all sat and it was like a drill.

And I'm saying to myself, "Oh my God, is she gorgeous. Would I love to see her in street clothes without her habit." Well, she sat in this big chair and no wonder it was so massive because she was just a big woman. She sat there and the little bursar from Windsor was sitting alongside her. She starts to say something in French and I says, "Sister, you don't have a problem because my friend, Mr. Jackie Kahane, can be my interpreter if you want to speak French."

So, she says something in French and Jackie says to me, "The bursar wants you to explain to the mother general what our problem is."

I says to Jackie, "Tell her in French that the Building Service Employees Union has organized the employees at the school in Windsor and they've asked the House of Parliament to certify them and the notice went to the school, but the poor little nuns didn't know what the hell it was and they never answered it so the government certified the union. That means that the school and the mother house will have to negotiate a union contract on behalf of their employees at the school."

Jackie tells her and she just glared at me with her arms crossed in her sleeves. She said something to the bursar and she asked me another question and I answered it and Jackie translated and she said something again to the bursar and whatever it was, all twelve of these little penguins got up in unison and all twelve shuffled out and left the mother general sitting there by herself with us.

After the door closed, she kind of leaned forward on the table and looked at me, and I'm staring straight at her, and I could have fallen backward off the chair because of what she said, and I didn't know whether to laugh or what because I was shocked. She says, in English, "All right, Mr. Franco, let's get down to brass tacks. What's wrong and what do we have to do to get this damn thing resolved?"

Jackie broke up laughing and he said something in French and she answered it and she started to laugh. Then we got down to brass tacks. She tells me she was born in Chicago and she became a nun when she was sixteen and she's fifty-two now and we don't need an interpreter. I just pulled the chair right up to the table and the three of us had our elbows on the table and we're putting our heads together to see how we're going to resolve this problem. I says, "If you let me alone, I'll go back to Windsor and, like I told the bursar, I'll call up the union and I'll tell the union to take a walk and that's the end of it. You people have been very nice to me and you've taken care of my children and I think I owe you one. You know Italian people, sister?"

She says, "Yes, I know Italians and I know Sicilians and I know their traditions and I know the way they react. I want to thank you, Mr. Franco. Now you go back to Windsor and, Mr. Franco, if you need any help, you just call me and then I'll get into the picture."

I says, "No, you don't have to do anything."

She says, "Well, you know I could pick up the telephone, too. Don't forget, I'm from Chicago and I do still have some friends there." It seems like she knows Bill McFetridge and a lot of other people.

So, I went back to Windsor and I got hold of the union and I says, "Hey, you're messing with the wrong lady. This lady is from Chicago and you'd better listen to me and you'd better forget about those applications and tell your people you can't do anything for them because this is a Catholic school. Do what you have to do, but get the hell out of there. One, I'm telling you. And number two, if you don't listen to me, this lady will pick up the phone and call some people in Chicago and you're going to have more problems than you think you've got right now."

Well, she didn't have to make those calls because they listened to me and they did the right thing and they walked away.

18

Franco had said that his dream was to be like Jimmy Hoffa. He had followed Hoffa's orders, done Hoffa's bidding, and tried to emulate Hoffa. In the 1960s, he was finding out just what price he would have to pay for that dream. In the fall of 1961, Hoffa was indicted for misusing Teamster pension funds in a shady Florida land scheme called Sun Valley, Inc. And that fall he went on trial in Nashville on charges that he had violated the Taft-Hartley Act by receiving about $1 million from a company called Commercial Carriers in connection with a firm supposedly owned by his wife and Bert Brennan's wife, Test Fleet Corporation. That trial ended in a hung jury, but Bob Kennedy's investigators had suspicions as to just how that jury had come to be deadlocked. They tried to prove their suspicions, which led in 1963 to the indictment of Hoffa on charges of tampering with the jury.

The Justice Department, though, was interested in more than merely getting Hoffa. It wanted to rid the Teamsters of what it considered corrupt influences and corrupt officials. In the process, if it could put enough pressure on some of those officials below Hoffa to give evidence against him in order to save themselves, so much the better. It had a weapon it might be able to use for just that purpose. The Landrum-Griffin Act, passed by Congress in 1959, mandated detailed reporting by unions and union officials of all income, expenditures, and other financial activities.

★ ★ ★

In 1959, we knew that the Landrum-Griffin Act was going to pass and we were aware that it was going to be a very effective law in restraining a lot of the activities of organizers such as myself, and it caused problems to our unions. So, we all took steps to meet those problems before the law went into effect, which was supposed to be January 1, 1960.

At that time, I worked for many international unions under Jimmy Hoffa's directions and I was traveling all over the United States, servicing those unions and the locals that I was supervising for Jim. If I had to go someplace because Jim would send me, to take a local into receivership or for some other reason, I would do so and like everybody else in America, I would use plastic cards to pay for everything.

Now, when we knew that Landrum-Griffin was going to happen, I talked to Jim and I talked to the heads of the other unions to see what we ought to do. I was asked to withdraw and hand in my resignation by some of them. Harry Dimeno, who was the general president of the Toy, Doll, and Novelty Workers, asked me to resign and he told me to take whatever membership I had and the five locals that I had and do whatever I wanted to do with them, and he said he would give me a check for whatever he owed me for servicing those locals, and he did give me a check for about $12,000. That check was deposited to the account of the Local 42, the General Employees local of the Distillery Workers. And I put my locals of the Toy and Novelty Workers into Local 42. I did the same thing with the locals I controlled of Sheet Metal Workers and some others, and the circus and carnivals I turned over to Harold Gibbons and his people in St. Louis. So, by the time the law was enacted, we were getting our house in order.

In August of 1959, we had an executive board meeting of Local 42, with the full executive board plus my attorney and my accountant. At that meeting, we decided to merge all the people that I had represented and take all the money and take all the business agents that were assigned to the other locals and the office staffs and make them all part of Local 42 so that nobody would lose employment, and everything else from those locals, like trucks and office equipment and everything else, would be given to Local 42.

At that board meeting, we agreed that all expenses that were incurred prior to that time would be approved by the board and paid by Local 42. And we agreed to give pay increases to the attorney and the accountant for their services, and they granted me a pay increase from $18,500 to $22,000 because of the increase in membership and because of what I was losing in pay from those other unions, though that increase didn't come close to compensating me for the loss.

Then we took up the money that was owed on the credit cards I had used. I was using American Express, Diners Club, and Carte Blanche, and they were all delinquent at that time. The board agreed that once the merger came about, all the cards would be paid off. The question was then asked of me, what part of those bills were the responsibility of the Toy and Novelty Workers and what part belonged to the Jewelry Workers and what part to the other unions and locals I was bringing in. I told the board I had no idea because I didn't keep records on that basis. All I would do was go out and do what I had to do, do my business and charge everything and mark it on the bill wherever I was, and that was it. And those bills would be approved in the normal executive board meetings we would have in the specific locals. But I couldn't divide a portion to this one or that one. So, what we did was to break the bills down into three or four parts so each local and each international union division would pay an equal part, and we thought that was the fairest way to do it. And the board approved it. And unlike a lot of other guys that ran union meetings, I used to tape all my executive board meetings. I had a very large tape recorder, but that one was broken that night, and so we taped it on a portable recorder.

The major bill that was outstanding was to American Express and it was for $1,832.50. What we agreed that night was that Local 42 would pay that $1,832.50, but due to the fact that I could not prove what part was used for Local 42, I would have to reimburse the local, and that's what happened. The local issued four checks—three for $500, each, and one for $332.50—and I paid them back in installments before December 15, 1959. So everything was cleared up and we merged the locals into Local 42 and we were ready to start 1960 with a whole set of new books and a clean slate.

In February 1960, I went down to Miami for the Teamsters conference and the international executive board meetings. I was staying at the Castaways and my secretary, Grace Martin, called me and told me the LM-2 financial report that was required by the Landrum-Griffin Act was all done and it would have to be signed and filed before March 15. I told her to send it to me because there was no way I could get home in time to go over it and get it off. So she sent it to me, and after I went over it, I called back to the office and I told the accountant, "I got it and I read it, but I don't understand it."

He says, "Joe, it's the only way I know how to prepare it. Don't forget, Joe, this is the first one of these that's ever been prepared and there's a lot of inquiries by the heads of many unions about interpreting the Landrum-Griffin Act, but there's been so many things coattailed onto it that nobody understands it. Even the Labor Department hasn't set up an office in Michigan yet to handle the questions. I just did it the best way I know how."

So, I signed it and sent it in. We did it again in 1961, for the record for 1960, and in 1962, for 1961, and in 1963, for 1962, and everything seemed to be going along without a hitch. Then, in 1963, the Labor Department issued a subpoena for all of my records back to 1959, not prior to 1959 because Landrum-Griffin didn't involve anything prior to that. And we had no problem with that. Our attorney, Joseph Louisell, raised all kinds of hell about the fact that they wanted our records and had to issue a subpoena instead of just asking, but we turned them over, because I didn't think there was anything to hide and I didn't think we had done anything wrong.

Well, what came out was that I got my first indictment out of that. They charged me with willful intent to defraud the United States government by filing an improper LM-2 report. What it was was that there was two columns on the report for listing moneys. Column A was supposed to be for direct and indirect expenses incurred by the union and column B was for loans made by the union. Since my expenses that I ran up on the American Express and the other credit cards was for union business, the accountant stuck the $1,832.50 that the union had paid out and that I had reimbursed the union in column A. In column B, he stuck a $300 loan I had with the union and a $1,000 loan that one of the business agents had. But the government said that was wrong and that the $1,832.50 was actually a loan and not expenses, direct or indirect, and that's what they indicted me for.

During all this, I met a man who was head of the Justice Department task force in Detroit. His name was Tom McKeon. We met in a restaurant a few times and we were on good talking terms.

And then I get another indictment. In 1963, I was going to buy a supper club and turn it into a nightclub. It was going to be a way to supplement my income, because I was strapped. It was costing me nearly $6,000 to send my girls to school and I had to take care of the home, the maid, and my son. I borrowed money from a very wealthy lady I was going with at the time, and I borrowed money against my insurance policy so I was able to put down $18,000 in escrow against purchasing this club, which I was going to call Jilly's, and I talked to Jilly Rizzo about it and he had no objection to my using the name.

The guy that had owned the club had passed away and his half-interest was with a receiver and the receiver had a lawyer and the other partner had a lawyer and I had a lawyer, James Rossi, who used to be the legal adviser to the state liquor control commission. Well, they all sat down and everything was drafted and I put the money down. And pending completion of the transfer of licenses to me, I got a letter from the liquor control commission saying that I had the right to go in and clean the place up and operate it under a management contract until everything was completed and the liquor license was transferred to my name, and I would then be the owner. But meanwhile, I was only operating it as a manager. Well, I went in there with a crew and we cleaned the place and decorated it with wall-to-wall carpeting and black carpeting on the walls and fixed up the kitchen and the bar and everything else and built a stage because I intended to have entertainment. Then I had to go into the hospital for surgery on my back, and I figured with my back and everything, there's nothing I can do to run the club. I got the word out that I'd like to sell it and maybe make some money on it even though the liquor license still hadn't been transferred to my name. I figured with the $18,000 I had put down and about $5,000 I had put into it, I had to get a little profit, and I was able to sell it for $27,000.

Now, the place is sold and a month or two goes by and I'm in bed and it's like seven-thirty in the morning. The kids are up and having breakfast and all of a sudden there's a tremendous bang on the door and damn near tore the door down. And in rushed four FBI agents and everybody's screaming and the kids are frightened. Two of these agents ran upstairs to my bedroom and grabbed me and said that I'm under arrest.

I says, "Whoa, hold it. You guys go back downstairs, let me put on a pair of pants and I'll come down and we'll see what this is all about."

They says, "No, we'll wait for you."

"You guys get the hell out of here, go downstairs, have a cup of coffee. I'm not running anyplace."

"We can't leave your side. We're not going to allow you to escape."

"Where the hell am I going to escape? I got kids in this house and you're scaring everybody to death."

I threw on a pair of pants and went downstairs and called my attorney and he says, "Go ahead and accept the arrest status and let them take you in and they're going to release you and we'll take it from there."

I got everybody out of the house, told them there was nothing to worry about, and then I turned to one of the guys and I says, "Now, what the hell is all this about?"

He gives me a piece of paper and it says I was being indicted for willful intent to defraud the United States government alcohol tax bureau of $32.50 for an alcohol tax license. I started to laugh and I says, "What the hell is this?"

One guy says, "I don't think it's anything funny. You've been indicted and you're under arrest. You intended to defraud the government for $32.50 for a liquor stamp."

"What the hell do I have to do with a liquor stamp?"

"Don't you own Jilly's nightclub?"

"No, I don't own it. I was intending to buy it. But all the money was in escrow and I was the manager of it."

"Well, we have you down as the hidden owner and you're

charged with defrauding the government of the money for the tax stamp."

"You got to be kidding me."

And I look out the window and there's four more agents in front of the house and four more in the back, and they got me surrounded like they thought I was John Dillinger or Scarface Al Capone or something. I says, "But my attorney says I should go with you. Okay. But let me go upstairs and get dressed."

One agent says, "No"

"What do you mean, no? I got to go to the toilet." I went right up the stairs and this son of a bitch went upstairs and stood right there.

I says, "What the hell is this all about?"

He says, "We don't want you to commit suicide."

"You don't what? Are you crazy? I'm gonna commit suicide for a goddamn $32.50 tax stamp I don't know nothing about and I'm not responsible for in the first place?"

He says, "A lot of guys get into trouble like you're in trouble with the other indictments you got . . ."

"What other indictments? You don't know what the hell you're talking about."

Anyway, I threw on a sweatshirt and a pair of old pants and they threw me in the backseat and handcuffed me and took me down and photographed me and took my fingerprints and threw me into the cooler until my attorney got there to get me out.

So, now I had another indictment. Then I got a call from Tom McKeon asking me and my attorney to come to his office. Joe Louisell had another case so he sent a young lawyer, Leo Fink. Tom sat at one end of the table and Leo and I sat at the other. Tom says to Leo, "I can't talk to your client, but I can talk to you. I will be willing to make a deal. If your client will plead guilty to the liquor stamp case, then I will drop the charges under the Landrum-Griffin Act. Maybe we don't have much of a case there, but we could go to court and cause Joe some embarrassment. But if Joe is willing to cop a plea on the liquor stamp case, that would not stop him from being an active officer of the local union."

What I found out was that if I pleaded guilty on that liquor stamp thing, I'd probably get a $500 fine and be told to apply for the stamp. I says to Leo, "I can't agree to that because I'll get myself into the jackpot because I don't own the license, I got nothing to do with the license, so how do I plead guilty to something I can't be guilty of?"

Tom says, "I can understand what the problem is. But you think about it and we'll see what we can work out."

We went back to the office and Ivan Baris, Joe Louisell's partner, says, "We're not going to cop a plea to anything. We're going to try this one right to the end."

I says, "No, don't. Tom's trying to do me a favor. He knows the liquor stamp deal is not going to stop me from being an officer in the union. All I got to do is pay a $500 fine and that's the end of it."

He says, "You want me as a lawyer, you'll have to do what I tell you to do."

"Okay." I knew goddamn well that I was making a big mistake listening to him.

Time goes by and I don't give Tom an answer one way or the other. Then I get another call and he asks me if I would come to his office. I says, "Sure. What's up?"

"I'd like to ask you some questions."

I told him I had no problem with that. At that point, I wasn't going to fight the government like I started out with, being snippy and snotty and very abusive. I figured Tom McKeon had been very straight up with me and the least I can do is to meet with him.

I went down to the federal building and Tom was behind the desk in his office. Right away, I noticed there was a door to another office and it was cracked maybe a couple of feet, and I kind of felt there must be somebody in that other office that wanted to hear what Tom McKeon and I had to say.

Tom started out, "You know, Joe, I tried to help you as much as I could, and I've been as fair with you as I could be and I offered you a deal on the alcohol tax license case. You've never given me an answer on that one, so we're going to proceed, and take you to trial for violation of the Landrum-Griffin Act."

I says, "Well, Tom, you know I'm only doing exactly what my counsel is telling me to do. As far as I'm concerned, I would accept the deal. I have no problem with it. But I hired the son of a bitch and what am I going to do? I'm stuck with this guy and I don't know what the hell I can do about it. That's the way Hoffa wants me to be. Hoffa assigned me to Louisell and Louisell assigned me to Ivan Baris and that's the game plan."

We start a little idle chatter that goes on for about ten minutes, and he tells me if there's anything I can do to help him, he can probably make it a little easier on me. If I would cooperate with them, they might still drop both charges.

"I don't know what you mean by cooperating with you, Tom. Maybe if you make yourself a little clearer." He starts hedging about what type of cooperation he wants, and I says, "Look, Tom, why don't you be straight with me? You've been straight right along, why don't you be straight with me right now? Somebody's in the other room. Why don't you tell them to come in here. You're stuttering and you're hedging and you either don't know how to get at me or you're more concerned about the other people listening to what you're trying to get across."

He says, "I'll tell you what. Excuse me for one minute, Joe." He gets up and he goes into the other room and he closes the door. Five or ten minutes went by and the door opened again and Tom McKeon came out and sure as hell, here comes Bobby Kennedy and behind him is Carmine Bellino. Bobby sat where Tom McKeon was sitting and Carmine Bellino sat on one side of him and Tom McKeon sat on the other side and I sat in front of the desk.

Bobby looks at me and he says, "So you're Joe Franco."

I says, "That's right. I don't think you have to introduce yourself. I know who you are. I'm sure you knew who I was before you came out of that office because I'm sure you've been tipped about me and you've seen pictures of me, otherwise you wouldn't be here today. Let's get that out of the way."

He says, "All you Teamsters think you're tough guys. You think you're just like Hoffa. Well, I'm going to get Hoffa, don't worry about that. And I'm going to get you, too."

"Hey, you know you get Hoffa, you get Hoffa; you get me, you get me. It's a goddamn big thing for you, I guess, but you're not going to get any publicity getting me. With Hoffa, you get national publicity. With me, you get shit."

He says, "Tom McKeon was hedging with you. I won't hedge with you. I'll tell you exactly what the fuck I want."

I says, "Ho-ho, you're getting down to my level now. You're using the language. You're pretty streetwise."

"You know goddamn well I'm streetwise."

Now this Carmine Bellino is just sitting there and not saying a thing and he's taking notes. I look at him and I says, "I hope you're writing everything down, because you can wipe your ass with it when we're done."

Bobby says, "You Teamsters, you're always the same. You never want to cooperate. It seems like Jimmy taught you guys and he taught you well, but you're all out of the same mold with him."

"Hey, I wish the hell I was like him because I'm damn proud of the man. I can't say that much for you. But take your best shot. What's on your mind, or are you just going to sit here and bullshit? I ain't got time for that, so let's get it out of the way."

"I got a deal to offer you."

"What kind of a deal? Let's see where you're coming from."

"One, I want information from you. I don't care if it's truthful or whether it's hearsay or fantasies or what. I want anything you can give me that I can use to bring Hoffa to trial. I want anything you can give me that I can use to bring Frank Fitzsimmons to trial. I can take anything you can give me on William E. Bufalino. If you can give me anything that will help me take these three guys to trial, or any one of the three, and get a conviction, I'll give you five years of federal immunity."

"What the hell does that mean?"

"All charges on your cases will be dropped. You will not have any federal charges brought against you for the next five years. No federal agency will touch you on any case whatsoever."

I looked at him and I says, "What if I went into a bank and held up a bank and I got caught?"

"I would see that all federal charges would be set aside."

"You got to be kidding."

"No, I'm not. That's the best deal I can give you."

"Well, I'll tell you one goddamn thing, it's a pretty tempting situation. Is it verbal or do I get it on paper?" I knew goddamn well he wasn't going to put that deal on paper.

"I can't give you anything in writing, but I can give you my word."

Well, at this point, maybe a little before, Tom McKeon got up and excused himself and walked out of the room. I don't think Tom wanted any part of this and I think he was a pretty straight guy. It was when he left the room that all this bullshit started to come down.

I turned to Bobby, I didn't call him Bobby, and I says, "Mr. Kennedy, let me tell you something. One, you can't give it to me in writing, so what you're telling me is as useless as tits on a bull. Two, if I did take your word, what happens if you're not around and your brother's not around and you don't have the power that you have today? All of a sudden, I'm left holding the bag. I'm going to go ahead and give you evidence so you can indict Hoffa and Fitzsimmons and Bufalino, and all of a sudden you're not around anymore or you have a bad memory. You know, I don't trust you. I might as well tell you straight out front. And I don't trust that fucking Italian sitting alongside of you. As far as I'm concerned, he's a fucking disgrace to the Italian people. So you see, right there, you made a mistake with me bringing this piece of shit with you, because that immediately chilled me off, knowing that he's Italian and he's having any part of this kind of a deal with another Italian. He knows better. You'd have been better off if you came in and sat down with me alone, Mr. Kennedy, instead of having him with you. Now, where do we go from that point? What do you want to know? First of all, you can't give it to me in writing and you can only give it to me verbally. But let's say that I do agree to go with you, what do you want to know?"

He says, "I don't care. I don't give a damn if you lie. All I want is that you go in front of a grand jury to state anything that you can state that will get us an indictment we can go to trial with. I'll make it my business to win that trial. All I want is enough to be able to go in front of a grand jury."

I says, "Well, that's a bad deal. One, Hoffa's my boss and my loyalty and my respect is to my boss. Number two, Fitz was my partner and I like the man and I've had a lot of close associations with that man and I can't say anything bad about Fitz because I don't know anything bad about him. Number three, as far as Bill Bufalino is concerned, whether you know it or you don't, Carmine Bellino will understand me, Bill is my *compare;* he baptized my son, his wife and him, and he's my son's godfather, and his daughter baptized my oldest daughter, Victoria, so she's my daughter Victoria's godmother. He also stood up for my children as far as the baptismals is concerned. Bill is like family to me, so you can't ask me to say anything bad about Bill Bufalino or his family. So that leaves out Bill. Now, what you really want is Hoffa; you don't give a damn about the other two. I want you to understand something, Mr. Kennedy, Mr. Hoffa doesn't tell me his private business. He doesn't take me into his full confidence in saying he's doing this and he's doing that, so I don't know what the hell you want from me. I can't tell you anything personal about the man or if he's involved with any businesses. I know what you're basically looking for, but that man doesn't tell me his business. I'm a little cog in a big wheel and Jimmy is the hub of the wheel. I don't have any inside information. So that eliminates all of that. Where do we go now? Who else are you looking for?"

He got real mad and he stood up and he slapped down on the desk and he says, "I want you to know one goddamn thing. If you don't cooperate with us, I'll have you in jail in the next two weeks and you can take my word for it. I'll have you in jail. And when I do that, what I'm going to do is take your four children away from you and put them in an orphanage and have you declared an unfit father."

With that, I blew my stack, I just saw red. I stood up and I slapped down on the desk and I built up as much spit as I possibly could in my mouth and I spit in his face and I says, "You son of a bitch. You dirty little fag bastard, like Jimmy told me you were. You fuck with my children, Bobby Kennedy, and I'll fuck all over you and your whole fucking family. I'll make a fucking vendetta on you like you wouldn't believe. Carmine, you tell this little asshole what it means when a Sicilian takes a vendetta on a family. I'll swear a vendetta on you and your whole family, Bobby Kennedy. I'm not James R. Hoffa. You can bet your ass, because I'll go down swinging and I'll take half your family with me before they get me. You can go fuck yourself."

I got up and I'm still yelling and I start to walk out, and he's looking at me. As I get to the door, he tells me he's giving me two weeks to change my mind and do like he says.

I got downstairs and I got in the car and went right over to Trumbull Avenue, and they got two federal cars tagging me the whole way, to see exactly where I was heading for. I went over to Teamster headquarters and went upstairs and went over to Local 299's office, which Fitz was now using as president with Jimmy in

Washington. I knocked at the door. Now the door has glass where you can look out of the office but you can't look in from the outside. I knocked and the girl tells me he's busy. I says, "Well, buzz him. Tell him he'd better open this goddamn door because I got something to tell him." I was fucking mad and I was mad at Fitz on top of it for making me stand outside and he knew I was standing there because I put my face right up against the glass. Well, the girl told him and he knew I was mad so he pushed the clicker and I opened the door and walked in. There were two or three guys in there and I says, "All you guys, outside. Get out. I got to talk to Fitz alone."

With that, I told Fitz exactly what took place, and I told him to call Jimmy and tell him, and I was going across the street where Bill had his office so I could tell him. Fitz got hold of Jimmy and Jimmy said he would be in on Saturday and we would meet and talk about it.

Now, when I told Bill what had gone down, he says he doesn't want to talk in the office, but he was going up to Ann Arbor to see a doctor to take some packing out of his nose that he'd just had an operation on and we should ride together. We got in the backseat and he had one of the business agents drive us. I told him word for word what took place. He says, "I'm glad you told Fitz because as far as we're concerned, Fitz is the weak link in the chain. If Fitz ever gets nailed . . . that's why Jimmy always protected Fitz in the old days, even with getting Fitz out of it when Mike Nicoletti and Sam Morasso and Frankie Collins had to go to jail and Jimmy got Fitz loose. Jimmy's always afraid if Fitz ever got behind bars, he'd probably open up and implicate him on something, so he's always protected Fitz. He doesn't think Fitz can stand up under pressure."

I says, "I don't know. As far as Fitz is concerned, we have always been real close and he always looked to me like a standup guy."

Comes Saturday and Bill gives me a call. He tells me Jimmy wants me in the office at ten o'clock but he's not going to be there, Jimmy just wants me and Fitz.

I went to the office and met with them and I told Jimmy the whole story from start to finish. Jimmy got a smile on his face and he says, "Well, you finally met the little fag bastard. And the other one, how do you like your countryman?"

I says, "Jimmy, don't go rubbing it in. I'm sorry he's Italian. He could just as well be Irish-Dutch like you. I told him to his face he's a disgrace to the Italian people."

He says, "Now you got some idea what I've had to contend with. He's desperate. He's trying to get everything he can to try to nail me, but I'm surprised he's getting that desperate that he wants Bill and he wants Fitz. When have you got your next meeting with him?"

"Well, he told me that I got two weeks and within two weeks I should give him a call and set up a meeting and give him a yes or no. I figure if we could get it on paper, we may have something we could work with."

"That's good thinking, but he would never give you a piece of paper. Forget about it. But I'll tell you what we can do. Fitz, you get hold of Bernie Spindel and have him meet with Franco. Franco, you have any objections if they wire you up and then you meet with Bobby and that way we'll record everything that comes down. If he makes this kind of deal with you, we've got it on tape and we can use it against him if we have to go into a courtroom."

I says, "Sure."

"Well, you have any objections to going in and having it transplanted because they may shake you down if you do meet with Bobby again? I'm surprised they didn't do it the first time. It probably was that he didn't think he would be exposed, he thought Tom McKeon would be the one who would make the deal with you. But this time they may be a little more cautious with you because now they're going to be looking for you to give them an answer on this deal."

I says, "What do you mean by transplant?"

"I mean implant. What they'll do is they'll make a little incision in your chest. They'll take you to the doctor's office and they'll give you a local shot and you won't feel any pain or anything, and they'll put a little microphone underneath your skin so if they shake you down, they won't feel any wires, they won't see anything, and within the two-week period, that will heal up."

"What do I do, walk around for the rest of my life with the transmitter inside me?"

"Nah. We'll take it out as soon as you get finished with your meeting."

"Nah, I have no objections."

"All right. Fitz, you handle it. You get hold of Bernie Spindel and set it up so Franco and you can get together with him, and take him over to Dr. Danny Cohen and have Danny put the transmitter inside."

We talked for a little after that and then Fitz left and Jim asked me to stick around, he wanted to talk to me. When Fitz was gone, he says, "What do you think?"

"Well, Jim, I don't know. You want me to do what you tell me, that's okay."

"No. What do you think of Fitz?"

"I don't know. I got funny vibes because now, after all the years I've known this man and much as I've done with him and the guy's always been standup with me. But I took a ride with Bill the other day and Bill tells me that you've always been afraid of him not being a standup guy and you saved his ass a couple or three times from going to jail and let him stay home and stay clean."

He says, and he nods his head like, yeah, a disgusted nod, "What am I going to do? Franco, I'm just not sure of him. In a lot of ways, Fitz is all right. But I've always had problems with Fitz. He does things. He fucks up things. I don't know. If it came to you, I wouldn't worry about it. If it came to Bill, I wouldn't worry. Most of the guys that are with us, I wouldn't worry. Fitz, I do worry about. I wanted to get your feelings."

"Well, I can only go by what Bill told me and I got funny vibes after that. If nobody would say nothing to me, I would still do things with Fitz."

"All right. Wait until Fitz gets hold of you and gets that thing put in and then call Kennedy and set up a meeting and let me know afterward and we'll have a sitdown."

Now, three, four weeks go by and I don't call Bobby Kennedy up and I don't hear from him and he don't hear from me. And I don't hear from Fitzsimmons. I get a telephone call from Jimmy. He says, "I'm coming in. I want to see you. Be in the office Saturday morning."

Saturday morning, I get to the office at nine o'clock and Jim's sitting there and he jumps up and his ears are tomato red, which means he's really pissed. I says, "Goddammit, what did I do wrong? Something happened?"

"Didn't I give you fucking instructions? Didn't I tell you to get that fucking deal set up with Spindel? Didn't Fitz tell you? Didn't I tell you in front of Fitz?"

"Yeah. What's wrong?"

"Fitz tells me you refused to do it."

"Where the fuck is Fitz at? Now I'm starting to believe what you told me and what Bill Bufalino told me. This dirty rotten Irish motherfucker that he is. Jimmy, you told me to do something. Goddammit, I've been waiting for Fitz. I've called him every fucking day for ten straight days. This son of a bitch won't even return my call on it. What am I supposed to do, come over there and grab him? The instructions from you was that he should get hold of Spindel and then Spindel and I would go to Dr. Cohen and get the goddamn thing done. Wasn't that the way it was supposed to be?"

"Yeah. But Fitz told me you refused."

"Where's he at?"

"He's across the street."

"Fine. Pick up the phone, call 299, and tell the bastard to come over here. Because I'll slap him right across his goddamn mouth if he stands there and lies to you. He lies to you behind my back. I'll make him tell you the truth in front of my face. Jim, it ain't me. I was willing to do it and the son of a bitch is lying to you. I should go to Bobby Kennedy and tell him some shit on him and fuck him, let him go down the tube now."

"No, don't do that. He's scared. I believe you, Franco."

"Get him over here."

"No, we don't have to do that. As long as I know where he's coming from, that's okay. There'll come a day, don't worry about it. I'll handle it my way."

"Long as you know. I'm still willing to do it. I don't know if Kennedy will answer my telephone calls or not anymore because it's already been four weeks that's gone by."

"Well, if he contacts you, you let me know and I'll have somebody else set it up. But don't you call him. Let him come back to you."

"All right."

And we sat there for a while talking about the kids and things and then I got up and says, "I got to get back home."

He says, "I'll talk to you during the week from Washington. Take care of yourself and say hello to the children for me."

I never heard from Fitz again after that in regards to this matter, and I never heard from Jimmy again in regards to that, and I never heard from Bobby Kennedy after that.

19

Robert Kennedy really didn't need Joe Franco's help in his pursuit of Jimmy Hoffa. Hoffa dug his own pit and Kennedy and the federal authorities were only too happy to provide whatever additional impetus was needed to shove him into it.

In February 1964, Hoffa went on trial in Chattanooga on the charge of tampering with the jury in the Test Fleet case two and a half years before. The trial took a month and when it was over, Hoffa stood convicted and sentenced to eight years in federal prison.

From Nashville it was on to Chicago for the Sun Valley case, the conspiracy to defraud the Teamster pension fund. Once more the jury brought in a verdict of guilty, and Hoffa was sentenced to eight years in federal prison to run concurrently with his other sentence.

If Hoffa could find any solace from all this, it was that he had not been convicted of violation of the Landrum-Griffin Act. He knew that when he served his time, he might be able to step right back into the office of general president of the Teamsters international.

★ ★ ★

I didn't go to Chattanooga for that trial. Jim sent back word for me to stay the hell away from there, he didn't want me around because he didn't want me exposed.

But, when he went to Chicago for that trial, I asked Allen Dorfman to ask him if I could come to see him. I told Allen to tell him that I was going through everything he was going through and they got more pictures of me than they got of Errol Flynn, and they got indictments against me and I was going to be going to trial, so I don't know why he's worried about exposing me and there's no way I'm going to hide my personality.

Allen calls and tells me that Jimmy's agreed to let me come over and see him at the trial because he figured I can't hide no more. I sat up there and watched the thing and then the judge called a recess and I went over to the rail and he came over to the rail and we shook hands and he cupped both of my hands and looked me right straight in the eye and he says, "How are you, Franco?"

I says, "I'm okay, boss. How do you feel?"

"Screw them. They think they're going to beat me, they're crazy. I'll fight them all the way down. How's your cases coming along?"

"Pretty good, Jim. It looks good. Everything's fine. Don't worry about me. Shit, you're fighting the battle here."

"Franco, I'm not worried about this. I'm going to go in and I'm going to do the time and I'll get the hell out and we'll start all over again. Well, not all over again. We'll pick up where we left off. Don't worry about it. Now, tell me, how are the kids?"

"The kids are fine."

"I know you, you son of a bitch. What are you doing for money for lawyers? I know it must be costing you an arm and a leg."

"Well, so far I get a piece here and give a little piece there and the lawyers are hanging on, hoping that we win the cases and I get out from underneath it and they know that eventually they're gonna get paid from me. The bills are running up. But what the hell are you asking me that for? I didn't come here for that, Jim. I came here because I miss you being out there. I miss the feelings that . . . you know, I don't like the feeling of you being behind bars." I started to get very emotional.

He says, "Cut it. You get into financial problems like you have in the past, I want you to go to Allen. You need anything, you go to Allen in case I'm not out there to help you. I'll talk to Allen." He flashed Allen to come over and Allen came over to the rail and Jim says, "I just told Franco if anything ever comes up and he needs help, he's to come to you. You take care of whatever Franco needs. I don't give a shit what it is. Make sure Franco and the kids are taken care of."

Allen says, "Don't worry about it. Joe knows well enough to come to me. And you know how my dad feels about him."

That's where we left it. I said goodbye to Jim. While he was in Chicago, I communicated with him through Allen. Of course, I saw him after that, until he went away, and then I would get messages to him through Bill Bufalino and Jimmy Jr.

As he had indicated to Hoffa, Franco's own troubles were multiplying during 1966. He began to feel he was living inside a pressure cooker with no safety valve. He was summoned by the Internal Revenue Service to explain a little matter of $800,000 in racetrack winnings over the previous two years on which he had paid no taxes.

He had an explanation.

They had introduced at the racetracks in Michigan and other places what they called the Twin Double, which was like a four-horse parlay, and I began reading about people winning like $70,000 or $80,000 or even more every night. What with running around the country and doing things for Jim, I hadn't been to the track in years. But, after the death of Alice, that kind of cooled off and I was around the office more. Now, this one night, I had just finished up a meeting and was sitting around and it was like seven o'clock and one of the kids who was trying to make an impression so he could become a business agent was hanging around, too, and he says to me, "Joe, if you ain't doing nothing, why don't we go out to the track?"

I says, okay, and we go out there and I run into Jay McCann, who was a Teamster business agent and my partner when I took over Local 614 in Jackson, Michigan in the old days, and Jay was an old harness tracker from way back and at one time I was partners with him on a horse. We got to talking and Jay explained the way the Twin Double worked, and we figured out a system. So, I says to Jay, "Who do you like in the fifth and the sixth and the eighth and the ninth?"

He gave me the horses. Then I saw an older trainer and driver named Joey Adams, and I says, "Listen, Joey, who do you got? I see you got a horse in the sixth and you got a horse in the ninth. What do they look like?"

He says, "I think I can win with both of them."

Then I saw a couple of other guys that owned horses and I got the word from them. So, I went ahead and started to bet and started to win, and I borrowed about $2,000 off of Jay and backed some horses, and the horses started winning, and by the end of the night, I was ahead $28,000. I paid off Jay and I was that much to the good.

Well, this twin double seemed like a good thing. I started going out just for the twin doubles and I was winning, and I started going around, to Yonkers and Denver and everywhere where they had the twin double and where I knew guys who owned horses. When I started making a lot, I knew there was going to be taxes to pay, so I called my accountant and I says, "How do I do this?"

He says, "Save your losing totes and put them in a box, because you can offset your winnings with your losses."

I did what he said and I threw all the losing tote tickets into this big carton. At the end of the year, he says, "How much did you win?"

I says, so much.

He says, "Have you got your losing tote tickets to offset that?"

"Yeah, no problem. They're in a big carton."

The same thing the next year. Then they called me in and they subpoenaed all my records back to 1957 and they did a net worth on me, because I had won $800,000 and I had lost $800,000, so it washed out as far as taxes was concerned. But they didn't like the way the whole thing looked and they was ready to indict me for tax fraud.

We go in, my accountant and me, and they start asking us and we turned over the whole box to the IRS so they could see that I had the losing totes to match up with the winning ones.

And that's where it stood for about eighteen months, into

1968, maybe 1969. Then we get called in again. I'm there this time with a tax attorney and the accountant, and the examiner from the IRS tells us they did a net worth on me and they can't find anything in it through the years except for a few hundred dollars here and few hundred there. But then they come to 1964 and 1965, and they find the $800,000 I declared in two years of playing the horses, and the $800,000 I lost which offset that. What they did was put those tote tickets into a log for every race I bet for two years, and the guy says, "Mr. Franco, we went through this and you did win $800,000. But we figured out that you lost $886,000. What we want to know is where you got that $86,000 to gamble with? It looks to us like undeclared income."

Now, I could have answered that. I was borrowing money to offset my betting and make sure I would break out with a winner, and then pay the money back, and this would give me additional tote tickets, and other things like that.

But, before I could answer, I got kicked on both sides, by my attorney and my accountant. They says to keep my mouth shut because the IRS was looking to get me on tax fraud and they would turn this over to the criminal department, and then I would have been looking at ten years, because I would have to prove where I got the $86,000 or go to jail. What I had to do was just take the $86,000 beef and shut up. I couldn't believe it. I think I'm the only man in history that ever got a tax rap for losing tote tickets. But I ended up doing it, and finally, in 1974, they agreed to a settlement of $51,000, which they got by confiscating my insurance policies and taking whatever other money they could capture and when I sold my home, they grabbed about 75 or 80 percent of that.

Franco's troubles were growing and Hoffa's had reached a climax. After his conviction in Chicago, there was little doubt that he would soon be going to federal prison. He might be able to run the Teamsters from his prison cell. Indeed, that was what he planned. But someone would have to act as his regent, to take care of all the day-to-day matters that constantly crossed the president's desk.

The logical man, perhaps the most respected Teamster leader —the man who might have taken some of the heat off the union—

was Harold Gibbons. Certainly the federal government would have breathed easier, and so would a lot of dissident Teamsters if Hoffa had handed the reigns to Gibbons.

Though Gibbons was still essentially loyal to his long-time friend and though he was an able, intelligent, and imaginative administrator, he was not Hoffa's idea of the man to keep his chair warm. It was not so much that Gibbons was honest or that he was a liberal Democrat, but mostly that Gibbons had shown an independent streak. He and Hoffa had a major falling out on November 22, 1963. On the day of the assassination of John F. Kennedy, Hoffa had not been in Washington. Gibbons was in charge of Teamster headquarters. Gibbons, like most Americans, was stricken by the event. He ordered the flags at the Teamster building lowered to half-mast and sent employees of the union home.

Hoffa was incensed. He railed at Gibbons, told him it was hypocritical to honor a man who had been the bitter enemy of the Teamsters and their leader. When Hoffa finished his tirade, Gibbons left the building and went back to St. Louis, and though he retained his position as a Teamster vice-president, he resigned as Hoffa's executive assistant and potential heir.

Over the next years, Gibbons and Hoffa patched up most of their differences, but the closeness that had once existed between them was gone. Hoffa believed that if Gibbons ran the union in his absence, he might turn into something other than a mere regent who followed orders. Hoffa's choice, then, was a man he was sure he could control—Frank E. Fitzsimmons. Hoffa was certain that Fitzsimmons would be the Teamster leader in name only.

★ ★ ★

Like always, I was planning to go to the convention in Miami in July. The kids were out of school and I was carrying a very bad guilt complex because I had put them in boarding schools. In order to make up, I decided that I would take them on a trip for the whole summer. I would buy a new station wagon and we would head out. We would go to Miami for the convention and then we would head out west. I put an ad in the papers for a young girl who might go along with us and take care of the children. This girl showed up and she was in her last year in college and she was majoring in child psychology and phys. ed., which was ideal. I hired her and off we went, down to Florida and got settled into the Castaways.

I went off to the Teamster conferences, and somebody I knew asked me to do them a favor. Would I go to Jimmy and set up a meeting for him with the wife of a guy named Frankie Carbo, who was out of Philadelphia and who was doing a long stretch for something to do with fixing a fight or killing somebody or something. So, I set things up and this very pretty little blonde woman comes into the lobby and I'm introduced to her and she says, "I understand you're a widower. If you want to bring your children over to my house, I'll be happy to take care of them while you're down here with the conference."

I says, "Thank you very much, but no, I have a babysitter."

We had lunch and then I took her over and introduced her to Jim and they sat down in the middle of the lobby at the Fountainbleu and they talked and it seemed that whatever the problems were, she got them resolved, because they were both smiling when she came over afterward and thanked me very much.

The next day, all hell broke loose. That's when Jimmy took the position of telling Harold Gibbons he was officially appointing Fitz the general vice-president of the international, to take care of things in case Jimmy would have to go to prison.

The word spread around that Harold was going to have a press conference and hand out a press release that he was going to challenge Fitz, which would have been a very bad thing to do because there was no sense in starting a pissing contest between Harold and Jimmy and Fitz. Everybody knew of my closeness to Harold, so quite a few guys started walking up to me. Babe Triscaro comes over and he says, "Well, your fucking friend is going to ask for a press conference and he's going to blast it all over the newspapers." And guys from New York and everywhere are telling me the same thing.

I says, "What the hell are you guys talking about?" Because right then, I really didn't know what had come down.

Babe says, "Jimmy just appointed Fitz as general vice-president and that put Harold down and Harold's pissed about it and he's going to blast it all over. And some guys are saying he's going to get up and run against Fitz."

"Well, look, if Harold said it, he was probably hot at the moment. Let me go talk to him."

I went up to Harold's suite and I sat down with him and I says, "Harold, what the hell is this I'm hearing?"

"I was hot, Joe. That's all."

"I know damn well you wouldn't do it. I'll tell you what you do. Beat everybody at their own game. Pick up the phone and I'll pick up the phone, and we'll invite everybody up here and we'll throw a cocktail party. Invite Jimmy and Josie, Fitz and his wife, invite everybody up, the guys from Ohio, all the key people that are really pissed at you now, and see if you can consolidate those people back into your corner again. They're not that crazy about Fitz, but they just don't like the idea of you making a public statement, of your going out and having a press conference."

Harold agreed with me. So we got on the phone immediately and started to set up a cocktail party for seven that evening. Harold called Jimmy personally and Jimmy accepted and everybody accepted. Now Harold had a young lady there with him, a Greek princess, I think, and Harold was married, even though they weren't living together anymore, but he knew what Jimmy's morals were on that point and that he didn't want strange women around, so Harold asked me, would I be her escort so that Jimmy wouldn't get all pissed. I did and I kind of played a host and made sure that everybody was having a drink and getting something to eat. Jim came up there and he and Harold got off into a corner and they talked and they shook hands and they cupped hands to show that their friendship was still there. I looked at Harold and winked at him and he grinned at me.

About then, Babe Triscaro walked up to me and he says, "Well, Joe, you got that one straightened out. Goddammit, Harold's a good man. I hated to see those two guys go on the edge. But what the fuck do we do now? We're stuck with Fitz. Nobody has any respect for Fitz. He's a nice guy, but he don't have the ability for the job Jimmy's throwing at him. God forbid something should happen to Jimmy tomorrow. Look what we'd be stuck with."

I says, "Well, Fitz ain't a bad guy. He's a nice man. He doesn't have the ability for it, but he's a nice guy. It'll be all right. Nothing's gonna happen to Jimmy."

So everything got straightened out there. But I was having

trouble with the girl I hired as a babysitter for my children. I found out that she was leaving the kids alone at the Castaways and going off to the beach by herself. I just picked her up and fired her and put her on a plane. But that left me without a babysitter. I got one of the girls that worked at the hotel to take care of the kids while I went to the conferences. That day, I was telling the Greek princess about it and she told me she had a neighbor who might be interested in taking the job. I told her that sounded good, but we were leaving for the West and going to California in a couple of days. She says that was a real coincidence because this girl was planning to head out that way, too, to see her mother and sister in San Francisco.

I met the girl, whose name was Barbara Chambliss, and I kinda took to her and so did the kids and I told her I'd give her five hundred dollars in cash if she went along as far as Denver and there I'd give her a plane ticket to San Francisco, or she could keep on with us to Las Vegas and then to Disneyland and she'd still get the five hundred dollars and anywhere she wanted, she could have the plane ticket.

She thought that was a good deal and we took off. We go to Denver and all of a sudden she started hemorrhaging and she collapsed and we rushed her to the hospital and she almost died. We stayed around for an extra week or ten days until she pulled out of it and got her strength back and she decided that she could keep on with us. In Las Vegas, she broke away and I gave her the ticket to San Francisco and I thought that was that.

We got back to Detroit at the end of August, and a couple of weeks later, I get a call from Barbara in San Francisco, and she says, "I know you don't have anyone to take care of your home and your children. I'm unemployed now. What would you think of the idea of paying me seventy-five dollars a week and I'll run your house and you can take the children out of boarding schools and I'll raise them for you?"

I was paying that much just for ordinary help to just clean the house. I told her come ahead, so she flew in and I told her I would give her two hundred dollars a week for whatever the house needed other than utilities, like food and her own clothes and the rest, and whatever she could save out of the two hundred dollars was hers. She agreed and after a while I took the kids out of school and

Barbara became part of the family. All my friends and all my family took a liking to her and pretty soon everybody was saying, "She's a nice lady. She takes care of your house, she takes good care of your kids. Why don't you marry her?"

In April 1967, Barbara and I finally got married by a circuit court judge who I helped get elected. Bill Bufalino was my best man. But that wasn't enough for Barbara. For some unknown reason, she wanted to get married in church. She started taking lessons and then we got married in church when she became a Catholic, and this time Sam and Dolly Lintine stood up for us.

Barbara and I went down to Florida for our honeymoon and we ran into Alan Drake and his wife, Wanda, and a young man named Tony Plate, whose real name was Tony Piato, and he was with a certain family out of New York, and later he disappeared from Florida. Anyway, Barbara and I and Alan and Wanda and Tony and his wife and another couple went out to dinner and who should we bump into but Frank Sinatra and his whole crew. Alan went over to say hello to Frank and Frank says they were going over to Dean Martin's place on the 79th Street Causeway and Alan and his party ought to come along. Alan must have said something that Joe Franco's here and he's on his honeymoon, and Frank just looked right over at me and didn't crack nothing, but he says everybody's invited.

Well, Tony Plate didn't want to go and the other couple didn't want to go, but Alan and Wanda wanted to go and so did Barbara because she was very much taken by Sinatra and everything else. She says, "Why can't we go?"

I says, "Okay, we'll go." We got into the limo that I had rented and we dropped everybody else off and went over to Dean Martin's place, and while we were pulling up, here comes a couple more limos with Frank and Dean and Joe Villa and the whole crew. There were nine or ten guys and only two or three girls and the whole crew was moving in and it was getting late, like two o'clock in the morning.

Well, I know what's gonna happen. They're gonna shut the door and it's going to be a very private deal. I says to Alan, "I don't think Wanda and Barbara should be exposed to that kind of a situation. You know what's gonna happen and I know what's gonna happen."

Now, here comes Frank. He walks right by me and he says hello to Alan and he nods his head to my wife and he don't say shit to me. Jilly comes up and he shakes hands and tells me congratulations and Pat Henry does the same and so does everybody in the troop.

I turned to Alan. "Look, if you and Wanda want to, go ahead. But Barbara and I, well . . ." And Barbara was looking kind of disappointed. I says, "Look, Barbara, you don't know what's gonna happen in there, and it might be something you may not want to be exposed to. I'm sure it's gonna be partytime, and I don't want any part of it. If I was single and you was single, that would be a different story. But we're married." So we left and went back to the hotel.

Later, Alan tells me, "Man, Frank was pissed. He was really pissed. He asked where's the other . . . he doesn't ask for you by name, Joe. He wanted to know where you went to. I told him you and Barbara didn't want to go because you were tired and you were on your honeymoon, and Wanda wasn't feeling good. I made the excuses. But he was pissed because we didn't all join the crowd. He thought you were stiffing him again."

20

On March 7, 1967, James R. Hoffa surrendered to federal authorities. The Supreme Court had turned down his final appeal, by a five-to-four vote. Chief Justice Earl Warren, writing the dissenting opinion, declared that the methods the Justice Department had used to convict Hoffa were "an affront to the quality and fairness of federal law enforcement." The chief witness against Hoffa in the jury tampering case, Edward Grady Partin, was employed by the government, Warren said, "not for the purpose of testifying to something that had already happened, but rather, for the purpose of infiltration, to see if crimes would in the future be committed. The government in its zeal even assisted him in gaining a position for which he could be witness to the confidential relationship of attorney and client. . . . Here the government reaches into the jail house to employ a man who was himself facing indictments far more serious than the one confronting the man against whom he offered to inform." Among those indictments facing Partin was one for perjury. Nevertheless, the Court majority upheld the conviction, and Hoffa was transported to the federal penitentiary at Lewisburg, Pennsylvania, to begin serving his eight years. If he behaved, even if he were never granted parole, he would be a free man again sometime around the middle of 1972.

★ ★ ★

I'll never forget the day he had to surrender. I sent a wire to him through Bill Bufalino and a message. I told Bill, "Tell Jimmy my feelings that he has to go to prison. I would have liked to serve his sentence for him so he could stay home. Tell him, he's closer to me than my own brothers are, and if there was any way I could go to prison instead of him, I'd be more than happy to do it."

Bill gave him the wire and the message and he sent back a short note saying he got it and he did appreciate it, and he knew I had my own battles to fight then.

Things went along and then in 1968, Harold Gibbons calls me up and he asks me to come into St. Louis and spend the weekend, and we'd play some golf, which was something Harold loved to do. I went over and while we were on the golf course, he says, "Joe, I want to hire you and put you on as chairman of the food division of the international union."

I says, "For you to ask me that, have you clearance from the little guy?" Meaning Hoffa.

"Yeah. I got word to him and he has no objections. He thinks you'd be a good man for it."

We finished up and we walked into the locker room and I says, "Harold, the only thing is, I make so much money a year and I can barely live on it. What do I do in this job?"

"Well, the first thing you do is you take your local, Local 42, and disperse it."

"I don't want to give it back to that international because, one, they don't deserve it because they never helped me to organize it, they never gave me any funds to do it, and all my funds came from Jimmy Hoffa, and all my help came from the Teamsters, so it's actually a Teamster local."

"You do what you want. You want to disperse it among other Teamster locals, you go ahead and do it. But you've got to divorce yourself from that local."

"That's no problem, as long as you tell me how much I'm going to make."

Harold told me that the chairman of the division would make around $42,000 a year and that was like $15,000 a year more than I was making. So I says, "Sure, I accept it. There'll be no problem."

We shook hands and we went to dinner that night with the

understanding that within a matter of thirty to sixty days, the whole thing would come through because Harold had the right to make the offer, seeing that he was chairman of the Central States Conference and also a vice-president of the international. Of course, Fitz was the general vice-president, running the union while Jimmy was in jail, but we didn't expect any trouble from Fitz, being that he was my ex-partner.

I went home and I was very happy and I told everybody and I started to make moves to get rid of the membership and everything else. Then all of a sudden, I get a telephone call saying to come to Chicago for the Central States meeting. At that meeting, Dave Previent, who was head of the legal department for the Teamsters, said to Fitz, "Joe Franco is a very capable guy and he can take over the division and run it with no trouble. But it just so happens that Joe Franco now has two indictments, and one is for violation of the Landrum-Griffin Act. Let Joe clear up those indictments and then let him come over and take over the division. But Joe shouldn't come over while he's got those indictments over his head because that will bring the heat down and we've got enough heat within the Teamsters without bringing Joe over and putting him in as head of some large division while he's going to be fighting his indictments in preference to taking care of the business he's got to take care of."

Well, Fitz listened to him and Fitz says to me, "You get your indictments cleaned up and then I'll appoint you, the executive board will appoint you, Harold Gibbons will appoint you, and you'll be chairman of the foods division of the international union."

I says okay. I wasn't worried. I thought both of those indictments were kind of crappy to begin with and the reason they'd been hanging around for such a long time was because the government was afraid to go to trial with them because they knew they were gonna lose. And when we did go to trial, we should be able to get rid of them without any trouble.

Then Harold calls me one day and he was going to throw one of his big charity affairs like he always threw where the tickets were like two hundred fifty dollars and five hundred dollars per person and all the money went to good causes, the three or four charities Harold supported.

So, I went in to go to the affair, and Josie Hoffa was there and Chuckie O'Brien was with her because he was supposed to be taking care of Josie no matter where she went. He was like a bodyguard with Jimmy in prison to make sure that nobody bothers her or takes advantage of her.

And there were a lot of other people there, too, since everybody came when Harold threw these things. One of the guys was Toots Shor, because he was very tight with Jimmy because Jimmy arranged for the money when Toots opened his new place in New York, and he was very tight with Harold, too. Now, Toots was a very big drinker, and he was not only a big drinker, he was a sloppy drunk. And sometimes Josie would have a drink and she would cut loose and get a little high. Me, I don't drink a lick, so I'm always sober. That was one of the things Hoffa liked about me. I never lost my cool because I can get into trouble without drinking. Jimmy used to say to me, "You know, Franco, you'd be fucking dangerous if you ever drank. Christ, you get into enough trouble being sober." Because I didn't drink, I was always the sober one and the guy who drove, and I was always the guy that stopped a beef or finished a beef. The rest of them were too goddamn drunk to do anything about it.

Well, this night of Harold's shindig, Sinatra was there with his whole entourage, because he was very close to Harold and he always showed up and did some of the entertaining. Two tables away from Frank, this guy got up and went over and tried to get Frank's autograph. And Frank had had a few drinks and he was pretty belligerent, the way he usually got when he had a few, and he told his bodyguard to flex the muscles and get the guy away. I couldn't understand that. Here was a guy that probably spent $1,000 for tickets and all he wanted was to get Frank's autograph and get his picture taken with Frank, and the bodyguard grabs him and a ruckus starts, which was the first one that night.

Well, then I look around and there's Toots Shor taking Josephine Hoffa over where it's darker and nobody's sitting and he gets her up against the wall and he starts to maul her, kissing her and everything else. Josie had just had one too many and she was just like jelly, and he was taking advantage of her and I guess he'd been drinking hard enough, like always, not to realize that he was taking advantage of that poor woman.

As far as I was concerned, that was the boss's wife and nobody's going to try to kiss this woman and make out with her and feel her up or anything else. Frank's bodyguard, a big ex-football player, is standing right near me and he sees it and he don't do nothing. I went over to Chuckie O'Brien and I touched him on the shoulder and I says, "Chuckie, are you going to do something about it or am I going to have to beat the shit out of Toots Shor?"

Chuckie says, "What am I going to do about it?"

"Come with me." I went over to Toots and I grabbed him by the shoulders and pinned him against the wall, and I cocked my right hand and I says, "You Irish cocksucker, you. The boss is in jail and you're fucking with his wife. Chuckie, take Josie upstairs and put her to bed. Get one of the girls to help you."

Now, I was going beat Toots's brains out. I got my left hand against his throat and I'm ready to cut loose when this ex-football player all of a sudden grabs my right arm and he says, "Don't do it, Joe. He's drunker than shit. He don't know what he's doing."

And here comes Harold. He says, "What are you doing, Joe?"

I says, "This goddamn pig, motherfucker that he is, he's got Josie over here and he's got his hand under her dress, copping a feel, trying to God knows what to her. And Josie's drunker than . . . she don't even know what's going on."

Harold says, "Hold it, Joe. Don't start no trouble." Then he grabs Toots and he says, "Come on, Toots, get your ass up to bed." He got a couple of his agents to take Toots upstairs and put him to bed.

Then Harold comes to me and he says, "Jesus, Joe, don't do that."

I says, "Harold, if that was your wife and somebody was doing it to your wife, I'd beat the fuck out of him, too. But it's the boss's wife and she's been drinking and having a good time and what do you call a piece of shit like him?"

He says, "I understand your feelings. You're right and he's wrong. The guy's dead drunk."

"It ain't over with. When I get into New York, I'll catch him when he's sober, in his own joint. I ain't gonna send word to the old man, because if I do that, you know what he'd ask me to do, he's gonna ask me to break his fucking legs for him to start with."

Harold says, "Jesus, Joe, don't start nothing."

"Harold, stay out of it. Don't go copping out for this drunken pig." And I walked away.

A couple of weeks go by and I'm in New York and I made it my business to go down to Toots Shor's. He saw me walking into his restaurant and he ran over and sat in a booth with some celebrities. I walked over to him and I stuck my finger in his face and I says, "I want to see you, you pig son of a bitch. If you want to be a man, step out of that booth, step outside, and I'll beat your ass for you." And I was yelling and everybody was looking up because they could all hear. What I don't say is why I'm saying this, because I don't want these people to know what he did.

He says, "Joe, I'm sorry. God, I'm sorry. I had too much to drink."

"The next time you see that lady, you'd better apologize. And I'd better hear about the fact that you apologized. Because I'll tell you something. I'll come back into New York and I'll make this room into a fucking bowling alley and you'll be the ball, and you know I'll do it."

"Oh, no, come on, I don't want you to be mad at me. Harold called me up and Harold hollered at me." He gets out of the booth because now he knows I'm not going to hit him then, and he takes me into the big circular bar they had and he wants to buy me a drink.

"I don't drink that shit. That shit's for you. You need it. I don't need it. You don't need to apologize to me. You apologize to that lady. She's a lady and on top of everything, she's the boss's wife. You dumb son of a bitch, you wouldn't have this joint if it wasn't for him. That's the kind of respect you have for him because he's behind bars? Don't you know that man's going to come out someday and find out what you did? You think he's going to be happy with you?"

"Joe, please, not so loud. I got a United States senator here." He grabs me by the arm and he takes me over and he introduces me to Senator Hubert Humphrey, who I already met a couple of times through Harold. And that calmed everything down.

In 1969, we finally went to trial. First we had to deal with that liquor stamp case. That trial went on for two days, and the Alcohol Tax unit and the IRS and the Labor Department and the Justice Department and the Liquor Control Commission, they all tried to make a big thing out of that $32.50, claiming that I had illegal income and I was a hidden owner, which was against the law, and all that crap. When it was over, Judge Fred Case told them that he had never seen anything so ridiculous in his life. He dismissed the whole thing and told them not ever to come back and try to use his courtroom to entrap any person again.

When we came out of the courtroom, there was this fat guy waiting, who was one of the agents that came to the house when they busted in and arrested me, and I'd been having plenty of trouble with him, and was he angry standing there, glaring. I walked by and I says, with a smile on my face, "You win some and you lose some." He looked like he was ready to come after me. I stood there and I says, "You want a piece of my ass, come on and get it." I wanted to hit him. Then I walked away.

Then we went to trial on the Landrum-Griffin thing, willful intent to defraud by filing a false LM-2, over that lousy $1,832.50. They start selecting the jury and I looked up and I saw a guy in the jury box that I hadn't seen since my days in the old neighborhood. I says, oh, I'd better not look, and I kind of turned around and looked the opposite way and looked at some friends and kind of winked at them and paid attention to them so this guy wouldn't see me. They started challenging the jurors and they came to this guy and he didn't know my name because that wasn't my name in the old neighborhood, it was Joe Valenti. And I didn't know his name, all I knew was his nickname, which was Matty the Rat, which the old-timers used to call him, him being much older than me. Well, this guy was a thief from the day he was born. I figured, well, if he sees me after they swear him in and he don't say nothing, he's going to hold out and at least I got one going for me. I wasn't worried about the case, but at least I'd have a little edge.

When the attorneys had all agreed on the jurors, Judge Tiger Thornton, and they called him Tiger because that's what he was, everybody said he was a government judge, he starts questioning the jurors very dramatically and I guess he scared the shit out of this Matty the Rat, because this guy says, "Your honor, I think I know him. I haven't seen him in twenty, twenty-five years, but he used to live in my neighborhood."

The judge says, "You're excused." And I looked at him and I

says to myself, you dumb son of a bitch, why didn't you keep your mouth shut?

Now my lawyer walks into the courtroom with a book, with a stopper in the page. I says, "Where's the records? Where's all the records and everything?" And the government came in with a box of records, some of my records for all the years, back before 1963 and from 1963 up to 1968. I mean, we gave them everything they asked for, we even gave them an office in the building to work out of and we extended them every courtesy. But my attorney's got this book and the section he's got marked is "willful intent." I look at him and I says, "Wait a minute. Let's not go on that basis. Let's go and throw a motion in there and say that the length of time it took us to get a trial . . ."

I finally got him to agree to make that motion and the judge ruled against it. Then I tell him to make another motion to get the thing thrown out, because they have all our records and we don't have anything and they took them and haven't given them back. So he made that motion and the judge threw it out.

The next thing I know, he's up in front of the judge with the government's attorney and they're talking and suddenly I hear they've all agreed that the accountant would not be called to testify on my behalf or the government's. I'm trying to figure out why my attorney would agree not to allow the accountant who prepared the books and prepared the LM-2 to testify, since the whole case was based on whether or not there was willful intent in my heart and not an honest mistake on the part of the accountant in putting figures in the wrong column. Well, I couldn't get an answer to that.

It seemed to me that the whole basis of the trial really depended on my accountant and my secretary. And they agreed not to call the accountant. And when they called my secretary, Betty Martin, they wouldn't let her explain anything. It was all answer yes or no. Like, did Mr. Franco tell you to do this? Just answer yes or no. Stuff like that. So she couldn't tell the jury that she was my bookkeeper, she was the one who prepared the files, she was the one that handled all the checks, she was the one who paid all the bills, she was there the night the executive board agreed to pay American Express and to be reimbursed by me and that the local would later reimburse me because it was just a matter of cleaning up the records.

When she was testifying yes and no, my attorney turns to me and he says, "I think you're in trouble."

"What do you mean I'm in trouble?"

"The way she's answering, yes and no, it looks like willful intent on your part and you told me there was no way they could find willful intent. Well, I'm going to have to put you up on the witness stand."

"What the hell for?"

"It's gotten to the point where if the jury likes you, you'll win your case. If they don't like you, you're going to lose your case."

"You mean to tell me I'm running a popularity contest? We're not here on the basis of law, we're here on the basis of whether I'm liked or disliked?"

"There's nothing else we can do."

I was wondering whether I could stop the whole thing there until I got another lawyer. I didn't know if I could legally do that. So I finally agreed to go up on the witness stand because I felt I had nothing to be afraid of and nothing to really hide, because I did run a clean local and I kept clean records.

I got up there and my own lawyer actually found me guilty. I mean, he asked me questions such as state how many years you worked for a union. I told him I worked since I was fourteen, fifteen years old and what locals and what unions. He says, "Mr. Franco, you're saying to me that you've worked two-thirds of your life in labor and you've represented unions."

"That's about right."

"How far did you go in school?"

"To the ninth grade."

"How much money do you make?"

"Twenty-eight thousand dollars a year."

Well, there's people in the jury box looking at me and saying, here's a guy that only went to school to the ninth grade and he's been spending all these years in the labor movement making this kind of money, where does he come off doing that with that kind of background?

And I would look over to the jury and I knew what they were thinking and they were looking at me like . . . well, I don't have the appearance of being a white Anglo Saxon and I give a very hard appearance no matter how I dress. I don't come across as a businessman, I come across as a hard individual.

And here's my attorney, asking me all these personal questions about how much money I make and my family background and the rest. And the government just picked up from that point. The attorney kept asking me the same things my lawyer was asking, and Judge Thornton kept throwing in the name of James R. Hoffa because some of the questions led to some of the checks that were issued to the Castaways in Miami Beach. The judge is asking, isn't that the hotel that Hoffa owns? Are you associated with James R. Hoffa, and things along that line. And before you know it, I'm being portrayed as a Hoffa henchman, and Hoffa's still very much in the headlines what with being in prison and the rest.

When they get through with me and I got back down to my table, I says to my lawyer, "Ivan, I think you buried me. I just got a gut feeling you buried me."

He just gave me a dirty look.

The whole trial lasted four hours one day and three hours the next day, including the time that the jury went out to deliberate. And they came back and they says, "We find in favor of the government and we find the defendant guilty of willful intent."

Now, the things that could have proved I wasn't guilty of willful intent was things like the books we'd turned over to the government, which they was saying they didn't have and my lawyers said they didn't have, and the tape of that executive board meeting which had got lost and nobody could find.

In 1970, I found that tape and I brought another lawyer into the case to make an appeal. But the bills for lawyers was running way up. I went to Chicago to see Allen Dorfman. I says, "Al, I don't want to bother you. I haven't in the last year. But the attorneys' fees are starting to get to me. I'm getting to the point where I can't survive. I can't take care of the house. I can't take care of the children. Everything is starting to clamp down. And the attorneys are starting to look to me for money and I'm looking at maybe $100,000 to $150,000 in attorneys' fees."

Allen says, "What do you want?"

"I don't know. Why don't we work something out? I understand that Mose Crislauv, the attorney out of Cleveland, is a good attorney and we're looking to appeal this to the Federal District Court in Cincinnati."

Well, Allen made arrangements for Mose Crislauv to represent me and he took care of all the costs and all the lawyers' fees. And there were several times when I was really hard up and Allen reached down into his drawer and pulled out packages with a few thousand in them and he says, "If you need more . . ."

I says, "Allen, I'm not going to come to you every day and say I need $2,000. This will take care of the bills and everything. But it's not going to pay the attorneys."

"Forget the fucking attorneys. Hoffa said for me to take care of that stuff and it's being taken care of."

The first thing we did was go back to Judge Thornton with the tape. He says, "Where did you find it?"

"I found it in a box of stuff that was given to the attorneys and the attorneys never brought it into court."

He says, "Well, those records were available to your attorneys and they were available to you." So he denied our motion for a new trial.

And then we found out that they had had me under electronic surveillance and they'd showed the transcripts of those bugs to Judge Thornton even though they never came out at my trial. So we asked if we could go and read those transcripts and if we found something in them, then maybe they would form the basis for another appeal. Well, they wouldn't let them out of the jurisdiction of the court, but they let us sit in the courtroom and read them. And I went through those sections where my name appeared.

What had been going on was that they were bugging and taping the offices of Home Juice Company of which Tony and Billy Giacalone were part owners, though Tony and Billy didn't know they were being taped. And the government listened in over a period of years. And there were a few meetings and conversations that I had with Billy and Tony Giacalone and they had them all down.

The thing is, there's a big difference between listening to somebody speak and reading what they say. I mean, if I says because I'm mad, "That dirty son of a bitch, what he did, I'll hit him across the head with a two-by-four and knock his brains out, I'll kill the bastard," that's just street talk in anger. It doesn't mean that I'm gonna go out and do it. But when you put it down and transcribe it and read it, it reads like the worst criminal that God ever put on the earth.

Well, I started to read those logs and I turned to Mose Crislauv and I says, "Close them. Because I'll tell you something, they don't look good when you read them. Forget about it. We blew this one. There's no chance whatsoever."

Mose agreed. And I say, "There's other shit in here that I don't even want to read about. So let's close it."

But we still had the tape of that executive board meeting that showed that the board had approved all the financial records and everything else. And Mose went to the Court of Appeals in Cincinnati with that and some other stuff, and we went in front of a three-judge panel.

While we were waiting outside, this young red-headed kid that was the government attorney came up to me and Barbara and he extended his hand and he says, "Joe, everybody in the department feels real bad about this, because we don't feel that you deserve the treatment you received and we think that they found a guilty verdict against you was really way out of line. I can't do anything because it'd be my neck. But I'll tell you what I will do. I'm entitled to twenty minutes. I'll only take five and I'll tell the judges that Mose Crislauv can have the additional fifteen minutes for his rebuttal."

We walk into the courtroom and one of the judges who comes out is Wade McCree who came to me many years before that when we had the Civic League Club and we endorsed him for office. He sees me and he nods his head to say hello and he looked kind of surprised to see me.

The next judge that comes out is Joseph Sullivan, who was also a friend of mine, and there's nobody in the court but me and Barbara and my attorney and the government attorney. Joe Sullivan looks at me and he says, "For chrissake, Franco, what the hell are you doing in this courtroom?"

"I don't know, your honor." It was very embarrassing to me. I didn't know what to say. Then I says, "Trying to protect my butt, I guess."

He laughed and he sat down, and then Judge Phillips, who was the chief judge, sat in the middle, and I'm thinking, I got two friends on this court and they're going to see where I got screwed and it'll be okay.

The government man got up and he took his five minutes and he didn't really say anything. And what he did say sounded like he was in favor of kicking the case back down to the lower court. And then Mose talked for thirty-five minutes and Joe Sullivan and Wade McCree questioned him and Judge Phillips never said a thing.

The way everything went, it looked like we were going to get a new trial, and everybody's telling me it looks like we won this round. And it looked like things were going to come out all right. The tax stamp thing, we won, and we agreed on a settlement with the IRS, and there was just this thing, and with what everybody was saying, it looked like I'd be moving into that job that Harold Gibbons offered me. Even the government attorney is telling me they're going to kick it back down and when they do, the government's not going back to retry it, they'll just ask for a dismissal.

I'm waiting for the court to hand down its rule, and I'm working like hell, organizing and other things. And then I get the decision, the document must have been an inch thick. What it came down was that they upheld the guilty verdict of the original court. And then the Supreme Court turned down our appeal for certiorari.

And then I got the order to get everything straightened away and surrender so I could go to prison.

The prospects for Franco as 1971 began were not for many happy new years. There stretched ahead of him a year in prison, or less perhaps with good behavior. But that was only the first part. For when he hit the streets again, he would still not be free man. He had been convicted under the Landrum-Griffin Act and that meant that for five years from the day of his release he would be forbidden to participate in the affairs of the union to which he had devoted himself for more than a quarter of a century.

Part V

21

There was much to do and very little time in which to do it. He felt he had to go to Washington and pay a visit to his old friend and one-time partner, Frank E. Fitzsimmons.

It was two or three weeks before I submitted myself to the federal marshals, and I sat there, and there was Jimmy's picture on the wall behind him and you could see the Capitol out his windows. I says, "Fitz, by the grace of God, you're sitting in the little man's seat. Look what you and I are looking at. We're looking at the Capitol. Isn't it amazing. Here I am on this side of the desk, ready to go to jail, and on the other hand, you're in the little man's spot. Fate is a funny thing. You're at the top and I'm going to prison."

He says, "Joe, don't worry. You and I have been together for a long time and every time I ever called on you, you were always there to help me. Don't think I'm going to walk away from you, because I won't. You're as close to me as anybody. I won't let you down."

"Well, you'll never have to worry about anything anymore."

He knew what I was talking about and he says, "Joe, the day he comes out, he can have this fucking job back anytime he wants it. Believe me when I tell you, if that man came walking out of prison tomorrow morning, I'd tell him to take this job and shove it right up his ass."

I says, "The little guy up on the wall behind you, Fitz, he just broke a smile. You know it as well as I know it, you've got the taste of the good life in your mouth and you ain't never going to give this thing up."

"Nah, Joe, it's too tough for me."

"Fitz, don't bullshit a bullshitter. Don't bullshit the guy that used to be your partner. I know you. You already made your deals, with Nixon and his guys. Do you think I'm blind? Everybody know it. Gibby told me, other people told me. You kissed with the devil and you're stuck with him. Now, the next question is, are you going to keep your commitment to the little guy, to Jimmy?"

"I'm working on it right now. Don't worry, I'm going to get him out."

"I believe you, Fitz. But keep your word. This organization was built by one man. Don't sell him down the river and don't sell this organization down the river. We sweated too much, we worked too hard for it, we gave up wives, we gave up blood. Just do the right thing."

Well, I got up and we shook hands and we hugged and he says, "Anytime you want something, Joe, anytime you need something, you call me, you have the wife call me. Make sure."

Franco was ordered to report to begin serving his one-year sentence at the end of February 1971.

I got the family together and we had dinner and I sat there with the children and told them that I would be gone for one year. I told them what I expected from them and laid down all the rules and regulations for their behavior and everything else. I told them to just think of me making a trip like I'd done many times before, but this time I'm just staying away longer than normal. Barbara and her mother, who was living with us then and who hated my guts for some unknown reason because I'd given her more than she ever had before in her life, they assured me that everything would be fine. I had made sure that the rent and everything would be paid and the personal stuff at home was taken care of. I had to be at the federal building at eight o'clock in the morning, and I figured I'd get everything over with in the evening to make it easier for me and the children, so there wouldn't be any tears and all that funny stuff going on when I left.

I got up early and kissed Barbara goodbye and told her she could come to see me at Lewisburg, which I'd made some arrangement to be sent to, after forty days. Then this young kid who worked for me, Billy Anton, picked me up and drove me down to the federal building where they handcuffed me and put me in a cage and then they transferred me to the county jail where I stayed for the next twenty-eight days. The amazing thing is, for all the years and all the things I've ever done in my life, this was the first time I ever spent more than twenty-four hours behind bars.

So, there I was and the fellow that was in the next cell was in there for killing a young boy and a young girl in lovers' lane in Pontiac, and the guy who was on the other side of me was in there for bank robbery, waiting to be sent to federal prison, and everybody that was in there except for three or four black guys that were there for pimping and breaking and entering and lower crimes like that, was in there for either murder or bank robbery and something on that order.

I'm there a little while and one guy comes by and he looks at me and he says, "What neighborhood did you come out of?"

I says, "Mack and Russell."

"Aren't you Blackie's brother?" Blackie was one of my older brothers.

"Yeah."

"You're Jo-Jo."

"Yeah. Who are you?"

He tells me and he's a guy I went to school with. I says, "What the hell happened?"

"Well, I finally got caught. After all these years, I finally got caught. Seems like you got caught, too. What the hell have you been doing?"

"Well, when I left the old neighborhood, I went with the Teamsters. I work for Jimmy Hoffa."

"Oh, yeah, I read about that man." He looks at me close and he says, "And I've seen your pictures in the paper, too."

"What are you in for?"

"I held up fifteen banks."

"Holy shit, fifteen banks."

"Yeah and they want the money back, but goddamn it, they won't get it from me, that money'll rot before I give it back to them."

"Maybe you can make a deal and get the hell out of here."

"Screw them. They ain't gonna make no deal with me."

"How much time did you get?"

"Forty-five years. With good time, I should get out in maybe thirty, thirty-five. How much time did you get?"

I'm starting to think if I tell this guy one year, I'm going to look like a piker. And I found out very quickly that they don't respect you in prison if you're a short-termer. Anything over three years, they respect you and they'll accept you. Less than that, they don't even want to make friends with you because they figure you ain't gonna be there long enough for them to even get to know your middle name. So, not even knowing what I was saying, I says, "Ten flat," which I learned meant ten years with no good time.

Well, that was very acceptable to him. And we were standing there bullshitting when this big tall kid comes walking up and I recognize him. He's the other guy's brother. He grabs me and hugs me and we start talking and I says, "What the hell are you doing here?"

He says, "Well, my brother's a piker. He only robbed fifteen. I robbed twenty-five banks, and if it wasn't for that son-of-a-bitch driver I hired on the last job, I'd have got away with that mother, too. But I didn't and I had to shoot it out with two FBI agents and I killed both of them."

"Holy shit, how much time are you doing?"

"I'm doing eighty years. They couldn't give me life because then I could get out in twenty. So they gave me eighty and they know goddamn well I ain't getting out, I ain't walking the street no more."

After a while, all I wanted was to get out of that place, because everything was going on. I mean, two little white kids got brought in and there was a line a mile long to punk them, and there was everything you could want and a lot of very bad things going on. I just wanted to get where I was going, which was to Lewisburg, where I could get settled where I was going to be, and see Jim and talk to him. But they kept delaying. But my nephew,

Joe Valenti, was organizing a law enforcement division for the
union and he had some connections, his wife being the niece of one
of the United States marshals. I told Joe to reach out and get me
the hell out of the county jail.

The next day, sure as hell, I got called out and taken over to
the federal building, got my papers processed, and then they shackled me, shackled my hands around my waist and they had a chain
around my waist down my legs and shackled both my legs, and
you would think I was Al Capone or some murderer or some
animal that they would have to chain up like that. We got into the
car and we head out, two marshals and me in the back seat. We
stopped at another prison on the way to pick up two more inmates
that they were going to take to Lewisburg, two young kids that
were doing twenty, twenty-five years for robbing banks, and all
they had on them was handcuffs. That was one hell of a ride. I
couldn't even reach for my cigarettes and my hands were starting
to swell up because the shackles was so tight, but it was a couple of
hours before the marshals agreed to even loosen them a little.
When I had to go to the bathroom, it was like a goddamn contor-
tionist and I couldn't pull my pants back up and I had to sit in the
booth waiting until the marshal broke the damn door down and
came in with his gun pulled like I was going to try to escape or
something, and he stood there with the gun pointing at me while
he unshackled me so I could pull my pants back up and then he
shackled me again.

We got to Lewisburg about eleven o'clock at night, and this
place is beautiful. From the outside, it looked like the Fountainbleu, a very European castle-type structure. I can hardly believe it.

As soon as we walk in, this guy, one of the trustees, comes
walking over to me and he says, "Are you Joe Franco?"

"Yeah."

"Jimmy Hoffa and Sam Berger said you was coming in and
when you got here they asked me to take care of you. Get yourself
processed and then I'll take you upstairs." Sam Berger was a book-
ing agent who was part of Berger, Steinman and Ross and he also
represented the trucking association and he got himself an indictment out of that and was serving two years.

Well, they took us back and I shaved and got a shower, and
then the screw came in and said, "Line up." So, we all line up

naked, and you really got to live through it to appreciate it, the shame they make you go through, the way they belittle you, they just humiliate you and do everything they can to destroy you. So, we line up and all of a sudden this screw who's got a big flashlight, which I'm wondering what the hell he's going to do with, he says, "All right, everybody raise your arms." He came up to each guy and looked in each armpit. "All right, spread your legs and pull your joint and your balls up." He puts the flashlight down there and looks on both sides of the groin. "All right, spread your cheeks." He takes the flashlight and he looks in my ass. I don't know what this is all about, but when we get through the guy that was waiting for me tells me they were looking for contraband. Guys come in who've done time before and they take a condom, which they call balloons, and they take money and anything else and grease the condom and shove it up their ass, so the screw is looking for something that may be hanging out.

Now, from there you're supposed to go into quarantine. But Jimmy had put the fix in for me and I was put in a private cell on the second floor, and the guy got me a T-shirt and a pair of baggy pants and a pair of paper slippers, which was supposed to do until I got my clothing allotment. And he says, "Okay, we'll see you at breakfast. As soon as I see Sam and Jimmy, I'll tell them you're here."

The next morning, I wake up and there's a big noise and the doors clang open and I can hear guys all shuffling out and going downstairs to breakfast. But I don't know what the hell I'm supposed to do, so I just walk out the door and down the stairs and onto the main floor and I'm walking around like a real hayseed that just hit New York City, gawking at everything. I'm in the main lobby of the Lewisburg Penitentiary, taking in this gothic-type lobby, and the only thing that was missing to make it a real castle was paintings on the wall. All of a sudden, a screw hollers out, "Hey, you."

I turn around and I says, "Are you calling me?"

He says, "Yeah, you get over here."

I walk over to what looks like a big podium. He says, "What's your number?"

"I don't know."

"When did you get in?"

"About eleven last night."

"Didn't they assign you a number?"

"No, sir."

"What's your name?"

"Joe Franco."

"All right, Joe, now write this goddamn number down in your brain. It's 3-7-5-8-0. When you hear that number, that's you. We won't be paging your goddamn name no more. It'll be 3-7-5-8-0, and you'd better goddamn answer. Now get downstairs and get yourself some breakfast and report back here."

I says, "Thank you," and I was going to say, "That comes from me to you, from 3-7-5-8-0." All of a sudden, I lost my identity and became a number.

I went down to the breakfast room, a huge cafeteria where you stood in line and they gave you a tray and you picked out stainless steel bowls that you ate out of instead of plates, and you took whatever you wanted, whether it was cereal and milk or bacon and eggs or whatever. I'll say one thing for the federal prison system, they have excellent food. Everything there was fresh. The only thing is, you never saw beef; you saw a hell of a lot of pork, but never beef. I'm sitting there eating when here comes Sam Berger. He hugged me and kissed me and he says, "When did you get in?"

"Last night."

"Did the guy take care of you?"

"Yeah, he introduced himself to me and he was real good, and he said he'd see me this morning."

Sam says, "Nah, I'll take care of you. What do you need?"

"I'm just about out of cigarettes."

"What do you smoke?"

"Tareytons."

"They don't have Tareytons here." He gave me a pack of Marlboro, so that's what I ended up smoking. He says, "Anything else, you let me know. It'll be at least three weeks before your money hits the commissary, so don't be ashamed. But whatever I'm giving you, I'm borrowing from somebody else, so just make damn sure I get it back so I can pay him back."

"Don't worry, Sam. I appreciate what you're doing."

"No, Joe, this is normal. This is the routine that everybody in the prison system does for newcomers that they know. They'll chip in and give you cigarettes and stuff until you get your commissary money. Now, finish your breakfast and we'll go down and see Jimmy."

"Yeah. I'd like to see the old man. What's he doing?"

Sam says, "He's already at work. But I want to tip you off right now, Joe. You knew Jimmy out on the street. It's not the same Jimmy."

"What do you mean, Sam?"

"These last four and a half years have been awful tough years for him and he's vicious. He's walking around like he's an animal and he's driving me crazy. He's really, really hard."

"Well, let's see what happens."

We go down there and Jimmy's in this little cage, it couldn't have been more than ten by ten, with a screen around it, and he's steam-pressing pants. That was his job, pressing pants and shirts and sheets and whatever. I ran over to the cage and I jumped up on the cage and because I didn't have any shoes on, I was able to grab it between my toes and I shook the cage like a chimpanzee would do, and I start to holler, "Get me out of here! Get me the hell out of here! I didn't do nothing! I'm innocent! Get me out of this fucking prison! I'm innocent! I'm innocent!"

A couple of screws at the other end start looking at me like I flipped my pizza. Jimmy stops what he's doing and looks at me and looks at Sam and he says, "When did that goofy bastard get in?"

Sam started to laugh and he says, "Last night."

I says, "Boss, you're here, I'm here. Where you go, I go. I'm only four years late, that's all. I'll spend the next year with you."

"Franco, get the goddamn hell off that cage before you get into trouble." He turns to Sam and he says, "Goddammit, Sam, what the hell did you bring him down here for? For four years, I had peace and quiet. Now we got that goddamn dago here and he'll ruin the whole goddamn penitentiary. The whole federal prison system is going to go to hell now because this guy's here. Would you believe we're stuck with this animal? He'll drive me crazy."

Sam says, "Hey, Jim, shut it down and let's go get something to eat. And then I've got to take him to get a haircut and get his clothes allotment."

And I'm still on the cage and I'm shouting, "I'm innocent. I'll get you out, Hoffa, if it takes me twenty years. I'll get you out."

By this time, two screws come running down and they say to Hoffa, "Everything okay, Hoffa?"

"Yeah. This screwball, he's all right. He's one of my guys." He turns off the press and he opens up the cage. And there were some beautiful new jackets up on a rack over there, like pea coats in navy blue and some army khakis with fur tops.

I says to Jim, "How does a guy get a chance to grab one of them?"

"Next time you come downstairs, we'll snatch a couple for you." Then he comes over and he gives me a hug and he says, "How do you feel?"

"I'm all right. How do you feel?"

"Aw, all right. I'm in here pressing shirts, making a living."

"Yeah, a hell of a living, a great job."

We went up to go get something to eat and Jim introduces me to a guy named Guido who's his right hand man in there. Guido was out of the labor movement from Baltimore and he was doing fifteen years.

Then Sam took me up and got me a haircut and took me over to get my clothing allotment, and they gave me a pair of shoes that were old paratrooper boots that must have been worn by twenty guys before me and they were full of paint and oil and tar, and the soles were an inch think and they must have weighed twenty pounds apiece, and they didn't fit. Sam tells me he's got to go check in and he walks away. I didn't know what the hell he meant; what he meant was that three times a day you have to be in your cell in order to be counted so they could know if there's a shortage of prisoners on each floor. Well, I didn't know about that, so I just wandered around and found myself out in the yard, which was three baseball diamonds inside a big wall that looked like here to heaven, with guards walking up and down on top of it and others in towers looking over everything, and there was a stamping plant over on one side where guys worked that didn't have money for commissary and where they get like fifteen, twenty cents an hour.

I get done wandering around and it became lunch time, which I didn't know about, and after lunch was over, here comes Jimmy and Sam and Guido. They saw me and they came over and Jim says, "Come on, we'll go over to the track." They had a quarter-mile running track. Jim says, "We'll walk a couple of miles."

We started walking, and we would do that every day, and those boots, I was breaking my feet into them and not breaking the boots into my feet, and on the first day, my feet were killing me and on the second, my feet were absolutely destroyed and on the third, I got blood blisters on the bottoms bigger than half-dollars and I says to Jim, "Hold it. That's it. I got 'em on my heels, I got 'em on my toes, I got 'em on the balls of my feet, I got 'em every-where. Boss, I got to fall out."

"You chickenshit son of a bitch, keep walking."

"Jim, I'm blistered to the point where they're blood."

"Don't worry about them, goddamnit, keep walking. They'll turn into calluses."

"Great. Then I'll have calluses all over my feet."

"They're better than blisters. They won't hurt. Keep walk-ing."

And he got me walking every day, two, three, four, five miles, and the blisters broke and the blisters became calluses, and I broke my feet into my shoes.

And he kept giving me tips about the way to behave in prison and make it through. He says, "Don't gamble, don't get too close to nobody, don't get involved, don't trust nobody because every-body's a stool pigeon, everybody, so nobody in here can tell on you if you don't open your mouth. When you take a shower, make sure you do it with the lights on and use your own bar of soap because there are sick son of a bitches in here who take razor blades and break them in half and stick them in soap to cut you all up. Don't take nothing unless you pay it right back." And he says, "I'll tell you how to survive in the goddamn joint, Franco. Work hard, walk hard, exercise hard, play ball, do what you have to do, only do it hard. Because what will beat you is not the prison system but your own mind. When you go to that bunk, and the door closes on you, the only thing you've got in that room is that light in that ceiling. When that goddamn light is on and you're lying there and you're looking at it and you can't sleep, then you're in trouble. You've got to be able to get into that bunk and lay down and go to sleep. That's the name of the game. So work yourself to the bone, walk, exercise, do what you have to do to be completely exhausted.

Comes eight, nine o'clock at night, when you go into that sack, don't let nothing bother you from going to sleep. You'll be too tired to think about all the crap out on the street. You'll be too tired to think about your family. Franco, that's what you have to do in order to survive. Believe me, I went through it. I'm telling you what it took me a year to learn. You set a routine for yourself and stay with that routine and you will survive whatever time you've got to put in here."

Everyday we used to meet, after lunch and at four-thirty and we would walk. And we would talk.

One time, he turns to Guido and he says, "Guido, you ask Franco, you ask him who the fuck was the boss on the streets? Ask him how long it would take us to go out there and start over again."

I says, "Well, it took us twenty years to get where we're at. Now we know all the tricks so it shouldn't take us more than a year, two years to get where we're at today with controlling the union."

He says, "See, see. You wouldn't listen to me. You think we're all washed up? You're full of shit. As soon as we get out, we'll take care of everybody. We'll get right back and we'll straighten that fucking mess out. Them rats, them sons of bitches, they're running out because they think the ship sank. They're full of shit. This ship ain't sinking. This ship is going to sail from now to hell freezes over. Ain't that right, Franco?"

"That's right, boss."

"Keep walking, Franco. Stay with me."

Another time, I says, "Jim, I read all that newspaper stuff about when you first walked in here they gave you a special job stuffing mattresses and you were beating the mattresses with a stick and saying, this one's for Bobby Kennedy."

He says, "They made that son of a bitch especially for me, to embarrass me and to try to belittle me and to break my spirit, because that's what they try to do in this place. When I first came in here, Franco, they took me down . . ." and he took me down to this little room, about thirty by thirty, and he says, "When I was here it was stacked up with mattresses that were either half-filled or old and needed repairing. I had to take crap and shove it in there and pack it and use a stick to pound it down and level it out and make it flat. That's what the flat stick was for. And, yeah, I probably said it, like anybody else, pounding and saying, this one's for Bobby Kennedy and this one's for . . . I might have used a hundred and one different names. It wasn't just a matter of using Bobby's name. It was getting the frustrations out. It wasn't that I was looking to get even with Bobby or anybody else. I was here. I had to do my time. I tried to do it the best way I knew how. I thought it was unfair for me being in here, but that's the way life is, Franco. You take the good with the bad."

The thing was, he was always ranting and raving, he was always saying, "Franco, let me tell you something. When we get out of this place, it's not going to be easy to go back out there and pick up where we left off. A lot of the rats that I made out there, they're going to be fighting me. I've got to know where I stand with some people. At least, you're here with me. You're going to be with me when we go out on the street?"

"Jim, I've been with you for nearly thirty years. I'm not going to change on you now. When you get out, and I'll be leaving before you, I'll be waiting for you."

"Franco, when I get out, you're going to be right with me and, by God, we'll do it. We'll get some of the old-timers back in again and we'll clean house and we'll get them sons of bitches straightened out and we'll get them back in line again. I'm the boss. I made the Teamsters. I'm Mr. Teamster. I'll do it again. Don't worry about it."

The things that went on. The violence. It was all the time. There was this one day I was coming in for lunch. I had met a guy and we had bummed cigarettes from each other and we had walked around the track together when Jim wasn't around. This guy's name was Bill. Well, I got there for lunch and I went down and got Jim, and Jim and Sam and Guido and I were standing in line and about fifteen or twenty guys in front of us was this guy, Bill. He turned around and waved at me and I waved back, sticking my finger up like saying I recognized him.

All of a sudden, I see him kind of slump over and fall and hit his head against the marble floor, hard like he had passed out. I started to get out of line to go over and see what was wrong and maybe I could help him. Jim grabs me by the waist in the back, and pulls me back. He says, "Keep your ass in line. Mind your own goddamn business."

"But, Jim, I know the guy."

"You hear what I told you? Mind your own goddamn business and keep in line. There's something wrong with him, let the goddamn screws do it."

"Okay, boss."

I just stood there and as we came up and got closer to him, I looked and there he was, laying on the floor. Somebody had come up behind him and stuck about a nine- or ten-inch butcher knife in his back and he was laying there in a puddle of blood. I just walked by and that was the end of my lunch.

Jim says to me, "See, you'd of got out of line, went over to him, and whoever did that would have thought that you were a friend of his, and probably nine out of ten times, he'd be looking to get you because he thinks that you're his friend and you might be looking for revenge. Don't ever get involved in anything that comes down in that kind of situation. Somebody gets stabbed, somebody gets cut, stay the hell away from it."

But I was sick to my stomach.

I was in Lewisburg for about sixty days before Barbara showed up to visit me, and she came with her mother. She starts telling me that things weren't working out very well for her and the kids were giving her a problem. There was something that she wanted to sit down with me and get an understanding with me about.

I kept saying, "What is it? What is it? What do you want to tell me? Just don't start something and don't finish it."

"Not now. I'll tell you on my next visit."

So, that wasn't a very good visit and she left me with a confused mind because I didn't know where the hell she was coming from.

She came in again and this is the third month and I've acclimated myself to the prison system and I'm starting to know the routine of the prison system and learning how to steal and everything else. If you're not a thief when you go to prison, they make you a thief while you're there. You're with every part of crime that you can think of. You're with bank robbers, you're with killers, you name it, it's there. You start talking to somebody about something and all of a sudden, he starts to give you ideas and hints in case you ever did it. Like this one kid that was a bank robber, he says, "Joe, I'll never make that mistake again of going in and not knowing that I'm being photographed. What I'd do now is I would get mercury and I would put mercury underneath my eyes and across my forehead and across my nose and chin."

"Why would you do that?"

"Because mercury will blur out that area of your face so that the closed-circuit camera will not be able to photograph you."

So, you can walk in there a straight kid and come out a well-groomed bank robber or whatever. You learn the whole trade in there.

Anyway, Barbara showed up with Danny Triglia, who I left the local union in care of, and Jimmy Prentice, who was the president of the local union and they wanted to pay me a visit, so they came up with her to keep her company. They were having problems with different companies and I gave them instructions as to the problems and how they should handle everything.

Then they went for a walk while Barbara and I had a private visit. And Barbara told me she was going to get a divorce. That floored me because I didn't expect it. I says to her, "No reason for you to do that now. You should have done it before. Is there somebody else involved?"

She kept assuring me there wasn't. Prior to going to prison, I never questioned her because I was there and she never got out of line because I would have just kicked her ass out of the house and that would have been the end of it. But she had me by the balls, because before I left to go to prison, I had to sign power of attorney over to her and I found out that she took all the money out of the bank, she even took my daughters' trust funds that the college cash goes into, and she took all the jewelry, and she cleaned me right out, and she was even trying to sell the house to a friend of mine, and they were willing to buy it at the price she wanted to sell it for.

When I found that out, I wrote to the guy and told him that under no circumstances was anybody allowed to buy the house while I'm in prison. They're going to have to wait until I get back home.

But when she told me all of this and that she was getting a divorce, I says, "Barbara, why did you go through everything that you went through, like becoming a Catholic? Why did you do it if you knew and you anticipated what you're doing today? I can't believe that you did this."

She says, "Well, I was afraid to tell you I haven't been happy for the last year."

"Jesus Christ, a year after we got married and then you're saying that you weren't happy? I just don't understand you."

"Well, I was afraid to leave you because I thought you'd hurt me."

"Barbara, if I was home right now and you said this, all I would tell you would be pack your clothes and get out. What the hell do I want to hurt you for? But now that you're telling me where I'm at now that I'm in prison, goddammit . . ." I got up and I chased her and I was going to grab her and choke the bitch to death and beat the shit right out of her in the visiting area.

Two screws come over and they grab me and they tell me, "Don't do it, Joe, because they'll throw you in the hole."

Well, I chased her right around the visiting area and chased her right out to the parking lot, which was where the screws grabbed me.

After that, I did a couple of months bad time. I just went berserk. I went through one hell of a period of mental distress, angry and frustrated because there was nothing I could do being behind bars. I think that frustrated me more than anything. On the one hand, I'm thinking, why don't I escape? On the other hand, I'm thinking, I've only got nine more months to do. So I just buried myself in work. I painted the whole goddamn prison, for chrissake, and the guys used to criticize me for doing it. I exercised. I just overdid everything and I ended up getting in shape again. I lost almost seventy pounds, went back down to a hundred ninety-eight pounds with a thirty-four-inch waist, and I was doing two hundred pushups and three hundred sit-ups every day. I used to push weights. I was punching a bag. I was playing handball. I did everything I could think of to get my mind off Barbara. Eventually, I came out of it, but when I got out, I was very angry and very frustrated and I wanted to seek revenge on Barbara.

I told Jim about it and I told him I was sure that there was something wrong and there was somebody out there and she was screwing around with somebody.

Jim says, "Don't let it bother you, Franco. It's going to be very easy for you to find out. When you get home, don't look any further than your closest friends. Ninety-nine out of a hundred times, when there is a problem like the one you're facing right now, it won't be a stranger, it'll be somebody close to you because that's the kind of a sick son of a bitch that'll take advantage of a situation like this."

After a while, I got transferred out of Lewisburg over to Allenwood, the prison farm. While I was there, I got very friendly with a guy from Brooklyn named Joe Shipani, who was the nicest guy in the world. He was living in a cell maybe two doors away from me.

He comes over to me one day and he says, "We got word from Jimmy Hoffa that Carmine DeSapio's coming in and he's a very, very sick man, he's going blind and he's got bronchitis and he's got pneumonia and he's got everything and they don't know whether this guy's gonna live. Jimmy wants us to take care of him."

I says, "Well, we can't keep him in the slum area. We got to get him the hell out of there."

I went over to Jack Berman who was a guy in the administration office and he was out of California and he knew Joey Bishop and a lot of other guys in show business who was writing to me. I says, "Jack, Carmine DeSapio's coming over here and that guy's a sick man. You better get us all transferred over to A or B or someplace so we can take care of him."

Immediately, he started shuffling the papers around and he says, "All right, get Joe Shep and Carmine and move them and yourself and move over to section B."

We got over there and we fixed ourselves up and we got Carmine's bed in order and I went over to the pill pusher who all he could do was give you aspirin and vitamins. I told the guy, "This guy could die on us. You got anything in mustard or something that I can sweat this guy? He's got a temperature like a hundred and four and I've got to sweat him out."

He gave me a whole big bottle of Vicks and a whole big bottle of aspirin and a bottle of Vitamin C. What we did was get settled and get Carmine settled and we hear the guys over in the next part, which was section A, which was separated from us in section B by a fifteen-foot aisleway. They're hollering, "Hey, you fucking dagos, who told you guys you could come into this section? Who the hell are you guys?"

I'm tucking in the end of my bed and I says to Joe Shep, "Is he talking to us?"

He says, "Yeah, and I guarantee the son of a bitch is talking to me." Because Joe Shep was like five one or five two.

I start trying to break the leg off the bed so I'd have something to beat this guy's brains in with. But all I could see was my shoes, the paratrooper boots. I grabbed the top of the buckle and made a nice handle out of it and the heel was a pretty good size so I could do some damage. Then I looked up and I says, "Are you talking to me?"

The guy says, "Yeah, you dago motherfucker."

"Yeah?" I jumped off the bed, over the cabinet, and I came down on the A side and I hit him right in the head with the shoe and split his head wide open. I just kept pounding the shit out of him. Before I knew it, there must have been ten guys on me trying to stop me from beating this guy half to death. And a lot of guys were laughing and they finally broke it up before the screws showed up. I guess a lot of them was laughing because it looked so ridiculous, beating a guy with a shoe. But that guy didn't show up again for a week, and when he did, he looked like a Hindu, all wrapped up.

Anyway, we got back to Carmine and Joe Shep and I took turns taking care of him. We stuck him in bed and we threw three blankets on him and we rubbed him down with Vicks and we popped three aspirins into him every two hours and we filled him full of vitamins and we got soup into him for three days, and we broke his fever. He started to get better and he started sitting up and we'd bring him breakfast and lunch, because we told him not to get out of bed. He started to get stronger and the weather turned nice, so he could go out.

Carmine didn't have a job, so I used to take him up on the side of the hill when I was going to work and I'd say, "Here's a blanket. You lay out here in the sun and I'll pick you up on the way back, about eleven-thirty, and we'll go to lunch." He'd sit up there and he'd read and he started to get a nice tan and started looking like himself again and was getting stronger. Every once in a while, we used to go out with the firetruck and pick wild berries and bring back a bucket full and we'd have them for breakfast. Carmine loved them with cereal. Joe Shep and I took real good care of Carmine DeSapio.

One day I was going into lunch and I see this little man, about five two or five three, with a corncob pipe come walking in and a big blond fair-looking guy was following him. He looked at me and he didn't say nothing. He just walked right past everybody. That's something you didn't do when it came to eating time because then you was cutting people, and the black people used to scream, "Hey, mother, get your ass back, there ain't no cuts in this line. You get your ass back in line and wait like everybody else does."

But nobody said nothing to this guy. For a couple of days he did that, breakfast, lunch, and dinner, and nobody would ever question him. He would go in and bypass everybody and sit down and the blond Greek Adonis would go over and get his food for him. That blond guy was a cold-looking son of a bitch. Good looking, but he sure was a cold, cold-looking man. He was probably in his early thirties, but he was built like a killer, strictly a killer, an out-and-out cold-ass killer.

Well, I was sitting there one afternoon and all of a sudden this old guy comes over to me and he sat down and he says, with a little bit of an Italian accent, not much, just a little bit, "I've been wanting to talk to you. Hoffa told me to say hello to you."

I says, "Oh, what do you need?" That's the first thing when somebody says to say hello, especially when it comes from an old man; it's my obligation to the old man. I says, "If Jimmy sent you, you need something, you need cigarettes, you need tobacco, you need commissary, something to hold you over until your commissary gets sent over?"

"No, no, no. I don't need nothing. I'm fine. Just that Jimmy talks a lot about you. He said for me to say hello to you."

"How's the man doing?"

"Oh, all right. He'll be all right. We've talked a lot in the last few years that we've been together."

"You been there a long time?"

"Yeah. Almost fifteen years."

"Oh God."

"How long you got to go?"

"I only got five, six months to go."

"Oh, you're what they call a short-timer." Then he starts talking to me and he says do you know so-and-so from the city of Detroit?

"No, I don't know him."

"Do you know Mr. Zerilli?"

"No. I've read about him but I don't know him."

"Do you know Mr. Pizziola?"

"No."

"Do you know Mr. Tocco?"

"No."

"Do you know Mr. Frank Costello? . . . Mr. Joe Bartolo?" He threw a lot of names at me.

"No. You're asking me about people, well . . ."

He says, "If you're a friend of Jimmy, how is it that Jimmy knows all these people and you don't know these people?"

"Well, Jimmy's in a bigger position than I am. I'm just a small little spoke in the wheel."

He slapped me across the face, as a sign of friendship, and he started to smile and laugh at me. He says, "I tell you, your mother and your father taught you well. Jimmy didn't teach you that. You were taught that when you were a little boy."

I says, and I started to smile, "I'll tell you something else I was taught. When you meet a man for the first time and he starts dropping names of people on you, you become very cautious and you don't expose yourself to that kind of a person, because they're name droppers and you know what name droppers are. They're just trying to find out where you're coming from and trying to find out where you're at and who you know, or they're trying to impress you with the names they're dropping on you."

He says, "I only used those names on you to see exactly what you would say."

"Well, I told you. I'm not well known."

"All right, you can stop the bullshit." I started to smile. He says, "I know you know them, so you don't have to say nothing. But I like you for it."

I says, "What are you doing? You've been here three or four days, what are you doing for work?"

"Nothing. I don't know what to do."

"How would you like a nice job by the church? I can get you a nice job over there. All you do is cut the grass, fix the flower beds, and in the back you can have a nice little garden, raise some tomatoes, some cucumbers, and that way we can have nice salads in three, four weeks. We can get some tomatoes before the fall hits in. We'll have nice fresh vegetables."

"Hey, that sounds like a good idea. Can you get it?"

"I'll talk to Jack Berman tomorrow."

In the morning, I talked to Jack Berman and I says, "Hey, Jack, there's a guy named Carmine just came in, probably in his sixties. Old man with a corncob."

He says, "Oh, I know Carmine. What do you want?"

"Give him a job over at the church because the guy that had it has just been transferred over to Pensacola."

He says, "Sure, the job's open. Tell him he's got it. Tell him to come in and see me."

Right away, I ran back and I told him, "Hey, Carmine, you've got the job." So that's where he was working from that time on, taking care of the gardens and everything around the church, which was a nice job for him. Every morning, I'd drive by in the truck and then I'd holler out in Italian, "Hello, signore," like they do in the old country.

He used to wave back and he used to say to me, "You're crazy, Franco, you're crazy. You always got a smile on your face, you're always laughing, you're always hollering. You're crazy."

I says, "No. You know what it reminds me of when I do that? It reminds me like if we're in the old country on the farm where they used to holler across the farms and say good morning to everybody. That's what it feels like to me."

When it came time for me to leave, I went over to Carmine and I shook hands and we embraced, and I says, "Hey, you wear my size shoe. Here's a couple of pairs of new shoes, one pair brown, one pair black. Here's some new clothes, some brand new clothes, take them." You see, by that time I had made a deal with a guy who was in the commissary and I used to tell him, "I'll give you two packs of cigarettes for every pair of pants and every blouse you get me, and I'll give you six packs of cigarettes for every brand new pair of shoes."

Well, with the exercise and all, my weight kept going down and I had a closet full of outfits in sizes all the way from forty-eights to forty, and three, four dozen T-shirts, and sweat socks and jockey shorts, and four, five pairs of shoes. Bobby Baker, Lyndon Johnson's guy, used to say I was the best-dressed con in the whole goddamn joint.

The funny thing about Carmine Galante was, it wasn't until I got out of prison and saw it in *Time* magazine and on different TV shows and other places that I really knew who Carmine Galante was, that he was a real powerhouse, that he was supposed to be what they call the *capo di tutti capi,* the boss of all bosses of the Italian families. I thought he was a nice man and I felt kind of sorry when they shot him later on after he got out.

All the time I was over at Allenwood, I still used to go back to Lewisburg. I had a bad ticker and a bad back and all I had to do was tell the pill pusher that I had to go over to the hospital and he would drive me over. When I was there, I used to drop by and see Jim and we'd have lunch and talk.

Now, it comes December and my time is coming to an end. By my computed time, I was supposed to leave on Christmas day. But the warden gave me what they call warden's amnesty, which he's allowed to give at Christmas and that's a three-day amnesty prior to Christmas. I was told to be ready to leave on Wednesday, December 22. On the twenty-first, I went over to Lewisburg and visited with Jim and we had lunch with Sam and Guido.

Jim says to me, "I hear you're leaving in a couple of days."

"Yeah, Jim, and I've got kind of mixed emotions, knowing that you've only got five or six months left to go and you'll have given them their full time. I kind of feel like I should stay here with you and wait until you're ready to go home. Now that I'm used to it and I've made a routine for myself, another couple of months won't bother me one way or another."

"No, you go home. I'll be home no later than June. I'm depending on you. You get home and you take care of yourself and don't get into no trouble. I need you. I want you to watch everything in that building, tell me who's doing what. I've got to know when I get home who's loyal to me and who's not loyal to me. You can tell them anything you want, that you and I didn't get along, whatever, but I've got to know who's loyal and who ain't. I don't want to make you a stool pigeon, Franco, but I've got to know. I'm not concerned about Fitz. He'll walk away when I get out."

"What about Harold?"

"Harold's with me 100 percent."

"Then what the hell are you worried about?"

"The rest of them guys. I'm getting reports that they're all goddamn rats, the guys I appointed to office. They're deserting me. That's what I got to know definitely when you get out there. You've got to find out for me."

"Don't worry about it, boss."

"I'll be home no later than June. They keep turning me down on parole, but now I ain't worried about that. They can't keep me after June. By then I will have given them all their time and they've got to legally release me."

"What about what Fitz has been working on, to get you out early?"

"He ain't got nothing done yet. And now I only got six more months to do and they're going to keep me in here to the bitter end, and you can bet on that."

I got up and I gave him a hug and I kissed him on the cheek and I says, "Boss, I'll see you in June."

I go back to Allenwood and that night we start getting rumors that Jim was getting a presidential pardon because Fitz had made a deal where he would support Nixon for reelection if Nixon got Jimmy out. I was sure as hell shocked because Jimmy didn't know a thing about it when we had lunch together that day, and he would have told me if he knew.

And I was getting ready to leave, too, and then they told me they were gonna hold me one more day, until December 23. I figured if Jim was getting out about then, if what we were hearing was true, maybe I could hitch a ride home with him. I tried to get word to him over at Lewisburg, but I couldn't.

On the twenty-third, we were watching television in the morning and I watched him on the TV walking out of those huge doors that I walked through and getting into a limousine with his son, Jimmy Jr., and the cameras and the reporters watching, and then driving off.

I went to the case worker then and I says, "I'd like to get my papers ready so I can leave."

The case worker says, "I'm sorry, Joe, but they've given all the girls the rest of the week off for the holidays and they didn't get your paperwork done, so you'll have to sit here until Monday."

"Wait a minute. The warden told me I was going to get three days' amnesty."

He says, "You want to call the warden?"

"Hell, yes. I picked that man as a man of his word." I called over to Lewisburg and they told me that the warden had left for Christmas vacation and nobody else had the authority to find out what had happened to the paperwork.

There wasn't anything I could do. I just bit my tongue and I stayed there and spent Christmas day there and Monday morning at five o'clock I walked out of there all dressed up, headed for Williamsport, and ready to grab a bus back home. It just so happened that some friends of mine came up and drove me home.

As soon as I got home, I called Jim and told him I was home. I says, "I saw you on the TV. I'm glad you're home and I'm glad you got a presidential pardon. You're out six months sooner."

"All right, Franco. Sit still and I'll get back to you as soon as I can."

What I didn't know and what Jim didn't know, because he had told me and he told everybody, was that somebody had written a thing on the back of the documents he had to sign saying that he agreed not to go back as president of the Teamsters or have anything to do with the Teamsters for eight years, until 1980. If he had known that was on there, he would never have signed it. He thought he was going to become general president again as soon as he walked out. If it had been there and he had known it, he would have sat in that prison and played hopscotch for another six months, which was all he had to do.

22

Bound by the restrictions not to get back into Teamster affairs until eight years had passed, Hoffa was livid and went on a concerted campaign to overturn those restrictions, which he claimed were not on the document he signed. Many observers agreed with him. Those restrictions had been added later, as part of the bargain between Frank Fitzsimmons, who had grown to love the emoluments and pomp that went with the Teamster presidency and was not about to give them up to Hoffa, and Richard Nixon and his cohorts. It was a campaign, increasingly bitter and tending toward violence, that would fill the next three and a half years of James Hoffa's life.

Joe Franco had his own problems. He had walked out the prison doors free but not free. Hanging over him was the five-year set-off of the Landrum-Griffin Act, preventing him from engaging in union affairs until the beginning of 1977. This restriction was not like the one on Hoffa's papers—a thing men could debate and try to overturn. The restriction on Franco was the law of the land, enacted by Congress as part of the statute. So, Franco had to find other work to support himself and his family. More immediate, though, was the problem in his family of Barbara filing for divorce.

It was some months after his release that Franco saw Hoffa again, this time at a banquet.

★ ★ ★

Jimmy saw me coming in and he waved to me to come up to the speakers' table. Myra Wolfgang was standing right alongside of him. Now, I had come out of prison with a pretty good tan and I grew a mustache and I had a nice suit on and shirt and a tie, which I seldom wore, and Myra looked at me kind of puzzled.

Jim says, "Why don't you say hello to him?"

Myra says, "Who the hell is he? He's beautiful. I'll marry him."

Jim says, "Quit bullshitting around, Myra. That's Joe Franco."

She says, "My God, Joe. Do you look great." And she came around and put her arms around me and hugged me and gave me a kiss. "What the hell did you do?"

"Myra, that son of a bitch worked me half to death while I was in the joint. He got me to lose all that weight, and I came out fit as a fiddle."

"You look great."

Jim says, "All right, Franco, you tell her. Who the hell was the boss in that joint? Who the hell could do that time?"

"Myra, he was the boss on the street and the boss inside the joint, and don't let anybody tell you any different. That man did the time and he could have done more time. He was the boss in there. Everybody would come to him. It was unbelievable. You thought you were on Trumbull Avenue when the carpet was rolled out in front of Jim's office. That's the way his cell was. I went up there one day and I saw the carpet and I broke up laughing," and then I says, "I seen two or three guys leaning up against the wall waiting to get in. He turned that goddamn prison into Trumbull Avenue. It was amazing how this guy was doing it in there."

That just made Jimmy's evening. He perked right up. He says, "See, Myra, goddamnit, I told you I was the goddamn boss. No question about it." Then he dragged me by the arm off to a corner and he says, "How are things with you?"

"All right, boss."

"You do what I tell you to do?"

"Yeah. I'm staying close to home. I'm starting to get my head straightened out a little bit."

"What happened to your wife?"

"That bitch, she left two days before I got home. She ran out with everything. She took all the money, she took everything, and she left the kids stranded over the Christmas holidays. When I got in on Monday, she was already gone a couple of days. She was probably afraid to stay there until I got home. I'll be getting a divorce in a couple of months; we're supposed to be going to trial pretty soon."

"All right. You need some help, holler."

"Okay. What I'll do is this, I'll work through Jim Jr."

"Okay, you call Jim Jr. because I'm making my office in Jim's office. So, anytime you want to get hold of me, get hold of Jim Jr. and I'll know you want to meet with me."

"All right. But I won't press it. I'll be waiting until you got yourself all straightened away and if you need me, I'll wait until you call."

He says, "You work it out anyway you want to work it out."

In that conversation that night, Franco told Hoffa some of the details of those first weeks at home and his attempt to get revenge against his wife.

What was coming back to me while I was in prison after Barbara told me she was getting a divorce, was that she was seeing another man and probably having an affair. When I got out, I was so screwed up mentally that I wanted revenge on her first, because you blame the girl, because if she don't open her legs, the guy can't get near her. And I blamed the guy, because the guy was a very close and dear friend of mine and he was showing disrespect for me while I was in prison. He's Italian, so he knows the moral situation about when a man's in prison, his family is held in the position of help, but you don't screw around with his wife and kids.

I plotted. Starting on a Friday night in February 1972, about sixty days after I got out of prison, I plotted where I would have an alibi. I got into the car with a shotgun and I found out where she lived, and I got there about twelve o'clock because I figured she would probably go out. I sat in front of her apartment where I can see the doorway and I wouldn't have any problem just taking a shotgun and blowing her head off. That's how bad I felt and that's how screwed up I was. I sat there with no lights on and the windows open and couldn't smoke and froze my fanny off until six o'clock in the morning. I figured, well, she ain't home by six o'clock, that means she stayed over at somebody's house or she's shacked up. So, I went home.

The next night, which was Saturday, I did the same thing. And then Sunday night, I did the same thing again. About one o'clock in the morning, I'm sitting there and I'm saying I got to be the biggest jackass in the world. Here I am, ready to kill this woman. My children, no matter if I get away with it, even though maybe I could have had the so-called perfect alibi, underneath it all, my children will know. I says, hey, to hell with this. I don't want my kids to think . . . they don't know what kind of a life I had before, but now they're at an age where they can put two-and-two together, and say, well, for Barb to get hit the way she got hit, it had to be dad, he either arranged for it or he did it himself. And, second, I'd be the first one that the cops would come and grab, and I'd have to go through that whole crap of going to jail, getting out on bail, getting a lawyer, fighting the whole goddamn thing. The hell with it. This bitch ain't worth it. Forget about it. I just rolled the window back up, lit a cigarette, turned the heater back on, and sat there until the car got warm, and went home and just washed it right out and that was the end of it. We got a divorce and it became final in the latter part of 1972.

Barred from his union, his wife gone, Franco did what he could in the next years while waiting for his Landrum-Griffin set-off to expire. He worked in a law office for a time. He got a job that would at least put him close to the union. He sold Teamster jackets, pins, emblems, buttons, and the like. He tried to stay on the good side of everybody despite the wars and rivalries that raged within the Teamsters, despite the battle lines that were being drawn between Hoffa and Fitzsimmons. He talked to Hoffa now and again, saw him occasionally. He talked to Fitzsimmons now and again, saw him occasionally. He talked often with old friends who were still part of the union structure, kept in touch with what was going on, went to what meetings and affairs he could, pieced together what was happening.

23

Hoffa was a man obsessed. He had lost his positions and he wanted them back. He had lost his power and he was determined to regain it. He was surrounded by traitors and he was going to pay them for their treachery and disloyalty. But he was hemmed in by those conditions on the back of his presidential pardon. He would do everything possible to rid himself of those chains.

He had emerged from prison at Christmas 1971 sure that Frank Fitzsimmons was doing no more than keeping his chair warm and would immediately step aside. When he discovered the conditions that had been attached to his pardon, he had thought that at the very least, he would rule the Teamsters from behind the scenes, giving orders that Fitzsimmons would obey without question. But Fitzsimmons had grown to relish the job he inherited. He would not step aside; he would not take orders; he would not be Hoffa's puppet. He told Hoffa to get lost. The union now belonged to Frank Fitzsimmons. James R. Hoffa was a man of the past, unneeded and unwanted.

It was bitter gall, and what made it even more bitter was the realization that the Teamsters belonged not to Fitzsimmons, but to President Richard M. Nixon. The power and majesty of the United States government would be used to keep Hoffa far away and to perpetuate Fitzsimmons's reign on the union throne.

When Fitzsimmons had first moved into Hoffa's office and

place, it had been only as caretaker. He did not even have the title of union president. Even in prison, Hoffa retained the title, and from prison he had given orders about running the union that Fitzsimmons had obeyed. The major task for Fitzsimmons had been to find some way to get Hoffa back on the street and back into office. And, indeed, he had tried. But that was 1967 and Lyndon Johnson was president; the Democrats were in power and the heirs of Robert Kennedy still ruled the Justice Department. Fitzsimmons's efforts had been greeted with scorn. Hoffa, the Democratic administration felt, was just where he ought to be and they would like to see him remain as long as the law allowed.

Fitzsimmons and Hoffa were stymied. But change was in the wind. An election would be held in 1968 and the Democrats, torn and in disarray as a result of the war in Vietnam, appeared destined for defeat. Fitzsimmons turned to the likely winner, and Richard Nixon eagerly accepted his terms: freedom for Hoffa in exchange for Teamster support, money, and votes, all of which went a long way toward providing the slender margin by which Nixon was able to defeat Democrat Hubert H. Humphrey.

If the campaign had been a courtship between Fitzsimmons and Nixon, a wedding took place once the new president was safely ensconced in the White House. Fitzsimmons had found that Hoffa's chair was growing comfortable, that he enjoyed being a man other men deferred to. If he still gave lip service to the idea that Hoffa ought to be released, his efforts in such a cause were more in the nature of delaying that release until a way could be found to prevent Hoffa from dislodging him.

Such thoughts passed on by Fitzsimmons to his new friends received a warm welcome in the White House. There was little desire among the Nixon people to see Hoffa back in power in the Teamsters. Hoffa was, when it came to the crunch, his own man going his own way, uncontrollable and so undependable. Fitzsimmons, however, was malleable. With the right incentives, such as an occasional private chat with the president and a little protection, he could be led easily in the right directions. And so the marriage was arranged and consummated, with each side getting what it wanted. Fitzsimmons would back Nixon and the Republicans down the line; his support and that of the Teamsters would be firm and undeviating; and underlining that support there would be plenty of cash to support the Nixon reelection campaign when it came in 1972, and for whatever other purposes the administration decided. For its part, the administration would back Fitzsimmons to the limit, would make sure he faced no real challenge or trouble from any source. And Teamster affairs would be handled only at the highest levels in the White House.

Thus when journalist Clark Mollenhoff—who had joined the administration as ombudsman to protect the public interest—heard rumors of a deal to free Hoffa, he sent an inquiry to John Ehrlichmann, along with H. R. Haldeman, the president's closest and most powerful adviser, asking what this was all about. Mollenhoff got a message back telling him to stay out of the Hoffa matter, that it was being handled personally by Ehrlichmann and Attorney General John Mitchell, and the president knew what they were doing and did not want Mollenhoff involved. Even more directly involved with the Teamster liaison, though, was another presidential assistant, Charles Colson. In his final days in the White House late in 1971, Mollenhoff decided to make further inquiries about the Teamster-Hoffa situation and discussed the subject with Colson. According to Mollenhoff, Colson told him that he "had concluded that Fitzsimmons would be content to run the Teamsters Union with Hoffa safely in prison." That suited Colson and Nixon just fine.

The administration did more to protect Fitzsimmons not only from Hoffa, but also from others who might be a danger to him. Law enforcement agencies around the country had begun to zero in on some of the financial irregularities that surrounded Fitzsimmons's career and on the questionable way loans from Teamster pension funds were being handed out to certain disreputable persons. According to law enforcement officials, word went out that Washington would not look kindly on any investigations of Fitzsimmons or the Teamsters.

But the problem of Hoffa would not go away. Within the union, there were mounting cries that not enough was being done to get the leader out of prison, that Fitzsimmons was being laggard in his efforts. With the clout that he supposedly had with the Nixon administration, he should have done more. Fitzsimmons would have to do something to quiet the outcry.

In the spring of 1971, Hoffa was about to appear once more

before the parole board to seek an early release. From Fitzsimmons and from people in the administration he was informed that he would have no chance of obtaining a parole so long as he continued to hold on to the union presidency and to vociferously maintain that he had every intention of taking up the reins again once he was released. Hoffa felt he was being offered a choice: a parole in exchange for relinquishing office. He was sure that once granted a parole, once out of the prison doors, Fitzsimmons would simply walk away, and he would easily be elected president of the union once more. Accordingly, he resigned. To his shock and fury, the parole was still denied. He would have to serve out his term barring some unlikely intervention from other sources.

Hoffa's resignation was greeted with relief, elation, and satisfaction by both the White House and Fitzsimmons. Almost immediately, Fitzsimmons convened a special meeting of the Teamster executive board to anoint him as union president, and two weeks later at the Teamster convention the delegates confirmed his ascension by electing him president for a full five-year term.

Still, Fitzsimmons did not feel safe. One day, probably by mid-1972, Hoffa would be a free man. And when he was free, he would promptly move to regain his old office. Fitzsimmons had lived in his shadow long enough to know that he would have considerable trouble standing up to Hoffa and resisting the demands when that day came. Something else would have to be done to protect him.

He discussed his problems with Colson, Attorney General John Mitchell, and other friends in the White House. As Christmas approached, they hit on a solution. Hoffa would be granted presidential clemency. But that pardon would have a restriction attached, forbidding Hoffa from resuming any union activities for eight years, until 1980, on pain of returning to prison. Hoffa, however, would not be told of those conditions. They would be added later. Years later, White House counsel John Dean would say, "John Mitchell ordered me to draw up the papers and he casually mentioned that Hoffa had agreed not to get involved in the union. So I said, 'Why not put that into the president's declaration?' He agreed. The whole thing was an afterthought added by us at the very last minute."

It was the ideal solution for everyone except Hoffa. He would claim that the Mitchell-Dean conditions were not on the papers he signed and must have been added later, and he became obsessed with proving that.

Fitzsimmons was very grateful, indeed, and he proceeded to show just how grateful he was. As the 1972 presidential campaign approached, he threw his personal support and that of the union behind Nixon, over the heated objections of Harold Gibbons.

Franco remembers that day and that scene very well. It took place at California's La Costa. Nixon sent Charles Colson out to the Teamster executive board meeting to make a pitch for major support and Fitzsimmons seconded everything that Colson said, promised to deliver the Teamsters to the president.

I was out there and you could hear Fitz and Harold screaming at each other. Everybody in the joint could hear the whole argument. Harold was really pissed. Fitz had sold out to Nixon and he was trying to turn the whole union over to him. Harold says, "Under no conditions will I ever endorse Richard Nixon for anything, including dog catcher. You can stick Nixon right up your ass if you expect me to support him."

Fitz just blew up and Harold came storming out and he walked over to me and he says, "Would you believe that shanty Irish son of a bitch wants me to endorse Nixon after what they've been doing? They've sold the fucking international to him and that Colson. I wouldn't trust that bastard as far as you could throw him. Joe, this man is ruining this international union."

And then Fitz got his revenge on Harold. He put him in a trick bag, which was that the health and welfare and pension program and the fringe benefits of the Teamster over-the-road contract is one of the highest paid contracts in the industry. A lot of the smaller companies couldn't afford that contract and stay in business. So, some of the locals in the Teamster council were setting up separate locals outside the council to organize these smaller companies and give them contracts they could live with. And Harold did just that out in St. Louis. That is a direct violation of the international constitution.

But everybody was doing it and Fitz was looking the other

way. But when it came to Harold, Fitz cited him and he took the chairmanship of the Central States Conference away from him, he took the chairmanship of the joint council in St. Louis away from him, he created a situation where Harold might lose his position with Local 688, he took his airplane away from him, he took everything away. The only thing he left Harold with was his vice-presidency of the international and Fitz even wanted him to resign that, but some of the guys raised a fuss and they said, "If you want to strip him, strip him all the way down, but don't take the vice-presidency away from him because Harold's very capable and we can use Harold and we can send him out on assignments." So, Fitz left him with that and then he began to give him some very difficult situations, such as the farm situation with Cesar Chavez out in California and other things nobody else could handle, always hoping Harold would fall on his face and be so embarrassed that Fitz would just dump him and nobody would put up a beef. But Harold stuck it out and he did a hell of a job.

Gibbons was the only dissenting voice, at least out loud. The rest of the Teamster executives went along and they went along when Fitzsimmons demanded that they all ante up $1,000 out of their own pockets to aid the Nixon campaign, to which he was personally contributing $4,000 of his own money. They offered no objections when he poured Teamster funds—nobody is sure how much but estimates run to in excess of $1 million—into the coffers of the Committee to Reelect the President, familiarly known as CREEP.

Once Nixon was swept back into office, Fitzsimmons proceeded to bestow even more Teamster bounty on those who had helped him. The Teamster legal affairs were yanked away from Edward Bennett Williams, who had handled them since the late 1950s when he defended Hoffa in one of his court cases, and handed over to Charles Colson; those affairs carried with them an annual retainer of $100,000. Richard Kleindienst, who succeeded John Mitchell as Attorney General, found it no trouble at all to get a multimillion-dollar insurance premium award from the Teamsters for a client, and those few hours of work earned him a fee of $125,000. And there were stories, never verified, that Colson collected another $500,000 in cash for the Nixon campaign from sources close to the Teamsters as a reward for having arranged the restrictions that were attached to Hoffa's pardon and for his help in squashing investigations into Teamster affairs.

With the weight and power of the federal government behind him, and Richard Nixon declaring with fervor, "My door is always open to President Fitzsimmons," Frank Fitzsimmons felt secure—secure enough to face down Jimmy Hoffa during one of their few meetings after Hoffa's release from prison. It happened in 1972 at the funeral of Tom Flynn, a Chicago Teamster leader whom Fitzsimmons had earlier named the union's secretary-treasurer over Hoffa's choice, Harold Gibbons.

In the funeral parlor, Jimmy turned to Fitz and he says, "I want you to appoint Harold Gibbons as secretary-treasurer of the international, which you didn't do when I told you before."

Fitz says, "No. I've already committed myself to Dusty Miller."

Jimmy says, "What do you mean, Dusty Miller? I know Dusty Miller. I made Dusty. He will have to step back and stand back because Harold is going to be the next secretary-treasurer."

Well, Fitz stood by his guns and he told him in no uncertain terms that he was not going to listen to Jim and he was not going to take Dusty out of that position and he had already committed himself and Dusty would be the next secretary-treasurer. Jim blew his stack and they had a real pissing contest right there in the funeral parlor and it never let up.

Fitzsimmons won that battle. But he was not so blind as to think that his victory had been either crushing or final. He knew Hoffa too well. Hoffa had never been a man to give in easily; he was vindictive to those who opposed him and he was growing more so as his frustrations grew. If he no longer had the authority and the power, he still had the ability to create fear. To survive, Fitzsimmons had to make those moves that would put Hoffa in a bind. One way was to make the ruling powers in the union beholden to him. In doing so, he could protect himself from the Hoffa threat and permit himself to enjoy the fruits of his position.

The thing about Fitz was that he just wanted to make money. He never wanted to be poor again because he knew what it was like. This man always had his left hand behind his back with an open palm, like put the money there before we go any further. And Fitz never did like responsibility. That's one of the reasons he always used to get into all kinds of trouble with Jimmy in the old days. He just wanted to be a little business agent to go out and do his things and maybe snatch a few dollars and take care of his family. He didn't want to be vice-president, he didn't want to be president, because that gave him responsibility. He used to come to me and say, "Goddammit, he gave me another detail. I got to go and do this and that. I do all the shit. I'm the fucking flunky around here. I wish he'd just leave me alone."

That was Fitz. Fitz didn't want to work. He wanted to go around and have lunch with this guy and have lunch with that guy and maybe make a deal here and make a deal there and pick up cash bucks here, a kickback, wherever he could make a buck.

When Fitz got elected general president, naturally he did what he thought he would like to have done if he was still just the vice-president. His theory was, I don't want to work. I just want to take that airplane and go fly around and play golf and be friends with important people.

So he said to all the vice-presidents, "I'm giving you the authority to run your own areas. If you get into trouble, don't come back to me. I don't want to hear about it. So, don't get into trouble. In the meantime, you have full authority to run your areas and I hold you responsible for those areas."

The guys turned around and they says, "Hey, Fitz, if you're giving us that responsibility, we're not happy with the money we're getting. How can we get a little money out of this thing?" That was something they could never do with Jimmy. You got responsibility with Jimmy, but there was never any money. That was the job you had and you'd better do it because he tells you to do it, but you'd better never come back and say, "Jimmy, how about a raise?"

He'd look at you and say, "I'll give you a raise. I'll give you a raise right out of that fucking chair."

But Fitz, they could be open with Fitz and they could make demands on Fitz because they knew Fitz wasn't going to argue and Fitz didn't want responsibility. So Fitz agreed to make all the vice-presidents general organizers, which is another $40,000 and more, and then he raised that up, and then he raised the salaries of all the international vice-presidents.

People say Fitz did all that to create loyalty from these guys and stop them from turning back to Jimmy. Fitz wasn't that brilliant. What he was doing was getting rid of responsibility and turning it over to everybody else. He was saying, "Here, boys, here's all the toys. Goodbye, leave me alone. I want to enjoy all the years I have left. I want to play golf. I don't want to hear trouble. I'll play politics. I'll run the office. I'll do the press conferences and the press releases. I'll go to all the dinners. But I'm not going to do what Hoffa did. I'm not going to Local 299 and hold meetings there, and I'm not going to go to your local unions and try to win your elections for you. That's your problem. You have a problem, you live with it, you resolve it, and that's it."

Fitz only wanted to enjoy whatever life he had left. He would rather rub elbows and give a little bit away, hell, give it all away, as long as he was left alone. He'd give it to Nixon, to Colson, whatever it was, so he would be clean and show the image of the great labor leader with a halo over his head who had no knowledge of no racket guys that were involved with the Teamsters or outside the Teamsters. Fitz didn't want to hear none of that shit. He just took the easy way.

When Jimmy was around, in order to get a grant for organizational purposes, Jimmy would oversee it, he would actually get into the area and before he would give a grant, he would want to know exactly where the money was going. Jimmy was an organizer. He was labor. Not Fitz. Fitz was just there. "This is what you need? Take the money. I'll give you what you want. Just don't bother me." It's not that he blackjacked anybody into supporting him. He just gave them the authority. Everybody had authority after Fitz took over. Prior to that, nobody had any authority to do a goddamn thing unless they cleared it with Jimmy first. Jimmy did not know how to delegate authority to his staff people. Fitz didn't know how to delegate authority to his staff people, either, other than to say, "Take the money, take the job, and just leave me alone."

It wasn't that Fitz double-crossed Jimmy. It was that the Teamsters was a good dowry for Fitz. He had $125,000 a year in salary, which was nearly twice what Jimmy made, and there was three homes he could live in, one in California, one in Florida, and another in Washington. He had access to a $3.5 million jet airplane that could carry him anywhere in the world, and all his expenses to be paid by the union. He didn't want to give that up.

Fitz was doing all this and Jimmy was out in the cold ranting and raving and planning his comeback. At that point, everybody in the country and in the international union took a stand-still position. Nobody dared to make any moves and say they were in favor of Hoffa or they were in favor of Fitz. They were caught between the devil and the deep blue sea. They were more scared of Hoffa than they were of Fitz, but Fitz was the general president and they had to live with him. And Fitz in his own way could be a very vicious man and a man who never forgot, he had a long memory, what people call an elephant's memory, and he wanted revenge on everything and everybody who belittled him from way back, which is one of the reasons he did what he did to Harold and other people.

And Jim was just not letting up trying to get back. He was spending money like a drunken sailor and he was doing this and that, and he never let up. I remember one time up at Shanty Creek, at the Michigan Conference of Teamsters. Jim Jr. turned to me and he says, "Joe I wish you would go out and see dad and sit down with him. He's driving mother absolutely crazy. He just sits there and raves all day long. He's going to kill her. I wish to God, my father never goes back to the Teamsters. I think mother and the rest of the family have had just enough of it. If he goes back, we're going to have to go through the whole thing again, and it's going to be worse. We've just had enough. If you could talk dad into doing something else and stop doing what he's doing, I'd be very grateful."

I says, "Jim, there's no way you can tell your dad to stop. You know he wants to be head of the Teamsters and there's no way of stopping him."

"I know it. He's like a raving maniac. But I really feel sorry for my mother. Everytime anything comes down, she gets the brunt of it."

They had a fiftieth birthday party for me in 1974 up at Shanty Creek. Fitz was there, telling me that he loved me but he would always remember the day he was sure I didn't pay him off over the Harold Johnson thing, and telling me I'm still Single-O Franco, and here comes his two sons, Dick and Don, with a cake with fifty marked on it and one candle. Fitz says, "Happy Birthday, Joe. You're fifty today."

I says, "Fitz, you son of a bitch."

He called Dick over then. Now, Dick was getting ready to run for president of Local 299 against Dave Johnson, and I was supporting Dick, getting him jackets and T-shirts and buttons and patches and everything he needed to hand out to the members to get votes. Dick kept saying how helpful I was to him, but he didn't say how much money I was putting out of my pocket and I really didn't have that kind of money in those days to be able to afford it, but I figured, hey, if the kid gets in, I'll be back in the Teamsters and I know Fitz will take care of me and he will forgive me for eating meat on Friday and those minor little sins that you go to purgatory for.

Fitz says to Dick, "You stay close to Joe. You listen to Franco. If he tells you something, you listen. It's like me talking to you. If you win that election, I want you to hire Joe. He can't go back. But I want you to hire him as an administrator or an adviser, as long as he doesn't have anything to do with the union or with the union contracts or negotiating or representing members of Local 299. I want him to work directly under you and advise you as to what you should do. That's my orders to you, son."

Dick says, "Whatever you say, Dad. You got my word."

I says, "Fitz, thank you very much."

Well, Dick blew it, he actually blew it for himself, so I had no chance of getting back at that level.

Supporting Dick Fitzsimmons had been a calculated risk taken by Franco. The aging Dave Johnson had not only been an integral part of Local 299 since the early days, he was also Hoffa's candidate. On one level it seemed that Franco was showing a measure of disloyalty to Hoffa. But, by supporting Dick Fitzsimmons, Franco was able to ingratiate himself with the then-Teamster president and so possibly ease his way back into union affairs, and he was also, in his way, able to serve as a Hoffa agent in the enemy camp.

In fact, during the early 1970s, Franco was playing a

dangerous game of Hoffa loyalist and Fitzsimmons friend. He
would not go against Hoffa, but neither would he publicly oppose
his old partner.

I got along good with Roy Williams and in many instances
over the years, Roy would call me or Sam Ancona, his executive
assistant in Kansas City, would call me and tell me that Roy wants
to see me. I'd go upstairs and the three of us would sit down and
Roy would ask my advice about certain things about Jimmy.

I would tell him what he should do and what he shouldn't do.
I told him, "Your loyalty has got to be to the boss and right now,
Fitz is the boss. If Jimmy tells you to do anything other than that,
just tell him in his own language that whoever is the head of the
Teamsters, that's where your loyalty goes to, no matter whether
you like him or not. You've got him and that's it, and you're stuck
with him. But you respect Jimmy and you give him loyalty, but
you're a Teamster, number one. If he tries to put you in the middle,
you tell him, "Jim, I love you. I love you as an individual. I love
you as a friend. But please don't ask me to go against Fitz out in
the open." That's what he did and I think Jimmy respected him for
it because there was always a good feeling between Jim and Roy all
the way to the end.

Hoffa didn't like it but he understood that Roy Williams and
Allen Dorfman and a lot of others had to put on a public show of
loyalty to Fitzsimmons if they were to maintain their positions. As
long as they continued to keep in touch, to assure him in private of
their devotion to him, he tolerated their public espousal of the
Fitzsimmons cause. He would need them when he came to power
again.

There were others who abandoned him. For them, he had only
contempt and a desire for revenge. Men like Bill Presser and
Dusty Miller and Bobby Holmes, he often declared, owed everything to him and had deserted him. They would pay. And he re-
served a special hatred for Chuckie O'Brien. O'Brien owed everything to Hoffa. His mother was a close friend of Josephine Hoffa,
and when she was widowed, Hoffa had gone out of his way to take
care of O'Brien, treating him almost as an adopted son. When
Chuckie O'Brien decided that school was not for him, Hoffa put

him on the payroll as a business agent for Local 299 and as a Teamster organizer. He often assigned O'Brien confidential errands, though O'Brien rarely carried them out with the efficiency and dispatch of the men who had served Hoffa through the years. Nevertheless, Hoffa forgave.

But as Hoffa's drive for a comeback was gathering momentum, O'Brien defected to the enemy. Fitzsimmons had control of the positions within the union. To O'Brien he showed what power he held. He sent him off to Alaska for a spell, then brought him back, under threat of banishment from the union itself if he sided with Hoffa. O'Brien realized that he had few qualifications that would enable him to find another job anywhere that would pay him the $40,000 a year salary like he was getting from the Teamsters. This seemed more important than his relationship with Hoffa. He threw what little weight he had behind Fitzsimmons, he became a Fitzsimmons sycophant, especially when the Teamster president held out prospects of a new job with the union in Florida.

Hoffa could never forgive O'Brien for his treachery and ingratitude. His desertion was worse than that of others who had swung behind Fitzsimmons, since he had been like a member of Hoffa's family since childhood. When Hoffa returned to power, O'Brien would pay dearly, as would all those other defectors.

And Hoffa would return to power. That was at the heart of all he was attempting to do. It was essential to overturn the restrictions that had been attached to his presidential pardon. In the 1960s, before going off to prison, he had spent hundreds of thousands of dollars trying to uncover or fabricate evidence that he had been the victim of a government frame-up. That had been unavailing. Now he was spending again. The money was pouring out of those sewer traps in his basement, at least $1 million and probably more, going to everyone and everything that could help him. There was money for teams of lawyers who would appeal on various grounds that the restrictions were illegal and unconstitutional. They were a violation of the constitutional separation of powers clause that barred a president, a member of the executive branch, from assuming a judicial role, which Nixon had done when he attached conditions to a pardon from a court-imposed sentence. There was as much money as needed for people in Washington and elsewhere who told Hoffa they could, for the right price, obtain documentary proof and affidavits that would clearly demonstrate that the restrictive wording on the back of the pardon had been added without Hoffa's knowledge after he had signed those papers.

He was also forging alliances with those who might help him once he was back on the Teamster throne. He might publicly proclaim that once he was union president again, he would rid the ranks of all the hoodlums and underworld figures, the ubiquitous "outside element," that had rallied around Fitzsimmons, who had given them, in exchange for support, almost unlimited access to Teamster pension fund loans and control of locals. But Hoffa had his own special relationships with many of these same people, and though they could not control him or influence him as they appeared to do with Fitzsimmons, they respected him and not Fitzsimmons. Now he was wooing some of them again. Things would not be so overt, and thus open to public condemnation and official investigation, as they had been in the past. But those who came to his side would be rewarded in the future.

One thing nobody doubted was that Hoffa would take sudden and violent revenge on those who had become his enemies. He talked about it. And Franco remembers a dinner one night in Florida when he and Roy Williams were suddenly alone at the table. Williams told him he had heard that Hoffa was once again in contact with Fidel Castro and had asked Castro to send in a team of specialists to dispatch one or more Teamster leaders who had deserted Hoffa for Fitzsimmons. Williams wasn't sure just who the targets might be.

But revenge would have to wait. It would mean little beyond self-satisfaction as long as the conditions on the pardon remained in force. Following the course laid down by law, Hoffa's lawyers first went to the pardons division of the Justice Department, arguing that the conditions would not hold because Hoffa was the only labor leader ever so bound. The response was an unequivocal rejection. The next step was an appeal to the Attorney General, Richard Kleindienst. Kleindienst didn't even wait to receive word that Hoffa intended to approach him. He said he had no intention of overturning the restrictions and if Hoffa did not abide by them, he would find himself back in prison. The next step was the courts. In 1974, the issue was brought before Judge John Pratt in United States District Court. Pratt ruled against Hoffa. But by now Hoffa

had new lawyers and an appeal was taken to the United States
Circuit Court of Appeals. The arguments would be heard in mid-
1975 and there were many constitutional authorities who believed
that Hoffa's argument of violation of the separation of power
clause was compelling and stood a very good chance of carrying
the day.

Hoffa, however, was not depending solely on the constitutional grounds to unshackle him. He was preparing to offer an
alternative defense of his position, that he had never signed documents containing the restrictions. His contacts, to whom he was
dispatching as much cash as they requested, were telling him by
mid-1975 that they were on the verge of obtaining that proof, that
they might even be able to obtain affidavits from John Dean, John
and Martha Mitchell, and others laying out just how the whole
pardon scheme had been developed.

As prospects brightened, Fitzsimmons grew more concerned.
There was little doubt in anyone's mind that a Hoffa freed from
chains would be swept back into office. His minion, Dave Johnson,
was prepared to either appoint Hoffa as a delegate to the Teamster
convention in 1976 from Local 299, which would give him a seat on
the convention floor, or even resign as president of Local 299 and
turn that office back to Hoffa to use as his springboard. Either
way, Hoffa would be right where he wanted to be and nothing
would stop him. A trucking industry survey in 1974 showed that 83
percent of Teamster members would support Hoffa over Fitzsimmons if a showdown came. The union wanted Hoffa back. Thus, his
mere appearance on the convention floor would obviously create
pandemonium, the bandwagon would roll, crushing everything that
stood in its way. Jimmy Hoffa would be swept back into office.

Hoffa was certain this was what the future held. Fitzsimmons
was very worried that Hoffa's certainty might be correct. And it
was not only Fitzsimmons who worried. There were a lot of other
people who feared Jimmy Hoffa, feared what he might uncover and
what he might do should he regain his old office. There were all
those Teamster leaders who had deserted him for Fitzsimmons.
There were those in the "outside element" who were riding the
Fitzsimmons gravy train and who might not find things quite so
easy or controllable with Hoffa back in Teamster headquarters.
There were the people of the Nixon administration who had

courted and married Frank Fitzsimmons. Nixon might be gone, resigned in disgrace to avoid the greater disgrace of impeachment, and many of those who served him loyally might be on their way to prison, but there were still those in government who played a role and who, thus, had much to lose should Hoffa succeed and Fitzsimmons depart. Even President Gerald Ford, when he took office, was wooing the Fitzsimmons-controlled Teamsters, praising the union and its leaders, hoping for Teamster support.

And so all watched and waited and considered what they could do to block Hoffa, especially as his confidence grew and he began to contact and draw around him those who had remained loyal through his years in the wilderness. He could not move without someone knowing about it. Federal agents kept watch on him and his homes, in Detroit and at Lake Orion, followed him wherever he went, listened in on his telephone conversations.

By the summer of 1975, the battle lines were drawn. In the balance hung the fate of Hoffa and Fitzsimmons, as well as the future of the Teamsters.

24

During the years following their release from prison Franco had not seen much of Hoffa. He had talked to him now and then, had met with him on occasion, had introduced him a few times to a woman much younger whom he had married late in 1973 during a time of loneliness. (This marriage did not take any better than his previous one and by 1975 it was coming apart.) But the contacts had been sporadic and without great substance. Franco had been waiting for that moment when Hoffa, about to triumph, would need him once more and call.

That call came in late spring of 1975. Hoffa and Franco met and Hoffa told him to be prepared for action, that the papers he had been waiting for would be available to him very soon, and so the climax of the long exile was approaching. Franco waited eagerly. For a time, he heard nothing. Then, on July 16, his phone rang.

★ ★ ★

I got this telephone call and the voice says, "Franco."

As soon as he said that, I knew who the hell it was. I says, "Who is this?"

"Quit the bullshit. You know who this is. Come on out to the cottage because I want to see you."

"You got company?"

"No, just Josie and I, that's it."

"Okay, I'll be out. But if you got company, I don't want to come out."

"No, just Josie and I."

"Okay, I'm on my way out."

It took me about forty-five minutes to get out to the cottage on Lake Orion. I walked up to the side entrance that was to the kitchen and Josie was waiting there for me. She gave me a hug and a kiss on the cheek and I returned it. It was like seeing family again for the first time in a long time. Josie and I sat down and he was in the front room laying on the couch, pretending like he's asleep. But I know this man.

Josie says, "Come on, Joe, have a cup of coffee."

So we sat down and I says, "How you been feeling?"

She says, "Fine. How are the children?"

"They're all getting big, Josie. One of these days . . ."

She says, "I want to see those kids."

"I'll bring them up this summer. Where's the old man?" And I winked at her, because I know he's laying on the couch.

"Oh, he's in the front room, sleeping."

"Is he behaving himself? Is he giving you any trouble, Josie? You know, he's getting old. He's out of shape. He's got to take an afternoon nap." I was deliberately throwing some crap out to see if I could get a roust out of him, because you can't say that about him. Jim was a health nut. He'd say, "Come on, I challenge you to a hundred pushups," and you'd have to do it.

That statement got him. He sat up and he says, "Listen, you dago bastard, I can take you anytime I want. With one hand tied behind my back."

I says to Josie, "Do you hear that bullshit? He woke up, huh? He was sleeping? No more sleeping than the goddamn man in the moon."

Jim comes out of the living room and we sit down and he says, "How're you doing, Franco?"

"It's getting pretty rough out there, Jim. You know I'm selling Teamster jackets and stuff, but it's one way I can stay close to the building to know, with the ear against the wall, what's going on. I'm getting very close to a lot of the local unions and they're just waiting for you to get back. They're just waiting for you to make your move. They're just riding the fence. They don't know whether to piss, shit, or holler because if they make any other moves, they're afraid Fitz will come down on them. So you got to go along with them."

"I don't want to hear that shit. The gutless, ball-less sons of bitches, they either stand up now or they'll fall by the wayside when I walk back in there. They either show me they're goddamn men when I need them or they'll get the hell out of there when I get back. And especially the English son of a bitch that sits there, the dirty gutless bastard that he is, Bobby Holmes. And I'll get that Irish son of a bitch out of there, too, if it's the last thing I do." Then he stopped for a minute, and he looked at me and he says, "What are you doing with your local?"

"Not a goddamn thing. I can't go back until seventy-seven."

"Bullshit. Grab the son of a bitching kid that you put in there, throw the guys out of there. Tell them to give you a paycheck every week."

"Jimmy, that local isn't worth it. I'm not going to touch that kid. He's making a living. He's got a very old family to take care of. Let him alone. I don't want to bother with him. I don't want that local. I don't need the heat that goes with it. When you go back, I'll go back when my time is ready to go back with you. No other way. I'm not going to go back any other way."

"Well, that's your goddamn business. But I'll tell you, Franco, I'm making a goddamn move. I'm gonna make the sons of bitches move. I'm gonna make every one of them sons of bitches in Washington squirm like rats on a sinking ship. That Colson to start with . . ."

He's starting to scream and holler, and Josie walks in and she says, "Hey, if you're going to start hollering and screaming and ranting and raving, the both of you get the hell out of here. Go out in the yard. Do all your hollering out there. I've got a headache."

So, Jimmy and I went out in the yard and sat at the picnic table. What she did by chasing us out was to get him calmed down a little bit. He says, "Franco, it wasn't easy for me to call you, even though I wanted to see you, to get you out here to talk."

"Why, Jim?"

"Because all my phones are tapped. That's why I didn't mention your name but short and quick. And that's why I cut you short. My phones are all tapped. Jimmy Jr.'s phones are all tapped. As a matter of fact, right over there on top of a hill, everything is being filmed. They know you're here now. You're already on film."

"You're shitting me, Jim."

"No. Take a look up there, on top of that pole, they got a camera. You can see the light flashing off the lens if you look real close."

I took a look and he was right.

He says, "Franco, they got me tied down so bad that if I whisper, they hear me, if I shit, they hear that. They're watching me and they're following me. I don't have a minute. When I drive downtown, I got an escort. The only place I can meet anybody safe is up here at the cottage or down in Jim Jr.'s office, because we got that place swept, we sweep it all the time to make sure. I don't meet people anyplace else."

"Jim, is there a chance for you to get back?"

"If it takes a million, if it takes two million, whatever it takes, I'll buy every political son of a bitch that had anything to do with that deal. I'll get the truth out no matter what I got to pay for it. I'm getting John Dean to tell the truth. I'm getting John Mitchell to tell the truth, and I'm getting that drunken bitch of a wife of his. But that Colson and that man that used to sit in the big chair in the Oval Office before they got him, they're the ones that fucked me, and I'll fuck them before I'm done. Sit still, Franco. It's only going to be another sixty days, maybe a lot less, and that son of a bitch is gonna hit and she'll blow right up. Then I'm going back. And when I go back, don't worry. Whatever you need, you got. I know what you need. I give you my word right now, when I go back, you'll never need to worry about selling anything. I will be back as general president. You may not be able to come back into the labor movement right away. But don't worry about it. You'll have a payroll coming for you and the kids. You've showed your loyalty. You've sat on the sidelines and you've waited. Now, just a few more months, maybe less, and this thing will hit the fan and then all the shit will blow."

He sat there looking at me and then he says, "When we get back in, we're gonna clean house. They'll need to follow me around with a fucking meat wagon. I got a list and they're all gonna go. Number one on that list is that fucking Irishman. Franco, I'm going to ask you to do something I never asked you to do before. I want you to hit Fitz."

I just looked at him and I started to say something, but he was all wound up and you couldn't stop him.

He says, "Number two is Bobby Holmes. That son of a bitch, that English bastard, I'll tell you something, Franco, I'll do him myself. Just wait until I get back into office. I'll take care of him myself. And number three is Dusty Miller. I made that mother-fucker. I took him from nothing and I made him an international organizer, I made him an international vice-president and he went over and he dumped me and he went with Fitz because Fitz made him secretary-treasurer over the fact that I wanted Harold in that job when Tom Flynn died, and Fitz appointed Dusty and Dusty wouldn't step down even when I told him to. He says to me, no, Fitz appointed me and I'm going to stay. Those three are the first ones. I want you to hit Fitz and I'll take Bobby Holmes and Dusty's gonna go, too. They turned on me. There's other guys that's all right. Roy Williams. At least Roy calls me and Roy talks to me and he listens to me and he's showing some loyalty to me. And at least Allen Dorfman comes to visit me and he talks to me and he stays in touch and he shows loyalty to me. I know he has to do business with Fitz, and I understand that, but he's still showing loyalty to me. And Harold's showing loyalty to me. But the rest of them sons of bitches. Fitz shows me no loyalty at all, and Bobby shows me no loyalty, he cut his own fucking deal with Fitz. And that fucking little bastard, Chuckie O'Brien. I brought that kid here from Kansas City because his mother wanted him here, and I raised him like he was my own, and I let him tell people that he's like my adopted son. That little son of a bitch, he's got nothing to do with me. I did it out of respect for his father and his mother. I did everything for that kid."

I says, "Jim, you don't have to tell me that. Everybody knows that."

"Go to hell, Franco. Look what he's done. He kissed and made up in bed with Fitz for a stinking job."

"Well, you know, Jim, some people when the wind blows north, the wind blows north, and when the wind blows south, the wind blows south. I'm sure when you get back, Chuckie will apologize and kiss and make up with you. So, I wouldn't be that hurt about him. He's a kid and I'm sure Chuckie still loves you, because I've talked to him, and he feels bad about it because you're pissed at him."

"I don't want to hear that shit, that little cocksucker. If I ever catch him, I'll beat his fucking brains out. I'll get him and I'll beat his fucking brains out, that two-faced bastard. Just let me see him and he won't know what hit him. All of them, all of them. I made them all, I did everything for all of them, all of them, they wouldn't be shit if it wasn't for me, and all of them are just sticking the knife in my back. They got to go. There's no two ways about it."

"I can't do it, Jim."

"What do you mean?"

"I can't do what you asked. I ain't gonna hit Fitz."

He got real pissed and he started ranting and raving at me that I wasn't showing him no loyalty. I told him that there wasn't anybody who showed him more loyalty. I loved him and I always did everything he asked, all the years, never asked a question, always did it. But for me to go out and kill Fitz, who used to be my partner and who I still liked, that was asking too much. There was plenty of people he could go to who would do the job. He didn't have to come to me, and I wasn't going to do that.

Well, he kind of calmed down after a while and we sat there and he started asking about the kids and other things, and then it got late and I got up to go. He says for me not to worry and he'd be in touch and it was only a matter of a very short time before we would be back where we belonged.

> *You've already read the names the government put out as the men responsible for Jim's disappearance, and there's no more proof now than there was then.*
>
> *So I'm not going to name them again. I can only tell you what I saw the day Jim Hoffa disappeared.*
>
> *—J.F.*

25

On the morning of July 30, 1975, two weeks after that meeting with Franco, Jimmy Hoffa got a telephone call. A few hours later, he left his home at Orion Lake to drive to Manchu's Red Fox restaurant in a shopping center at Fourteen Mile Road and Telegraph in Detroit. He never returned. Late that afternoon, his car was found in the shopping center's parking lot, unlocked and abandoned. There was no sign of Hoffa. He had vanished. He was never to reappear.

In the days, weeks, and months that followed, a scenario of Hoffa's last day was put forth by the Justice Department and the FBI and fed in bits and pieces to eager journalists, investigators, and the public. It came to be accepted as the truth. It goes something like this:

The call Hoffa received that morning was from one of two men, or someone purporting to represent them, requesting a meeting early that afternoon at the Red Fox. Hoffa knew both men well, had dealt with them through the years. One was a ruler of an important Eastern Teamster Local, rising to that exalted position through the ranks of one of the East's major crime families. He ruled his local with an iron and violent hand, and challenges to him were not met with kindness. From the early days, he had been a friend and supporter of Hoffa. In the mid-1960s, he was convicted of extortion and served almost five years in prison at the same time

s Hoffa. There are stories, not entirely reliable, that he and Hoffa
ad several bitter quarrels and, as a result, their friendship was
hattered. After his release, he became one of Fitzsimmons's major
ources of strength in the East.

As for the other man, he was, according to various investiga-
ive agencies, a leading figure in Detroit organized crime circles
nd an enforcer of mob dicta. He had been arrested over the years
ourteen times for almost every conceivable crime but had been
onvicted only once, of bribing a police officer. A frequent honored
uest at Teamster conventions and conclaves, though he held no
nown office in the union and was not a member, he was a close
riend of many Teamster leaders, including Hoffa, whom he had
nown for years. It was he who was supposedly trying to set up the
neeting between Hoffa and his former friend at the Red Fox. The
xpressed purpose was to make peace between the two men.

A little before noon, Hoffa left home, telling his wife that he
vas going to a meeting with two of his colleagues at the Red Fox
nd would be home late in the afternoon. On his way to the rendez-
ous, he stopped at the offices of Airport Service Lines, a limou-
ine service, to see the purported owner, Louis Linteau, a one-time
fficer of a Teamster local in Pontiac who had lost his job after a
onviction for embezzlement. Linteau was out to lunch. Hoffa
vaited awhile and while he waited, he chatted with employees of
he limousine company, telling them that he was on his way to a
neeting at the Red Fox and he wanted to have Linteau with him.
When Linteau didn't return, an impatient Hoffa got back into his
ar and drove off.

He reached the Red Fox at just about the time agreed on for
he meeting. It was early afternoon. He waited a half hour and
hen called Linteau, who had by then returned to his office. Hoffa
old him, "The bastards are late." Indeed, according to theory, the
nen were not only late, they had no intention of appearing; one
vas actually in New Jersey and the other was at a Detroit athletic
lub getting a massage and a haircut.

After talking to Linteau, Hoffa called his wife to say that the
nen he was meeting were late but that he would hang around and
vait for them. He returned to his car. At least two bystanders later
aid they saw him at about two in the afternoon standing by his car
n the parking lot, apparently waiting for someone. One of the

bystanders said that about then a maroon Lincoln or Mercury drove up. Three men were inside. The car was very much like one owned by the son of one of the men who was supposedly going to meet with him. A second man, the driver, had switched allegiance when Hoffa was in prison. The meeting was peaceful and friendly. After a brief conversation, Hoffa got into the back seat of the maroon car and it drove away.

Once in the car, Hoffa was knocked unconscious and either shot or strangled during the trip away from the shopping center into Detroit. His body was disposed of in an incinerator.

In the more than a decade that has passed since Hoffa was last seen, this has come to be a generally accepted explanation of the events that occurred that day at the end of July 1975, expounded by journalists, spread by the FBI, the Justice Department, and other investigative agencies.

Joe Franco says it won't wash. And it won't wash for many reasons.

★ ★ ★

First of all, Jimmy would never have told Josie where he was going or who he was going to meet. That wasn't his way. Jimmy would have said, "I'm going out and you'll see me when you see me," and Josie would have accepted that. She would have been shocked if it was any other way.

Second, Jimmy was supposed to have left home and made a meeting with two former colleagues at the Red Fox, which was very far from his home at Lake Orion, and he was supposed to have stopped to see Louis Linteau. Louis was an old friend of mine; he used to work as a business agent for Local 614 in Pontiac, which Tommy Burke and I went into to straighten out when they were having trouble. Louis got into some trouble and he was an officer of that local and got defeated. Louis didn't have a dime but as soon as Jimmy got home, he gave Louis the money to become the owner of the airport limousine service where he was working before that. That gave Jimmy a piece of the business, which he was doing all the time and which there is no paperwork on, but which ran into the millions. Now, if Jimmy stopped there and Louis wasn't there, the last thing in the world Jimmy would have done was to go in and talk to some employees, some flunkies, and tell them, "I've got a meeting over at the Red Fox and I'm meeting with important people," and naming them. Anybody who knows Jimmy knows that's bullshit. He wasn't the type to do that. Who the hell are these people that he would confide in them? He would not disclose his personal business to anyone, let alone the employees that worked for Louis Linteau. For all the years that I've known him, he would just say, "Come on, Franco, take a ride with me. I've got to go downtown to meet with someone." He would never say who he's meeting with or what the meeting with so-and-so was for or anything else. He would never mention the names of people he had meetings with.

Now, we get to the Red Fox. When Jimmy set a time for lunch or a meeting or something, you'd better be there right on the dot. He's not going to stop off someplace and have conversations with people and then go to the place, and you'd better not, either. He would never be late; he would be prompt. He would have waited maybe fifteen minutes and if the people didn't show up, he would have got into his car and left. The only reason he would possibly have waited beyond that, which they said he was doing, was not because he was waiting for someone who wanted to patch up a quarrel, but because he was waiting for someone to come with the information he was waiting for, which he had told me about.

Now, they say two other guys known to Jim showed up in a maroon car and Jimmy got in and drove off. No way on God's earth. The night before Jimmy disappeared, I was with the supposed driver. I ran into him in my nephew Joe Valenti's office at Teamster headquarters where he used to hang around. And he says to me, "Joe, do me a favor, drive me home."

I says, "Sure, I'm on my way out toward there, anyway."

So, I drove him out and we stopped off at the golf course and we spent a few minutes out there with Dick Fitzsimmons and other guys, and then we went on our way. And he told me he was borrowing Walter Shuler's trailer in the morning to drive down to Florida with all his belongings, because he was getting married or he had just got married and he was setting up a home down there. And while we were driving, he started talking about Jim and telling me how much he really loved Jimmy and how sorry he was for the things that he did and it wasn't really worth the job or anything else. He says, "I tried to talk to him but he won't answer my calls and when he does get on the phone, Joe, he calls me every name under the sun."

I says, "Well, friend, just leave it alone and do what you've got to do to survive and once he gets back into office, I'm sure that all the anger and all the viciousness he's got into him will kind of ease off. You've just got to give him time. He's screaming and hollering, but let things go his way and you'll see, he'll get back to being the same old Hoffa that he was."

And he says, "I sure hope so, Joe. Because right now, if Jimmy ever saw me, he'd slap me across the face so hard I'd see stars for a year and he'd probably stick his foot up my ass so far they'd have to amputate it at the knee."

That's just what Jimmy would have done if that guy showed up at the Red Fox. He'd just have started screaming and ranting so everybody would have come running, thinking there was a riot going on, and he'd have hit him and laid him out.

So, it couldn't have been that guy that showed up. And if it was anybody else, people he didn't know, he sure as hell wouldn't have gone along peaceful. He would have bit and scratched and hollered and put up one hell of a fight right to the end, so they'd have had to take him right on the spot and drag him into the car. And with people watching? No way.

And besides, all this speculating about who he was going to meet and who met him and the rest, that's pure bullshit. They had the taps on his phones, so they knew damn well who he was going to meet. Weren't they listening that day? And they were following him everywhere he went, like his shadow. How come that particular day they pulled off and left him free?

It wasn't anything like they said. I know. Because I was there and I seen it all and I know what happened.

What Joe Franco says he saw that summer afternoon was not intended for his eyes or for the eyes of anyone who knew Jimmy Hoffa and understood how he reacted to the expected, and to the unexpected. What Franco says he saw that afternoon gives a lie to the accepted truth, to the theories and official versions propounded and propagated by the FBI, by the police, by those in power.
What Franco says he saw that afternoon—and held in silence for

more than a decade for what he considered good reasons, and now reveals here for the first time—points to a criminal conspiracy reaching into the very highest levels of the American government.

I had a meeting that afternoon up in Flint, and the Red Fox shopping center was on the way and I stopped off there to take care of some personal business having to do with my wife, Leslie, who I was busting up with at the time. It was starting to get late and I was getting worried that I was going to be an hour late for lunch and the meeting and everything when I spotted Hoffa. He was standing and walking around near his car like a bantam rooster. I sure as hell didn't want him to see me. Because if he'd have seen me there, he'd have said, "Franco, what the hell are you doing here?" and he'd have been thinking I was following him or spying on him or something. And I knew if he started to question me and I told him I was there because of personal business having to do with Leslie, he would have been real pissed because he took a liking to her and Jimmy was very moral, he was a family man and he just couldn't stomach divorces and bad scenes between husbands and wives. It wasn't his thing.

So, I just stayed where I was, wondering how long I could hang around before I had to head out for Flint. And I could see that Jim was waiting for someone, and I figured, from what he told me out at the lake when we met, that he was waiting for the guy to deliver the documentation he was expecting that he could take to court and have all restrictions against him lifted.

I knew I couldn't hang around much longer or he sure as hell would spot me. So, I was getting ready to head out when a car drove up to him. It was a black Ford LTD, four-door. There was a black driver and two white guys, and these guys got out. They were typical Ivy Leaguers, with sport jackets and shirts and ties, and you could see that they were either federal marshals or federal agents, one of the two. Being in the business as long as I been in the business, it doesn't take too much for me to smell it or to see it; I can tell right away unless the guy is really underground and really disguising himself. But you knew right away these two guys were definitely either marshals or agents.

Now, Jimmy was standing there, ready to get into his car like he was going to take off when this black Ford pulled up in front of him. These two white guys got out and they went into their pockets and they came out flashing their wallets, and you could see the identification tags were coming out from both of them. It was all done very quietly and very smoothly and very professionally. They flashed their identification and they said something to Jim, which, knowing how they work, was probably, "We're with the government and here is our ID's and we've got some questions we'd like to ask you, so would you please come with us." And Jim would have gone, because he was used to that kind of thing. It happened all the time.

He got into the back of the car with these two guys, and they took off. There wasn't no trouble or anything. They headed up toward Pontiac and I tagged after them a little way and then I turned off to go on to Flint. That was the last I ever saw of Jim.

The road they were on was heading straight for the airport at Pontiac. Later on, I began to think that maybe they must have had a plane waiting there to take Jim away and get rid of him where nobody would ever find him. But nobody ever looked into that or tried to find out if there were any private planes leaving Pontiac that afternoon, if there were even any records. But you've got a lot of big lakes—Michigan, Huron, and Superior—within easy flying distance and they're all pretty damn deep.

After they started investigating, and they were talking to everybody and dragging everybody before the grand jury, I got called down to the grand jury five different times. They says to me every time, "Mr. Franco, we would like you to be a cooperative witness."

I says, "If you want to give me immunity, I'll answer every question you give me, and I may add a little more to it than what you're asking. But unless you give me immunity, there's no way you'll get me into a grand jury because you've not got a cherry with me. I've been in there more goddamn times than you have and you ain't gonna put me in a trick bag again."

One guy says, "There's no way I will give you immunity. The only way I will take you in there is if you will be a cooperative witness."

"Well, then, I'm going to tell you right out here in the corridor, I'm going to take the Fifth Amendment and if you want to waste time with me, you take me in and I'll have you in and out of federal court every five minutes. So, now you know the name of the game; if you want to bother with it, go ahead."

"Well, I know your reputation. I can't give you immunity, Mr. Franco. If you're not going to be a cooperative witness, we'll just call you another time."

They did that four more times and never out of all those times did they offer me immunity and never out of all those times did I answer any questions in regard to the disappearance of James R. Hoffa.

But if they had given me immunity, I would have told them exactly what I saw out at the Red Fox and what happened there.

26

Hoffa was gone. Franco, the loyalist, knew he would not return to help and protect him. He was on his own now and his one desire was to get back into the Teamsters, as soon as his five-year set-off under the Landrum-Griffin Act expired. His hope for that lay in his old friend and one-time partner, Frank Fitzsimmons. With Hoffa's demise, Fitzsimmons was now the unchallenged president of the union. But Franco was getting mixed signals from Fitzsimmons.

One time he says to me, "If you would have stayed loyal to me, gone along with me and not Hoffa, I would have shared everything with you, Joe. I loved you as much as I loved my son. You would have been alongside of me because I know the things that you've done for me. I knew every time I needed you, you were always there. But you were Hoffa's man. You were never my man."

Another time, he says to me, "Joe, I promise you this. When your five years are over, I will definitely put you back to work."

"Okay, Fitz. I talked to Roy Williams and Roy gave me a commitment that as soon as my time was up, Roy would help me in the central states. There'll be a spot for me someplace and I can go back into the movement."

Fitz says, "Well, that's good. Either one of us. It makes no difference. As long as we get you back to work."

While I was waiting through that set-off, we were out at LaCosta for one of those tournaments that Fitz was throwing every year. We had just come off the golf course, and Fitz came over to me and he put his arm around me and he says, "You see that big house I've got up on the hill? That's my house, Joe. And you want to know what I did the other day? They brought me five fucking million dollars in cash. If you would have stayed loyal to me, I would have shared."

And then something happened that still gets me. I won the Class B golf tournament that year and I won two hundred sixty-five dollars. Fitz sent a friend of his named Art Stone, who was a good golfer and who used to be part of the Young Democrats in Michigan with me. Art comes over and he says, "Fitz says where is his end of the two hundred sixty-five dollars."

I looked at Art and Art's laughing his ass off. I says, "That dirty son of a bitch. He wants a piece of that fucking two hundred sixty-five dollars? I won't give him the benefit of ever saying I didn't cut up a buck with him when I made a buck, whether it's legitimate or illegitimate. Tell Fitz he'll get his."

I went out the next day and I bought him a raglan sleeve sweater in the pro shop. It costs one hundred fifty dollars, so he got one hundred fifty dollars out of the two hundred sixty-five dollars that I won. I sent it to his home. Do you think he would ever turn to me and say, thank you, I got your gift? Not a word. But that was Fitz. If you made a nickel, he would put that hand behind him and he'd expect two-and-a-half cents, otherwise you don't make a nickel with Fitz. And I guess when he told me they gave him five million cash, he was telling me the truth and it was on the basis that he gave a Teamster loan to somebody and he was getting his share.

Later on, when Fitz got cancer and he was dying, he had made a commitment to Roy Williams that Roy would be the next president if anything should happen to him. Now, I knew that was coming because of things I heard and smelled and I used to tell guys that Roy was going to be the man. A lot of guys believed me and they consolidated their positions with Roy and went along with him, and they came out all right. And a lot of guys didn't and they didn't do too well when it came Roy's turn.

But Fitz. Just before he died, somehow Pat, who was his wife, got very friendly with Joe Morgan's wife, and Joe was international vice-president from the southern conference, and all of a sudden there became a very close relationship between Fitz and Joe Morgan.

On his death bed, there was three or four vice-presidents in the room and Joe Morgan and Roy Williams. Now, Fitz got it in the throat and he was only able to whisper. He turns to Roy and Joe Morgan and he whispers, "I want Joe Morgan to be the next general president. He's got my blessings."

Roy says, "Fuck you on your death bed. You're not going to tell me in the last few minutes of your life that after two years that you've told me and committed yourself to me, and everybody in this room knows that you committed yourself and the executive board, all of a sudden you're switching and telling me I've got to step down and you're going to give it to Joe Morgan. Fuck you."

Well, Fitz couldn't argue with that because he's dying and he couldn't hardly talk. And everybody in that room says, "Forget about what he's saying on his death bed." So Joe Morgan backed right off and he says, "Roy, forget about it."

Fitz died a day or two after that and at the convention, Roy got elected general president.

In the Teamsters, you got a structure like in the army, so when you got to do something, you go by the procedures and you don't bypass anybody. So, late in 1976, I went to Bobby Holmes, who was the vice-president for the state of Michigan and also the head of the joint council. I had already talked to Roy and Roy says, "Don't worry. As of the first of the year, when you're off the paper, give yourself fifteen days over just in case of time, because the government could just use one day to call you in violation, and you'll be back at work. Now, you go back to Bobby and talk to Bobby, but don't tell him you talked to me about it. Let Bobby make his move."

So I went to Bobby and Bobby says, "Joe, you got no problem with me. Go do your homework."

"I already did my homework. My homework's done. What I

need is you to go into the executive board and ask for an approval for me to come back to work."

"No problem."

Right away, I contacted Sam Ancona and Roy Williams and I says, "I just talked to Holmes and he told me he has no problem with it and he will come up to the next executive board meeting and recommend that I be reinstated and put back to work until I am able to retire."

Roy says, "Good."

The next conference was at the Arlington Park Towers Hotel outside of Chicago. I was waiting downstairs in the lobby with a guy named Neil Dalton and McMasters and Bob Coy, and we're waiting for the executive board to break up. I'm waiting for the good news that I would go back to work on like January 15, 1977. Here comes Bobby Holmes and he don't say shit to me. Here comes Roy and Roy turns to Bobby and he says, "I'm going to tell you something, Holmes. If you walked out of that meeting without bringing Joe's name up, I would have put Joe on the central states conference payroll. I told you, goddamnit, why do I have to remind you every time there's got to be something done?"

It turned out that Bobby didn't bring my name up while the meeting was in session. Just before Fitz adjourned it, Roy says, "Wait a minute, Fitz. Mr. Holmes has a request to make."

Fitz says, "What's that about?"

Roy says, "He told Franco that he is going to request that Franco be put back to work as soon as his time was off. It seems like he's got a loss of memory."

And Bobby Holmes says, "Oh, I did forget. Mr. Chairman, I'd like to put it on record that as soon as Joe Franco is off the paper, that he be reinstated into the Teamster movement and given a job."

And when Roy came out that's when he was laying into Bobby, telling him, "Why can't you do it the way you tell people you're supposed to do it? If I didn't jump on it, Fitz would never have known what was coming down. But I would have hired Joe. I would have put him to work. In spite of you, Bobby, I would have put him to work."

Now, Bob Coy's standing there and Bob says, "Where the hell do I put him?"

Roy says, "I don't give a shit where you put him. I'll even give you the money. I'll give you a grant. Make a request. If you don't, I'll keep him in the central states."

Bob Coy turns around and he says, "Well, hell, I'll take Joe." Bob Coy and I were real close in those days.

And Neil Dalton says, "Jesus Christ, if it wasn't that Joe lives in Detroit and I'm up in Saginaw, I'd take Joe."

And Bob Coy says, "No, I'll take him."

I says, "Don't argue about it, fellows. Let me stay with Bob Coy. At least he's in Detroit. At least get me back in, then we can work the wrinkles out."

Roy looked at me and he kind of smiled. "Well, let's get one thing straight. He goes back to work right after the first of the year, one way or the other. With no stipulations. He goes back to work until this man wants to retire or is able to retire."

And everybody agreed. So, I went back into the Teamster movement on January 15, 1977, and I worked for Bob Coy as a general organizer for three years and then he transferred me over to Joint Council 43, and I stayed out the balance of the five years with the joint council. Then they laid me off because of a political fight between Bob Coy, Bobby Holmes, and Roy Williams.

So, after thirty-six years as a Teamster—less the year he spent in prison and the five years he had been forbidden to return to the union—Franco was no longer a Teamster. But at least he would have his pension to look forward to, the pension fund set up by Allen Dorfman for Jimmy Hoffa and the union.

Allen was in a lot of trouble then, getting ready to go to trial again and people were spreading rumors that Allen was saying he wasn't going to go to the can again for anybody and that if he has to, he'd be a government witness against everybody. Neil Dalton was one of the guys that told me that, and I told Neil, "I don't believe that. I know Allen and he's not afraid to do another couple of years, which is all he is looking at. He comes from the old school. He was trained by his father. He was trained by Jimmy, he was trained by the outside people that he belongs to. Somebody's spreading some goddamn rumor and it's going to get him in trouble. You mark my words, somebody keeps that shit up, it's going to hurt Allen."

As far as the Teamsters is concerned, the quickest way to ruin somebody's reputation is to start a rumor that he's a stool pigeon. All of a sudden, the people that you're associated with, they're scared of you, they don't want to talk to you, all of sudden, you've got leprosy. And the word is coming down that at the next meeting Allen's going to talk about who he was getting moneys from and who he was paying off and he was going to be a government witness against Roy Williams and everybody else. I didn't believe it then and I don't believe it now.

I talked to Allen in regards to my pension and he assured me, "Don't worry about it. I'll punch you in and you'll be all right."

Then I called him up again and he started to scream and holler at me and he says, "How the fuck can you call me up and ask me for fucking favors? Jesus Christ, Franco, ain't I got enough troubles? I'm going to the fucking can. People are saying things about me. And you're calling me up and asking me for fucking favors. Son of a bitch, I told you before, you ain't got a thing to worry about. I'll take care of it."

Finally, I calmed him down and he says, "Jesus, Joe, I'm sorry. They just got me fucking crazy. I'm going to the can, no question about it. Just make sure you keep writing to me. You wrote me the first time and that helped, so keep writing and we'll stay in touch."

Two weeks later, somebody hit him coming out of the hotel in Chicago. That kid did not deserve to be hit. Whoever did it made a big mistake. They were killing the goose that laid the golden egg and that's not sound business.

Still, Franco had Allen Dorfman's word that nothing would interfere with his pension. He had the promise of others in the union hierarchy. He had all those years he had put into the movement, backed by the words of those who had known him and worked with him.

Bobby Holmes, who had risen through the ranks to become president of Joint Council 43 and then, finally, fourth vice-president of the Teamster international, swore out an affidavit stating that he had known Franco since early 1946 when "he was servicing the request of our general president James R. Hoffa, working as an organizer under Jimmy's personal direction. Sometime in or about 1951, again under the direction of Mr. Hoffa, he assumed responsibility of a Distillery Salesmen Local Union No. 42 in the city of Detroit. From January 1977 to December 1979, Joint Council No. 43 authorized an organizational grant to Local Union No. 243, which enabled Local Union No. 243 to employ Mr. Franco as an organizer. From January 1980 to December 1981, Mr. Franco was employed as an organizer for Joint Council No. 43."

Dave Johnson, the Hoffa loyalist who had been president of Local 299 until his retirement, seconded Holmes, saying that he had "a very good recollection of Mr. Franco's early Teamster organizational activities under Mr. James Hoffa's personal direction from 1946 through the 1950s in organizing the cab drivers, the Ford dealership salesmen and mechanics, and various other groups. While Mr. Franco worked for the Distillery Workers' Local No. 42, he also assisted Teamster Joint Council No. 43 in many of its organizational and related activities."

Affidavits and statements from others poured in, recalling the early days and the early activities of Franco under the personal direction of Hoffa. It seemed solid backing for Franco's claim that he deserved a pension from the union when he retired.

But to some in the Teamsters, who remembered Hoffa only vaguely and those around Hoffa hardly at all, there were questions. In the late spring of 1986, a hearing was held to determine if Franco was eligible for a pension. When it was over, Franco was informed:

> The Board of Trustees has determined that Mr. Franco is not eligible for a Twenty-Year service pension for the following reasons:
>
> he sustained a break in service for the period from 1971 to 1976 inclusive; and
>
> he did not meet the minimum service requirement of twenty years (due to his not having earned at least ten years contributory service credit).

Mr. Franco was not working in covered service from 1971 to 1976, a period in excess of three years, and therefore, he sustained a break in service which caused a loss of all noncontributory service credit he had earned from 1946 to 1971.

If, in a sense, that marked a final period to all the years Franco had devoted to the Teamsters and to his leader, Jimmy Hoffa, still the Teamsters union was no longer the union he had known. Under Hoffa, it had been hard, cynical, tough, driving, expansive, growing, and corrupt. By 1968, it was soft, shrinking, fat, and still corrupt.

Once, there had been Jimmy Hoffa. He had driven the union and had used the union to his own ends and to the ends of those he served as president, and the Teamsters had grown to more than 2.25 million members. The union was still growing and prospering, and still creating, as Hoffa desired, fear in the hearts of its antagonists.

But Jimmy Hoffa went to prison and Jimmy Hoffa vanished, and then there was Frank E. Fitzsimmons, and the Teamsters began to grow soft and flabby, and the greed and the payoffs were hardly hidden any longer.

And then there was Roy Williams, when Fitzsimmons departed, and Roy Williams proved weak and corrupt and hardly able to rule or inspire respect and confidence, and the Teamsters began to shrink. Williams went to prison for trying to bribe a senator and he was implicated in corrupt practices of all kinds, and he admitted to his own close ties with underworld figures.

So Williams departed, a sick man in a wheelchair with an oxygen tank always nearby. In his place there came Jackie Presser, son of Bill Presser, and he was a fat man who liked the good life and who raised his own salary so that he became the highest paid labor leader in the United States, earning a wage that would make many corporate presidents envious. And Jackie Presser, it turned out, was something more. He was and had been for some years a stool pigeon for the FBI. And the membership of the Teamsters under him continued to fall, to under one million eight hundred thousand.

So, the Teamsters had come to be something Jimmy Hoffa

never would have recognized. Once there had been Hoffa, who considered himself the working man's friend, spokesman, and leader; and business was the natural enemy of labor. Now there was Jackie Presser, who put a large distance between the working men he was supposed to lead and himself, who acted not as an antagonist to business but as a businessman himself, interested mainly in enriching himself and, no matter the cost, entrenching himself.

★ ★ ★

I was at the international convention in Las Vegas in May of 1986. It was disheartening. On Tuesday morning, there was a committee headed by Bob Coy that came out with a resolution to try to take the name of James R. Hoffa off the Teamster honor roll. To this day, Jimmy is still president emeritus, as if he had retired. But this committee introduced a resolution to take Jimmy's name off as president emeritus and remove Jimmy's name from all the records and documents and anything that has to do with the Teamsters whatever, and take down any pictures and statues or anything that has to do with him.

Thank God, when they introduced that resolution, you could hear all the delegates chanting, "As long as there's Teamsters, there'll always be Hoffa." They defeated the resolution.

Let me tell you, as far as the rank-and-file of the Teamsters are concerned, as long as there's Teamsters, there'll always be Hoffa. He was Mr. Teamster. His name is still magic. He was the man who raised the standard of living of his people. The truck drivers and warehousemen were known as ruffians, real lowlifes of the blue-collar people, they were looked down on, and this man came along and raised them up into the middle class and gave them a good life and they became respectable. He built the Teamsters and it's been going down ever since he went away.

And now the officials of the Teamsters, Jackie Presser and the people around him, his flunkies, they don't even want to recognize that this man ever existed.

I refused to go to the convention after Tuesday. I never left the hotel after that. I've been back to Teamster headquarters since, but I'm not part of the new team. They made that clear to me. And

I know why. I was and will always be Jimmy Hoffa's man. And you know what? I wouldn't have it any other way.

Franco believes that everything he did, that everything Hoffa ordered him to do, that everything Hoffa did was, ultimately, for the benefit of the American working man, for the Teamsters. He did what he had to do. That he believes.

AFTERWORD

The reader may be curious as to the fate of some of those who moved through Franco's life and career.

Mort Brandenberg continued to run the Distillery Workers Union for years after Franco's departure. He died in 1973 at the age of sixty-three.

Bill Bufalino, essential to Hoffa in offering legal and other advice, and a close friend to Franco, continues to practice law in Detroit.

Tom Burke had a brief moment in the sun in 1958 when he was called before the McClellan Committee to testify as to some of his activities on behalf of the Teamsters. He rambled and obfuscated and finally, with resignation, he was dismissed from the witness table. In the late 1960s, he died of cirrhosis of the liver in a hotel room, alone and broke.

Johnny Dio, who, it was said, never turned an honest dollar in his life, was an early Hoffa ally, and was rarely out of trouble with the law. He was indicted but never tried for a role in the acid blinding of crusading labor columnist Victor Riesel. Through the 1950s and 1960s, he was constantly in and out of court and in and out of prison. In 1967, he was convicted of stock fraud and sentenced to five years in prison. Almost as soon as he was released, he was tried and convicted again, this time of bankruptcy fraud. He died in federal prison in 1979 at the age of sixty-four.

Allen Dorfman, who developed the Teamster pension and welfare funds with his stepfather, Paul Dorfman, was convicted in 1972 of taking a kickback for arranging a pension fund loan and served ten months in federal prison. Once released, he went back to work in his old fields. A decade later, along with President Roy Williams, he was convicted of conspiracy to bribe Nevada Senator Howard Cannon. In January 1983, a month after the end of the trial, he was gunned down in a Chicago hotel parking lot after lunching with friends. No one has ever been charged with his murder.

Paul "Red" Dorfman, stepfather to Allen, a man whose ties with organized crime in Chicago went way back, died of natural causes in the early 1970s.

Harold Gibbons reached a truce with Frank Fitzsimmons following Hoffa's disappearance. There were some disaffected Teamsters who wanted him to run for union president against Fitzsimmons in 1976. He toyed with the idea for a time, and then struck his bargain with Fitzsimmons. He withdrew from the race and Fitzsimmons restored most of his old jobs, including that of head of the Central Conference of Teamsters. He died in 1982 at the age of seventy-two of a ruptured aneurysm while on a union trip to California.

Miltie Holt, long-time secretary-treasurer of Teamster Local 805 in New York and very close to Johnny Dio among others, took refuge in the Fifth Amendment when called before the McClellan Committee. He walked out of the hearing room and back to his old job where he remained until 1971 when he was indicted and convicted of extortion. He died following his release from prison.

Harry Karsh also used the Fifth Amendment before the McClellan Committee to avoid answering questions about his organizing and other activities related to circuses and carnivals. He continued to work at his trade until his death some years later.

Bill McFetridge was honored as an honest, conservative, and dedicated unionist through his many years as president of the Building Service Employees Union and vice-president of the AFL-CIO. He died in 1969 at seventy-five.

Johnny O'Rourke, head of the Teamster Joint Council in New York and an international vice-president, had been an early Hoffa supporter. But he broke with the Teamster president in 1962 over the issue of nationwide bargaining and a master contract covering all Teamsters, which he opposed. He died of a heart attack in 1965 at the age of sixty-five.

Sam Perrone who, along with Hoffa, had been one of those who had warned Franco of the dangers that an automobile could contain, got into his own car one day in the 1950s outside a Detroit car wash he owned and which Franco had helped him finance. True to his own teachings, he kept half his body outside while he turned on the ignition. The car was rigged. It blew up and blew Perrone out the open door, and blew off one leg. Because of the caution he preached and practiced, he survived and continued to be a fearsome power in Detroit until his death of natural causes a few years later. He had made so many enemies by his violent ways that nobody knew where to look to seek whoever had planted the bomb in his car.

Bill Presser, the Teamster power in Ohio, served two months in prison in 1960 for contempt of Congress for mutilating certain Teamster documents demanded by the McClellan Committee. In 1961, he served another six months for obstruction of justice. In 1971, he pleaded guilty to eight counts of shaking down employers and was fined rather than sentenced to prison. In 1976, in poor health, he retired as head of the Teamster Joint Council in northern Ohio and international vice-president, but not before he won the promise and the endorsement by Frank Fitzsimmons of his son, Jackie Presser, to be his successor. He died in 1981.

Babe Salupo went to a union conference in Detroit in the late 1950s only a few months after suffering a heart attack. While relaxing in his hotel room with Joe Franco and other Teamsters, he had a fatal heart attack.

Babe Triscaro, the former boxer and long-time partner of Bill Presser in Cleveland, sought shelter in the Fifth Amendment when called to testify before the McClellan Committee. From the hearing room, he went back to being a Teamster ruler. In an interview with a reporter in the late 1970s, Jackie Presser, by then head of the Joint Council in Ohio, described his father's old partner as "the kind of hood we have to clean out of here." Presser was not as good as his words. Triscaro remained a union officer until his retirement and death in the early 1980s.

Myra Wolfgang joined the union movement soon after her graduation from Carnegie Tech in the mid-1930s. She was recognized throughout her career as perhaps the most prominent and successful woman in this male-dominated field. She died in 1976.

Frank Fitzsimmons died of cancer in 1981.

Roy Williams succeeded Fitzsimmons, only to resign as Teamster president in 1983, following his conviction for conspiracy to bribe Senator Howard Cannon. He was sentenced to ten years in prison. In order to delay as long as possible the start of the sentence, the ailing Williams, confined to a wheelchair and breathing bottled oxygen, agreed to testify for the government at various trials of men accused of organized crime conspiracies. Among other things, he admitted that he had been receiving $1,500 a month from mob figures since 1974 in exchange for arranging loans for them through the Teamster pension fund.

Jackie Presser, now the Teamster president, came under federal investigation on charges of various corrupt practices and was indicted in mid-1986 on charges of labor racketeering, embezzlement, and filing false reports with the Labor Department. But Presser's attorney, backed by statements of several FBI agents, claimed that all the illegal acts that Presser was charged with had been authorized and concocted by the FBI in order for the Teamster president to gather evidence for the investigators as part of a secret existence as a government informant. This revelation did not seem to do him any harm with the union hierarchy. At the Teamster convention that summer, he was reelected union president.

Index